165
Pageant

This map is adapted from the official chart used by the United States Air Force. Strategists term the area between the 30th and 65th parallels the key zone since all modern wars have started there. Star shows geographical center of the U. S. Reprinted by permission of The New York Times.

THE PRICE OF POWER

BOOKS BY HANSON W. BALDWIN

MEN AND SHIPS OF STEEL
(With Wayne Francis Palmer)
THE CAISSONS ROLL
WE SAW IT HAPPEN, Edited, with Shepard Stone
ADMIRAL DEATH
UNITED WE STAND
WHAT THE CITIZEN SHOULD KNOW ABOUT THE NAVY
STRATEGY FOR VICTORY
THE NAVY AT WAR

Hanson W. Baldwin

THE PRICE OF POWER

Published for the
COUNCIL ON FOREIGN RELATIONS
By

HARPER & BROTHERS · PUBLISHERS
NEW YORK · AND · LONDON

"Justice without force is impotent.
Force without justice is tyrannical.
We must therefore combine justice with force."

PASCAL.

TABLE OF CONTENTS

CONTENTS

SECTION III
THE EFFECT OF THE FACTS
POLICY REVISED—THE COURSE WE MUST FOLLOW

PREFACE

This book is a fission product. It was born at Hiroshima and nurtured on Park Avenue. It cut its eyeteeth around a long green baize-covered table in the library of the Harold Pratt House in New York City—the home of the Council on Foreign Relations. It grew to maturity in a room of the Council house. It represents the product of collective thought, careful research, group discussion and individual opinion.

The atomic bomb altered the face of war and changed the course of history. But it was not the only instrument produced by World War II which revolutionized war and politics, strategy and time. The technological revolution accompanying the tremendous ferment of political change which the war represented confronted man with a completely new world—but, alas, not a "brave new world." The old order had vanished; Europe was no longer the center of world power; the age of air power and of the rocket, the bomb and the germ was at hand.

So awful and so portentous and so sweeping were the changes thus indicated that the Council on Foreign Relations, an organization which is concerned with a continuing study and evaluation of the foreign policy of the United States, decided to constitute a study group on "National Power and Foreign Policy," to investigate "The Power Position of the United States" in this postwar era. This group—which really continued and extended a series of politico-military studies made during the war under the auspices of the Council in close collaboration with the government—was first convened on October 18, 1945, shortly after the war's end, when the awful power of the atomic bomb and the bright dreams of a real world order impressed the minds of men. The group, under the chairmanship of the author, held a series of eighteen study and discussion meetings, the last on April 10, 1947, when the dreams had faded and most of mankind had come back to realism with a thud, convinced that the millennium was not at hand and that we were living in the same old world with patches on it.

Thus, the Council group ran the gamut of emotional and mental experience common to the average American in these past two years—but, for this group, at least, disillusionment has not been the product of it. For the study goal was a realistic one—to discuss the meaning of the technological and political revolution to the strategic position of the United States and to determine, if possible, the consequential effects upon our military and foreign policies. This was a large order, and it was realized before study was started that no complete answer would, or could, be found. Nevertheless, the data presented and the discussions recorded represented, in the opinion of the study group and of the Council itself, statistics and analyses which, it was felt, should reach a wider audience. The chairman of the group, the author of this book, was "elected" to weave the material into book form. This book is the result.

The Price of Power represents, therefore, collective thought and collective effort, but it is not literary collectivism; if there be mistakes they are mine, and the blemishes in style are the author's own peculiarities. Nor was it possible or desirable, of course, to "impersonalize" this book and to try, probably with futility, to make it represent in all details the concensus of a score of active individual minds. Therefore, the opinions are not group opinions, but "mine own"; and I must also be held responsible for most of the analyses and conclusions, even though, in many instances, a majority of the group agreed with the views here recorded. It should be clearly understood, therefore, that this book, though published under the sponsorship of the Council on Foreign Relations, cannot be said to speak for the Council, nor does it represent the views of any government department or of the study group on "National Power and Foreign Policy" either collectively or individually.

Nevertheless, the keenness and enthusiasm of this study group, and the body of facts which its individual members produced, make the following men, in a sense, collaborators of the author, who should share in whatever merit the book may possess but should not be blamed for its obvious deficiencies:

Maj. Gen. Maxwell D. Taylor—Superintendent, United States Military Academy
Captain A. B. Vosseller—United States Navy
Maj. Gen. Otto P. Weyland—United States Air Force
Langbourne M. Williams—President, Freeport Sulphur Company
Eugene E. Wilson—Vice-Chairman, United Aircraft Corporation

In addition to those listed, one or two members of the group preferred to remain anonymous. Several other persons, some of them quoted from time to time in the pages of this book, made "guest appearances" at one or more meetings as experts in their particular specialties and contributed data or ideas of importance.

Many of those listed above, particularly the permanent members of the Council's staff, lent major service to the author during the actual preparation of the book. I have also drawn heavily upon various articles, reports and data that I have prepared for the *New York Times* and have used phrases or material from articles in *Harper's Magazine* and from a lecture delivered at the University of Chicago. My wife, as always, has been wisely helpful and patient during the crisis of composition.

Last but not least, both the author and the Council owe a debt of appreciation to Arthur H. Sulzberger and the editors and management of the *New York Times* who envisaged this book as a public service and made it possible for the author to write it.

HANSON W. BALDWIN

New York City, December 1947

INTRODUCTION

THE PROBLEM

> For it is a knell
> That summons thee to heaven or to hell.
>
> *Macbeth*

CHAPTER I

THE PROBLEM

Rules of action are only snares . . . till they run out of the empty head into the hands, by use.

LAWRENCE, *Seven Pillars of Wisdom*

THERE is a basic paradox—political and strategic—in the coupling of the word "defense" with modern military means and methods.

The atomic bomb, the long-range plane, the giant missile and biological agents have demolished so many of our most cherished "security" concepts that "defense," measured by any military yardstick, has been reduced well-nigh to the absurd, and has become, practically, chiefly a reflex of retaliation. The modern weapons of war are legion and "total"; man, in his search for "defense," has broken the boundaries of space and solved some of the mysteries of nature, and, ironically, has made himself far less secure than ever before in history.

The rise of nation-states, population growth, the industrial revolution, and now the technological revolution have made war "total" in the widest sense, and "defense," if it dominates the military thinking of a nation, a term synonymous with defeat and completely incompatible with modern reality. No theory of "limited liability" or defensive strategy or tactics can win the war of tomorrow. Nor are man's attempts to limit the extensive destructiveness and outlaw some of the far-reaching horror of war likely to succeed unless power is linked to reality and both to morality. Moral scruples— such common international *mores* and customs and laws as earth's divided peoples have come to accept—and international conventions and treaties may serve as deterrents to strong-arm diplomacy, but the fear of a swift counter-punch, or retaliation in kind, is, until men accept a true common code, a weightier argument against aggression.

The problem of the twentieth century, therefore (as it has been the problem of all past centuries), is to harness justice with power, idealism with realism. Its solution, however, is more pressing than in ages past, for modern communications have destroyed many of the barriers of terrain and the handicaps of distance; the plane has "burst the bonds of earth," and today's genii have raised the lid of science on a Pandora's Box of evils.

To some, the revolution in weapons and the totality of modern war threaten what Leslie Paul has called "The Annihilation of Man," and the solution of man's perennial problem, therefore, is, at least to man, of transcendental importance. But though the emergency be dire and the urgency extreme one does not need to paint the problem in extremes to stress its importance. Man is a traditionally persistent creature; somehow, despite the cataclysms through which the earth has passed, he has managed, though seemingly threatened with periodic extinction, to survive, to evolve, to grow. The scientific revolution which produced the atomic bomb and the social and moral stagnation which produced "total war," though perhaps the greatest threat man has yet faced, are, nevertheless, not likely to lead to his extinction. Nor will civilization perish as long as there is a library in Peru or a volume of Shakespeare or a painting of Goya or a symphony of Beethoven or a copy of the Bible upon this earth. What we need really fear, therefore, in this atomic age, is not the extinction of man or the end of all civilization, but a return of the world to the Dark Ages. What Tennyson wrote in a time gone by is prophetic today:

> The children born of thee are sword and fire,
> Red ruin and the breaking up of law.

It will be small comfort to the sons and daughters of this generation of Americans to know that a Lima library still stands if American culture and Western civilization are destroyed.

The problem, then—though world-wide and common to all men —must, for the sake of clarity and realism, be "localized." It is primarily and specifically the problem of preserving and perpetuating American man and Western culture. Nor is this a narrow or a selfish concept. For America, alone, among the major countries of the West is the only nation which has never experienced the ravages of modern war; America alone represents the final undamaged citadel of Western civilization. We are, therefore, in "localizing" the problem of atomic-age security, accomplishing far more than mere "defense" of the United States; we are trying to guard the heritage of the West and to insure the future of the only world area where the rank weeds of ruin are not choking and impeding the development of man. If we succeed, without vital damage, in fostering the growth of the democratic ideal and protecting the roots of the tree of liberty we shall have served the world and not only the West.

The problem of American power and its proper use in the atomic age—to which this book is addressed—is one to which no easy or complete solution can be found. Most of the so-called "solutions" and world panaceas offered since the war smack somewhat of that beautifully simple formula: "Oh, if only everybody would do what's right . . ."

Too many of these formulas err on the side of the extremes; they are either too artistically idealistic or too brutally realistic. What is needed is an eyes-on-the-stars-feet-in-the-mud approach.

But there can be no objective approach, no real understanding of the problem, unless we rid our minds of the cluttering shibboleths —military and psychological—and the tragic fallacies that tend to make us view the world scene with astigmatic lenses. To pose clearly the strategic problem confronting the United States we must first examine and dismiss some of the untruths that have colored or are coloring our contemporary military thinking.

First—"peace in our time."

This fallacy now needs little belaboring. Yet twice in a quarter century millions of the American people thought they were fighting the "last war"—the "war to end wars." After World War I we brought up a generation of youth, taught in the sheltered school of idealism to ignore the facts of power and the nature of man. The result, in the stormy Thirties and as another war came to the world, was disillusionment and cynicism, a "lost generation." It was expressed in a "to-hell-with-the-world-I'll-get-mine" attitude, a shirking of public duty for private ease known so well to our Army in the last war as "gold-bricking." Despite this lesson in current history, many Americans believed for a few brief months after World War II that the United Nations would be a sure-fire recipe for perpetual peace.

As a people we are prone to wishful thinking, lack the long view of history. There is no evidence whatsoever in past history (or in the study of present-day man) for the belief that the millennium is just around the corner. Permanent peace—a world without war —has been the goal of generations; it is a "consummation devoutly to be wished." But there is no likelihood that all war will be abolished in our generation, or, indeed, for generations to come. For peace is not only a state of mind but a process of education, and man learns slowly. Each succeeding generation, it seems, must relearn some of the bitter lessons of the past. Yet there is progress; the United Nations, weak though it may be, is stronger than the League of Nations; the effort for peace, the effort to abolish war has achieved in the twentieth century world-wide organization, world-wide support. There is no reason for black despair or bitter disillusionment in the fact that some kind of war recurs through the centuries with almost monotonous regularity; war, even if it comes, does not *have* to mean a return to the Dark Ages. Today the widespread scope of war, and its instruments of devastating horror, are, per se, a check upon its inception, yet we should build no dream castles upon so slight a foundation. International controls may limit, but will not abolish, war; the United Nations will help but will not cure.

Nor will the world state, in any form, be a cure-all for the pernicious malady of conflict. To quote Nicholas John Spykman:[1]

World federation is still far off. This is perhaps just as well, because the world state would probably be a great disappointment to its advocates and very different from what they had anticipated. Brotherly love would not automatically replace conflict, and the struggle for power would continue. Diplomacy would become lobbying and log-rolling, and international wars would become civil wars and insurrections, but man would continue to fight for what he thought worth while and violence would not disappear from the earth. . . . From an ethical point of view power can be considered only as a means to an end. It is, therefore, important that the use which is made of it should be constantly subjected to moral judgments, but to hope for a world that will operate without coercion and to decry man's desire to obtain power is an attempt to escape from reality into a world of dreams. Man creates society through co-operation, accommodation, and conflict, and all three are essential and integral parts of social life.

The world state in any form is not likely, therefore, to eliminate war. But the concept of a democratic world order, a "Parliament of Man, the Federation of the World," is one of the higher aspirations of the human being; it represents a goal, an objective, an ideal, a dream, a vision, the force of which is no less real though it cannot be attained. As Browning wrote, "a man's reach should exceed his grasp, or what's a Heaven for?"

Yet we cannot take refuge from the real in the ideal; "Heaven" is not yet here on earth. We must be pragmatic in our interpretations of experience.

A study of the past indicates that major wars rarely tread upon each other's heels, but the lessons of history teach us that a large war may again blight the earth within a half century.

Second—"we were unprepared."

This half-truth has been applied, with almost repetitious monotony, to the state of the U.S. armed forces before World War I, World War II, in fact all our wars. But the statement is sophistry; for what were we "unprepared"? Preparedness is relative, not absolute; there are degrees of preparedness. Before the Second World War this nation had a Navy equal to any and the best long-range bomber in the world; the National Guard had been federalized, conscription had started, and the factories of the country already had commenced the manufacture of war orders. Nevertheless, we were, of course, "unprepared" for the war that developed, and we shall always be unprepared; for there is no such thing as *absolute* preparedness, and it is futile to strive for it. Germany, for instance, was prepared for the Polish campaign, but not for the war she got; not even totalitarian states, much less democracies, can indulge in the luxury of *absolute* preparedness in time of peace. *Absolute* preparedness is the will-o'-the-wisp of history which has led any country that attempted it to destruction. *Relative* preparedness, on the other hand, if the yardstick of relativity is sound, is a wise form of national insurance.

Third—"A strong army and navy will prevent war."

This is the beguiling complement of the foregoing "unpreparedness" argument. The assertion that armaments mean security has the imperative negation of history. Like preparedness, there is no such thing as *absolute* security, either in the political, the military or in any other field; the world would be a dull place if there were. The greatest armaments—those of Sparta, Persia, Macedonia, Rome, Carthage, France, Germany, Japan, Russia—have never meant either inviolability against attack or certainty of victory. The greater the armaments, the greater the temptation to embark upon imperialist war, upon unlimited war, the greater the tendency to strive for *absolute* preparedness with the rest of the world cast in the role of potential enemies. There is no safety in excessive armaments, nor is there safety in flabby weakness. Excessive military weakness can invite attack. But excessive military strength can precipitate war. There is a happy mean in armaments as in politics.

Fourth—"Disarmament means insecurity."[2]

This, the corollary of the foregoing fallacy, stems from a distorted view of the politico-military history of the 1920's, a view always popular in chauvinistic minds and one which has found wide acceptance during this postwar crisis. This view of history holds that the gallant and idealistic United States was the dupe of clever international politicians; that at the Washington Disarmament Conference of 1921 we were hornswoggled out of our rightful power and reduced to an inferior position and that all the wrongs of the earth (including the Hitler regime) can be traced directly to this naïve mistake. No deep research is necessary to refute the bias and prejudice of this argument. The Washington Conference halted a rapidly growing naval race between the United States and Britain, reduced for a period of at least a decade the international friction caused by excessive naval competition and formalized for the United States a position of naval parity with Britain. Our mistakes in the Twenties were not in the field of armaments limitations, but in the political realm; we granted Japan virtual strategic hegemony over the Western Pacific, and our failure to enter the League

of Nations doomed the effectiveness of that organization and
nullified the political, psychological and military results achieved
by the armaments-limitations conferences.

Samuel Eliot Morison, in his *The Battle of the Atlantic—History
of United States Naval Operations in World War II*,[3] adds an important postscript:

Naval officers on both sides of the Atlantic (Britain and the
United States) blame this unpreparedness (for World War II,
specifically for anti-submarine warfare) on the naval-limitation
treaties, but actually each country might have built up a better-
rounded fleet within the treaty framework, had it been willing to
pay the cost.

William T. R. Fox clarifies this episode of history in his *The
Super Powers*:[4]

It is now fashionable to assert that the Washington Conference
was an Anglo-American disaster and a triumph for Japanese duplicity. Walter Lippmann in his recent *U.S. Foreign Policy* speaks of
"the exorbitant folly of the Washington Disarmament Conference."
. . . (But) Civilian leadership brought a halt to a disastrous naval
competition.

The argument can be made that the fault of the Washington
Conference was not too *much* naval limitation, but not *enough*.
Battleships, battle cruisers and aircraft carriers were limited by the
treaty in numbers and tonnage; cruisers, destroyers and submarines
were not. Hence naval competition in the smaller types of war
vessels ensued, checked temporarily by the London Naval Conference of 1930. However, the world's political situation and our
failure to support international organization through the League
of Nations had then reaped their bitter results.

As Mr. Fox points out, the real mistake of the Washington Conference was not, therefore, in the principle, or the achievement, of
naval limitation, but:[5]

The treaty of self-abnegation by which the United States and
Great Britain bound themselves not to increase their fortifications
in Western Pacific waters was a blunder based on an inadequate
grasp of the expansionist basis of Japanese policy.

The limitation of armaments does *not* mean insecurity, unless a great power indulges in disarmament unilaterally, something we have never done. Limitation of armaments will not end war, for armaments are not the primary cause of war, but rather surface evidence of an infection in the body politic. But excessive armaments encourage an armaments race, breed fear and insecurity and add to the multiple frictions which bring on war, and arms limitation, though it will not abolish war, does tend to limit it, which is no minor goal.

Fifth—"The United States will be the first area to be attacked in any future war."

This glib assertion, which is only a half-truth, has had considerable popular acceptance now for a quarter of a century, though it has not yet been proved valid. Postwar military prophets after World War I warned that the next war would bring the weight of enemy attack *first* upon U.S. soil. They were, of course, wrong. They may well be entirely wrong again, unless U.S. diplomacy becomes utterly bankrupt. For the basis of our whole past strategy has been to fight our wars overseas. And the basis of our diplomacy (as applied to strategy) sometimes has been, always should have been, and henceforth must be to insure for the United States positions (bases) in readiness overseas from which our military power could be applied to the enemy, and allies-in-being so that we would not fight a war alone. These "alliances" heretofore have been *de facto* rather than "treaty" or *de jure*, and the term "allies" has been neither fashionable nor politically possible in the past until after we had entered a war. Nevertheless, our diplomacy while avoiding "entangling alliances" has tried—and is still trying—to win us friends and "allies." The technological revolution in weapons and the great range of the plane and the missile which will make through-the-air transoceanic attack possible make the proposition that the United States will be the first to be attacked less fallacious than ever before. Nevertheless, it represents only a half-truth. Our soil may be *among* the first places to be attacked in any future war, but no potential enemy could possibly afford to neglect the danger spots nearer his own borders from which we might launch attacks against him. So long as the United States possesses "allies" and bases overseas a primary objective of any enemy must be elimination, neutralization or conquest of those positions. A concurrent attack upon the continental United States would be, of course, possible and perhaps probable, but our own advantage would be considerable so long as we possessed positions overseas and the enemy did not.

Sixth—"Invasion of the United States is now possible."

Neither now nor in the foreseeable future is the large-scale physical invasion of the continental United States probable; today it is virtually impossible. Invading forces can come to the United States only by sea or air, and distance and geography, though foreshortened in the air age, still have strategical and, above all, logistical meaning. Only at the Bering Strait, where Alaska abuts closely like a jagged escarpment to the land mass of Eurasia, are the distances separating us from potential enemies small enough to permit the large-scale transport of armies by air. But in Alaska and the contiguous coast of Asia communications are almost nonexistent, and the climate is so severe that large-scale air-borne operations would be exceedingly difficult. Only by sea or by air can enemy forces invade our land. So long as we "control" the sea and the air no large-scale physical invasion (like the Normandy invasion or the other amphibious and air-borne operations made famous during the war) are possible. Small-scale air-borne operations, involving the transportation of regiments or even a division of men, might be accomplished, though without air superiority they would be very difficult.

The history of air-borne operations attests to their complexity, and the sizable transoceanic distances that still separate us from potential enemies make any large-scale invasion through the air impossible in the immediate future, whether or not the enemy enjoys air superiority, and exceedingly difficult, though not impossible, in the more distant future. In other words invasion, in the sense of the actual landing on our shores of large bodies of armed men, is not, and never has been, a major problem of this nation. Yet such are the range, flexibility and speed of modern weapons that physical invasion, as subsequent chapters will explain, may not be necessary to future conquest. In the twentieth century of the atomic bomb, supersonic missiles, long-range jet planes and high-speed submarines, the strategic problem for the United States is *not* defense against massive *invasion*, but protection against massive *assault*.

Yet assault, in the modern age, does not have to be physical. There is, therefore, a seventh and final fallacy which must be scotched.

Seventh—"The United States must be attacked before it will enter war."

To most people such "attack" means physical assault. Yet "attack" can have compound forms, and the United States might be "attacked" in insidious ways, other than by mass killers. The weapons of ideas, attacks on the minds and souls of men, economic attacks, political attacks—all these are possible in total war; indeed such preliminary assaults already have taken place in the "cold war" now joined between the United States and Russia. Nor is another Pearl Harbor a fundamental precedent to United States participation in another war. Wars rarely start without preceding periods of tension and "build-up"; the overt act merely caps the climax. We can be drawn into war today by a variety of means and through an almost imperceptible process, for conflict is part of the life of man and conflict today between nation-states is a compound of the complex social structure of those states. "Defense," therefore, comprehends far more than defense against physical attack; today it means, in the words of the President's Advisory Commission on Universal Training, a "strong, united, healthy and informed nation." We must forever remember that war does not have to start with physical attack upon American cities; it *can* start in the kingdom of our minds, or in Afghanistan or Thailand, Austria or Peru.

Stripped of the gaudy trappings of myth and half-truth, fallacy and invention, the dimensions of the United States' strategic problem in the atomic age come into clearer perspective. Yet that problem cannot be stated, even in general terms, without first considering some of the broad lessons taught us—with blood and mourning, tears and sweat and misery—in World War II. For those lessons lead us, as later chapters will show, to the basic paradox of our age.

World War II did not develop new basic *principles*. For the *principles* of war—that is, the broad "rules" of the art of fighting —are immutable; "their interpretation and application will vary greatly (through the ages), but their substance is the same."[6]

Many air enthusiasts, bred on the doctrines of Douhet, Mitchell and Seversky, have claimed that "strategic bombardment" or air attack upon cities, civilian populations and factories introduces a new *principle* of war in that it focuses military effort upon the civilian rather than the military populations of the warring nations. But pressure *behind* the military lines has been an old tactic of warfare since the days when Attila the Hun and Genghis Khan ravaged, burned and looted Europe. The naval blockade is an indirect form of such pressure; the siege and sack of walled cities in the Middle Ages, Sherman's devastation of Georgia and Sheridan's of the Shenandoah Valley are all examples of precisely the same tactic that the air age has produced, the application of military power to civilian and behind-the-line installations. The instruments have changed and the plane and the (atomic) bomb have extended the potential area of devastation of the scourged and ravaged earth to the infinite, but the principle of ruthlessness is still the same.

Hannibal annihilated the legions of Rome in the "perfect" battle at Cannae in 216 B.C. Eisenhower, using precisely the same tactic of the "double envelopment," crushed the last cohesive German armies of the West in the Battle of the Ruhr in 1945.

Despite the universality of war's principles, it is well to recall and to emphasize that war still is, and always has been, an art, not a science. It utilizes and transcends all sciences, but military operations are not, per se, scientific; they cannot be marshaled in the exact phalanx of equations. Particularly today in this era of total war they represent, not merely the clash of armed men and the movements of vehicles, planes, ships and supplies, but the ebb and flow of intangible forces, the surge of national wills, the power of the spirit. The inexact and the intangible are as much a part of modern war as the finite; a glint of sunshine on plane wing or gun barrel may change the course of history.

It is necessary to emphasize this point specifically in this age of the technological revolution in warfare, lest we tend to think of future war solely as a scientific manifestation and in "push-button" terms. Science and the armed forces must, of course, be closely harnessed, but war remains an unscientific occupation.

Like genius, the art of war represents, too, an infinite capacity for taking pains; yet the art of taking pains can lead to its own confusion. The Germanic cult for precision and the propensity the

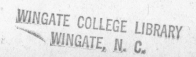

Prussians have shown for trying to reduce esoteric subjects to finite dimensions (viz., some of the mumbo-jumbo and pseudo-science produced under the cloak of "geopolitics") have not been without influence in the United States. But the human factor, man himself, is still the dominant unknown in war or peace, and we must guard against oversimplified solutions or easy analyses that do not give full weight to this and other intangibles.

Such a preface is necessary to any discussion of the lessons of World War II. For in this era of political revolution, economic flux and technological change, any lessons from the *past* will be applicable to the *future* only so long as their relationship to man is stressed and understood. Such lessons, to be viable, must be under constant re-examination and reinterpretation, lest we tend to prepare for the next war in terms of the last.

With such qualifications we may list a few of the major strategical lessons of World War II.

First—

Victory in modern war is no longer won by the big battalions but by the big factories, backed by the big laboratories and the busy scientists. This has been increasingly true since the industrial revolution; Forrest's "to git thar fust with the most" now must be paraphrased to "git thar fust with the greatest fire power." The Russian front in the war just passed would seem to refute this lesson, and it is true that massed man power still is a factor of military strength. But the mass army (with man power as the yardstick of strength) has declined steadily in importance as Hoffman Nickerson has noted,[7] and the technological revolution in weapons, superimposed upon the industrial revolution, has further reduced in importance *numbers* of fighting men as an index of strength.

Our victory in World War II was primarily and fundamentally an industrial victory, a victory in which the factories of America supplied not only our own armies but the forces of our Allies. The United States was, irrefutably, the "arsenal of democracy"; the statistics of our industrial effort are Gargantuan, unprecedented, even undreamed of, by any other nation. It used to be said, for instance, that a nation must fight a war with the navy it possessed at the outbreak (so complex and so difficult is the construction of men-of-war), yet we produced during World War II fleets that completely dwarfed our prewar Navy; the ships—naval and mercantile—that went down our ways easily exceeded the combined tonnage of all the fleets of the world. Our factories produced by far the greatest air force in history, one without previous concept or yardstick, and gave us an army more thoroughly equipped than any that had ever gone forth to battle. We shipped to our Allies, over thousands of miles of sea and despite the best efforts of our foes to prevent it, $46,000,000,000 worth of munitions, the equivalent in dollar value of enough military equipment to outfit completely six great air forces, and 2,000 infantry divisions and 558 armored divisions—more divisions, by far, than there were in all the world. In short, the big factories of America won the war.[8]

Incidental to the growth of the importance of industrial strength—of the massed machines rather than of massed man power as the determinant of victory—was the decline in importance of generalship (though not of leadership). Generals (and admirals, though particularly generals) became, at least in the highest ranks, general managers rather than tacticians and strategists. There was still a premium, particularly in the early days before the industrial output of war material had risen to such unprecedented peaks, on skill in maneuver and a nice sense of terrain and timing, and Rommel, who did much with little, exemplified this "dying" art of generalship perhaps better than any other individual of World War II. But for the most part the higher-ranking generals had to be a combination of politician, personnel manager, inventory clerk and general manager, and—once the big factories of America had outstripped the factories of the Axis—the Allies could scarcely have lost the war no matter what mistakes in generalship were made. After 1943 there was no single American general or admiral of whom it could be said, as it was of Jellicoe at Jutland, that he could "lose the war in an afternoon." For the factories of America, the industrial know-how of America, and the mechanical competence of America, those very materialistic achievements which have made us as a nation great in physical stature (but perhaps weak in spirit), won the war. Industrial strength is, therefore, a major factor in military power and a major measure of national power in the modern world.

Second—

The continental United States is not only arsenal and supply base, but is now the main *operating* base for our armed forces. This development, the beginnings of which were evident in World War II, is speeded as the range of weapons increases. During the war our entire global strategy was directed from Washington; headquarters was not, as in Lee's day or Napoleon's time, on horseback or in the field. Our B-29 Superfortresses were directed strategically and sometimes even tactically from Washington. The Navy's "floating-base" system, which utilized supply ships, floating machine shops, barracks ships, etc., etc., to support the combatant ships rather than fixed and immobile advanced land installations, was provisioned, supplied, stocked and prepared in the continental United States. More and more as the war progressed not only supplies but operations tended to stem outward from the United States, the main base, to the foci of fighting. This trend, marked during the war, is likely to become more and more pronounced in the atomic and rocket age. As transoceanic, transpolar, and ultimately transworld ranges are achieved, the continental United States will tend to become more and more completely the main operating base of our armed forces as well as their main manufacturing and supply base.

Third—

The offense has so far outstripped the defense, largely because of the technological revolution in warfare, that our strategic concepts have been altered fundamentally. This superiority of offense over defense, which reversed the trend of World War I, when the machine gun and the trench system locked the fighting fronts in bloody stalemate, became apparent almost as soon as World War II commenced. The basic theory of "Blitzkrieg" is movement, and the Germans maintained their mobility—something the opposing armies had been unable to do a quarter century before—by coupling fire power to the plane-tank spearhead. As the war developed, and the bomber came into its frightful heritage, the offense gained even greater ascendancy. By skillful choice of terrain, prodigious feats of fortification and very careful use of maneuver and counterattack, a nation fighting a defensive war might hope for a time to ward off its enemy's ground attacks, but there was little hope in the air of averting altogether all bombing attacks. The ascendancy of the offensive, which was temporarily checked by the development of the anti-tank gun, radar and other equipment, became more and more pronounced in the closing years of the war, with the introduction of the robot V-1 "flying bomb," the supersonic V-2, the submarine with "schnorchel" and high underwater speed, and the atomic bomb.

These last weapons heralded the nature of the technological revolution in war through which we are passing, and foreshadowed the nature of the next war. The evolution, thus begun, has scarcely closed its first chapter. Weapons are reaching toward the ultimate in range, power and speed; clearly forecast on the world's proving grounds and laboratories are more atomic bombs, supersonic transoceanic missiles; high-speed submersibles with rocket-firing facilities—the first true submersibles in history, able to cross the oceans under water; biological poisons; radioactive dusts; and gases far more toxic than the German "Tabun" wartime series, never used (which outmoded all previously known war gases). These and other frightful agents of destruction have conferred upon the offense a great and growing lead over the defense, and have altered —particularly the coming intercontinental and transworld missiles—all American strategic concepts.

The United States is now, therefore, more vulnerable to assault than ever before in history; for the first time in history we have "live" frontiers—frontiers of the air through which missiles may move across the Pole or across the seas at supersonic speeds, frontiers of the underseas, from whence modern and unseen leviathans may launch devastating attack upon our coasts.

These "live" frontiers, and the increasing "lead" of the offensive tactic vis-à-vis the defensive system, seem to make hopeless the problem of American defense, using the word in its narrow and specialized sense. Against atomic bombs, long-range, globe-girdling planes, intercontinental missiles and induced plagues, the best defense, in fact, the only true defense, would appear to be a strong offense, the threat of *retaliation in kind*, the threat of worse blows against the enemy homeland than any the enemy can deliver against us. This means reorientation of our traditional American military policy to an offensive concept, the active preparation and main-

tenance of a mobile force in being with complete equipment, ready
for instant *offensive* action.

Fourth—

Modern war is "total" far beyond the imagination of even those
who coined the phrase; it enlists the whole effort of the nation
and directs the flowing stream of history. The "totality" of effort
of the United States and of all other major nations that participated
in the Second World War far exceeded national efforts in any
preceding wars. Yet the evolution is not complete, and powerful
forces vector the state-at-war toward the "nation-in-arms," the
"garrison state," the "arsenal state." The trends have been inevitable
since the industrial revolution and the growing importance of the
big factories as compared to the big battalions put a wartime
premium upon the man behind the lines. The plane—which has
made possible the *attaque brusquée* upon civilian morale, civilian
homes and civilian-manned factories—has made the civilian a part
of the war machine. Missiles and atomic bombs extend and strengthen
these trends. In the next war, labor as well as fighting power will
probably be drafted; in the next war, every phase of national effort
that does not contribute to victory will probably be eliminated.
The totality of war includes the mind and spirit as well as the body
and the machine. The immense importance in any future conflict—
and in the "peacetime" preparatory stages of that conflict—of the
"big ideas" as well as the big industries has been but lightly outlined by the last war. Total war means total effort, and the peacetime preparations for it must be as comprehensive, at least in outline form, as the execution of it. Consequently the effects of total
war transcend the period of hostilities; they wrench and distort
and twist the body politic and the body economic not only *after*
a war (as we are now seeing) but *prior* to war (as we shall soon
see).

These "lessons," tentative and subject to perennial re-examination
though they may be, do serve to delimit and define the nature of
the modern American strategical problem. It is a problem as portentous as it is seemingly insoluble.

For if we take a long view of history, if we keep our feet in the mud while our eyes are on the stars, we must recognize that another war, some time, somewhere, of some nature, is extremely probable. We must also recognize that neither the United Nations nor a federalized world order are likely to avert permanently the recurrence of conflict. National military strength, therefore, is still essential—in fact, more essential than ever, in the age of atomic bombs and swift, globe-girdling missiles. But we have seen that armaments, per se, do not mean security, and that undue emphasis upon armaments can make for war.

And the frame of experience in which we have just set the American strategic problem in the atomic age compels us to confront the greatest and most puzzling dilemma in our military, or indeed in our political, history.

What is this dilemma?

It can be best stated in the form of three statements and ancillary questions:

1. We have seen that the continental United States is now not only the manufacturing arsenal and supply base of any American military effort, but is also the main operating base of our armed forces. Because of this triple importance, because, especially, of the value of mass industry to war effort, it is more important than ever before in history to protect the continental United States against assault. Yet we have also seen that, because of the technological revolution and the ascendancy of the offensive, the United States is now more vulnerable than ever before in history. How, then, do we "defend" the continental United States?

2. Offense today is by far the best defense. But how can we develop in peacetime in a peace-loving, non-imperialist democracy an offensive force of suitable type, ready for instant action?

3. (an extension of, and corollary to, No. 2). The atomic bomb and the age of total war make mandatory an increase in military efficiency. This logically means, if maximum military efficiency is the ultimate goal, a direction of all phases of national life toward military strength, the extension of the influence of the military into all phases of life. Yet how can we thus increase military efficiency without weakening our democracy, how can we prepare for total war without becoming a "garrison state" and destroying the very qualities and virtues and principles we originally set about to save?

This, then is the grand dilemma, this, the puzzling problem of our age.

Notes—Chapter I

1. *America's Strategy in World Politics*, by Nicholas John Spykman, Harcourt, Brace & Company. Pages 458 and 12.

2. For "disarmament" should be read "limitation of armaments." The word is loosely and incorrectly applied, for real "disarmament" never has been considered seriously at any of the so-called "disarmament" conferences and never has been practiced by any major nation, except when imposed by victor upon vanquished. Real "disarmament" belongs to the millennium and probably will not be achieved in a score of generations, but "limitation of armaments" is a practical possibility of today.

3. *The Battle of the Atlantic—History of United States Naval Operations in World War II*, by Samuel Eliot Morison, Little, Brown & Company. Page 11.

4. *The Super Powers*, by William T. R. Fox, Harcourt, Brace & Company, Page 53.

5. Ibid., page 53.

6. Wallace Goforth, in an address to the L'Institut Militaire de Quebec, June 1947.

7. *The Armed Horde, 1793–1939*, by Hoffman Nickerson, Putnam. See also *Arms and Policy, 1939–1944*, Putnam, by the same author.

8. It is, of course, an oversimplification, purposely indulged in for the sake of clarity and emphasis, to say that any single factor "won the war." What is meant is that the "big factories" were the predominant factor, *not* that the machine can replace man. Man is always the soul of battle. Mass production was our outstanding advantage vis-à-vis the enemy. We had no such advantage in "spirit" or "morale"; indeed, we were often at a disadvantage. (See Chapter V.)

SECTION I

THE FACTS

WORLD IN FLUX—CHANGES IN U. S. POWER POSITION

Facts do not cease to exist because they are ignored.
ALDOUS HUXLEY

CHAPTER II

THE POLITICAL POSITION

> . . . international society will continue to operate with the same fundamental power patterns. It will be a world of power politics in which the interests of the United States will continue to demand the preservation of a balance in Europe and Asia. . . .
>
> NICHOLAS JOHN SPYKMAN[1]

THE political position of the United States, as the second half of the twentieth century approaches, is one of strength in a world "inherently unstable, always shifting, always changing."[2]

The surging tidal wave of war swept away peoples, undermined empires, brought down governments, destroyed political systems, and continued a process of political "fractionalization," coupled with great power concentration, that commenced at the turn of the century. When the backwash of conflict ebbed two great powers, the United States and Russia—their collective resources so far exceeding all others that they have been dubbed "super-states"— were left supreme in the new political world, principal arbiters of the destinies of our times. A third state, entitled to the description "great power," but not comparable in strength to the "super-states," is Great Britain, which draws accrued force from its dominions and colonies. Despite that diplomatic euphemism which includes France and China among the "Big Five" of the United Nations, there are *not* five front-rank powers in the world today but only three, with two of them, in the terms of Hollywood, "super-colossal."

None of these three is primarily European (save in cultural background); the power foci of the world have shifted away from Europe to the "heartland" of Eurasia, the "new world" of the Western Hemisphere and the tenuous sea empire of Britain. Politically, militarily, ideologically, culturally and economically Europe is no longer the center of the world; the "spotlight" of history has shifted from the so-called "dying"[3] continent to new areas.

The process of political fractionalization has accompanied the process of great power concentration. Since the beginning of the century, in Europe and elsewhere throughout the world, more than thirty independent small states have emerged from the chrysalis of history; only seven[4] have disappeared, and new ones are now in the process of formation. The breakup of the great empires of the nineteenth century accounts for some of this process of cellular destruction and cellular growth, but the spread of industrialization, and the Wilsonian concept of the self-determination of peoples were powerful spurs to this historical trend.

Some of these smaller powers are not homogeneous either politically or ethnically, and a few represent geographic and economic absurdities, but others are sound cells in the great body politic. But none of them, not even a nation like France, which strictly speaking is not a small power but a "middle power," possesses sufficient inherent strength to rank with the "Big Three"; none of them, alone, possesses the strength to preserve a balance of power in Europe, in Asia or in the world.

We have, therefore, in the postwar world a shift away from the old balance-of-power system to a so-called condition of "bi-polarity." Actually this change, though fundamental in the histories of the participating nations, is less basic, in the mechanism of power, than it seems. For power politics[5] still dominates the contemporary scene, and some equilibrium of world power is still a requisite for peace.

"Bi-polarity" already is exerting "lines of force" across the world. More and more the small and medium powers of the earth resemble steel filings caught in a magnetic field: many of them are attracted to the positive pole; many to the negative. In between, where the pulls are equal, the filings are in uneasy equilibrium. Such is the inevitable result of the emergence of two great super-states; the world is not "one world"[6] but two great power groupings.

This tendency toward "choosing sides," with the frictions that result, has been hastened by the "shrinkage" of the earth, as well as by the great expansion, due to the war, of Russian and American interests. Modern communications have reduced the time-space factor to such a degree that two super-states in the same world inevitably jostle each other and step on each other's toes. There is, no longer, in Grayson Kirk's words, any neutral "middle ground." There are zones of lesser and greater interest but no zones without any interest. The interests of the "super-states" coincide or collide at half a dozen global points; the immutable facts of industrial economics, of twentieth-century politics and of the technological revolution in war make Russia and the United States reach out far beyond their borders.

To the United States a world role and world-wide interests are unavoidable; we have had greatness thrust upon us. American isolationism was once a logical political by-product of our geographical position, and that geographical position still has importance today. But our complete insularity—and the real validity which isolationism once enjoyed—now have been destroyed[7] by the foreshortened nature of our world, and in the coming age of guided missiles distance will have still less meaning.

Strategically, a world role for the United States is vital. Strategically, the United States fought the last war to prevent the "encirclement" of our "continental island" by hostile forces. If we could not then permit all of the coast of Western Europe or all of Eastern Asia to fall under the sway of any one power or of any two allied powers, how much more important is it today, in the age of the atomic bomb and the supersonic robot, to oppose similar domination. Strategically, therefore, American interests now must reach far beyond our coasts.

Economically, too, we are now increasingly aware of the interdependence of the world. Depression abroad may mean depression here; certainly our economic well-being is now more and more dependent upon foreign trade and export markets. No longer can we anticipate virtual self-sufficiency in raw materials;[8] the new weapons require in quantity raw materials which we have never possessed, and the war depleted some of our important mineral reserves—notably oil and high-grade iron ore. We must, therefore, have access to overseas minerals or we cannot remain a great power.

The United States has obligations on a world-wide basis which make impossible any return to isolationism or detachment. Our obligation to defend the Philippines, for instance, against any aggressor, despite the newly won independence of that republic, is an unwritten moral covenant. And our very participation in the United Nations, which is a child of our loins, involves an inescapable moral responsibility which commits us to the role of world power.

These considerations frame and define the role of the United States in the modern world. It is a role similar in some ways to that once occupied by Great Britain; we are now the banker nation, the creditor nation, the exporting nation, the great sea power, the great air power, the nexus of world communications. Much as Rome was the center of the world of its day, Washington is the center of the Western world in the twentieth century.

But there is a rival capital—and its name is Moscow. For any realistic statement of political facts must recognize that the world today is two worlds, and that conflict between Moscow and the West, another chapter in the vast eternal struggles of man, already has been joined.

This conflict is as real as the air about us, and as palpable as the earth; we cannot escape it or change it or avert it by Nice Nelly thoughts or by believing only what we wish to believe. Historical experience proves it; great power groupings inevitably develop friction points. But there is more than the experience of history to prove the existence of conflict between Russia and the West. The political, economic and ideological differences between Russia and the United States are too major to blink. A frank understanding and recognition of these differences must be the basis upon which any American policy is based.

There is the conflict of economies—the economy of capitalism with its profit incentive, its free-enterprise system and its past record of tremendous productivity and cyclic strain, and the economy of communism, with state ownership and control, elimination of capital gains, and the governmentally controlled utilization of man power, including slave labor, as an economic commodity.

There is the ideological conflict between the preachings of Western democracy, that the state exists for man, and the practices of communism, that man is a tool of the state. There is the basic conflict between the Christian ethics of the West and the militant fanaticism of the Bolshevist-anarchist code that the end justifies any means—proselytizing, subverting, spying, overthrowing and undermining, "liquidating" or removing all men and governments who do not bow down to the holy religion of the "party line."

There is the political struggle between a relatively primitive, partially industrialized, totalitarian dictatorship, a police state, which lends lip service only to democratic forms, and an easy-living but energetic, highly industrialized democracy which sometimes confuses license with freedom but which has produced the highest material standards of living in the world.

This conflict is inescapable, for Russia, too, is a world power; she, too, has world commitments, and she, too, has world interests. Like the United States, she has felt the strategic necessity, in the age of guided missiles and of "foreshortened geography,"[9] of exerting influence and securing bases beyond her frontiers. Like the United States, Russia has world-wide economic interests; she badly needs the manufactured products of the West to build up her own industry, and in time—though in the distant, not the immediate, future—she may even become a great exporting nation. And like the United States, Russia has world-wide political and moral obligations, the obligations to international communism which the men in the Kremlin have always honored despite wartime "recantations."

There is, therefore, inescapable conflict in today's world, with Russia and the United States as the chief protagonists. The United States must face the facts of this struggle. But a frank acknowledgment of conflict does not necessarily mean that a shooting war with Russia is inevitable or even probable; certainly it does not portend its imminence. For the men in the Kremlin do not want war, if they can achieve their aims without it. But those aims, which can be simplified to one aim, the conquest of power, will, I think, continue to guide Russian foreign policy as long as the Communist party rules Russia, and the Politburo will utilize any and all tactics, including, if necessary, eventual war, to accomplish the objective.

We can hope, therefore, if we follow the right policies,[10] to postpone or avert shooting war with Russia and to ease considerably the present strain and friction, but we can never hope, given the Russian Czarist traditions overlarded with Communist ambitions, to achieve really friendly, easy give-and-take relationships, so long as totalitarian communism faces democratic capitalism.

"X," the anonymous author (popularly supposed to be George

Kennan, of the State Department), summarized the situation objectively in an article, "The Sources of Soviet Conduct" in the July 1947 *Foreign Affairs*:

... there can never be on Moscow's side any sincere assumption of a community of aims between the Soviet Union and powers which are regarded as capitalist.

... we are going to continue for a long time to find the Russians difficult to deal with. It does not mean that they should be considered as embarked upon a do-or-die program to overthrow our society by a given date. The theory of the inevitability of the eventual fall of capitalism has the fortunate connotation that there is no hurry about it. The forces of progress can take their time in preparing the final *coup de grâce*. Meanwhile, what is vital is that the "Socialist fatherland"—that oasis of power which has been already won for socialism in the person of the Soviet Union—should be cherished and defended by all good Communists at home and abroad, its fortunes promoted, its enemies badgered and confounded. . . . The cause of socialism is the support and promotion of Soviet power, as defined in Moscow.

The political bi-polar world in which we live, which neither the UN nor any other agency can, at present, really weld into one[11] is, thus, whether we like it or not, a *fait accompli*, and we must build our policies upon acceptance of this fact.

But it is necessary to assess and analyze, if we are to understand the power position of the United States from the political viewpoint, the strengths and weaknesses of our potential friends and potential enemies in this bi-polar world, and to understand the changed political grouping and strategic situation the shift in power has helped to bring about.

As noted, the "security zones" of the "super-states" do not stop at their frontiers; both Russia and the United States have what might be described as "inner" and "outer" security zones. The nations contiguous to Russia's frontiers are in Russia's "inner security zone"; these states, in Kremlin opinion, must have governments friendly to Moscow, and that means either completely Communist-dominated governments, or left-wing coalition governments, with Communists in key positions,[12] or puppet areas controlled by force of Communist arms. This aim Russia already has accomplished not only in Europe but along vast reaches of her entire frontier—in Finland, Poland, Czechoslovakia, Yugoslavia, Bulgaria, Hungary, Rumania, Albania, Sinkiang, Outer Mongolia, Manchuria, Northern Korea. Of the nations contiguous to Russia, only Turkey, backed by the United States and Britain, and Iran— the latter the only really successful (yet transitory) example of United Nations' action against aggression—have, at writing, escaped such political domination,[13] and Northern Iran, at least, is plainly within Russia's strategic orbit and subject to political domination at some future time.

Russia's "outer security" zone might be defined as most of the rest of the world; initially, at least, it includes Greece, Austria, Italy, France, Germany, South Korea, and North China. Here the Soviet objective is precisely the same as in the "inner security" zone—establishment of governments friendly to Russia; namely, Communist-dominated governments. But the methods are different, and the means more subtle. In Western Europe the party line does not have the immediate backing of military force, nor are the ruthless tyrannies, internal espionage systems, and totalitarian methods to which the Balkan countries have been accustomed for so long, under no matter what government, well adapted to the culture of the West. Neither in Western Europe nor in Eastern Asia can Moscow claim the bond of Slavic blood and (paradoxically, in a Godless state) the Orthodox religion, which have proved an important tie in most of the Balkans.

In Russia's outer security zone the Communist tactics are termitic; sooner or later power is to be seized, if possible, from within the state by that faithful bank of Kremlin proselytizers who in all nations call themselves Communists, or who disavow the faith publicly but never oppose its edicts.

In the countries of this outer zone Communist parties and Communist influences have, generally speaking, recruited considerable strength during and since the war. This leftward swing was not unexpected. Prewar Europe was a land too often ridden by dead traditions and ancient forms; Asia was in economic and political chaos; the masses of both continents could not look to the old order for relief but could pin their hopes only upon the radical, the new, the untried. The great war achievements of Russia, the sheer propinquity of Russian mass, the effective participation of Communists in the wartime resistance movements, and the mistakes of the right and even of the left (non-Communist) political parties all contributed to the trend.

Working from within, the Communists in France, Italy and elsewhere entered coalition governments and commenced carefully to rehearse the familiar ritual of betrayal and conquest. In some cases they succeeded, within the legal framework of a country, in cutting the ground from beneath the feet of the left-center and liberal parties.

For a time in the war and postwar period, the Communists, in their pursuit of the conquest of power, substituted the tactic of legalism and political gradualism for their traditional preachment of illegal and violent revolution. In most European countries the ostensible political goals held out to the masses by Communist parties and left-center parties alike were seemingly identical—social reforms, nationalization of industry, etc. The chief political differences did not seem to lie in the ends but in the means; only the Communists stood in the public mind for accomplishment of these ends by force. The wartime switch of the party line which transferred the policy accent from "revolution" to a "gradualist" and legal approach was one of the factors that in the immediate postwar period helped to steal the thunder of the non-Communist left, and—given the greater fanaticism, aggressiveness, discipline and organization of the Communists—won votes for the Communists from left and center. To the liberals of any country the only other alternative to the program of the leftist parties—maintenance of the status quo and preservation of a "free enterprise" system[14]—seemed, in the postwar era of change, to have little appeal.

This Communist opportunism had its greatest and only complete successes in areas where political demagoguery was effectively supported by Russian armed force. In such countries the reduction in political effectiveness of the non-Communist left-wing parties was usually followed by absorption of these parties by the Communist party and eventually by domination by the Communists.

But in Western Europe the conquest of power was unable to progress by legal and gradualistic methods to such an end, and today the parties of the non-Communist left, particularly the peasants' and workers' parties, have regained a considerable measure of their influence and they remain the foremost enemy, in Communist estimation, of the Moscow-directed program.

The 1947 announcement of the creation of an international

"Cominform," in some respects a thinly disguised reavowal of the prewar "Comintern," in effect acknowledges a partial failure of the opportunistic policy of gradualism and a return to the ruthless tactic of revolt. Actually these political maneuverings have far less significance than the unalterable Communist aim which now, as in prewar days, remains the "security" of the Communist mother state, Russia, and, in second priority, the communizing by any and all means of as large a part of the world as possible.

The formation of the international "Communist Information Bureau" and the ousting of Communists from various of the Western European governments represented, however, a frank admission that the Communists' first postwar political attack upon the citadels of Western Europe, particularly France and Italy, had failed, and that a new tactic was to be tried. Togliatti, Communist leader in Italy, has threatened armed revolt, and inspired street riots in Paris and elsewhere indicated the resumption of the "illegal" and violent approach. This tactic, too, is opportunistic and perhaps transitory; it, too, can be abruptly changed at any time and in any country if the "party line" considers another approach more profitable.

Despite these mutations in Communist fortune, the net Communist gain, as compared to prewar days, is major, and Communist parties hold the balance of political power or exercise considerable influence upon the governments of many of the world's nations.

Russia, therefore, has been making considerable progress in the postwar years—not only in dominating her inner security zone, but (to a much lesser extent) in organizing and extending her influence in the outer security zone.

But the United States, too, has defined its own inner and outer security zones, and it, too, has been busy organizing these zones, though with the different weapons of democracy. The "inner zone," which a few years ago might have been defined as North America, Central America, the Caribbean, and the Eastern Pacific, has certainly been broadened since the war to include the Western Hemisphere, Hawaii and Greenland inclusive. The Monroe Doctrine, one of the few traditional pillars of American foreign policy, has been virtually restated, strengthened and amplified, all within the elastic terms of Article 52[15] of the United Nations Charter, first by the agreement of Chapultepec, and then by the inter American treaty of Rio de Janeiro of August 1947. To fortify these agreements separate defense arrangements have been reached with Canada, and various devices of presidential visits, military staff talks, military and diplomatic missions, economic aid and cultural interchange have been used to solidify the American republics insofar as possible into an American "bloc."

The outer defense zone of the United States, like that of Russia, is virtually world-wide. It certainly includes the Far Western islands of the Pacific, the British Isles, Iceland, the Azores and, as already indicated, the coastal littorals of Europe and Asia. Significantly, too, the spreading scope of our "defense" zones is now, like Russia's, concentric—not linear; the age of the Mercàtor projection has ended, and the new charts of the air-power age are oriented upon the polar regions. Politically, we have made since the war some progress in organizing this "outer zone"; we have been far from idle. Greece, Turkey and Korea, China and Italy (in addition to occupied Germany and Japan) are among the nations where American influence and American power are looming large, and most of Western Europe and Eastern Asia build their future upon the dollar. Nor is this merely a crass example of "dollar imperialism"—though without doubt the pull of power (in this case financial and industrial power) has acted as a lodestone upon many of these nations. For the physical materialism of America is, in the opinion of many of these nations, far less objectionable, tinctured as it is with a strange blend of idealism, than the philosophical materialism and cold, hard pragmatism of the Russians. Moreover, in these political skirmish grounds, the doctrine of international communism has now and again met major obstacles in nationalism; the interests of Russia, intelligent Frenchmen (or Englishmen or Italians) often perceived, conflicted with the interests of France (or England or Italy).

The political position of the United States, therefore, in the postwar world is still one of considerable strength.[16] But our position, as this chapter has tried to show, is not dependent upon ourselves alone. The strengths and weaknesses of our friends and foes (actual and potential) must inevitably alter the world's power balance.

RUSSIA—

The USSR has the strengths and weaknesses of a great land power and of a great dictatorship. The strength of its geographical position in what Mackinder, the British geopolitician, described as the Eurasian "heartland" has been dubbed, somewhat inaccurately, "incomparable."[17] There is no doubt that its vast sweep of territory over the greatest land mass in the world and straddling two continents gives Russia a dominating land position which practically defies complete conquest[18] (if by conquest is meant occupation and exploitation). That position also makes possible relatively easy extension of Russian power by land into Western Europe or Eastern Asia. However, large areas of Russia lie in climatic extremes; much is arid, and great spaces of tundra in the frozen north are of very limited strategic, political or economic value; only about 13 per cent is tillable. The USSR so far is a landlocked power. The conditions of her geography have imposed upon her throughout history the inevitability of inferiority at sea. Only in the Pacific do her mainlands debouch upon the open ocean, and there she is hemmed in by islands, many of which she does not hold. The Baltic and the Black are land-girt—their entrances controlled by other powers—the Caspian, an inland sea. The Arctic is ice-locked by nature. These geographical factors have been the basis of Russia's traditional drive toward an ice-free high-seas port. These disadvantages, which have helped to keep Russia a land power instead of a sea power, are also an element of strength, for her mainlands are protected from direct assault by sea. Though less vulnerable than any other power to amphibious assault, she is not, however, immune to such assault. And today, the plane, the atomic bomb, the missile—which enable direct attack upon industrial targets in Russia's vast hinterland—have destroyed much of the "heartland's" strategic invulnerability, just as they have weakened our own strategic position.

Soviet population and prospective population growth is another source of Russian strength; the USSR numbers between 190,000,000 and 200,000,000 persons today (as compared to 145,000,000 in the United States), and, it is estimated, will reach more than 250,000,000 by 1970. To this huge pool of strength, which, as the years pass, probably will continue to be a "younger" population than our own,[19] must be added 160,000,000 more peoples in lands already dominated by the Soviets (Rumania, etc.), plus perhaps 10,000,000 to 12,000,000 Communists in Russia's "outer security zone"—Britain, France, the United States, Asia, etc. This population, particularly the Russian elements of it, is tough, tenacious, loyal to "Mother Russia," brave and able to subsist on little. It is backward mechanically and is deficient in knowledge and technical skills. Some of its elements, particularly the non-Russian minorities in the USSR (some of the Ukrainians, for example) and the non-Communist majorities in Russian-dominated satellites, are dissident and give only lip service to Communist tenets.

In potential resources, the Soviet Union is possibly without a peer, but many of her resources lie in such inaccessible regions or are so difficult and expensive to exploit that they will remain for many years potential rather than actual. In developed resources the USSR ranks well behind the United States and seems to be particularly weak in tin, tungsten, mercury, sulphur and perhaps uranium. Nevertheless Russia possesses within her present territory virtually all the materials needed for her economic development and military potential.

In industrial production Russia is again second only to the United States (for a detailed statistical analysis of this comparative data, see the appendices), but the development of her industry, particularly her heavy industry, has been rapid in recent years, and her first postwar Five-Year Plan, though behind schedule in some particulars, and weak in agriculture and consumers' goods, seems to be making progress.

Contrary to popular impression, Russian industry is *more* (not less) concentrated, and *more* (not less) vulnerable to atomic (or conventional) bombing than U.S. industry. This is because the United States possesses a far larger *number* of plants, and because Russian industry has more transportation and production bottlenecks. The principal metallurgical areas in Russia (which means also the areas where heavy industry is most thickly concentrated) are the Ukraine, the Urals and the Altai-Sayan mountains of Siberia (the so-called Kuznetsk complex), with the Kazak area, the Lake Baikal area, and the Amur River area in Siberia of lesser but growing importance.[20] These are widely separated areas, each far-flung in scope, but they depend upon a tenuous and inefficient network of communications, and above all there are one or two facilities in each area which are bottlenecks in the whole producing process and which, if destroyed, would virtually cripple Soviet industry.

The ideology of the Communist cause and the totalitarian authoritarianism of the Soviet Government are factors which add considerable strength (and some weaknesses) to the Russian balance sheet. Virulent fanaticism on an international scale which does not stop at any means and which fosters the creation of termitic cells in the body politic of other nations is a major weapon of the Kremlin. The ability of the Politburo to concentrate the full power of the nation upon the task in hand, with a ruthlessness unparalleled in Western nations, is another weighty asset. But these factors are somewhat offset by the antipathies and antagonisms which fanaticism always breeds, and by the inflexibility of the Russian bureaucratic system. Russia has the ponderous might and power and mass of a glacier—and something of the same inflexibility.

In a military sense the Russian colossus has the strengths and weaknesses of mass. Technically, her army is somewhat backward, and generally speaking its equipment, with notable exceptions, is not comparable in quantity or quality[21] with that of Western armies. But in potential military man power Soviet Russia has unequaled resources (China, which is not, in the full sense of the term, a "nation," excepted). In the USSR in 1950 there will be about 13,000,000 males between the ages of eighteen and twenty-four—the best military age—and "the young men growing up in Russia will, between now and 1960, be able to outnumber the combined forces of U.S.A., Britain, the Dominions, the Low Countries and Scandinavia."[22] The Soviet Army is not, however, motorized or mechanized as are Western armies; "shanks' mare," horses, mules, troikas, busses—anything that moves is pressed into service by the Red Army. Essentially, it is an army of foot troops and its tactics are primarily those of mass.

The Red Army has developed some brilliant generals, who have been immeasurably aided in their campaigns by the virtually inexhaustible supply of Russian man power; casualties are no deterrent, and no price is too high to pay for a position. The restraint of death, therefore, has little effect upon the Red Army.[23] Its medical services, sanitation, discipline and supply (except in the best units) are backward. Its convulsive movements in retreat or in attack during World War II resembled none of the ordered chaos of Western armies on the move but rather the terrible surge[24] of the hordes of Genghis Khan—cavalry, tanks, busses, carriages, mules, oxen, cows driven along for meat and milk, soldiers, women, camp followers, all joined in inexorable mass movement. But most of the man power is fighting man power; there is little "overhead" in the

American sense and none of the vast appendages of OSS (Office of Strategic Services), graves-registration services,[25] medical personnel, special staff sections, etc. etc. which in the American Army divert so many men from the task of fighting. The Russian supply problem, too, is less complicated than ours; they have fewer vehicles and less mobility, but the Red Army, like the Japanese, lives in part off the country and moves up what it requires by sheer muscle power. Today, the Soviet Army (except for crack units) is an army of mass, half-trained troops with loose discipline, but tough and hardy; but it was and is, though not an efficient army, a highly effective one. Its weaknesses, moreover, are being remedied slowly.

The strength of Russia is the strength of the land; her strategy always has been geared to an army concept. This strength is at the same time a weakness; Russia's air force, is, like her land strength, a service of mass rather than quality. She has a great number of planes, particularly day fighters, and a large fighter and light-bomber production capacity. Her attack planes and close-support or "tactical" aviation are good, and she has some fast fighters, including jet models derived from the Germans. Russian copies of our B-29 Superfortresses have been made, but the USSR has no strategic bomber force comparable to our own. Air-raid warning systems, radar and fighter control techniques, and co-ordination of anti-aircraft guns and fighters are very weak; during the war her night fighter defense was conspicuous by its absence, and the Germans raided virtually at will.[26]

On the sea Russian naval strength (relative to our own) is negligible—though sufficient, against other Baltic and Black Sea states, to control those two seas. However, the Red Navy like the Red Air Force is benefiting from other powers. Fast, late-type German submarines and sunken German surface ships raised by the Russians as well as vessels transferred from Britain and the United States under lend-lease and taken over from the Italian Navy have added somewhat to the prewar strength of the Red Fleet and have undoubtedly proved a powerful stimulus to Russian naval designers. But today neither the Russian Navy nor the Russian Air Force could possibly keep the coasts of Europe secure against invasion.

Russia's traditional foreign policy has been blended of a strange mixture of offensive and defensive concepts. A warm-water port always has been included in her expansionist ambitions; control of the Dardanelles is another traditional objective. The introspective Russian mind, on the other hand, has tended to look inward toward the vast undeveloped spaces of "Mother Russia"; a species of isolationism always has distinguished the Russian outlook. Today, under the spur of Soviet industrial development, this has taken, at least for a time, the form of economic isolationism; Russia is striving to become industrially self-sufficient. But this nationalistic trend is accompanied and paralleled by an ideological internationalism, as expressed in "The Internationale"—the "international party shall be the human race."

GREAT BRITAIN AND THE DOMINIONS—

Strategically, Great Britain in the atomic age is part of Europe, and her past invulnerability to attack (so long as she controlled the seas) has gone forever. As a base for military power the isles are far less secure than ever before in history but no less important; they offer a defense in depth to Europe and they still lie athwart the principal shipping and air routes to the continent. Britain's new-found vulnerability in the age of the air, and the transformation of her nineteenth-century empire into a twentieth-century fraternal association of nations has led her to seek some strategic and territorial "compensation" for the lands that once were imperially British and which now no longer offer bases or "positions-in-readiness" for British forces. On the world scale Britain's attitude has been, on the whole, one of withdrawal, of "pulling in." India, Burma, Palestine, Egypt and most of the Middle East are now no longer "British" in the generic or the military sense; the sun is setting on the empire on which the sun never sets. But significantly in one world area, the general British policy of reducing commitments and withdrawing forces is being reversed. Africa, not India, is the new Mecca of London, and South Africa—geographically removed from the centers of European power, difficult to attack, rich in raw materials, gateway to a fabulously wealthy and undeveloped continent and strategically important to the sea and air routes to the Orient and the Pacific—plays a large part in Britain's future plans.

The so-called Mediterranean-Suez life line, reduced in basic importance with the British withdrawal from India, Burma, Egypt and Palestine, was, in any case, shown to be vulnerable in the last war to land-based aviation and to mines. The instability of the Middle Eastern political situation which renders that area an insecure base for British power, and the advent of the atomic and guided missile age make the Suez Canal-Mediterranean route potentially indefensible. Although Britain has by no means withdrawn from that sea, or from the Middle East, and is "hedging" her strategic bets by holding on to Cyprus, Malta and Gibraltar, the strategic-economic importance of Africa looms large on the canvas of Britain's future. The African positions offer Britain the ability to establish alternative relatively secure sea-air routes around the Cape of Good Hope, or across Africa, to replace, if need be, the misnamed Mediterranean-Suez "life line." South Africa, with its non-homogeneous population—British, Boers, natives, Hindus, many of them with little loyalty for Britain—has been held together politically and "saved" for England by one man, Jan Christian Smuts. When he passes from the stage of history, South Africa may become a politically unstable base for British power; clearly the recent visit of the royal family to this area was an attempt to consolidate latent loyalties. In any case, there is not much doubt that South Africa, its then political complexion permitting, has been selected tentatively as the site of an alternate British capital if London, in the next war, should be demolished or too greatly threatened by atomic bombs and guided missiles.

Britain's concentration upon Africa is not only in the South; Rhodesia and Kenya, East and West Africa and the Sudan are all undergoing development and experiencing immigration perhaps unprecedented in their history. Kenya is replacing Palestine and Egypt as the principal British military supply base in this whole vast area; the air routes across Africa, pioneered during the war by American fliers, are to be developed and extended by British pilots, and Britain is showing an understandable and lively interest in the future of the former Italian African colonies. The sea route around the Cape of Good Hope is being safeguarded by the development of naval and air bases and by the annexation, by South Africa and Australia, of the Prince Edward Island Group and Heard Island in the remote South Indian Ocean.

Britain's geographical weaknesses—her economic insularity which makes her dependent upon sea-borne imports for existence plus her strategic vulnerability to continental air power and missiles—is somewhat compensated by the "defense in depth" which Africa and her world-wide dominions offer. Canada and Australia particularly, each with active energetic white populations and with growing industries and large resources, are powerful increments of imperial strength and, remote from the world's power sources, they offer some of the attributes of a secure base which Britain lacks.

Economically Britain's position is far less sound and even more imperiled than her geographical one. She is trying to pull herself up by her boot straps and to restore prewar standards of living in an island which, in this modern world, may be overpopulated. Many of her industries are technologically backward, and quantitatively they are far outstripped by the United States and Russia, and the growing industrialization of the rest of the world and the loosening bonds of empire threaten her economic existence. Coal has long been one of the basic bulwarks of British economic power; her coal exports to Europe helped materially to "pay" Britain's way. But the mines have come upon bad days; Britain's postwar coal production has been, until recently, insufficient for her own use, much less for export. There are many technological and other reasons for Britain's impoverished economy. The terrible toll of British life in World War I, the loss of the best and bravest of several generations, and the liquidation of a considerable part of Britain's overseas investments during World War II are part of the background. The fact remains that Britain's economic situation today is grim, nor can true but irrelevant remarks about the "stout old British character" alleviate that grimness.

Nevertheless, the coal of Britain—if it can be gotten out of the ground; the mineral resources of the Empire, and the factories of the British Isles, particularly the shipyards and aircraft factories—are powerful factors of enduring strength.

Politically and psychologically Britain is also "sick"; she is struggling to regain her prewar position by socializing or "nationalizing" many of her resources, and, so far, has tried to cure economic ills by imposing more and more controls, always a doubtful and dangerous expedient. In a psychological sense the British people, though resigned, hardy, brave and tenacious, have too little incentive; high taxes and the elimination of the profit system (in certain fields); the lack of consumer goods, and the social and economic stratifications of British life, plus the increasingly onerous "controls" and restrictions of government have reduced the urge to work hard to a minimum.[27]

Just as the economic situation in Britain requires drastic cures—perhaps wholesale emigration, or the creation of a new African empire, for instance—so the psychological situation calls for emphatic measures. The "sickness" of the British people, though not advanced and not yet pronounced, has been evidenced since the war in the (for stable, stolid Britain) increase of extremists. Anti-Semitism, fed, of course, by the unforgivable murders and terroristic policies of sections of the Jewish "underground" in Palestine, has flourished, and the Mosley brand of British Fascists has battened on it. Communism has also recruited a few members from those who naturally recoil in horror from the excesses of the right, and the British middle class, long the solid backbone of the "tight little isle," already impoverished and pinched economically, is now caught politically and psychologically between the millstones of fanaticism. Extremism is not likely to be the ultimate outcome, however, unless hungry desperation stalks London's streets. The British, in George Orwell's words, have the "habit of not killing one another," and an Englishman, in a letter to the Manchester *Guardian* (quoted by Herbert Matthews), expressed the national trait concisely when he wrote: "The English taste for art is confined to the art of living together." Indeed the solid, objective stable qualities of the British probably doom the extremist; Britons may express their resentment about the shape of things by voting the Conservatives back into power!

Militarily the world-wide system of British bases offers her great advantages in position, and the number and excellent quality of her planes, ships and equipment make her a major factor at sea or in the air. Britain still possesses many of the long-term elements of military greatness, resources, bases, skills and aptitudes and character. But her native population is small and she cannot depend for mass man power upon the peoples of the empire. Britain may be expected to make great progress in military research and development, but her economic stringencies have reduced her short-term capacity for maintaining military strength; she cannot afford the "insurance" of a large navy, army, or air force. For the first time since Drake's day, the British Home Fleet has been virtually decommissioned; it contains a pitiful modicum of vessels; her army is being cut gradually from 800,000 men in 1947 to perhaps 200,000 men, approximately its prewar strength, and the R.A.F., now considered perhaps the most important of the services, is relatively small in size though excellent in quality. Her economic and population weaknesses and her losses in both World Wars will probably impose long-term military restrictions, which, if war should come, might limit Britain's effort.

Britain, despite her Socialist government, is still tied—inevitably —to the United States, upon whom she is dependent economically as well as politically.

Traditionally, British foreign policy has been that of "the free hand." Throughout the period of Empire greatness, Britain opposed consistently the domination of the continent of Europe by any one power, and implemented her policy by limiting her political and military commitments, and, in war, by throwing the power of the British pound, the British fleet and limited army strength into the scales against any nation that sought to achieve continental domination. But precisely the same factors that have invalidated the geographic concepts of isolationism have delivered a death blow to the "free hand" policy of Britain. Neither "splendid isolationism" nor real detachment is possible in the modern world of atomic bombs and guided missiles; there are no longer any neutrals, and Britain is not an island any more.

. . . the hand of Britain is not free as it was two generations ago . . . ; and though she may be driven back on the "free hand" as her general line of policy, it would be difficult to execute and clearly no more than a makeshift.[28]

Britain and the United States are tied, by the facts of power in the postwar world, to common policies.

This *de facto* "alliance" is more than a product of sentiment, ideology, common language and common tradition. It represents common interest; Britain's traditional policy (and it is now a life-or-death policy) still opposes the forcible domination of Europe by any one power. To the United States, the British Isles are an essential advanced base; to Britain, the United States must represent the "defense in depth" which her proximity to the continent does not permit. But there is an even more compelling factor which emphasizes the strategic interdependence of Britain and the United States and which, for at least the foreseeable future, would seem to make impossible any British "neutrality" and would force Britain on the side of the United States in any future world conflict. That factor is the fate of the Commonwealth, which—widespread across the world—is now almost completely dependent for protection and for economic unity upon American sea-air power.

For all countries of the Commonwealth good relations with the United States in particular are of vital importance and every care must be taken to maintain harmony. . . .[29]

FRANCE—

France is still suffering from the old *malaise*—the illness of division and political dissension, economic, demographic and psychological weaknesses that brought her to downfall in 1940. Today, she is a medium power with potentialities of extreme weakness if past trends continue.

The strategic importance of France was well illustrated by the last war. She is a key to Western Europe; through the "gates" of the Lowlands, the conquerors of the past have swept from France into Germany and vice versa. France guards the natural barrier of the Rhine, and her Alpine passes control communications into Italy. Her Atlantic and Mediterranean coasts offer, through her great ports, natural gateways into Europe, and the proximity of France to England makes a strategic rapprochement between France and England vital to the British Isles. As a colonial power France also has great importance. Her North and West African colonies are not only a source of military man power and economic wealth, but they flank the sea routes through the Mediterranean and around Africa, a fact of particular importance to Britain, now engaged in a reorientation of her strategy, with Africa cast in a role of greatly expanded importance.

The French military position is one of weakness. The old prewar complacency—"the French soldier is much better than he looks"; "the French Army is the best in the world"—has perhaps forever vanished; today's weaknesses are recognized and may, indeed, be overstated. Because of economic stringencies and a falling birth rate, the French armed forces are small in size and at present obsolescent in equipment. The Air Force seems particularly backward, and the French factories probably are incapable of producing planes in sufficient quantities to maintain superiority over the air space of France. The Navy is making a valiant effort to recover some of its prewar strength with the aid of a carrier loaned by Britain, small vessels transferred to it by the United States and prizes of war. Though small in size compared to the gigantic fleets of the United States, the French Navy today is the world's fourth largest, and its ships are more modern than those of Russia.

France's economic weaknesses are not as pronounced as those of Britain, for she has always been, with the aid of her African colonies, a far more self-sufficient nation. Her coal and other resources, complemented now by the resources of the French-controlled German Saar, her land and her frugal peasant stock are continuing items in the black in the economic balance sheet. Financial and currency reform, plus some rehabilitation of her industry and transportation, could draw much real wealth out of hiding and could eliminate the black market, which now has a strangle hold upon French life.

The French future, however, is plainly mortgaged to politics. The disunity of the prewar years, marked by a multiplicity of parties at cross purposes and a consequent instability of government and program, has continued to characterize postwar France. The psychological result induced, partly, of course, by the French Communists, the shadow of Russia and the fear of the average Frenchman of being caught "in the middle" between the United States and Russia, has been confusion and lack of confidence. For a time the Communists capitalized strongly on this weakness, but the fall of 1947 seemed to have marked at least a temporary turning point in the fortunes of the French Communist party. Its strength was not diminished absolutely, but relatively the Communists lost ground as large segments of French opinion crystallized and combined into an anti-Communist combination. Noteworthy was the re-emergence as a powerful force in French politics of General de Gaulle's Reunion of the French People, a political movement centered in the austere, egoistic but strong personality of one man.

Psychologically and politically the Gallic temperament has at once great qualities of durable strength and excitable propensities for mercurial and instable action. The French are essentially individualist and democratic, but they are susceptible to the persuasions of a flaming cause or the rounded periods of a great leader. The future of France depends upon their reactions.

CHINA—

A disparate country—never, in modern times, a nation in the Western sense. Torn by civil strife, inchoate, massive, half-feudal, the giant stirs but has not yet fully awakened; its unification as a nation still seems a process of decades or even centuries.

China's strategic importance is that of mass and position; her vast land area occupies much of Eastern Asia and dominates the coastal islands from Okinawa to the Philippines. Her territory offers certain natural, though difficult, routes of invasion into the heart of Eurasia, but her primitive transportation and communication network and her great distances restrict materially the feasibility of extensive land military operations. Her limited number of modern ports and logistic and political difficulties make maintenance of large air bases on Chinese soil difficult. Strategically, Manchuria and the contiguous area of Korea, both already Communist-dominated by virtue of Yalta and other agreements and postwar developments, are the most important areas in the China sphere. North China, with its relatively rich mineral deposits, is a gateway to all the southern coastal littoral, and the Shantung peninsula, opposite Dairen and Port Arthur, is an important base for control of the Yellow Sea.

China's military strength is almost solely that of mass man power; she has virtually no major industry; her equipment is poor, her leadership bad, her methods extremely primitive, her armies weak psychologically and divided into warring Communist and anti-Communist groups. Given ammunition, adequate weapons, modern training, and good leadership, the Chinese peasant can become a patient, dogged soldier; today his military strength is chiefly that of a great guerrilla land force. Chinese air strength is minor and is wholly dependent upon outside sources of supply. The Chinese Navy, by virtue of an American training mission and the transfer of American supplies, is probably the most efficient of the armed services, but is capable of little more than coast-guard action and limited amphibious transport. Nevertheless, it is, next to the Russian, the most important navy in the Far East today (U.S. and the colonial powers, Holland, England, etc., excepted).

China's great economic weaknesses, partially war-induced, are both short-term and long-term. She has the strength (and weaknesses) of a tremendous population, but her population is too large for the primitive methods of land cultivation employed, and periodic famines occur. Her peoples are largely illiterate and backward; China has very little industry, her transportation and communications network are inadequate, and though rather important sources of raw materials are known to exist they have been but little exploited. She is also subject to a violent run-away inflation and black market, and graft and corruption probably unequalled elsewhere.

The political problem of China also seems largely insoluble. Americans have made the profound mistake of viewing China as a nation in the Western sense, although she has never been in modern history a homogenous whole. We have also tended to recoil in holy horror from revelations of graft, corruption, bribery and bureaucracy in Chiang Kai-shek's government, although the practice of "cumshaw" and the excesses of bureaucracy have behind them in China the validity of centuries of tradition. Because certain sections of Communist-dominated China did offer, to the visiting American, a pleasing contrast to the sordid and decadent qualities of Chungking and Nanking, some of our peoples have advocated support of the Chinese Communists as the lesser of two evils. These Communists, we have been told, are not real Communists; they are not tied to Russia. Such a judgment represents a profound mistake; no matter what the Chinese Communist movement may once have been, no matter what its agrarian origins, no matter what the roots of its justification, it is today part of the international Communist movement, supported by Russia, encouraged by Russia, and its general plans and policies worked out to follow the Communist party line (modified, of course, as it always is, to fit local conditions). Chiang Kai-shek, therefore, rather than the Communists, is the lesser of two evils.

Neither he nor the Communists, however, offer hope of any quick political solution in China; indeed, we may have to face the virtual disintegration of China into two or three or more virtually autonomous regions, with the Communists controlling in the North, Chiang in the Yangtse valley area, and "war lords" elsewhere.

GERMANY—

In power potential, if Russia be excluded, Germany is still the strongest nation of Europe. Today, divided, conquered, occupied, her cities in ruins and her industries working at reduced capacity, the Reich is not a military power, but a political hodge-podge, a psychological monstrosity, and an economic volcano. Nevertheless, the potentialities which once made Germany a great power able to fight half the world still exist. Raw materials in the Ruhr, Silesia, etc., the discipline, energy and skills of her peoples, her unexcelled scientific and technological capabilities, industries, when reparations dismantling is completed, roughly equivalent in capacity to that of 1936, and the organizational brains and military skills of the ex-enemy make the Germans a potentially formidable people. Germany's power, however, is potential only, dependent strictly upon unification of her peoples and a concentration of the national purpose upon some objective. No one can yet say what effect her terrible defeat will have upon German psychology, but to a people nurtured on the doctrine of Nietzsche and the dark epics of Wagner, the carnage of defeat will probably do no more than foster a persecution mania. Hitlerism is not dead; the essential nature of the German people is unchanged. As Harold Nicolson writes in *The Congress of Vienna*:[30]

> . . . the neurotic Prussian is congenitally subject to sudden alternations of extreme confidence and apathetic despair. . . . how natural it was for the average Prussian, or indeed the average German, to pass (as it were in a night) from a sense of destiny to a sense of doom, and again from the helpless acceptance of doom to a feverishly active faith in destiny.

The Germans, in the march of history, have been outstripped industrially and in population, and the changes in the world political situation, plus the crushing nature of their defeat and the facts of their partition, indicate that even a revived Germany, truncated as she would be, would be a limited menace to the peace of the world unless allied with a super-state or other great or medium powers.

But German technological capacity and industrial efficiency, allied for instance with Russian mass, would be a formidable combination indeed. Nor has the potential strength of such an alliance

,escaped the attention of the men in the Kremlin. Long before the war ended, the "Free Germany National Committee" and the "Union of German Officers," headed by German Communists and by the captured German generals, Field Marshal General Friederich von Paulus and Major General Walther von Seydlitz, had become formidable instruments of propaganda. These groups are still retained by Moscow in altered form: (1) to cement the military-industrial relations between Russian-occupied Germany and Russia; (2) to serve as a potential political instrument to govern Eastern Germany, and to weld Germany into a Communist "ally" of Russia when the Western allied armies are withdrawn. The "Free Germany" committee, now called the "German National Liberation Committee," not only has the formidable force of international communism, and particularly German communism, behind it, but its military members are calculated to appeal to the German conservatives and ex-veterans to persuade them of the righteousness of the cause. Moscow also has organized, as an implement to back up the "Free Germany National Committee" (and, incidentally, to increase Russian military strength) an army of German prisoners of war, variously estimated in size from 100,000 to 1,000,000 strong. The nature of this Russian-dominated German army and the details of its organization are shrouded by the "iron curtain," but there is no doubt that hundreds of thousands of Germans have been organized in military or semi-military formations and have been at least partially equipped with arms. Germany today is a battleground, its fate still undetermined, a country trying to rise to new power by exploiting the differences between the East and West. Tomorrow, renascent Germany, rather than Russia, may be the world's problem.

JAPAN—

Japanese military power, like German, has been temporarily eliminated, but the basic nature of the Japanese people has not been altered; their capacities for militarism still exist. The nature of a people is not changed in two or three or five or ten years of occupation, despite the best-thought-out democratization and re-education policies. Our educational methods in Germany and Japan have not been more than superficially effective; "de-Nazification" is a phrase and a legal process, not a reformation of the mind.

The insular position of the Japanese islands off the coast of Asia gives them strategic importance similar to Britain's, but unlike the British Isles, the Japanese islands lie off a relatively undeveloped land mass, with the great hinterland of China a power vacuum. Japan is deficient in raw materials, excessive in population; her future, if she is to have one, must lie in external activities—trade, emigration, shipping, alliance with another power. The energy, submission to discipline and courage of the Japanese people are still major military assets, but like Germany, Japan's immediate future as a world factor is as an ally. But she does not have either the continental position or the industrial and technological capacity of Germany. Under her new constitution, Japan is supposed to have renounced for all time all military forces, but already some second thoughts on this subject by Americans as well as Japanese indicate this renunciation is merely temporary. In the immediate future, without armed strength of her own and economically impoverished as she has been by the war, Japan, like China, is something of a power vacuum. Thus vast areas of the Orient, once at least in uneasy equilibrium, now are temporarily powerless pawns, influenced by the chess masters, Russia and the United States. Like Europe, the Orient today is no longer a power center in its own right. For the time being, at least, so vulnerable is Japan to sea blockade,[31] the Pacific ex-enemy is clearly dependent upon, and therefore under the influence of, the United States. This will be true even when our troops are withdrawn from the main Japanese islands, for the nearby American positions in the Marianas and Okinawa dominate Japan strategically. The short-term future of Japan, therefore, is inevitably linked with the United States.

But the men in the Kremlin and Japanese Communists, though they have so far had little success, have not abandoned the "conquest of power" in the Orient, and they will be aided by the major economic and political difficulties Japan certainly faces in the future. The Russians still hold hundreds of thousands of captives of Japan's Kwantung army, to what end and for what purpose (save as slave labor) is not yet clear. And Russia dominates Manchuria and Korea, the continental positions directly opposite Japan.

ITALY—

Italy has far less inherent power—politically, industrially and in population—than either of the other former Axis powers. But her geographical position in the Mediterranean, dominating the central portion of that sea and flanking Greece, and her ship-building facilities and the heavy industries of the Po Valley make her an important factor in European politics. The land routes through the Alps, traversing Italian soil, offer one gateway (though of limited importance) from east to west, and ideologically Italy (Rome), as the center of Catholicism and traditionally one of the great cradles of the culture of the Western world, has tremendous significance. Traditionally, Italy tends to side with the West, but disappointment over peace-treaty terms directed particularly against England, the propinquity of Communist-dominated Yugoslavia, hard economic conditions and the bitterness of defeat have aided the Communist drive for domination.

Such are some of the principal strengths and weaknesses of some of our friends and enemies in the bi-polar world of today. Scores of other nations—some of them deserving ranking as "medium" powers, most of them small, none without importance—add great individual and collective strength to the world total. Yugoslavia, Communist-dominated, has a large army of stout fighters; Turkey controls the Dardanelles, flanks the Middle East and has a tough, large army (though badly equipped). The Scandinavian countries, with iron ore and industry, shipping and food, are important in the picture of the North, and Spain, bitterly anti-Communist but no friend of the democracies, is an important factor in Mediterranean strategy. Greece, torn, like China, by civil strife largely induced by Communist policy, is a battleground, with Mediterranean influence and control of the Aegean approaches to the Dardanelles as the prize.

The great importance of the smaller countries in the conflict for power which already has been joined in this bi-polar world is geographical and collective; they offer positions and bases and areas of strategic necessity to the "super-states," and their pooled strength is formidable. These smaller states are, indeed, the battleground of ideologies, economies, politics; collectively they may determine the future history of the world.

No fully accurate international balance sheet in this bi-polar world can be drawn up, for the world is not all black and all white, not all Communist, or anti-Communist; there are many gradations of political and ideological loyalties, many areas of gray, and in vast regions of the earth the struggle still is undetermined. Because the interests of the United States and of Western civilization require a clear conception, however, of the world's present political structure, it is useful to list, insofar as it is possible to do, the Communist, or Communist-dominated states, dominated *politically* and/or *economically* and/or *strategically*—and those influenced by or favorable to the United States. This listing, of course, is subject to change as the struggle for power goes on.

THE UNITED STATES

Great Britain	Belgium
Eire	Holland
Canada	Philippines
Australia	Japan
New Zealand	Latin-America
South Africa	Portugal

RUSSIA

Manchuria	Hungary
Outer Mongolia	Yugoslavia
Korea	Albania
Sinkiang	Poland
Rumania	Finland
Bulgaria	Czechoslovakia

UNEASY WOULD-BE NEUTRALS

Norway, Sweden, Denmark
Switzerland

NO MAN'S FRIEND

Spain

THE BATTLEGROUNDS

Austria	The Middle and Near East
Italy	China

France   India
Germany   Burma
Free Territory of Trieste   The Malay States
Greece   The Netherlands East Indies
Turkey   Siam
Iran

The mere listing of such a "line-up" does not adequately suggest the importance of the facts.

The world is two worlds. The "heartland" of Eurasia—the world's greatest land mass—is Russian territory. Eastern Europe is under Russian political and strategic domination. This means, so far, that Eastern Europe is also under Russian economic domination, and in turn this poses a major problem to the United States, in its attempts to aid and help and influence the nations of its "outer security" zone. For before the war the countries of Eastern Europe, exactly those countries that are now in the Soviet sphere of influence, exported some 80 per cent of their products to Western Europe and obtained almost an equal percentage of their imports from Europe. Eastern and Southeastern Europe provided a small but essential percentage of the foodstuffs of the West. But they are now being economically "integrated" insofar as possible into the Soviet orbit, and the food supplies formerly available to the West from the East have not been available in the postwar period. This is part of the background of the so-called Truman-Marshall plan; that plan not only is attempting to rehabilitate and stabilize Europe, and to "stop" communism but to help the West reorient its economy temporarily in the hope that eventually trade with Eastern Europe may be resumed. This divisive trend, the result of war dislocation and destruction, which has pulled an economic iron curtain as well as a psychological one across the middle of Europe, may be, in part, transitory—must, indeed, be temporary, if economic stabilization is to occur. Czechoslovakia, for instance, has found she needs American products and American markets, and Poland, which sent more than 90 per cent of her exports to Russia in 1945, reduced that to 63 per cent in 1946 and to about 43 per cent in the first six months of 1947. But even if the economic division of Europe is in part temporary, the facts of Soviet strategic domination in Eastern Europe are plain. Russia controls the Baltic, and Sweden stands in her long shadow, which also looms ominously over Greece, the

Middle East and Turkey. The Soviets probably could, if they were willing to face the consequences of war, shut off the supply of high-grade Swedish iron ore to Western Europe and cut the flow of oil through the Mediterranean from the Middle East.

Russia occupies a similarly advantageous strategic position in northeastern Asia. She exercises directly by virtue of the Yalta and Potsdam agreements, and indirectly through the power of the Chinese Communist armies, effective strategic control over Manchuria, which in itself has long been the industrial heart of the mainland of Eastern Asia. The Communist armies of China also control or threaten great stretches of territory in North China, site of some of Asia's wealthiest mineral deposits. American forces occupy Southern Korea but, aside from their numbers, which are small as compared to the Russian garrison, they are in an indefensible position, for most of the industrial production and 90 per cent of all the power in Korea comes from the Soviet-occupied zone.

Russia, therefore, is solidifying control of her "inner security" zone and has great strategic and ideological and some economic influence upon nations in her "outer zone."

But the United States is not weak. We, too, have "solidified," though by less arbitrary methods, most of the Western Hemisphere in an "American bloc," and in our outer security zone, the industrial products which only America can furnish and the food which America is furnishing are potent arguments.

Such are the facts of power in the political world of the twentieth century. From them various writers, James Burnham probably most unequivocally,[32] have drawn the conclusion that a struggle for the world, with world domination as the fruit of victory, is inevitable. To support this thesis they have drawn heavily upon Toynbee,[33] whose epic treatment of the history of civilizations seems to trace a pattern common to them all. Judged by this background, the world has approached a period in our present civilization called the "Time of Troubles," when two "super-states" have risen, by wars and power, to world dominance. The next cycle, Toynbee infers, may be the emergence of one of them—probably through war—to outstanding dominance and the downfall of the other, followed possibly by a final implacable step in the cycle, the decay and dissolution of the entire civilization. But this inexorable Greek tragedy, which, with variations, has been repeated periodically in the life cycle of men and nations, requires centuries for fulfillment, and, in any case, as Harold Nicolson has well observed: ". . . if history can teach us anything it can teach us the folly of prophecy and the wisdom of patience."[34]

And one engaged in a short-term review of our national security does not need either to accept or to reject the Toynbee thesis to understand the political bi-polarity, with all its strategic implications, of the modern world.

NOTES—Chapter II

1. *America's Strategy in World Politics*, by Nicholas John Spykman, Harcourt, Brace & Company. Page 461.

2. Ibid., page 472.

3. It would be premature to bury Europe; that continent often has been moribund, but never has expired. Its population is more than double that of North America, and its resources are great.

4. "Disappeared": Austria-Hungary; Estonia; Latvia; Lithuania; Serbia; Montenegro; Manchukuo. To which might be added Danzig and Fiume.

5. The term "power politics" is opprobrious to most Americans, but actually it does not deserve its ill repute. "Power politics" is a redundancy, for there are no politics without power and no power without politics. And power politics can be applied to progressive and forward-looking purposes as well as to evil and conquest.

6. Willkie's famous phrase "one world," though idealistic, was always unrealistic; "one world" is, and has been, impossible until the education of man erases the prejudices of man.

7. This does not mean that isolationism, as a political manifestation, is "dead." Far from it. Isolationism, in modern guise, is still an influence in domestic politics, but strategically and geographically the once valid concepts upon which isolationism rested are now obsolete. See Chapter V.

8. See Chapter IV and Appendix I and II.

9. How much Russia has appreciated the strategic implications of the new weapons remains to be seen. Her expansion into Eastern Europe, however, seems more a result of past (and bitter) experience than an assessment of future needs. Three times in a little more than a generation she has been subjected to violent and extensive land invasions from the west; her policy today is in some sense that of the Czars—to build up buffer states and land masses between her and the power centers of Western Europe. But it has less excuse today, with Western Europe in ruins and air power rather than land power the real threat.

10. See Section III.

11. To reiterate a previous footnote: One world in a real sense will have to be the product of long-term effort—the effort of centuries; it will not be achieved by formulas or organization but only from the mind and the spirit,

by education and experience. James Burnham thinks it can be achieved only by the personal mental and moral renunciation of power.

12. Communist-dominated governments nearly always find Communists heading the departments of security (or interior); in other words, controlling the internal police power of the country in question. The next step in the Communist technique of the "conquest of power" is capture of a nation's judicial processes and armed forces.

13. This "domination" by Russia is of course more or less complete, depending upon the stage reached in the Communists' conquest of power. It is absolute in Rumania, Bulgaria and Yugoslavia, and strategic, more than political, in Finland and Czechoslovakia.

14. American policy in Europe has too often seemed to offer only these goals.

15. Article 52 of the United Nations Charter permits regional agreements within the framework of the UN.

16. The details of our power position—military, economic and psychological—are developed in succeeding chapters.

17. *The Struggle for the World*, by James Burnham, the John Day Company. Page 114.

18. The sheer mass of Russia would seem to defy complete conquest even in the atomic age. But great border fringes have been attacked and conquered and sundered from the main Russian mass many times in past history.

19. These figures are a compromise of population statistics found in the following books: *The Population of the Soviet Union*, by Frank Lorimer, League of Nations, 1946; *The Peoples of the Soviet Union*, by Corliss Lamont, Harcourt, Brace & Company, New York, 1945; *The Future Population of Europe and the Soviet Union*, by Frank Notestein and others, League of Nations, 1944; *The Statesman's Year Book*, the Macmillan Company, New York, 1946.

20. From an article by George B. Cressey, "Siberia's Role in Soviet Strategy" in *Compass of the World*, edited by Hans W. Weigert and Vilhjalmur Stefansson, The Macmillan Company. This book contains a disparate but interesting discussion of geopolitical factors, particularly the provocative chapter by the Rev. Edmund A. Walsh, S.J., on "Geopolitics and International Morals." See also the article by "X," "The Sources of Soviet Conduct" in July 1947 *Foreign Affairs*. "X" comments: "Soviet economic development . . . has been precariously spotty and uneven. . . . Here is a nation striving to become in a short period one of the great industrial nations of the world while it still has no highway network worthy of the name and only a relatively primitive network of railways. . . . Maintenance is still a crying deficiency of all Soviet economy. Construction is hasty and poor in quality. Depreciation must be enormous. . . ."

21. Although the Soviet Army is not as well equipped as Western armies, the Russians have always manufactured good artillery, and their theory of artillery support is a corollary to their whole mass army concept. Their World War II heavy tanks were excellent combat vehicles though they owed some of that excellence to basic American and British design features.

22. "Soviet Military Potential," by Colin Clark, in *Soundings*, London, September 1947.

23. This human profligacy has its drawbacks; it tends to "freeze" tactical concepts of mass.

24. These comments about the relatively primitive logistics and equipment of the Russian Army are *not* applicable to a number of excellently trained, well-equipped and thoroughly disciplined units. These form, however, a distinct minority.

25. Low-ranking Russian casualties are not reported. If a Russian private does not come home his family must assume he is dead. They may never know.

26. See *The Strange Alliance*, by Major General John Russell Deane, the Viking Press. Pages 121-22.

27. Britain never has been, in the American sense, either an economic or social democracy; there have never been opportunities for advancement for the common man comparable to those enjoyed in this country.

28. *British Security*—a report by a Chatham House Study Group, Royal Institute of International Affairs. Page 156.

29. Ibid., page 78.

30. Harold Nicolson, *The Congress of Vienna*, Harcourt, Brace & Company. Page 22.

31. The war demonstrated the vulnerability of Japan to sea blockade. Contrary to popular opinion, the blockade of Japan was the primary cause of her defeat—not the air bombardment. Japan was already defeated before the two atomic bombs were added to the huge fire raids which destroyed so many Japanese cities. Even before the first conventional bomb was dropped on Japan, Japanese raw materials were scarce; food rationing was severe, and her industrial output had declined.

32. *The Struggle for the World*, by James Burnham, the John Day Company.

33. *A Study of History*, by Arnold J. Toynbee. Abridgment by D. C. Somervell, Oxford.

34. *The Congress of Vienna*, by Harold Nicolson, Harcourt, Brace & Company. Introduction.

CHAPTER III

THE MILITARY POSITION—THE NEW FACE OF WAR

O Hercules, the valour of man is at an end!

ARCHIDAMUS

THE fate of man in a "bi-polar" world, always politically complex and economically difficult, has been rendered infinitely hazardous by the technological revolution in warfare.

Politically, there have been bi-polar worlds before in history—Greece and Persia; Greece and Rome; Rome and Carthage; England and Spain. But never before have weapons approached the infinite in speed, range and destructiveness; never before have the technical means been presented to man by which he might hope to exercise dominion of all the world—or destroy much of it in the process.

From out the first flint axe and bended bow has at length emerged a Frankenstein monster—the inventiveness of today—that is destroying man's own work, his own culture, his own civilization, his past, his present and his future.[1]

Never before have weapons transformed the world, in a time-space sense, into "one world";[2] never before has war even approximated its present "totality." The Huns, the Vandals, the Mongols and the Goths scourged and destroyed, ravaged and burned, but never with such awful scope and horrible efficiency as today.

The trend toward totality and absolutism in war has been marked since Napoleon when "armies were quadrupled in size and battles in slaughter."[3] Jomini remarked prophetically a century ago that war might well become "wars of peoples . . . a bloody and most unreasonable struggle between great masses equipped with weapons of unimaginable power,"[4] and Spengler recorded bitterly in 1922, "this is the century of gigantic permanent armies and universal compulsory service. . . ."[5]

The industrial revolution, the rise of powerful nation-states, the degradation of morals have all contributed to this manic destructiveness, but the capstone and climax of horrors has been achieved by scientific discovery and engineering development—the technological revolution of today.

Range, destructiveness and mobility always have determined the dominant weapons of their day. Of these characteristics range was, and is, the most dominant. Like a boxer's reach it is a highly important coefficient of combat efficiency; if one ean hit an enemy and the enemy cannot hit you, the battle is won. The slingshot and spear outranged the club and were in turn superseded by the bow and arrow, the smoothbore, the rifle, the cannon, the long-range naval guns and field pieces of today—and currently by the plane and the long-range guided missile. The range of weapons, soon to be measured in transoceanic and intercontinental terms, is now approaching the limits of our world and may, in real truth, almost achieve the infinite in globe-girdling, satellite missiles capable of circling the earth endlessly.

Destructiveness, similarly, has achieved new dimensions with the startling suddenness of a geometric progression. The single-shot, one-kill weapon was quickly superseded by weapons of mass destruction—the machine gun, gas, etc.—and this trend is now approaching totality when one bomb, with lethal impersonality, can destroy 100,000 people whom the bombardier never sees.

Similarly, mobility has achieved climactic superlatives. The speed of the plane and the speed of the missile, both of them now measured in terms of the speed of sound, are becoming the standard yardsticks of military mobility.

Range, destructiveness, mobility—modern science and modern engineering have pushed back the horizons of nature and broadened the frontiers of knowledge. But—to what end? To let us gaze— "we, who are about to die"—upon the death mask of the new face of war?

An understanding of the present capabilities and limitations of the new weapons, their future potentialities and their military significance, is fundamental to any comprehension of America's present power position.

This chapter will attempt to describe in language the layman can understand the new weapons of war.

THE ATOMIC BOMB

The atomic bomb is a finite, not an infinite weapon, a weapon with definite limitations, but also with terrifying capabilities. It is more than "just another bomb," but less than "the absolute weapon," though, for the purposes of the common man, it comes close enough to the latter to lend little comfort.

It is, first of all, a bomb, and hence must be carried to its objective by some mechanism. Its explosive substance, plutonium or uranium 235 (both derivatives of uranium),[6] is the basis of its power; the atoms of this material at the instant of detonation are sundered, or "fissioned," giving the bomb a theoretical explosive power (in the case of all bombs so far used) equivalent to roughly 20,000 tons of TNT.

Actually, just as 20,000 tons of TNT, if it could be exploded in one bomb, would *not* be as effective a destructive agent as 20,000 tons of TNT detonated in many separate bombs, so the atomic bomb is considerably less destructive than its theoretical potential. For large bombs are less efficient destructive agents, in proportion to their size, than small bombs. The area of damage caused by small bombs increases about as the 4/3 power of the weight; damage due to medium-size bombs increases in approximately direct proportion to the weight; in large bombs, the damage area increases as the 2/3 power of the weight. For very powerful bombs, like the atomic bomb, a thousandfold increase in power would be required to give a hundredfold increase in damage area. The Strategic Bombing Survey has calculated that the damage done and casualties caused by the atomic bombs detonated over Hiroshima and Nagasaki were equivalent to that caused by 2,700 tons of conventional bombs. In other words one B-29 Superfortress with one atomic bomb did as much damage in a single raid as 270 B-29's each carrying ten tons of conventional bombs.

The atomic bomb achieves its destructiveness, as do conventional explosives, by releasing, at the instant of explosion, energy in the form of pressure or blast waves and heat, but in prodigious amounts.

In addition the atomic bomb adds an insidious killer, never heretofore faced by man in the long history of war—intense radioactivity, similar to that given off by radium or X-ray machines, but highly penetrating and lethal. Some of these radioactive fission products with "half lives" of years' duration may contaminate the area in which they are released, much as mustard gas does, and can, under certain circumstances, "deny" the area to man or beast for long periods.

The bomb's effects upon structures and human beings at Nagasaki and Hiroshima, both land targets, have been collated and published by the United States Strategic Bombing Survey.[7] The findings should be read by every American:

The Heat Effects of the Explosions—

Fires were started directly by the intense flash heat, some of them 10,000 feet (almost two miles) from "ground zero," the point on the ground directly beneath the point in the air where the bomb exploded (in both cases probably 500 to 1,500 feet above the earth). Telephone poles were charred 13,000 feet from "ground zero." Roof tiles "bubbled" with the heat out to 13,000 feet from the center; granitic rocks scarred and peeled a mile from "ground zero." Burns of unprotected skin were reported up to 13,000 feet; serious burns within 4,500 feet, but even light clothing provided considerable protection against these flash burns.

The Effects of Blast, Pressure or Shock—

Some blast effects, minor shattering of glass, reportedly were felt eight miles from "ground zero," but generally speaking even light damage was limited to about a four-mile radius. Destruction or structural damage to modern reinforced concrete buildings "of good construction" was limited to within a few hundred feet of "ground zero," though serious damage to such structures occurred over a larger area. Destruction or severe damage to light steel frame, wooden or brick buildings extended to far wider areas, most of them, however, within a radius of a mile and a half of "ground zero."

The Effects of Radiation—

"The rays proved lethal for an average radius of 3,000 feet from 'ground zero.' They caused loss of hair up to 7,500 feet . . . the

radiation apparently had no lasting effects on the soil or vegetation
. . . subsurface soil showed earthworms and other life only a few
inches below the surface . . . evidence of lingering radioactivity . . .
slight . . . [but] strong enough to leave open the ominous possibility of a different situation had the bomb[s] exploded at ground
level."[8]

In lay terms all this means that *one* atomic bomb if used without
warning against the average world city might destroy about four
to five square miles of that city (the five boroughs of New York
include within their limits about 322.8 square miles), cause major
additional damage to five to ten more square miles and might
cause 60,000 to 200,000 casualties, half of them dead.

The Bikini tests proved the terrible nature of the bomb against
sea targets.[9] Both of the tests at Bikini involved ships of all types
anchored in a lagoon and deliberately arranged in a target pattern
smaller and of considerably greater density than would ordinarily
be found, except in "tight" harbors like New York and Pearl
Harbor.

The first test—an air burst high above the target ships—did somewhat less damage than expected and showed that steel men-of-war
withstand blast and flash heat better than the huddled masonry
structures of a city. Gamma rays, released at the instant of the
explosion, would have been lethal to exposed personnel near the
center of the target, and extensive damage to superstructures, radio
antenna and upper works occurred, which indicated the necessity
for considerable revisions of naval design. Five ships—two transports, two destroyers and a light cruiser—were sunk, and numerous
vessels damaged.

The second, or underwater test, which simulated the explosion
of an atomic bomb in a port or harbor of average depth, produced,
however, a number of unexpected consequences. The underwater
shock wave not only crushed bottoms and opened seams, thus sink-
ing two battleships and an aircraft carrier and five smaller vessels,
but hurled engines or boilers from their bed plates, distorted pro-
peller shafts and did other serious naval damage to half a dozen
vessels. But the most terrible effect of the underwater bomb burst
was the intensity and persistence of the radioactivity. In the air
bursts, which probably would have killed or made ill all personnel
within a mile of the burst, the gamma, neutron and other rays and

the radioactive fission particles were to a large extent dissipated in the air. (It is theoretically possible, however, for these particles to be "trapped" in a cloud and to be deposited on the earth, perhaps a hundred miles or more from the scene of the original explosion, in a literal rain of death. This has not occurred, however, in any of the world's five atomic explosions.) But in the underwater burst the fission particles were "trapped" by the water and in turn "impregnated" the surrounding water, algae, seaweed, silt and the bottom of the lagoon with radioactivity. Thousands of tons of contaminated radioactive water were hurled hundreds of feet into the air by the explosion and drenched the decks of the target ships; some of the observing ships which steamed into the lagoon after the explosion sucked up contaminated water into their condensers, evaporators and fire mains, and the radioactive particles clung to oil slicks and the sea growth on the ships' bottoms.

In Bikini lagoon itself unusual radioactivity was dissipated, except on the bottom in the vicinity of the explosion, within a year after the underwater detonation, but parts of some of the target ships were still dangerously contaminated fourteen months later. Even a few of the observing ships were "hot" months after the explosion and had to undergo an extensive but only partially satisfactory program of decontamination. This does not mean that these ships could not be boarded; even some of the "hottest" target ships were boarded for brief periods a few days after the explosion. But it does mean that certain places in these ships where members of the crew would ordinarily have to live and work were still so contaminated a year to fourteen months afterward that indefinite occupation of these quarters might endanger health, or even life.

The Bikini tests, therefore, again demonstrated the terrific power of the bomb. They indicated, however, that cities, built-up urban areas, and factory complexes, rather than navies, were its "natural" targets. A fleet at sea or in big lagoons like that at Bikini would be too dispersed to fear "annihilation" by one or two or three atomic bombs,[10] but in narrow "tight" ports one bomb could not only do major damage to shipping, but could spray the docks and surrounding areas with so many fission particles that large parts of that port would be "denied," or effectively "blockaded," for weeks or months.

Navies were not made obsolete by Bikini, but naval design and naval tactics were affected, and the persistent radioactivity introduced a new problem to military medicine and to military morale.[11]

In addition to the bomb's use against land and sea targets it has potential importance as a weapon of saboteurs. This potentiality has been greatly exaggerated. The bomb is such a "precious" weapon that nations would hesitate to risk a bomb's loss in such a doubtful venture. Moreover the bomb is not a child's toy which can be carried around in a suitcase. Only three types of planes now in operation can transport it—the B-29 Boeing Superfortress (with modified bomb bay); the new Consolidated B-36, largest combat plane in the world, just coming off the production line; and the Navy's record-breaking distance champion, the Lockheed P 2 V-Neptune. The B-29, only one of these three available during the war, had to be specially altered, Glenn Martin, the aircraft designer, has testified, so that the bomb could be fitted into its bays. The two separate bays of the normal B-29, each eighteen feet in length (and six feet wide) were modified with special bomb-bay doors. The atomic bomb, therefore, is probably more than eighteen feet but less than thirty-six feet in length, perhaps less than six feet in diameter, and it weighs less than ten tons (probably considerably less), the top capacity of the B-29.

Such a sizable object could be carried by saboteurs into a cellar or workshop near a vital industrial area, but if it was to be done, the bomb would have to be "broken down" into many suitcase or trunk loads, or concealed and disguised in a huge packing case. This would obviously entail considerable risk of discovery. Once assembled, however, a sabotage bomb could be detonated by clockwork mechanism or radio "trigger," and the bomb's great radius of destruction would probably make it effective against the objective it was intended to destroy, even if it were detonated as much as a mile from the guarded gates of a vital area.

A sabotage bomb could also be hidden in the hold of an expendable merchant ship. The bomb could be timed to detonate while the ship was passing through the Panama Canal, for instance, or after it had berthed at a New York pier. Rigid ship inspection could provide at least partial protection against such sabotage use.

Such are some of the characteristics and capacities of the present atomic bomb. What are its limitations and potentialities?

It *has* limitations, for it is a *finite* weapon.[12]

First, it is a bomb, not a projectile; it must be transported to its target.

It has a definite, and not an unlimited, destructive and casualty-causing effect. One bomb will *not* destroy all of a great city, although one bomb, properly placed, can carve the central core from a great city. One bomb, designed to penetrate by force of gravity deep into the earth before exploding, will *not* rack down all the buildings of a great city, will *not* crush all underground shelters over many miles. For the force of an atomic bomb, exploded underground, cannot be more than a tiny fractional value of the cataclysmic force of an earthquake, and earthquake-resistant construction stands up well to even the worst tremors.

Nor is there any satisfactory evidence as yet that the simultaneous or near-simultaneous explosion of, say one hundred atomic bombs would deluge the upper atmosphere with such a mass of radioactive fission products that life on earth would become unbearable. There is, however, no certainty on this point. Radioactivity is one of the greatest "unknowns" in atomic war, and informed speculation on this phase of atomic explosion is all that is possible. Some scientists fear the simultaneous or near-simultaneous explosion of several atomic bombs might "saturate" part of the atmosphere with radioactivity and create havoc in certain areas of the earth. Others question this. Most, however, agree that a "chain reaction," which would "destroy" the atmosphere, is impossible.

It is, or will be, mathematically possible to increase the amount of energy released, or the explosive force, of the atomic bomb, but by just what amount is still a matter of debate among scientists. Theoretically, atomic explosion could be made one thousand times more efficient; practically this is, as far as can now be foreseen, completely impossible. The nature of the atomic bomb is such that an explosion occurs only when the mass of fissionable or explosive material—plutonium or U-235—is a certain size. When the mass of material reaches the "critical" size nothing can stop the explosion, and the "chain reaction" or explosion releases such a tremendous amount of energy and occurs so rapidly that the explosive material is blown apart very rapidly and the chain reaction halted before more than a small number of the total atoms in the material are fractured.[13] This is the reason why the actual explosive force of the atomic bomb is so much less than its theoretical potential power.

Thus the technical problem in designing an atomic bomb is to secure a device which will assemble an amount of fissionable material substantially greater than the critical amount, and do it in a time so short as to prevent a premature (and inefficient) explosion. The solution of this problem is the secret of the atomic bomb.

Reduction in the time required to bring the subcritical explosive masses together, which, of course, is only a fraction of a second, perhaps some increase in the *number*, or size, of the subcritical masses, plus an increase in the speed of the chain reaction (or explosion) itself would mean an increase in the explosive force of the bomb.

A multiple of two, three or four—far, indeed, from the factor of one thousand so loosely used—would seem to be the limit to which the explosive efficiency of an atomic bomb might possibly be increased over the course of years. Scientists are in sharp disagreement as to whether or not it will be possible to build a more powerful bomb than this.

But even if an atomic bomb could be designed, the explosive force of which would equal that of 100,000 tons of TNT (or five times that of the present bomb), its destructive effect, as we have seen, would in no sense be comparable to such a detonation. For the present bomb's destructive capacity against cities is roughly equivalent to 2,700 tons of conventional bombs; the prospective destructive effect of a single atomic bomb with five times the power of the present bomb would be roughly equivalent to 9,000 tons of conventional bombs.[14]

Since the larger and more powerful the bomb the less its destructive efficiency in proportion to its weight, there would not seem to be much point, even if it were feasible, in increasing indefinitely the power of the bomb, especially since the present bomb can "eat" four to five square miles out of the heart of the average city. Three atomic bombs of the present type would do as much damage as a single bomb five times as powerful, and there would not be so many military eggs in one basket.

Just as the "size" or power of a single atomic bomb is limited, so, too, there is today a definite limit on the numbers available. Again, theoretically, that limit is astronomical, or at least limited only by five figures. But, practically, there are today finite restrictions.

The first of these is the quantity of fissionable or explosive material available. So far only U-235 and plutonium, both of them painfully derived from vast masses of uranium ore, have been used for the bomb. Thorium can be used, but probably only in "association with uranium";[15] in time other minerals *may* lend themselves to fission, but very few, if any. Today uranium is the only practical raw material. Theoretically, uranium is a fairly plentiful material— about four parts in 1,000,000 in the earth's crust, more plentiful than gold. But though uranium is contained in over a hundred minerals, the present known methods of extraction indicate that carnotite and pitchblende are the only important raw materials. There are some known, but limited, rich deposits of these raw materials.[16] But the so-called pure U-235, which must be extracted from uranium, represents only seven tenths of one per cent, or one one hundred and fortieth of the total weight of uranium, and uranium itself is a derivative of pitchblende and carnotite, and, when purified, represents only a tiny fraction of the raw ore. Plutonium, in turn, depends upon the basic raw material, uranium.

Practically, therefore, the present *known* deposits of pitchblende and carnotite and the amounts that can be taken from the earth limit the present output of fissionable material. This limitation, however, can be expected to diminish in importance as new deposits are discovered and new fissionable materials found.[17]

Another limiting factor on the number of bombs produced is the sheer size, complexity and expense of the process required. Great numbers of men, skilled and unskilled, trained and expert scientists, grade A engineers and technicians and vast and elaborate industrial plants with extensive mechanical "know-how" were required to produce the first atomic bomb, and, on lesser scale, are still required to continue the process. It is true that the process of production— particularly the production of plutonium—has been, and undoubtedly will be, simplified and cheapened and it is also true that additional capital investment in atomic-energy plants will increase our rate of production. Hanford Engineer Works, for instance, probably can be duplicated, and the amount of fissionable material produced thus doubled, with an investment of less than the $350,-000,000 Hanford originally cost. But practically it is not so simple in the United States to appropriate such huge sums in peacetime, and there is, in any case, a limiting factor in the number of skilled technical men available. In the case of Russia, this limitation is not so much dollars or man power as it is engineering ability, production know-how, industrial facilities and technical skill. The production of the atomic bomb required industrial achievements that taxed all the great plants of the United States and involved the design and production of valves, gauges, meters and other devices which had never even been dreamed of before.

As George Fielding Eliot wrote in the New York *Evening Post* of November 3, 1947:

. . . in the construction of the Hanford plutonium plant the Du Pont company let about 10,000 subcontracts, more than 50 per cent of which required highly skilled technical design and labor in their fulfillment.

Power is another potential limiting factor in the manufacture of atomic bombs, although the various methods of producing fissionable material and new developments in manufacture make this factor of doubtful importance. Nevertheless, the United States has a virtual "corner" on the world's large electrical power stations. Twenty-five out of twenty-nine stations with a capacity of more than 500,000 kilowatts are located in the United States and Canada; eight with a capacity of more than 1,000,000 kilowatts are all in North America.[18]

All these things, therefore, combine to prevent real mass production of the atomic bomb, and it is safe to say that that bomb can never be used during the lifetime of this generation with anything like the prodigality and abandon with which conventional bombs were used in the last war.

Practically, the limitations on numbers are even more precise. The atomic scientists have said that it would be easy to accumulate a stock pile of 10,000 atomic bombs, and the implication of the statement is that this could be done quickly. Actually, however, there is very little possibility that it could be done quickly. For some time to come our available atomic bombs, which means all the atomic bombs in the world, will, I believe, be *very* limited in number.[19]

The limited number of atomic bombs now on hand has been

stressed, for one bomb, contrary to misleading impressions, will not destroy a city, and if a nation has bombs numbered only in two figures, or even in three figures, the most careful strategic calculations must govern their use. The Air Coordinating Committee[20] in a postwar report estimated that perhaps six atomic bombs would be required to "eliminate all of the important [aircraft] plants" centered around Los Angeles. To talk therefore, of completely destroying the industry of the United States with fifty bombs, or even with one hundred bombs, of the Hiroshima type, is oversimplification, particularly since some bombs in actual warfare would be wasted and not all, by any means, could be put on—or near—their targets. Fifty bombs delivered precisely against carefully selected industrial areas could, of course, do terrific and dangerous damage, but the great extent of our industrial empire and the probability in war of bomb wastage would somewhat cushion the effects of such mass atomic bombardment.

There is one final limitation of considerable importance. Today, and for the immediate future, it seems probable that only great powers can make atomic bombs. There is, in the strictest scientific sense, no "secret" to be kept, but there are many mechanical and technical "know-how" secrets, and, above all, the industrial establishment and total effort required to make more than one or two atomic bombs is so major that—some of the atomic scientists to the contrary—there is, I believe, little immediate chance that a small power, unaided, can make the bomb. The only powers that appear to have the economic capacity and the raw materials necessary to make the bomb in the foreseeable future are the United States, Russia and Great Britain (inclusive of the Dominions), and Britain is definitely handicapped, perhaps fatally, by her stringent economic situation and man-power shortage. France and Sweden, however, and perhaps other countries will be able in time to build small atomic piles for power purposes.

In 1948 only the United States is producing atomic bombs or fissionable material,[21] and in 1948 only the United States has accumulated a stock pile of bombs. But the bomb's so-called "secret" is a transitory one, and Russia and very possibly Britain, less possibly France, will acquire in time the industrial plant and mechanical and engineering ability to produce the atomic bomb. In time, if her capital investment is a large enough one (and in Russia capital investment means man power, and the complete concentration of man power upon the task in hand is a factor of Soviet strength), Russia's production rate might—but probably will not—outstrip our present production rate.

But we have a major time advantage. December 1945 might be said to mark the beginning of intensive Russian effort (in an industrial and mechanical sense) on the atomic bomb. Authorities think it will take the Russians a minimum of five or six years, perhaps ten or twelve years, to produce the first bomb, and another considerable period to accumulate bombs numbered in two figures. Some estimates are considerably less, some considerably more; a few range as high as twenty or twenty-five years. I am inclined to think it will require a longer rather than a shorter time, but we cannot count upon it. Sometime between 1950 and 1957, the Soviet state will probably "have" an atomic bomb; sometime between 1960 and 1970 the Russian stock pile may be numbered in three or even four figures.

For Russia and the United States the limitations enumerated—as to numbers of bombs available and the production rate of the bomb—are, it is important to remember, *short-term* limitations; time will probably nullify some or all of them. Some scientists believe, for instance, that the present limiting factor of plant facilities and capital investment which restricts our present output of the bomb could be eliminated almost "overnight" by unrestricted concentration of U.S. resources upon atomic-bomb manufacture. They point, with some reason, to our annual prewar production of military aircraft, numbered in the hundreds, and to the wartime production of close to 100,000 planes in one year. In the case of Russia, the lack of sufficient technical man power and the limited industrial "know-how" of the country would make the elimination of this factor more difficult. It is conceivable, however, *if additional sources of uranium ore are found*, that atomic warfare, now strictly limited quantitatively, could become, in the distant future, atomic warfare unlimited. And it has always been true, at least since Napoleon's day, that the trend of warfare has been toward unlimited methods; in the stress of a future war we might well find new ways of making atomic explosives and even more dangerous ways of using and applying them.

But today and for quite a few years to come there is a definite limit on numbers of bombs available; there will be *few* available to any nation, not *many*. Those who correctly stressed the potentialities of the atomic bomb when it was new to the world telescoped and confused the time factors; they pictured the ultimate as possible now. Two years ago atomic scientists were talking glibly of 10,000 atomic bombs as if they were an accomplished fact; we were assured repeatedly that Russia could catch up and overtake the United States in short order, and the bomb was pictured as virtually an infinite weapon. The sober reappraisal that has occurred makes the bomb a finite and not an infinite or "absolute" weapon, it probably assures us of a commanding lead in the atomic race for some decades, and it relieves some of the terrific sense of urgency that overhung all atomic-bomb discussions in 1945 and early 1946. There still is time. Whether this is a benefit and will permit more mature, more reasoned and less passionate and hasty decisions or whether elimination of the sense of urgency will induce complacency, only the future can tell.

But the atomic bomb, powerful weapon though it is, is only one of the instruments of the revolution in war; there are other mass killers of perhaps even more lethal potency.

ATOMIC DUST AND GASES

These insidious poisons are a "kissing cousin" of the atomic bomb. They can be released, as has been explained, by the actual explosion of an atomic bomb, but such an explosion is not necessary to produce them. Our production of fissionable materials has shown us the way to produce quantities of highly lethal radioactive dusts or gases which might be sprayed from planes, distributed in aerosol solutions (a very fine spray) or scattered by detonation of conventional explosives over a city, harbor or water reservoir. What effect these would have, the underwater test at Bikini has indicated.

The famous "Smyth Report"[22] states that it was "concluded that the fission products produced in one day's run of a 100,000-kilowatt chain-reacting pile might be sufficient to make a large area uninhabitable."

Translated into laymen's language, this means that atomic power plants, used for peaceful purposes, produce as by-products radioactive poisons of tremendous potency. The quantities now being produced are large but insufficient to "drench" an entire nation.

There are some limitations on the use of such poisonous particles. Their military efficacy depends largely upon the "life" (or strictly speaking the "half-life") of the fission products; if their "lives" were of short duration, the poison dusts could not be stored indefinitely, it would be impossible to build up a stock pile, and it would be difficult to transport them to a target before their potency had gone. The Bikini tests indicated that many of the fission products of an atomic-bomb explosion (though not necessarily those of a slow-reacting atomic-power plant) had "lives" measured in years. If quantities of these "long-lived" particles could be dumped on a city, that area might truly become as desolate and inanimate as salted fields. But the length of the radioactive "lives" of these particles—by-products of a slow-reaction atomic pile—and the quantity available would impose limits upon the military utility of atomic dusts.

Another important limitation on the use of radioactive poisons would be the necessity of shielding and protecting the users against their effects. If transported in a plane, heavy lead or similar shields would be required to protect the crew; if transported in a missile some means of protecting the launching crew would be required. Radioactive dusts could, however, be used by "suitcase" saboteurs with efficiency, though the "suitcase" would have to be small and heavily lined with lead.

But the chief problem in the use of radioactive poisons would seem to be the problem of distribution; the aerosol method of spreading the dusts in a fine spray of air-borne droplets has not yet been fully perfected.

Chemical Gases

Gases, one of the first, and to the layman still one of the most terrifying, of war's mass weapons of destruction are synthetic chemical agents that have toxic or irritant effects upon the human body. Gas was not used, or was but little used, in the last war, but the new gases that were developed during or since the war indicate by their present characteristics and future potentialities that gas has by no means reached its limit of lethal effectiveness and that it may be employed in another war.

The Germans developed during the war but never used a so-called "Tabun" or "Green Ring 3" series of gases (so called from the method of designation). These gases were two to ten times more toxic than any of the standard chemical agents previously used—mustard, phosgene, lewisite, etc. The "Tabun" series were virtually odorless and, like mustard gas, they had a considerable "persistency"; they clung to woods, swamps, and low areas for hours, days, weeks or even months. These gases are blood and nerve poisons; inhalation of the vapor causes headaches, difficulty in sight and a tightness in the chest. Exposure to a high concentration causes instant death. The "Tabun" series do not burn as mustard does, but are capable of penetrating the skin and causing death by systemic poisoning. Though relatively instable and difficult to manufacture and store, their lethal efficacy is major.

Since the war, gases, or "substances," not ten, but a thousand times more toxic than previous known agents,[23] have been proven to be at least theoretically practical, and the end is not yet.

The distribution of these new agents will undoubtedly prove to be difficult, but the increased toxicity of even the "Tabun" series already has made obsolete the World War II gas mask and protective clothing. The new mask and clothing must provide "all-round" or complete protection; it seems certain that not a square inch of skin can be safely exposed. Each man must carry his own oxygen supply, or his gas-mask filters must be unusually effective and of long "life."

BIOLOGICAL AGENTS

Biological warfare, the newest of war's mass killers, has never been used extensively in war. Several nations have experimented extensively with a few of its possibilities, and the United States, in the laboratories at Camp Detrick, near Frederick, Maryland, and elsewhere, has made such notable discoveries during and since the war that the feasibility of "B.W." seems to have been demonstrated. The Germans did some experimentation, chiefly with typhus, in an effort to discover methods of control; the British have conducted extensive researches, and the Russians are known to have taken over in Manchuria a Japanese biological-warfare "factory" which was actually producing toxins or bacteriological poisons. The Japanese are believed to have used biological agents (bubonic plague) in one instance against a Chinese town, and Japan's Manchurian factory is known to have developed a crude anthrax "bomb."

During the war American forces sprayed oil on Japanese truck gardens in New Guinea and the Pacific islands, and as the war ended a shipment of biological agents was on its way to the Pacific which was to have been used against the Japanese rice crop in the home islands.[24]

The experiences of the war and postwar era, therefore, have shown that it is entirely feasible to "mass produce" in quantity lethal toxins, bacteria and viruses that can kill or produce disease or cause growth changes in men, animals and plants. The feasibility of the actual dissemination of these agents has not yet been proved in actual warfare, except in the case of plant life, but experimentation has indicated the possibility that several agents could be utilized successfully against men and animals.

Biological warfare cannot and should not be viewed in any narrow frame. It is a novitiate branch of the armed services, and even scientists do not yet comprehend more than a fraction of its vast possibilities. It offers literally death unlimited, or life hideously changed. To too many, "B.W." is envisaged merely as "germ warfare" and dismissed as the notion of cranks or knaves. But it is far broader than "germ warfare." In one sense it comprehends and includes, for instance, the atomic bomb, radioactive dusts and poisons and even common chemical agents, for any and all of these can cause mutational changes in men, animals or plants which could have profound effect not only upon the course of a war but upon the future of the human race. The atomic bomb, indeed, is perhaps the most powerful mutational agent known, though its exact effects are not yet understood. But biological agents, common chemicals or radioactive particles might, for instance, produce changes in the shape of the human blood cells. Some scientists believe that the "miseries" and "pains" to which so many Negroes are subject are possibly the result of sickle-shaped blood cells, characteristic of a sizable fraction of the world's Negro population, caused by some mutation of the past. Gates' *Human Genetics*[25] opens a few doors to this little-known and mysterious field of human life and to the possibilities of altering human growth. Plant life can be similarly blighted or forced or changed. "B.W.," therefore, is far more than "germ warfare"; it has horizons unlimited.

The agents of biological warfare in addition to those mentioned are many and varied, and their effects different and complex; only a few of the disease agents can be indicated here:[26]

Anthrax. This bacillus can infect man as well as beast. Can be transmitted through contaminated soil, pasturage, fodder, or through the air. This is not only a dread disease for cattle, but pulmonary anthrax in man is almost invariably fatal.

Botulinus Toxin. Perhaps the most lethal poison known to man, it produces botulism, which is more widely known to housewives as "food poisoning" and is found in improperly canned foods. Case mortality has varied from 16 to 82 per cent; paralysis usually sets in in twelve to twenty-four hours and death occurs in from twenty-four hours to ten days, or recovery requires two to four months. Can be transmitted through drinking water, or possibly through the air.

Tularemia (*Rabbit Fever*). This is highly infectious, the patient has a prolonged and completely prostrating illness, but usually recovers. Can be transmitted in many different ways.

Psittacosis ("*Parrot Disease*"). Can be transmitted through the air and is highly infectious. Produces a disabling and debilitating illness, frequently resulting in death.

Pneumonic Plague. Can be distributed through the air and is "superlatively" infectious; could easily produce a "devastating epidemic."[27] Sulfa drugs have, however, yielded good results in reducing the mortality rate.

These are only a few of the disease agents which lend themselves to military use. There are at least twenty-six other diseases which would appear to have military application, and there are at least nine different types (and many subtypes) of plant diseases, including cankers, blights, rots, fungous and insect diseases which can be utilized.

These agents have so many different properties and can be distributed in so many different ways that biological warfare is—potentially, though not yet actually—one of the most flexible forms of warfare. It can destroy plant, animal or human life. It can create a tremendous and raging pandemic. In the words of Dr. Franklin S. Cooper[28] it attacks the enemy, no matter where he may be. Different types of agents can create different effects; an "attrition attack," launched before war starts, can weaken an entire nation by epidemics, or a sudden severe "assault" can decimate a localized area. Certain types of agents, like poison gas, can kill or disable all persons who come in contact with them but will have no effect beyond the limited contaminated area. Other types are "self-propagating"; they spread like a prairie fire or human conflagration and reach out endlessly beyond the area where they were first spread. Some agents can cause temporary disabling illnesses without death. None of them, unlike other weapons, destroy property; "B.W." could therefore eliminate an enemy without destroying his industrial riches. "B.W." is also an ideal weapon of saboteurs; disease organisms, unlike the atomic bomb, can literally be carried into a city or to a water supply in a suitcase. Like the atomic bomb, "B.W." would appear to be primarily an "anti-civilian" weapon; it could cause social and economic disorganization of a great city or perhaps an entire nation, and could produce, as did the great plagues of the Middle Ages, wholesale and hair-raising panic.

Such are some of the potential capabilities of biological agents. It is important to emphasize that they are, at the moment, potential and untested in actual warfare, with the exceptions noted. For there are some major limitations in the use of biological agents, and though this new form of mass killing is shrouded in governmental secrecy, the indications are that these have not yet been entirely overcome.

"B.W." is, first, a two-edged sword; many of its agents could "backfire" and infect friend as well as foe. Immunization of the army and the nation that first employed such an agent would, therefore, be necessary, and any such wholesale immunization might give warning of impending use. It would be possible, however, to prepare certain virulent disease organisms for propagation in a foreign country, and at the same time to produce antitoxins to protect our own forces. Immunization against all forms of "B.W." agents is impossible.

Second, by various protective, decontamination and sanitary measures, practically 100 per cent protection can be given to small groups—such as the leaders of a government, or to small localized areas (though not to a whole nation or entire army).

Third, immunization against some of the most infectious diseases, though not against all, is possible.

Fourth, certain agents would have to be distributed in such large quantities that the scale of military effort required would probably not be worth the result; in other words, other weapons would do a more efficient job. It has been estimated, for instance, though without benefit of official or scientific sanction, that some 270,000 heavy bomber sorties would be required to transport enough "B.W." material to "kill" the wheat crop of Russia. There were only 1,440,000 Allied bomber sorties in the entire course of World War II.

Fifth, the problem of dissemination has not yet been solved adequately. Distribution through the air, like gas, is the most effective method, but a satisfactory aerosol (or fine spray) system has not yet been devised. Nevertheless, the problem of dissemination of *infectious* organisms—like pneumonic plague, which infected half the population of Harbin some years ago in a "wildfire epidemic"—is not so difficult, since once started it spreads contagiously and spontaneously. The problem then, however, becomes isolation and control.

For all these reasons "B.W." is not yet of military age. But its practicability seems to have been proved satisfactorily, and there is not much doubt that the major powers will have some biological agents ready for extensive use by 1955.

Such are some of the principal mass agents of destruction which have revolutionized war. None of them, save in a sense biological agents, carry their own motive power. All of these agents—the bomb, bacteria, gas—must be transported to the target by a "carrier" of some type, plane or missile.

It is fortunate for the world that today the means of destruction are more advanced than the means of getting those agents of destruction to an enemy.

PLANES

It is trite, in this air age, to reiterate that the plane alone has changed the whole face of war. It has become, probably the dominant arm, certainly an arm at least co-equal in importance to the surface services. If air superiority was not always absolutely essential to victory in the last war, it, at the very least, greatly decreased the cost of victory for the side that possessed it. If strategic bombardment of the enemy's cities and factories and transportation systems did not alone win the war, Douhet notwithstanding, that bombardment did accomplish effective "blockade" and the slow attrition of the enemy's "behind-the-lines" strength. Air power contributed tremendously to victory in World War II.

But in the last phases of, and especially since, the war, air power has had a powerful increment of strength, which at once alters its entire technical and tactical concept and enormously increases its potential destructive power. Air power today is indispensable to offensive, defensive and supporting operations, and to victory itself. The atomic bomb and jet propulsion have revolutionized the weapon which already has revolutionized war. But the cycle is by no means complete. The development of atomic power for planes and missiles, still in the embryo stage of progress,[29] will in turn revolutionize the entire aircraft and missile propulsion field. The potentialities of the bomb already have been discussed. The airplane and its successor, the missile, equipped now with new power are the principal instruments of the mechanistic war of the air age. Today, the piloted plane is still "Queen of the Air"; tomorrow, the robot missile may supplant it.

Look first at the plane—its present capabilities and future potentialities.

Today, the United States possesses three operational planes that can carry the atomic bomb. One of them, the Navy's Lockheed Neptune, holds the world record for one-way non-stop flight— 11,236 miles. Another, the giant Consolidated B-36, the so-called "10,000-mile-10,000-pounds-of-bombs" plane, is probably the longest-range bomber and the biggest weight lifter in the world. However, neither of these planes, nor the older B-29, now classified as a medium bomber, is a real "intercontinental" or "transpolar" bomber. The actual tactical operating radius of the first B-36's which are coming off the production line at Fort Worth in 1948 is about 3,000 miles; that is, they would almost, but not quite, be able to reach Ireland from bases in Newfoundland and return. The Russians have built some "Chinese copies" of our own B-29 Superfortress which have considerably less range than our B-36, and the latest British bombers will have operational radii which may be almost comparable to that of the B-36.

Today, therefore, no nation has, as far as is known, any bomber capable of sustained two-way operations across the oceans or across the Pole. All the great powers have, or will have, however (with the United States at the moment in the lead), bombers capable of striking targets 3,000 miles from their base and returning. This present limitation on combat operating radius—3,000 miles—is likely to define the outer limits of air power's effectiveness until at least 1952, perhaps longer. This does not mean that world distance records will not be broken in the meantime. But the time required for the design, development and testing of a new plane is at least four to seven years—from blueprint to production—and the giant new long-range weight lifters present a very great production problem. We shall not have, for instance, one-hundred B-36's until mid-1949, if then, and it would probably take until 1950 and cost about $120,000,000 to prepare to produce B-36's at the rate of one-hundred a month. Improved B-36's and new planes to supersede this type will be coming along, but no country is likely to have a fleet of bombers with *tactical* radii exceeding three-thousand miles before 1952, if then.

However, in the long-term view the world's the limit on range. In time, perhaps by 1955 or 1960, perhaps sooner, true ocean-hopping and transpolar bombers will be in operation, in limited quantities, and in time non-stop world-girdling planes will be feasible. Tomorrow all the new bombers will be able to carry the atomic bomb.

In size, as in range, planes are achieving new superlatives. The largest combat plane today is the B-36, designed for a maximum bomb load of 72,000 pounds, or thirty-six tons. Under overload conditions, and with a special rig, it is expected to be able to carry for short distances two of the new 42,000-pound conventional bombs. It will easily carry the atomic bomb, which weighs less than ten tons (possibly half that amount).

The future size of planes, and hence their weight-carrying capacity, appears to be more sharply limited by practical considerations than does their potential range. First is the cost, complexity and difficulty of manufacturing the huge sky giants.[30] Second is the problem of airports. Giant planes, like the B-36, not only require long runways for landing and take-off,[31] but strong concrete taxiing and take-off strips, and particularly very strong "hardstands" or parking strips. For the B-36, the present problem is not so much the runway or the taxiing strips. It has been estimated that some fifty-seven military and commercial airfields in the United States have runways adequate to the weight of the new sky giant (though how many are available overseas is another question). "Jets" or "jet-assisted take-off"—rockets to give the plane an extra boost of power—could be used on short runways.

But most of the parking strips of the nation's airports are too thin to permit adequate "static" testing, the "revving up" of engines of the parked planes; the pressure upon the landing wheels would be so great that the wheels would break through the concrete and sink deep into the earth.

This problem of airports can be licked in two ways, and both solutions are being tried. One way is to strengthen existing airports or to build new ones—either an expensive and long-term job, since the weight of the new giants may require the careful laying of many additional inches of concrete. The second is redesign of the landing-gear structure to "spread out" the weight of the plane over larger surface areas. New multiple landing wheels and new tire pressures offer a temporary improvement, but tracked landing gear, which operates much like the tractor treads of a tank, seems the most hopeful eventual solution. This development is far from perfected; so far it has been shown to be technically feasible, but present designs are heavy and bulky, and the great problem of folding a tracked gear into the thin wings or small fuselage of a high-speed bomber has by no means been solved.

The airport problem is not a major, long-term limitation on the use of giant planes, at least in this country. Airfields of the requisite size and strength can be, and are being, built in the United States, despite costs and time involved. But the airport limitation is, and will be, a serious one at overseas points (until tracked landing gear is developed), particularly if those points are not available to our military forces in time of peace. To construct a single airstrip for use by the B-36 type twenty shiploads of cement would be required. The tremendous construction, supply, maintenance and operating problems of giant planes—and of great airports for them —also create a limiting logistical factor.

Limitations on the weight and size of future planes are, therefore, very real, though not insuperable. And the relatively small weight of the atomic bomb, less than ten tons, is not an incentive to build bigger and bigger planes. Nevertheless, if the requirement exists, it seems probable that *operational* bombers (and/or military transports) capable of lifting fifty to seventy-five tons of bombs or "payload" for short distances can be developed by 1960 or thereabouts.[32]

In speed, as in range, planes are making phenomenal strides. Jet propulsion (which will be further described and explained in the section on missiles) has given the aviation industry the *power* for speeds faster than sound (761 miles per hour at sea level), but aerodynamic problems and problems of aircraft structure and control have so far limited man-controlled flight. Those limits are real and major, for the so-called "sonic barrier," which sets up an invisible "wall" of extreme air turbulence and tremendous stresses when planes reach the speed of sound, is still but imperfectly understood, and much experimentation and research is necessary. Nevertheless, the present operational maximums of the fastest military fighters now range in the 500-to-600-mile-an-hour zone, while aircraft speed records, made by non-operational planes, are in the 600-to-750 mile-an-hour range. Planes like the Army's jet Lockheed P-80 and Republic P-84 fighters, or the Navy's carrier-based North American XFJ-1, the McDonnell Banshee and Phantom jets and the Grumman Panther are blazing new operational trails in the skies, and still faster fighters will soon follow.

It seems highly probable that man will break completely through the "sonic barrier" and, in time, will be able to fly in the "supersonic" (faster than sound—from 900 miles per hour to infinity) zones, where flight is smoother and easier and theoretically any speeds are possible. When that will be, it is impossible to say; it may occur with experimental planes like the Army's XS-1 or the Navy's Skyrocket in a few months, or it may take years. Both of these tiny "flying laboratories" have in fact, "nudged" the sonic barrier —and the XS-1, at high altitude has exceeded sound's speed. But the early optimism of the immediate postwar era that supersonic piloted flight in operating (not experimental) planes was imminent has now given way to a fuller understanding of the tremendous scientific and engineering problems involved, and a few authorities are still qualifying their predictions with an "if ever." For supersonic speeds will have very little military utility and cannot be adapted to military operations until a host of complementary problems are solved.

High speeds have completely altered the whole technique of aerial war and have created a thousand problems. New methods for ejecting bombs must, for instance, be developed. The opening of bomb-bay doors at high speeds might upset the whole aerodynamic balance of the plane or might even tear off the doors. Forced ejection of the bombs, possibly through a chute, or like a rocket, may be one of the answers. Bombs themselves must be redesigned for the new speeds to prevent fins being torn off and to lessen or eliminate tumbling. A much improved high-speed bomb sight will have to be devised if extreme dispersion and great inaccuracy are to be avoided. So far such high-speed (subsonic) bombing as has been done has resulted chiefly in strewing bombs over large sections of the landscape. New methods of high-speed navigation, new radios, internal cockpit antennas instead of external antennas which cannot be torn away by the sheer force of hurtling through the skies at 600 or 700 miles an hour; new armament; new sighting and fire-control equipment; proper "insulation" for a plane heated almost red hot by rushing violently through space, and new tactics must be devised, and above all some methods of protecting and "acclimating" men to such speeds must be worked out. Normal *operational* transsonic[33] or supersonic speeds for piloted military aircraft are not likely, therefore, before 1952, at the earliest, and probably not before 1958, although numerous military planes will be on the very "edge" of the supersonic barrier long before then.

If the problems of high speed, long range and great size are difficult, how much more difficult it is to combine the optimums of each in one plane. That cannot, of course, be done; each plane design represents a compromise of desired combat characteristics. But it is important to work toward the optimum desirable plane, a bomber that will carry the atomic bomb (or less than ten tons of weight) from United States soil to any point in the world and return *at supersonic speeds*. The latter qualification—"*supersonic speeds*," or at least transsonic speeds, or speeds in the 600-to-900-mile-an-hour range—is highly important. For large slow bombers which move sedately across the skies, like the first models of the B-36, will soon be easy prey for the new fast fighters, and easier prey for the new anti-aircraft missiles. High speed in bombers is therefore particularly important. No such optimum bomber as the one outlined above is in existence today and none is in sight. Some of the Navy's projected carrier-based aircraft, though limited in size and payload, will undoubtedly be able to carry the atomic bomb at very high speeds over considerable distances. But those planes that seem to come closest to the desired ideal are, as far as is known, land-based and all American—the heavy, jet-powered Northrop B-49 flying wing; the medium Boeing B-50, a much faster and bigger version of the B-29 with Pratt and Whitney reciprocating engines; the Boeing B-47, six-jet, rocket-assisted bomber, with swept-back wings, and some of the Navy's land-based bombers.

MISSILES

Missiles are the ominous creatures of the much-heralded but still remote "push-button war." They are robot mechanisms, equipped with explosive charges, that fly through the air under their own power, guided by their own automatic control devices. By ancient definition a stone thrown by a catapult would have been called a missile. Today the modern terminology of ballistics would probably classify that stone as a *projectile*; i.e., a device like a shell or a bullet which flies through the air to which an initial velocity is imparted by a surface launcher, but which has no motive power or guidance mechanism of its own. A rocket, therefore, is a missile, though the bazooka rocket, made famous during the war, is not a *guided* missile; it has its own motive power but no guidance mechanism. Today nearly everything that flies through the air that is not piloted by man or fired from a gun or dropped like a bomb can be classified under the generic term, missiles.

But there are endless types and varieties of missiles; the Germans, for instance, who were far ahead of the rest of the world in this, as in most, branches of military science, developed some 138 guided missiles or modifications during the war. The new science, still in its infancy, has not yet achieved a simplified classification or easy characterization of the different types of missiles, so that there is no easy royal road to missile knowledge.

Missiles can be classified: aerodynamically, as winged or wingless; by range—short, medium or long-range; by function—artillery, anti-aircraft, air-to-air, air-to-ground, air-to-ship, ship-to-air, ship-to-shore, etc.; by motive power—aeropulse, ramjet, turbojet, rocket, etc.; or by guidance systems—pre-set, guided and target-seeking, etc.

Unlike planes, but like projectiles, some missiles already travel at supersonic speeds, and the power plants are becoming available to give them even greater speeds and greater ranges. The power plants can be conventional aircraft engines; for instance, the remote-controlled drone B-17 Flying Fortresses with which the United States has been experimenting are, in one sense, missiles. But the newest missile power plants are all jet; that is, they push the missile through the air by issuing a powerful jet of burning gases from the rear.

The jet types of missile power plants (some of which also power the new jet planes) are of four principal types:

1. The rocket. This uses either solid powder or liquid chemical propellants (liquids are exclusively used for the larger rockets). It differs from other jets in that it carries its own oxygen with it and hence can operate beyond the earth's atmosphere and even in a vacuum. However, the oxygen adds much weight, so that the payload, explosive charge or range is reduced. The giant German V-2 rocket (*Vergeltungswaffe-2*, "Revenge Weapon No. 2"), which bombarded London, burns liquid oxygen and alcohol as fuel, but it must carry three pounds of fuel for every pound of other weight.

2. The ramjet. This is also known as the athodyd, and nicknamed the "Flying Stovepipe," which it resembles. Simplest of all engines (and hence easy and cheap to produce), it has no moving parts. It rams its way through the atmosphere, scooping the air into a cylindrical duct open at both ends which consists simply of an air diffuser at the front end, a combustion chamber into which fuel, usually kerosene, is injected, and a nozzle or "venturi tube" for the exhaust gases at the rear end. The air is "rammed" by the passage of the ramjet through the atmosphere into the combustion chamber, mixed and burned with the fuel and expands out the rear, the reaction of the expanding gases pushing the device ahead. Theoretically, this little "gadget" has the attractive characteristic that the faster it goes the faster it goes (since increased speed simply increases the compression of the air rammed in the front end, and hence the efficiency). Actually, there are limits; the flame tends to blow out and the "stovepipe," despite its shape, "piles up" "solid" masses of air or "shock waves" in front of it which impede faster

progress. What the limits are we don't know—perhaps 1,500 to 2,500 miles an hour, perhaps considerably more. The device requires a 400-mile-an-hour launching by a catapult, rockets, or other means before it will function, and it is limited to the earth's atmosphere.

3. Turbojet. There are many different types; some are geared to propellers. This engine powers most of the world's new jet planes. It has the great advantage of requiring no launching device and is more easily susceptible to human control and alterations in speeds than the other jet engines. Air scooped into the front end is compressed by a mechanical compressor; then passes into the combustion chamber, where a fuel-injection system mixes it with kerosene (or gasoline). The burning mixture passes through a turbine which drives the compressor and then expands through the rear nozzles in a flaming jet, producing a force which pushes the plane or missile forward. Used chiefly in planes but has limited use for missiles. Expensive and complicated to build and limited to the atmosphere.

4. Aeropulse. So named, because spring-loaded shutters "pulse" open and shut periodically to admit air through the air scoop into the combustion chamber, where it is mixed with kerosene or gasoline, is burned and expands in a jet out the rear. This simple engine, cheap and easy to make, powered the German V-1 or flying bomb which bombarded London. It requires, however, a catapult for launching and is limited to the earth's atmosphere. Most important, it seems to be limited in speed to the subsonic or transsonic zone, perhaps 600 or 700 miles an hour or less, and for this reason it is powering very few postwar missiles or planes, except target drones and experimental devices.

Complicated though the power plants of missiles are, the guidance systems are far more complex. Few of them have been perfected; all of them are still in the bare beginnings of research and development. The problems presented test the knowledge and the ingenuity of a score of sciences and will tax even the engineering and industrial capabilities of America.

Even though missiles are robots and the actual guidance must be done mechanically in split seconds, the real *guided* missile is subject to control from the ground (or from shipboard, or from piloted plane) with man still the final authority and ultimate brain. The factor of human error, therefore, can be reduced in missile warfare but never completely eliminated; the problem is almost to put the brain of man into a robot.

Any guidance system in a real guided missile comprises three elements—a tracking system to "track" the target; a computing system to figure out mechanically the course the missile should take to reach its target, and a directing system to keep the missile directed on that course.

In general a missile can be controlled by a "command-guidance" system, in which the control is exercised remotely from the surface, or from a plane, or it can contain its own control and guidance mechanisms.

There are many different guidance systems; only the principal ones can be explained briefly here:

1. Pre-set system. In this system, used in the German V-2,[34] man has virtually no control over the missile once it is launched. The data to take the missile on the course desired is set into the mechanism before launching; the robot takes over after launching, and if the target changes position, errors creep in, or the mechanism fails, nothing can be done about it. The pre-set system is often inaccurate against anything except area targets—particularly at long ranges—but it is not subject to enemy jamming and a large number of missiles can be hurled into the air simultaneously.

2. Beam-rider. This type of missile control is particularly applicable to anti-aircraft missiles of relatively short range. The missile "rides" up a radar beam (or up converging beams) directed from the ground (or ship or plane) upon the target. The beam actuates the missile's control mechanism; as the target moves, the beam moves and the missile moves. Theoretically, this should result in collision between target and missile, but actually the beam may lose the missile, or the control mechanisms may have to move so rapidly to keep "on" a fast-moving target that the missile will go "wild." The potential advantages of this system when perfected are accuracy and ability to fire many missiles rapidly; its chief disadvantage is that the enemy can "distort" or "jam" the beam. This type of control may also have application to longer-range missiles. Though radar is limited to line-of-sight or straight-line distances and will not follow the earth's curvature, a "rocket at 150 miles altitude is within line-of-sight from about 1,100 miles away."[35]

3. Long-range systems. There are many possible combinations

The use of "Loran" or a system of long-range radar navigation is feasible for missile ranges up to 1,000 miles or more, but requires an elaborate system of "master" and "slave" Loran stations and very accurate controlling mechanisms. Another system contemplated would direct a missile by making it automatically follow a line of magnetic force. Another would utilize the well-known methods of celestial navigation by building into the missile small telescopes which would be kept constantly trained, during the missile's course, by a gyroscope, on selected stars. As the telescopes moved, a computing mechanism would figure out constantly the course required to bring the missile to its target and would in turn transmit its orders to the directing unit. Such a system could not be jammed by the enemy. Navigation by radar strip map is still another possible means of directing guided missiles. The radar in the missile, constantly scanning the earth over which it was passing, would match its "image" with the corresponding image on a radar strip map of the territory, fitted into the missile before it was launched. Such a process would, of course, require radar mapping of all the territory intervening between launching point and objective, and would be of little value over the sea.

4. Target-seeking devices. These "homing" mechanisms "take charge" of the missile only when it has approached the proximity of the target. They pick up and "home" on radio, radar, infrared rays, heat or light emitted by the target and automatically direct the missile to seek the target. They can be fitted into any type missile.

Such are some of the robots that man is devising today. They have all the fiendish possibilities that literature has so often celebrated in the form of the mechanized man who "comes to life." But it is important to emphasize that these devices, terrible though the future implications are, are still possibilities or potentialities, not present-day actualities; the age of "pushbutton war" is *not* just around the corner.

For the science of missiles is so new and the problems presented so huge that the collective difficulties dwarf even the problems solved in producing the atomic bomb. These problems are so many and so major that only a few (of the simplest ones) can be indicated here.

1. The atomic bomb, in the form of warhead, has not yet been

fitted to a missile. This sounds like a simple problem, but it is not. The bomb itself is a ponderous and intricate mechanism; before dropping it has to be "armed" or "cocked" by humans; it is heavy and long. It must be redesigned into warhead, equipped with safety devices to prevent premature explosion, or explosion over friendly territory in case a missile goes wild, and yet fitted with an automatic "arming" and detonating device which will insure explosion when it strikes its target.[36] In other words the atomic bomb and the missile have not yet been "married," although they will be, probably by 1950 or so.

2. New liquid propellants that must be used in the new missiles are but little known, and nearly all of them, to quote a scientist at the California Institute of Technology, are "explosive, corrosive, toxic and volatile."

3. Combustion temperatures in jet engines are ranging far beyond anything hitherto known. About 1,500 to 2,500 degrees Fahrenheit is about the maximum possible in turbojets today, 6,000 degrees the maximum for projected rockets, but we must contemplate future temperatures of 15,000 or even 20,000 degrees, as compared to working temperatures of about 550 degrees for aircraft piston engines. This means intricate cooling systems, or new materials or alloys, hitherto unknown, capable of withstanding such heat.

4. The gyroscope is the basis of all guidance and control mechanisms. But the gyroscope has never before been called on to perform with complete precision-accuracy in a missile hurtling 5,000 miles in one hour, through all sorts of extremes of heat and cold and in a "platform" undergoing violent oscillations. A gyroscope's factor of accuracy is the amount of friction it generates as it spins on its bearings; to do the job required in long-range guided missiles, gyroscopes ten thousand times more accurate than any ever built before in this country (which means an almost frictionless, "perpetual-motion machine") are required.

5. Accurate mapping is absolutely essential to any system of long-range firing or long-range bombing. It has been discovered since the invention of radar that existing maps of large portions of the world (which supposedly had been accurately mapped) are in error; places are actually, as computed by radar, half a mile, a mile or more from their indicated positions as shown by existing maps. This is true of many of the West Indian Islands and of some of

North America; it was found to be true during the war of certain places in the Mediterranean, and is probably true of much of the world, since all mapping, prior to the technological revolution, was done by much the same system. As a bewildered Army officer said, when this unexpected complication came to light: "Where the hell is Minsk really *at?*"[37] This problem of virtually remapping the world is one of the most difficult and urgent now faced. The United States has done some extensive and intensive postwar mapping, particularly in the Arctic regions. But mapping Russia or its contiguous territories presents another problem. We apparently have attempted this; that is one reason why the Russians have been so chary about permitting American planes in the Russian airspace. In 1947 the Polish Government, despite American requests, refused to allow our military attaché in Warsaw to use his plane in Poland. They correctly declared that the plane was not used merely for courier or liaison flights, but that an aerial photographer, equipped with mapping cameras, was part of its crew. But conventional mapping, important though it is, will not be adequate in the guided-missile age. If missile "homing" devices are to function, "heat" or "infrared" maps must be prepared which will show accurately the heat differentials between the airspace over London, for instance, and the airspace over the adjacent county of Kent.

These difficulties are enough to indicate that "pushbutton war" or missile war is still largely potential.

Here is the approximate situation in 1948, and the potentialities (measured against time) insofar as we can judge them:

Short-range ground-to-ground missiles: Used during the war, field artillery rockets, anti-tank missiles, etc., are now a fully accepted and important part of the ground army. No outstanding developments since the war, but experimentation with better rocket powder continuing. This type does not have rifled gun accuracy but delivers a terrific volume of barrage fire against area targets. Will improve slowly but definitely in accuracy, range and size.

Short-range ship-to-shore: About the same observations apply to this classification of rockets.

Short-range air-to-surface: Fourteen-inch rockets, bigger than the Navy's famous wartime "Tiny Tim," are now in existence which give a plane the hitting power of a fourteen-inch gun. Bigger and longer-range missiles with target-seeking mechanism will gradually evolve.

Short-range air-to-air: All sorts of new developments in this field are to be expected, but accuracy and the problem of launching from high-speed planes are still incompletely solved.

Anti-aircraft: Tremendous developments have occurred in this classification since the war, and the ramjet beam-riders, or anti-aircraft rockets, fitted with both target-seeking devices and proximity fuses (which detonate the missile when it passes close enough to the target), will alter shortly the entire science of anti-aircraft gunnery. Good, reliable anti-aircraft missiles may be available for initial pilot production between 1949 and 1953, and will extend the vertical range of anti-aircraft perhaps to 200,000 feet, certainly to 100,000. These will not eliminate the gun but will supplement it and extend its range. There is a "blind space" in guided missiles which probably means guns will have to be used against planes flying below 15,000 or 20,000 feet. But the new guns will have to have tremendous velocity and high rate of fire.

Medium range: The new concepts of war which now view interstellar space as the only limitation on range would now classify the 220-to-230-mile V-2 as a "medium-range" rocket. None other equal to the V-2 is yet ready for production. However, basic improvements in the German model including the addition of real guidance mechanisms have been tested, and a better American version of the V-2 could probably be ready for mass production in late 1949. The German-designed V-1 aeropulse flying bomb, American-built and equipped with U.S. guidance mechanisms, has been launched successfully from U.S. submarines, but it is purely an experimental vehicle, already has been outmoded, and will not be mass-produced. It has 150-mile range. An experimental prototype of a giant 500-mile rocket may be ready for test between the end of 1949 and 1952, but its accuracy will probably be questionable.[38]

Long-range missiles: Judged by our new yardsticks of space, no really long-range missile, of more than 1,000-mile range, is in sight today, unless one includes drone remote-controlled aircraft (like the B-17 drones used at Bikini), which so far are limited to subsonic speeds.

Two types of "drones," or crewless aeroplanes, have been developed. The B-17 and Navy drones used at Bikini were controlled by means of television and radar by "mother ships" flying near the drones; the maximum distance from the mother ships at which the drones can be successfully controlled is probably about seventy-five miles. This is a remote-control system; there are no fully automatic control mechanisms in the drones themselves, but they must be guided by the "remote" pilot.

A truer "missile" is the type of "drone" that flew across the Atlantic in the fall of 1947 with no human hand on the controls. The controls of this plane are of the "pre-set" type; the mechanism is set up before take-off to guide the plane, which is controlled by an automatic pilot, on a certain course, at a certain speed and at a certain altitude. Automatic navigational corrections are made by the mechanism along the course when the plane comes within radio range of radio beacons. At the end of the pre-set course, a homing device "guides" the plane toward the final radio beacon and then into the glide path for the landing. Flaps, landing gear, gas-tank switches, brakes, etc., are all automatically controlled. This latter type of drone seems to have less combat applicability than the Bikini type. Radio beacons for homing and navigational purposes would not normally be available in wartime, and accuracy without these aids would be impossible. The Bikini-type drones, however, can be accurately controlled and directed to the target visually by a mother ship which can itself remain on the outskirts or fringes of the most dangerous anti-aircraft area.

These "drone" planes, or missiles, though possible today up to ranges limited only by the ranges of the plane itself, are only primitive examples of what may be expected in the long-range category tomorrow. Between 1955 and 1965 supersonic pilotless aircraft of transatlantic ranges and reasonable area accuracy may be expected. But even so the first transoceanic missile will probably travel in level flight at relatively low altitudes. Such missiles present, therefore, far less a problem to the defense than the high-altitude parabolic flight of a rocket. A 5,000-mile-an-hour rocket—development of the V-2—which zooms 100 to 200 miles high into the ionosphere and then drops with sickening speed upon its target, is obviously the ultimate in missiles.

The Germans had planned a long-range missile of this type during the war, with which they hoped to bombard the United States. The principle was simple; the robot was to be merely a "multi-stage" or "step" V-2 rocket. Two or more of the V-2 power plants were to be harnessed together in tandem. Each plant would function separately; the rear one would take the rocket off the earth and into the first stage of its trajectory; when its fuel was exhausted, an explosive mechanism would detach it from the rest of the rocket assembly and the spent motor would drop to the surface. The second "stage" would then function, and the next motor would propel the rocket on its way until its fuel, too, was exhausted, when it, too, would "fall off." Thus, the great disability of the rocket, the tremendous weight of the fuel and oxygen it must carry, would be overcome, and the weight would lessen as the range increased. Only the final "stage" would carry an explosive warhead.

The German design, though simple in theory, was, and is, extremely difficult to work out practically, and since no system of guidance has yet been developed that is practicable for long ranges, the accuracy of any such intercontinental rocket would be, as of today, subject to tremendous error. The Germans had no real solution of the long-range guidance and control problem involved in bringing a 3,000-mile missile "home," even to a target as large as Greater New York City. The reader with some knowledge of physics can easily imagine the difficulties of controlling or changing the course of a missile traveling at high speed above, or in the upper reaches of, the earth's atmosphere. It can be done only by applying a fully controlled force, in time, magnitude and direction—all carried within the missile itself!

The day of the transoceanic or transpolar curved-trajectory missile, with ranges of 3,000 miles or more, supersonic speeds, accuracy sufficient to hit any big city, and capable of carrying an atomic warhead, is still far off; it will probably be 1958 at the earliest, more probably 1965 or later, before huge operational missiles of this type are practicable.

The process of evolution from present available weapons to intercontinental missiles will therefore be gradual and will be marked by several stages of development.

We are now in the long-range-bomber era, of relatively slow lumbering "boxcars" not yet able to conduct two-way transoceanic raids.

Then, threatened by the development of anti-aircraft missiles and improved anti-aircraft guns and detection devices, the bombers will step up ranges and speeds and either increase their altitudes to the maximum to escape anti-aircraft fire or "come down on the deck" to treetop level to escape radar detection. Some of them may become drones or crewless aircraft.

Concurrently, or later, medium-range guided missiles (both low-altitude level-flight and high-altitude curved-trajectory types) launched from naval vessels, planes or advanced bases 100 to 500 miles from the target, will become available. Then these ranges will be increased.

Then will come the low-altitude, level-flight, supersonic trans-oceanic missile, possibly powered by ramjet or turbojet.

The ultimate step will be the supersonic, curved-trajectory, high-altitude intercontinental missile, probably rocket-powered, with a warhead of mass destruction—atomic explosives, biological agents or other means of dealing out death wholesale.

All of the great powers are now engaged in this race for missile supremacy. At the moment, with the help of German knowledge obtained after the war, we are probably equal to any, perhaps ahead of all. Yet self-confidence can sometimes be a snare. The Russians were ahead of us during the war in the development of artillery rockets, and the USSR also rounded up a considerable number of German technicians and had available in their portion of conquered Germany the component parts for 1,000 to 2,000 V-2's. But today no nation is ready for extensive missile war, for intercontinental air war or for transpolar war. No nation has combat models of supersonic planes, no nation has yet been able to send a piloted plane above the point—63,000 feet—where human blood "boils," and no nation has a plane with combat range sufficient for two-way bombing raids across the oceans or the polar icecap.

But we are as yet in the early stages of the race for air and missile supremacy.

The missile combines in one implement three of war's tools—the plane, the pilot and the gun. This is why it is, in the fullest sense, the instrument of "pushbutton war." That type of warfare is not yet possible, will not be fully possible for fifteen, twenty or thirty years, and man, in any case, will always be the controlling brain. Today missiles are still relatively inaccurate, chiefly valuable for use in barrage fire or against area targets. Tomorrow they will be ocean-spanning and all but human.

INSTRUMENTS, THE RAYS, INFRARED, ULTRAVIOLET, ETC., SOUND,
ELECTRIC GUNS

The guidance of missiles, the efficacy of planes, and the accuracy of gunfire are completely dependent in modern war upon proper instrumentation—particularly radar. Radar, with its ability to track targets hidden by clouds or smoke or night and unseen by human eyes, revolutionized the art of gunnery and of bombing during the war, and provided a means for detecting an otherwise unseen foe. It had approached a high peak of development at the war's end, and probably future advancements will be less spectacular and more gradual.

Today, radar is limited in effectiveness to straight-line distance; it will not follow the curvature of the earth; it is blanked off by mountains.[39] Radar range depends to a great extent, therefore, on the altitude of the radar station—or conversely, the altitude of the target being tracked—above sea level. Straight-line, or line-of-sight, distance between a rocket at 150 miles altitude above the earth (an entirely possible figure; the V-2 has exceeded 100 miles altitude) and a radar station at sea level can be as much as 1,100 miles before the curvature of the earth interferes. Theoretically, therefore, radar ranges, at least for high-flying missiles, would seem to be almost unlimited, but practically there are many limitations. We found, for instance, in some of the first tests of the V-2 in New Mexico that our radar could track the missile in the upper portions of its trajectory, but "missed" it in the lower. This was later rectified, and recent radars have traced the V-2's parabolic course, 100 miles range and 100 miles in the air, throughout its flight.

Normally, however, the maximum effective range of "search" radar equipment, at no more than 100 feet or so above sea level, is perhaps 200 miles. But even that distance is too great to permit fully accurate range estimation; the so-called "gunlaying" radars are precise only at shorter distances, and the radar used in bombing measures its accuracy in miles.

The first requirement for the guided-missiles age, therefore, is a new "long-range" radar, or other device, which will permit man to "see" and measure accurately beyond the horizon. This has not yet been perfected.

Short radio waves (which must be used rather than long waves in locating an object) travel only in straight lines; the problem, therefore, is to bend or "refract" or "reflect" these waves in such a manner that they will detect an object, if necessary on the other side of the earth. This might be done, theoretically, by establishing "sky" relaying stations in planes, or, as has actually been suggested by reputable scientists, by means of a satellite missile radar station circling the earth, or, but not until much more knowledge is available, by reflecting the short waves from the so-called "Heaviside layer"[40] in the ionosphere. However, even if a "long-range" radar can be developed, it will take much time to perfect one that is operationally suitable, for the task it must do is immense—detect accurately and instantly the launching of a missile, 1,000 to 5,000 miles away, track that missile as it moves at 5,000 miles an hour towards its target and measure its range continuously.

No such radars are available today; they may, indeed, never be available, but in radar development and technique and radio control we, and the British, are well ahead of the world. This was one field in which the Germans lagged; their scientists were not able to transmit much of value to the Russians, and it is significant that one of the primary objectives of the Russian-controlled Canadian spy ring was radar.

Television is another instrument which may have some promise, though far more limited than radar, for the future; today its military uses—as a guidance mechanism for short-range missiles, in "drone" planes, etc.—are of definite but limited utility.

The various "rays"—infrared and ultraviolet—already have been partially harnessed to war. Infrared was used in a limited way during the war by the Germans for firing tank guns at night; by parachute troops as "pathfinder" equipment; by our motor-vehicle drivers to enable them to drive rapidly along a blacked-out road, and, in the so-called "snooperscope" and "sniperscope," to illuminate a night battlefield with invisible sources of light and to enable a sniper to "sight" and pick off an enemy at night. But the ultimate in infrared development has by no means been reached. A detection apparatus which will pick up infrared rays given off by man or machine (without the necessity of "illuminating" the area with a source of infrared light) is under development and will make possible "invisible warfare." Infrared applications will be applicable to the "homing" mechanism of missiles, in planes for night bombing and night fighting, carrier landings and take-offs, in aircraft detection, and in many other ways.

Military applications of ultraviolet rays, and of cosmic rays, are not clear, but experimentation is continuing.

Other developments in instrumentation deserve brief mention, if only because instruments, though unspectacular and undramatic, are the soul of the machine; they "control" and make possible modern war.

Aerial photography will be of primary importance in the next few decades, for the mapping already described as essential to missile war, and, in war, for recording the results of combat and for new mapping. Three-dimensional, shutterless, continuing-strip cameras, now in use, enable the mapping of 16,000 square miles in fifty-one minutes; by such means a missile's course from launching site to target could be literally mapped in a day.

Bolometers, or heat-measuring devices, used in homing mechanisms, and electronic eyes are other gadgets of prime importance in a score of weapons. A new sixteen-inch tracking telescope, mounted on a 90-mm. anti-aircraft gun platform, has followed successfully the 100-mile-high flight of a V-2 rocket.

The Navy has developed "radac"—"rapid digital automatic computation"—which has been hailed by John R. Steelman, chairman of the President's Scientific Research Board, as phenomenal. It presages, Mr. Steelman reported, a "technical revolution in the field of automatic computers . . . of military significance comparable to radar in that radac constitutes a revolutionary method of analyzing and handling information in the same sense that radar is a revolutionary method of collecting information." The new "gadget" is of "almost unlimited accuracy,"[41] and of high speed and great capacity; it will affect fire control, missile control, communications, logistics and other branches of the military art, and may even enable the successful shooting down or interception of high-speed guided missiles.

The other novel possibilities in the armory of Mars are legion. The Germans had experimented with both an electric gun and a sound gun. The former, which expelled a projectile through solenoids or loops encircling a steel track, was cumbersome, heavy, and required major power sources, but the projectile was given terrific velocity, and if mechanical difficulties can be overcome, the electric gun would seem to have some application to anti-aircraft and naval use.

The electric gun would be flashless and silent and hence the ordinary means of locating artillery positions, by sound and flash (supplemented now, and probably soon to be superseded, by radar location), would not suffice.

The application of this or some similar principle to small arms, the invention, for instance, of a silent, flashless, rifle or machine gun —something that is by no means impossible—would add a new silent terror to the battlefield and would, of course, greatly aid the army that possessed such a device.

The utilization of sound as a weapon is another possibility. The German "sound" gun was in the laboratory stage, but could kill a man by blast or pressure effect at 180 feet and could disable him at 300 yards. This weapon, because of its limited range and its unfavorable comparison with other weapons even more potent and more simple, seemed to present a military dead end, but unexpected discoveries may alter this view. Certainly sound as a weapon cannot be dismissed in view of the sicknesses reported and difficulties caused to men who have worked for long periods around jet engines which emit a terrific cyclic roar.

THE NEW NAVIES

Nearly all of the weapons and instruments previously discussed have definite application to sea warfare. Missiles, for instance, have been and will be used from naval launching platforms; new jet planes have flown from carrier decks; in time ship-based planes will be able to carry the atomic bomb.

But there are other naval weapons peculiar to navies which must have special mention.

Foremost of these is the new submarine, the first true submersible in world history. Like so many other military superlatives it must be credited to the Germans. At the close of the war, the Nazis had built or designed two types of U-boats which revolutionized all prior submarine design and would have made obsolete overnight our entire anti-submarine technique.

Some of these new submarines were equipped with so-called "schnorchels," or long tubes which "inhaled and exhaled" air from the submarine's hull. These tubes, approximately as long as a peri-

scope and of about the same diameter, were equipped with automatically closing flapper valves to prevent accidental flooding of
the hull structure. They permitted German submarines to cruise,
if desired, at periscope depth across the Atlantic; there was no
necessity, as in the older type, to surface every twenty-four hours
to recharge batteries. The advantages of this almost complete submergence were, and are, tremendous. Periscopes and "schnorchels"
were coated with anti-radar paint, and in any case extended such
a short distance above the surface and presented so small a "target"
for search radars or for the human eye that the job of finding them
was like looking for a needle in a haystack.

The new submarines were also able to make far higher underwater
speeds than had been thought possible. Hull design was altered; the
newest high-speed submarines are now the shape of a raindrop, with
the bow end thick and heavy but streamlined like the lower portion
of a raindrop, the stern tapered. Their engines, influenced by the
fundamental changes in naval propulsion machinery now commencing, are far more powerful than prior submarine engines. The German Type 21 submarine, with a very large battery capacity, had
a maximum submerged speed of more than fifteen knots, as compared to prior maximums of eight or nine. The Type 26 was to be
equipped with an auxiliary Walter hydrogen-peroxide turbine
engine, which carried its own oxygen and thus made it possible to
combine, for the first time in the world's history, very high speed
and *complete* submergence. The Type 26 was to have been capable
of short bursts of speed up to twenty-four or twenty-five knots
submerged.

Such speeds, and far stronger pressure hulls which permitted
submergence to depths up to 1,000 feet, meant greatly improved
combat characteristics. The submarine, moving at periscope depth
and hence practically invisible, was now able to track and *overtake*
even the highest-speed convoys, something it could not have done
in the past without surfacing. It meant that all submarine attacks
could now be submerged attacks. The complicated nature of the
problem thus presented to the defense can be best indicated by one
fact. The sound-detection and ranging equipment (so-called "sonar"
gear) which our ships use to locate (at short distances) submerged
submarines was not effective, in 1946, at surface speeds much greater
than eighteen to twenty knots. This meant that if our surface ships

picked up a 25-knot submarine on their "sonar" gear, they could not "overtake" without "losing" him. New "sonar" gear is being manufactured, and other detection instruments, such as the "MAD," or magnetic air-borne detector, promise future development. High-frequency radio direction finders; the "sonobuoy," a floating radio broadcaster equipped with a hydrophone to pick up any noise from nearby submarines, and other devices will, when improved, tend to balance the present ascendancy of the submersible.

Nevertheless the submarine may be the capital ship of tomorrow's navy, for the ultimate in size, speed, submergence depths and power has not yet been reached. The future submarine will be equipped with missiles with atomic warheads to be fired from the *submerged* vessel,[42] or with V-1-type flying bombs, which already have been launched from surfaced American submarines. The submarine thus becomes not only a commerce raider but a powerful assault ship. Cargo submarines, transport submarines, fast, small, one- or two-man types for coastal work or harbor attack, great submarine aircraft carriers, or submarines as radar picket or warning boats or as "master" or intermediate guidance stations for transoceanic missiles—the varieties and potentialities are enormous. And today, the improvements in naval design and naval engineering make those potentialities realizable.

Today, the nautical world stands on the threshold of the gas-turbine era of propulsion, of which the Walter hydrogen-peroxide engine is one example. The elimination of boilers and the substitution of chemical reaction for energy instead of steam will increase speeds, ranges and efficiency. The application of jet engines to ships, particularly in the form of the hydrojet, or water jet, is a more distant possibility, but ultimately, perhaps by 1960, atomic power for ships will become practicable. An atomic pile aboard a man-of-war will require much heavy shielding to protect the crew against dangerous radiation, but it will provide a practically inexhaustible source of power; frequent "refueling" will not be necessary as in the past, and range will be indefinite. Obviously such developments not only alter the technology of navies and their tactics, but also their strategy and their logistics; advance bases will no longer be of such imperative necessity.

Surface ships of new and radical design will also play major roles in the navies of tomorrow. Missile ships,[43] drone launchers, perhaps even radio-controlled robot assault vessels,[44] will be developed. The V-2 already has been launched from shipboard; drones have taken off from carrier decks. The ships of the Navy—in the past, gun platforms to control the seas—are now becoming launching platforms for planes and missiles, instruments to intervene, not alone at sea but in the air and on land, in the "war of the world" which the new technology makes possible.

The new ships will be armed with the best weapons of the last war and the newest developments of tomorrow. New torpedoes, driven by electric or hydrogen-peroxide engines, or the so-called hydro-bombs (jet-driven and dropped from planes into the water) will, in time, increase torpedo speeds to seventy-five or eighty knots and ranges to perhaps 60,000 yards. The new torpedoes will "home" on enemy targets, either by sound or magnetically or by heat, and their warheads may someday include atomic explosives.[45]

New "oyster" mines of the "pressure" type which will detonate only when ships of a certain size pass above them already have been added to the Navy's conventional mines; new types undoubtedly will be devised.

Defensive devices have not been neglected; artificial fog, produced by a new method, can—under good conditions—obscure a fleet in a very few minutes.

And finally naval architecture must adapt itself to the atomic age. Ships can never be built that cannot be sunk, but damage can be limited by strengthening superstructures, etc.; personnel can be shielded from the worst effects of blast, heat and radiation, and safety can be sought, probably not so much in armor as in speed, mobility and numbers—in other words, dispersion.

These naval developments will not be immediate but gradual. It will take time to accomplish them; in the near future, the ships that won World War II will still have validity. But it is probable that by 1960, or thereabouts, most of the world's great naval powers will have completed conversion of their submarine fleets, at least, to the new-type high-speed, schnorchel-equipped vessel. And also by 1960, atomic power may commence to play an *operational* part in naval design.

In most of these naval developments, except possibly in the technique of anti-submarine warfare in which the British are equal or superior to us, the United States has a clear lead. The Russian Navy is negligible; the Russians have never been distinguished for naval design and were dependent until 1940 (and probably still are) upon foreign sources for the manufacture of large naval guns and heavy armor.

But the Russians, like the British and ourselves, secured some Type 21 submarines after the collapse of Germany;[46] they have had access to German scientists and German engineers and technicians, and Stalin has announced with emphasis the Soviet intention of building a deep-water fleet.

· THE NEW ARMIES

The new armies, like the new navies, are adapting to the specialized use of the ground battlefield many of the weapons, devices and developments already described.

Atomic explosives and atomic power have not, and probably will not be, utilized by ground armies for years to come, but the trend toward increased power, increased range and greater mobility, marked during the war, will continue.

Field artillery has by no means approached the ultimate in power; supplemented by rockets, and perhaps utilizing the rocket-assisted shell (a shell fired from a gun, but equipped with a rocket engine, which "takes over" halfway in flight and increases range), it will multiply its fire power many times and "lengthen" ranges to perhaps 100,000 yards.

Armor is still the "king" of the ground battlefield, although it is clear that the terrific velocities of new guns, the increasing power of new explosives, the greater and greater use of ground mines and the growing predominance of the plane and the missile have tended to decrease its relative importance. The trend toward tracked, armored vehicles is pronounced; the field artillery of tomorrow will consist almost entirely of self-propelled guns, or a species of tank. The merging of armor and the other ground arms will become more and more complete, and tanks will become rocket launchers, artillery pieces and personnel carriers, the spearhead of the ground armies.

The tank restored mobility to the ground battlefield in World War II and gave the soldier the punch and protection of armor. Recent technical and design developments will make possible still more powerful armed forces. The design trend is toward greater gun power, greater mobility and greater armor protection, in that order of priority. All of these qualities are being combined today on a single tank hull to a degree that would have appeared unbelievable a few years ago. A new 25-ton light tank will mount a high velocity 76-mm. gun in a gyro-stabilized turret. A computing sight and a range finder, plus an automatic loading device, should make possible for the first time in tank warfare fast and accurate gunnery from a *moving* tank against a *moving* tank. Developments such as this mean that armor will continue, as long as ground troops fight, to play a leading role in war.

Perhaps the greatest change to be expected in the technique of ground warfare, one which is still largely potential, will be its "marriage" to the air, for the use of the plane to transport ground armies and to supply them is an art yet in its infancy. This trend, which will someday enormously increase short-distance or *tactical*, and long-distance or *strategic*, mobility of the ground arms is following two complementary lines. *Air-borne* developments are starting with the lessons of the last war, when our paratroopers, glider-borne infantry and specially organized air-borne divisions used planes to give them *tactical* mobility and to enable them to accomplish, through the air, the vertical envelopment of the enemy. *Air transportability* is, on the other hand, a relatively new postwar concept. It contemplates the air transport of ground forces, not necessarily directly to the battlefield as in the use of air-borne troops, but to a theater of action. In air-borne work men, equipment and munitions must come down out of the skies prepared for instant battle; air-transported troops, on the other hand, may expect to land at a prepared airport and to reorganize and concentrate before going into action. The ultimate objective of the American Army, and presumably of all other armies, is to develop air-borne techniques to the maximum and to make *all* ground forces air-transportable. These are major and ambitious aims, and there are many difficulties in the way of accomplishing them.

In *air-borne* work, the glider-borne infantryman and the paratrooper are still the key elements, but new ideas and new concepts, if developed successfully, *may* make both gliders and parachutes obsolete. Today, the "chute" is still used, but the British general staff believes the individual "chute" may be obsolete for air-borne purposes in seven years. Gliders, towed by short metal towbars, instead of long nylon towlines, are also still in use; one of the latest American types is the CG-18A, a 16,000-pound all-metal glider which can carry thirty troops, pilot and co-pilot, and which can be towed at a higher rate of speed, 180 miles an hour, than wartime gliders. But both gliders and parachutes suffer from one disability: gliders cannot be towed at very high speeds, and planes have to slow down to a maximum today of about 125 to 150 miles an hour when mass parachute jumps are made; otherwise the terrific opening jerk of the harness on the man's body is too great. Use of the German ribbon chute and other devices may enable relatively high-speed jumps, perhaps at 250 or 300 miles an hour, but even so there is little immediate hope that gliders can be towed at such speeds. This means that glider-tows will be "sitting ducks" for the new anti-aircraft weapons and fighter planes, and it also means that when paratroop planes slow down to permit jumps, they, too, will be easy targets. Parachutes, in any case, are somewhat unsatisfactory means of lowering a soldier to the ground; a unit tends to become scattered and disorganized, and powerless gliders are hard to control and tend to produce large casualties.

Efforts to find more satisfactory means of putting air-borne troops on the battlefield now center around two concepts. The development of a so-called "assault transport," in some ways a powered glider, with large capacity but very low landing speeds, equipped with skids or tracked landing gear which would enable landing in rough fields or even over ditches or logs, may offer a possible solution. But even so, the "assault transport" would still suffer from the disability of low cruising speeds. Another and perhaps more hopeful solution contemplates the development of "air trailers," fashioned after the ground concept of prime movers and truck trailers. Designs for this device envisage a metal rectangular or cylindrical box or "capsule," capable of attachment to the underside of a mother plane's fuselage. The "capsules" would have ramps for easy loading and skids for landing. The plane "prime mover" would pick up one of these "capsules," loaded with men, equipment or guns, at its take-off field and would carry it, slung beneath its fuselage, to the drop point. There the mother plane would either: (1) land, with the aid of tracked gear, detach the capsule and take off again; (2) unsling the capsule in flight and lower it by large parachute; (3) skim low at low speeds over the landing area, a few feet off the ground, drop the capsule and allow it to skid to a stop.

Still another possibility is the utilization of helicopters as cargo and troop carriers. The Piasicki XR-16, a dual-engined helicopter, can carry 12,000 pounds of cargo for short distances, and could be equipped with a boxlike fuselage, which could be detached and lowered by cables to the ground while the helicopter hovered above the landing area.

None of these ideas are, as yet, much more than ideas, and all of them suffer from the same disadvantage—low speed at the time of the drop or the landing. For this reason it seems probable that a landing area undefended by an enemy, or one previously cleared by air attack or other means, will have to be found if air-borne operations of the future are not to suffer very severe casualties. It also seems probable that the individual parachute and the individual para-trooper will still have validity for a long time to come even if new mass-carrying devices and mass-landing devices are perfected.

In *air-borne* work all equipment that is integrally part of the air-borne forces must be so designed that it can be carried without disassembly in plane or glider, or lowered by parachute. The devel-opment of recoilless guns and powerful light tanks and the perfec-tion of giant parachutes which enable the lowering of even large field pieces and jeeps from the skies makes this less impossible than it sounds.

Air *transportability*, on the other hand, contemplates the transport of all items of ground equipment, but some of the heavier ones, it is recognized, must be disassembled and perhaps distributed through several planes because of bulk or weight. The design of new equip-ment, however, is being done with air transportability in mind; for instance, a new 155-mm. self-propelled howitzer is being constructed in such a manner that portions of its armor can be easily removed to permit its air transportation by 50,000-pound cargo transports.

By such means a major increase in the strategic or long-range mobility and in the tactical or short-range mobility of ground armies is a realizable possibility in the future. But the limitations and restric-tions on the mass transport of armies by air are so considerable that the vision of entire armies moving at high speed above oceans through the clouds is still a Wellsian one, and is likely to remain an imaginative, rather than a practical, concept for many years to come.

The first and most important of these limitations is the industrial and technical and tactical problem of constructing and operating giant transport and cargo planes or the tremendous fleets of smaller transports necessary to carry a great ground force. Bigger and bigger planes will be built, but the huge expense and complexity, already noted, of building and operating great fleets of them, particularly over *long* distances, make the 100-per-cent air transport of large armies virtually impossible for the foreseeable future. The 46-ton tank, standard equipment of our Army today, cannot be transported by any single plane available in 1948,[47] and even if one were built, some eighty-seven of these sky giants would be required to transport simultaneously the medium tanks (exclusive of other equipment or men) of *one* armored division. Heavy engineering equipment cannot be loaded into any plane now available, and 12,000 pounds operational payload is the top limit of the C-82, Fairchild Packet, present "workhorse" of our air-borne divisions. During the war no entire division was ever "air-lifted" at one time; 1,200 C-47 cargo planes (the standard "workhorse" then available, now superseded by the Fairchild Packet) would have been required to put, *one* entire air-borne division into the air at one time. The immense problems involved in logistics, supplies, availability and suitability of airfields, traffic control, extensive fighter protection for the transports, etc., dictated the actual procedure. "Parts" of divisions were ferried in by air; then the transport planes would return to base for another load. Such a procedure, of course, is logistically feasible and militarily practical only over short distances, not now measured and not soon to be measured in transatlantic terms.

Planes, therefore, are unlikely to supersede ships, railroads, or motor vehicles in the transport of bulk cargoes or great armies, and until 4,000- or 5,000-mile high-speed, transoceanic transport planes of large capacity are developed, perhaps by 1960, even small air-borne or air-transportable operations at great distances will not be militarily practicable. But the landing of small saboteur or "suicide" groups by air in the heart of an enemy country is possible today, and it will be within the capacity of all great powers in the future to pick up one or two divisions of ground troops and set them down on the other side of the world,[48] provided, of course, the hostile air force has first been neutralized. These divisions would not be equipped with heavy tanks or field pieces or bulky engineering equipment, but the development of light, recoilless guns (used in World War II) and improvements in light tank armor and armament would give them fire power and mobility superior to the infantry divisions of the last war.

In one other respect—the development of amphibious techniques and the tactical mobility of ground units—the armies of tomorrow may be expected to make important strides. Amphibious tanks for landing operations were in the first stages of development when the last war ended; great sea-land monsters of tremendous fire power, some of them perhaps robots and radio-controlled, may be developed in the future. One such device, dubbed the "creep"—a sixty-foot landing barge—bucks, rears and jumps out of the water, up a beach and through swamps by means of a propulsion system hitherto unknown to war. Amphibious tanks especially designed to be transported by cargo submarines will also be evolved, and will lend great strength to small parties of "Commandos" or saboteurs. Helicopters may also prove to have considerable utility in "airphibious" work— the transfer by air of men and cargo from ship to shore.

On land, speed, cross-country mobility and armor will be combined. Tracked vehicles, or new types of rugged, wheeled vehicles, armored to provide protection against small-arms fire for the personnel they carry, will be standardized.

The tempo of war is ever increasing; speed and range are reaching out to the ultimate on land, on sea and in the air.

In most of these developments, the American Army in 1948 is equal to, or ahead of, the world. In theory, ideas and blueprints of new equipment, we also lead the way in air-borne development, but too much of our postwar air-borne work has been on paper. The Russians, with perhaps 100,000 trained air-borne troops, have considerable strength in this arm, but their man power exceeds their available transport power, and most of their present air transports are old and slow.

Such is the grim profile of the new face of war. The weapons and equipment described have completely revolutionized—and the word is too soft—not only the techniques and technology of war but also its tactics and strategic concepts (as explained in Section II). They have added tremendous power and terrible range to Mars.

Today, the United States, with the atomic bomb, the beginnings of guided missiles, biological and chemical agents, good, long-range planes, the world's finest (and largest) navy and the best-equipped army, holds a definite technological advantage, which means, in this age, a strategic advantage. That advantage is, as of 1948, a considerable one. But Pandora's box of evils is still open, and there can issue from it, at any time, new genii to change the world.

Notes—Chapter III

1. *Armament and History*, by Major General J. F. C. Fuller, Scribner's. Page xiv.

2. But not in a political or psychological sense. See Chapters I and II.

3. Fuller, ibid., page 107.

4. Quoted by Fuller, ibid., page 107, from *Makers of Modern Strategy*, edited by Earle, Craig and Gilbert, Princeton University Press. Pages 91-92.

5. *The Decline of the West*, by Oswald Spengler, English edition, Volume II, Alfred A. Knopf, Inc. Page 428. Also quoted by Fuller, ibid., page 107.

6. Plutonium is also found, but in infinitesimal quantities, in nature.

7. *The United States Strategic Bombing Survey—The Effects of Atomic Bombs on Hiroshima and Nagasaki*, U. S. Government Printing Office.

8. For additional details see table compiled by the Strategic Bombing Survey reproduced in Appendix III.

9. This author witnessed the second, or underwater, test.

10. The indications of the Bikini tests were that an air or underwater burst would sink or cripple all ships of any type within five-hundred yards, seriously damage all within half a mile, and would inflict relatively light damage, diminishing to negligible, to all those three quarters of a mile to one mile or more away. Fleet cruising dispositions at sea and fleet anchorages in all except "tight" ports are spread out over far greater space than this.

11. Radioactivity also has grave implications for civilians. Mystery always breeds fear, and mystery still surrounds the atomic bomb. Radioactivity, too, is an insidious, stealthy killer. A crew of a ship or a battalion of infantry or a family in an apartment house might be superficially unharmed by the explosion of an atomic bomb, but nevertheless doomed to certain death. When a man—military or civilian—knows he is doomed, and yet, for the common good, must carry on with his work as long as he can stand, a new problem in mass psychology and national morale is introduced.

Radioactivity may cause almost immediate death if a person is heavily exposed, or it may cause death within a few days to a month. The radiation attacks the bone marrow and the blood corpuscles; nausea, weakness, temperature, general debility, the breakdown of the cellular structure of the body, internal hemorrhages and sometimes bleeding through the skin result. There is no known curative if the exposure has been intense enough, but remedial measures which hasten recovery and check the invasion of the weakened body by infection include rest and nursing care, and whole blood and plasma transfusions.

12. It is, of course, impossible to be specific about details of the atomic bomb, since those details have been guarded with great secrecy. It is even more difficult to be accurate and specific about all the characteristics and limitations of the atomic bomb, since the world's atomic knowledge is still in its adolescence and many of the characteristics and limitations, when the bomb is used in certain ways or under certain conditions, are the result of informed extrapolation or, in other words, scientific "speculation," and are not the result of experience or actual measurement. This is particularly applicable to the remarks in this chapter about anticipated damage effects when an atomic bomb is exploded at or below ground level, something that has not yet been done. At writing, the Army is planning a series of tests in Utah with conventional explosives, some of which will simulate atomic explosion, to test the effect of "earth shock" on underground structures.

13. The Hiroshima and Nagasaki bombs were probably less than one tenth of one per cent efficient. The Smyth Report states that "the energy released in uranium fission corresponds to the utilization of only about one tenth of one per cent of its mass."

14. See Page 58.

15. *Documents under Discussion by the Atomic Energy Commission of the United Nations*, compiled by the U.S. mission to the United Nations, page 19. Protoactinium could be used as a fissionable material according to the Smyth Report, but "can be eliminated because of its scarcity in nature."

16. For the U.S. position in this and other minerals see the next chapter.

17. But Eugene P. Wigner in "Roots of the Atomic Age," a chapter in *One World or None*, Whittlesey House, McGraw-Hill, estimates on page 15 that "an almost unlimited amount of plutonium could be made within not too many years, enough for a very large number of bombs. . . ."

18. According to Stefan T. Possony, "Who's Who in the Atomic Race," *U. S. Naval Institute Proceedings*, February 1946.

19. See Bernard Brodie, *The Absolute Weapon*, Harcourt, Brace & Company. Brodie concludes (page 59): "Thus, while the bomb may remain, for the next fifteen or twenty years at least, scarce enough to dictate to its would-be users a fairly rigorous selection of targets and means of delivery, it will not be scarce enough to spare any nation against which it is used from a destruction immeasurably more devastating than that endured by Germany in World War II." See, too, the excellent discussion by Ansley J. Coale in *The Problem of Reducing Vulnerability to Atomic Bombs*, Princeton University Press. Mr. Coale's calculations of bomb size and *potential* production differ somewhat from mine. Both these studies err, I believe, in assuming too large an actual production.

An anonymous Army officer, interviewed in Hawaii in 1946, made a public estimate that we were probably producing bombs at the rate of about one a week. But he, like the rest of us, probably was guessing. His estimates appeared in *The New York Times* of July 30, 1946, Page 8, col. 3.

20. *Report to the Air Coordinating Committee of the Sub-Committee on Demobilization of the Aircraft Industry*, 11 October, 1945, U. S. Government Printing Office.

21. Russia does not "have" an atomic bomb today, according to best available information and opinion. She *could* have, but very probably has *not*, produced an atomic bomb. But when she does at any time from 1948 on we may not know it until long after the event, though there is some slight possibility that radioactivity from a test-bomb explosion in Russia might be detected beyond her border.

22. *A General Account of the Development of Methods of Using Atomic Energy for Military Purposes under the Auspices of the United States Government*, by H. D. Smyth, Princeton University Press, page 45. This is the "Bible" of all would-be writers on atomic energy and has been heretofore referred to as the "Smyth Report."

23. Major-General Alden H. Waitt, Chief of the Chemical Corps of the Army, spoke of these new toxic agents as "substances." They may not be synthetic gases, but biological agents or radioactive poisons.

24. The agents which were to have been used against the Japanese rice crop were synthetic hormones which produce a cancerlike derangement of the growth processes of plants.

25. *Human Genetics*, by Reginald Russell Gates, the Macmillan Company.

26. A thorough treatment of biological-warfare agents will be found in *The Journal of Immunology*, May, 1947, "Bacterial Warfare," by Theodor Rosebury and Elvin A. Kabat, with the assistance of Martin H. Boldt, and in Appendix IV, a discussion by Dr. Franklin S. Cooper. See also an excellent discussion, "B.W.," by Gerard Piel, in *Life*, November 18, 1945. I have drawn upon these studies in this section.

27. "Bacterial Warfare," *The Journal of Immunology*. May, 1947.

28. See Note 26.

29. The development of atomic power for aircraft has been adjudged feasible in time. More than a year of postwar study of the problem was made by the Fairchild Engine and Airplane Corporation and associated concerns, and the feasibility, though probably far off, of such a propulsion system was believed to have been definitely shown. The difficulties, however, are immense.

30. For more details see next chapter.

31. The length is not so important, however, if "JATO"—or "jet-assisted-take-off" rockets to give the plane an extra boost of power—is used.

32. Theoretically the C-99, transport version of the B-36 (largest land plane in the world), will have a payload of about 100,000 pounds (or more than 400 troops) but it is the only plane of its kind in the world. Only one has been ordered, and its service tests are incomplete. Howard Hughes' giant plywood sea mammoth, sometimes called the "Hercules," the largest aircraft ever built, is designed for a theoretical capacity of perhaps 700 people, but it, too, is incompletely tested. Both of these giants may provide valuable design and construction lessons for the future, but they are definitely experimental, not operating, planes.

33. Transsonic is that "twilight" zone where speeds about equal that of

sound; i. e., from about 600 to 900 miles an hour. It is in this zone that the greatest scientific, aerodynamic and control problems are encountered.

34. In the V-2, fuel could be shut off by radio from the ground, but no alteration of course was possible.

35. *The Problem of Reducing Vulnerability to Atomic Bombs*, by Ansley J. Coale, Princeton University Press. Page 84.

36. Absolute insurance of detonation apparently has not yet been achieved with the atomic bomb.

37. Quoted from an article, "Are We Ready for a Pushbutton War?" by Joseph and Stewart Alsop in the *Saturday Evening Post*, September 3, 1947.

38. All the time estimates in this chapter are at best informed guesses, for in the present state of missile development no one can say what unforeseen problems in this field may occur. The time required to produce a certain weapon is entirely proportional to the effort put upon it. The peacetime effort of the United States in this field, though major, is far more leisurely than was the wartime concentration. The estimates given here are based upon a continuation of about the same expenditures and concentration of about the same effort as in the postwar years 1946–47.

39. That is why "hedge-hopping" planes skimming closely over the earth's surface frequently avoid radar detection. Radar also can be "jammed" by "windows" (the wartime term) of metallic bits of paper released from a raiding plane. These reflect the short radio waves and appear on the radar screen in the form of hundreds of pinpoints of "blobs" of light, thus confusing the operator and "hiding" the raiding plane. Radar by no means insures 100 per cent detection.

40. This electrically charged "layer" of atmosphere has the property of generally, but not always, reflecting radio waves.

41. From *The Federal Research Program*, a report by John R. Steelman for the fiscal year ending June 30, 1947, U. S. Government Printing Office.

42. The Germans had conducted experiments in the firing of a V-2-type missile from beneath many feet of water. The water apparently does not interfere materially with the ballistic qualities of the missile, as the California Institute of Technology has discovered.

43. The hulls of the *Kentucky*, laid down as a battleship, and of the battle cruiser *Hawaii* are to serve as the experimental platforms for the Navy's first missile ships. But design has not yet been completed; in fact the required missiles (of at least 100,000-yard range) have not yet been developed.

44. Radio-controlled drone boats were tried during the war and were, of course, used at Bikini. Their controls, however, are not entirely reliable; they may go wild, and the radio channels which control them may be jammed by the enemy. "In the Mediterranean the Germans actually succeeded in wresting control from us and then insulted us by saying over the radio, "Dey vos your darlings yesterday; dey are ours today." (*Combat Scientists*, by Lincoln R. Thiesmeyer and John E. Burchard, Office of Scientific Research. and Development, Atlantic, Little, Brown. Page 363, Footnote 3.)

45. But this is far off; fissionable material, as yet scarce, is too much needed for bombs.

46. The Russians secured about six German Type VII-C and four type XXI U-boats, and many others in component, or unassembled, form—perhaps fifty in all. In addition, they have secured or salvaged some surface ships of the German Navy, including the aircraft carrier *Graf Zeppelin* (damaged and never finished); the obsolete battleship *Schleswig-Holstein* (badly damaged); the cruiser *Luetzow* (damaged); the cruiser *Nürnberg* (renamed the *Admiral Makarov*); ten German destroyers of the *Narvik* and *Elbing* classes; and seven torpedo boats.

47. The Consolidated C-99, one of which is in existence, has a top rated payload of 100,000 pounds, but the medium tank is too big for its fuselage. See Note 32.

48. Whether or not divisions, thus air transported or air borne, can be *supplied* by air at great distances from base is a different question. The use of the cargo or supply submarine in conjunction with surprise air-borne operations, particularly those involving raids, may be quite important.

CHAPTER IV

THE ECONOMIC POSITION

... the technique of war ... presses all mechanical possibilities of the time relentlessly into its purpose, and under pressure of military necessity even opens up new domains hitherto unexploited. ... .[1]

SPENGLER

HALF a century ago Brooks Adams foresaw the economic supremacy of the world centered in the United States.[2]
But even his unusual prescience which enabled Adams to visualize, fifty years before it occurred, a bi-polar world could not have predicted the sheer magnitude and scope of the American supremacy. With but 6 per cent of the world's population, the United States has a quarter of its national income, half of its telephones, 35 per cent of its railroad mileage, 65 per cent of its petroleum production, 40 per cent of the coal production, and more than half of its steel and a quarter of its copper production. The little nation which Brooks Adams wrote about when it turned the corner of destiny in the Spanish-American War has now become a romance in statistics—a giant among pygmies.

The economic position of the United States in the postwar world is one of tremendous power, relatively or absolutely, and of some weaknesses.

It used to be said that total war was too expensive to fight, that any nation that tried it would bankrupt itself. In one sense this is true. Total war often means the liquidation of overseas investments and unbalanced national ledgers. But the prospect of bankruptcy has rarely acted as a deterrent to conflict. With wishful hope we predicted, in the dark decade of the Thirties, the financial downfall of Germany and Japan; they could not, we held, "afford" conquest. The realities of history have blasted the chimeras of the past. War, we now know, is never too expensive to fight in the terms of dollars or pounds or francs or rubles, for the generation that fights wars never fully pays for them (except in sweat and blood) but transmits its burden of increased taxation and reduced resources from generation unto generation. And money in any case is but a symbol of real wealth, either in economic or in military terms.

The real productivity of war, like the productivity of peace, is but a sum of man- and machine-hours; the economic position of a nation depends fundamentally upon its peoples, its industrial facilities and their output, its transportation, its agricultural production, and its supply and production of raw materials. In all these elements the United States is strong, and it is well that this is so, for the big factories rather than the big battalions dominated the past war, and a tremendous, varied and flexible industrial plant plus a general economic position of great strength is essential—as previous chapters have shown—to development and production of the new weapons.

The population of the United States, often cited as a potential weakness in comparison to that of other powers, is, despite present and prospective limitations in numbers, a factor of great strength.[3] A little of the prewar demographic pessimism about America's future, which was a result of the decreasing birth rate, has been relieved by the phenomenal increase in the birth rate in recent years. This increase is by no means conclusive, but, at the moment, we are in no immediate danger of becoming an "old" or a static people. Our population, though far smaller than the enormous masses of China and India, and somewhat smaller than that of Russia, is qualitatively much further advanced than any other peoples. Educational levels are far higher and skills and aptitudes better developed than in the mass-population countries, and our workmen are backed up by far more horsepower and many more machines. In productivity per man-hour the United States is unequaled; extensive industrialization, power development, and the technical and mechanical skills of American workmen far more than compensate for inferiority in numbers.[4]

In industrial facilities and industrial output we have no peer; today there is not even a very close second. The prodigies of wartime production are too recent in memory[5] to require much elaboration. The United States produces half of the world's power, does some 40 per cent or more of the horsepower hours of work performed in the world, and turns out 35 to 50 per cent of the world's industrial production.[6]

In heavy industries, shipbuilding, plane and automotive construction and munitions-making the war showed the unrivaled economic strength of the United States.

Similarly, the transportation index of our economic vigor is large. Our commercial passenger and freight airlines, our automobiles, busses and trucks and railroads have no equals in transportation mileage, passengers carried, or cargo transported.[7] Only the merchant marine, of major importance in our foreign relations in peace and in war, shows elements of major weakness. In these postwar years, it seems to be following the same retrogressive course which led to the decline and decay of American commercial sea power after the First World War. The merchant marine must, of course, be reduced in size from its unnaturally inflated and uneconomic wartime peak. But in 1948, there was danger that the process of "deflation" would go too far. Labor unrest, extravagant unionism fostered in part by deliberate Communist attempts to seize control of the transportation unions and in part by backward and reactionary owner practices, inadequate governmental policies,[8] the exceedingly high costs of American ship construction and ship operation, and growing competition with the British, more experienced in the carrying trade, threaten to weaken the American merchant marine dangerously. Nevertheless, partly because of our tremendous ship-construction program during the war, partly because the traditional maritime nations had not yet been able to rebuild their merchant fleets, the operating American merchant marine in 1947 numbered 2,349 vessels, displacing a grand total of 27,181,000 dead-weight tons, or about 27½ per cent of the world's total tonnage.[9]

Despite the growing industrialization and urbanization of the United States, the "remarkable maintenance of high levels of American agricultural production is a source of strength for our national security."[10] During the war, the United States increased total agricultural production by 25 per cent, food production by 33 per cent, despite the migration of 8,000,000 persons from agriculture.

New techniques and new farm machinery, plus the expansion of soil-conservation practices, promise in the immediate future continued high levels of agricultural production—although the farm,

of course, is far more sensitive to droughts, floods, and other cataclysmic "acts of God" than nearly any other occupation of man.
The farm, and hence its productivity, is also very much at the
mercy of sudden shifts in prices incident to the instability of our
industrial economy. A cyclic rise and fall in wheat production, corn
crops and livestock is, therefore, to be anticipated, and the continuation of a one-crop economy or the deforestation of the plains may
bring about a recurrence, in some parts of the country, of the
disastrous "dust bowl" conditions of the Thirties.

The urgent necessity for the extension of soil-conservation practices and for reforestation is underscored by government estimates
that one third of our topsoil has been dissipated and about one fifth
of our original tillable land is no longer productive. Half a million
of our 460,000,000 tillable acres are being lost each twelve months
to erosion.[11]

Intensive cultivation of the remainder and the extensive use of
fertilizers, pest control, mechanical farming aids and "scientific"
farming have nevertheless increased our total agricultural production, as noted, by phenomenal figures. But this very productivity
can be a long-term danger as well as a short-term blessing. For
improper cultivation, particularly one-crop economy, can ruin the
land; a few years of overexploitation can destroy the work of a
thousand years of nature. From an agricultural point of view, our
long-term danger is clearly depicted; as Robert S. Bird put it in the
New York *Herald Tribune*, "in the United States land fertility is
draining away and the population is rising fast."[12] Contour planting,
strip cropping, terracing and flood-control work, better crop rotation, and the more intelligent use of increased amounts of fertilizer
are vital if our soil fertility is to be preserved. We cannot feed the
world today or tomorrow; Russia, Manchuria and Argentina have
greater areas of rich soil than we do and, potentially, greater agricultural production. Nevertheless, we are today a tremendous food-
producing nation—one of the greatest agricultural nations of all
time.

This high level of agricultural production does not, of course,
imply complete self-sufficiency in all the elements of our diet.
Coffee, olive oil, tea, cocoa, bananas, many tropical fruits, and various other elements of the foods dearly loved by Americans come
from without our borders, but unlike England, unlike Germany,
but like Russia, we produce more than enough in our own country

to maintain our population in health; we cannot be starved by blockade.

Our raw-material position, too, is *relatively* satisfactory. There are, however, certain major weaknesses in our minerals position, both absolutely and relatively. William G. Hotchkiss outlined the absolute weakness well, in an article, "Our Declining Mineral Reserves," in the Autumn 1947 *Yale Review*:

The fact that we of the present generation have consumed more minerals than our ancestors used before us in all the history of the race is either unknown to the average citizen or he regards it as a mere academic matter. When he can't get a new automobile, or a new battery for his old car, or a telephone, he puts the whole blame on the slowness of "reconversion" and thinks that everything will be all right by another year. He would be better advised if he looked upon some of these shortages as foretastes of possible chronic conditions when the present great appetite for minerals lifts current needs above world production.[13]

In other words world consumption of certain minerals, particularly copper, lead and zinc, appears to be overtaking total world production, and it is possible that world shortages may ensue.

In the case of the United States certain relative weaknesses (perhaps best illustrated by the tables in the appendices) add to our problem, although there is no doubt that, as of today, the United States leads the world in *developed* raw materials.

Much has been made of our decreasing reserve of petroleum products, and the approaching "exhaustion" of the Mesabi Range of high-grade iron ore. However, the Bureau of Mines and the U. S. Geological Survey have estimated, based on 1935–44 average-use rates, that we still have some fifteen years' proved reserve of petroleum products, and possibly seventy-six years' reserve of iron ore. If so-called "submarginal and highly speculative" and low-grade reserves are proven workable (as a result of new prospecting and processing) we may actually have an indefinite reserve of petroleum and over five hundred years' reserve of iron ore. These figures, though comforting, are not, of course, conclusive, and they must immediately be qualified.

In the case of petroleum products domestic oil demand has risen phenomenally since the war and production is at a high peak, but no great new discoveries of oil in this country have been made for some years. The known and proved reserves will last, even at the postwar-use rate, for at least a decade, and the probability of new discoveries or of more economical methods of extracting oil from shales, etc., indicate that a measured optimism, though it should be qualified, is probably not misplaced. Nevertheless, insofar as *natural* oils are concerned, and barring the possibility of new and great discoveries, we are becoming a *net* importer of oil, instead of one of the world's greatest exporters. Our reduced petroleum reserve is sufficient to explain our great interest in the Middle East oil fields, the production of which is *not* of great *direct* strategic importance[14] to the nation but is of tremendous indirect importance. The development of the Middle Eastern fields can supplement American production and can provide oil for European markets, which would otherwise be drained from American or Venezuelan wells. The Middle East, however, is too exposed and too distant to represent a sound strategic source of oil in an emergency. Thus, it is fortunate that the Venezuela-Caribbean fields are relatively rich and well developed and that new oil-rich areas of promise comparable to Venezuela, which can be developed in perhaps a decade, have been discovered in Peru and Ecuador. The Navy's Point Barrow explorations in Alaska may also result in new discoveries. The development of economic methods of utilizing oil shales and other submarginal deposits also offers insurance against the future. From a military point of view, the reduction in proved petroleum reserves in the continental United States is not of *vital* consequence, since synthetic liquid fuels, adequate for all except a few purposes (some lubricants excepted) can be produced from natural gas and coal, and we have a reserve of more than 4,300 years of bituminous coal and lignite, and a reserve of 187 years of anthracite coal.[15]

Iron ore presents a potentially somewhat less serious case than petroleum. The Mesabi or Minnesota ranges are believed to have about 40 per cent of the original high-grade reserves remaining, enough for our needs for a period variously estimated as a decade to forty years. When this rich deposit is worked out, the United States will have to depend on low-grade taconite deposits in this area, or on low-grade deposits in New York and elsewhere in the United States, and in Labrador and Latin America. A new project for producing high-grade iron concentrate from taconite, a rock formation with low iron content, was started recently in the Mesabi region. If successful, this process will provide all our needs (though at increased steel costs) for many years, since there are an estimated 60 billion tons of taconite in the Mesabi-Great Lakes area. If the taconite concentration process does not prove feasible on a large scale, recourse will have to be had to other low-grade iron-ore deposits, which means the economic dislocation of the whole iron-ore industry, heretofore concentrated around the Mesabi Range. The problem in iron ore is basically a technological and production one; it takes time to devise a new concentration process or to readjust a whole industry to new geographic locations. And time is precious in modern war and in the preparations for it. The present iron-ore situation in the nation indicates the eventual need, though not a vital need in our generation, for new sources of iron ore outside the United States.

But rubber, as the war showed, is no longer of such great concern (perhaps in time there will even be a substitute for steel). Our mass production of synthetic rubber has proven that we can be virtually independent, if necessary, of overseas sources of natural crude rubber, although an irreducible minimum of natural crude will probably always be necessary for mixtures and for specialized purposes.

We are not, therefore, in danger of becoming a "have not" nation in iron ore, petroleum or rubber. But to produce enough of each of these products *within our borders*, for our long-term needs, does pose a major economic problem to the nation. The production of synthetics or the exploitation of low-grade reserves (like oil shale and taconite) implies more labor and more equipment—i.e., higher costs—per unit of product obtained. As the new processes are perfected, costs and man- and machine-hours required for production will probably decrease, but until that time we would have to devote in a war emergency increased amounts of labor and equipment to the job of producing raw materials at a time when all types of labor and equipment would be in great demand. These processes and facilities cannot be improvised overnight; they must be ready before war comes. This potential weakness, incident to our declining mineral reserves, cannot be ignored; nevertheless we are, relatively speaking, well off in iron ore, rubber and petroleum.

In many other minerals we are far less fortunate. There are reserves of at least nine important materials which should last more than a hundred years, nine sufficient for twenty-five to a hundred years (based on the average-rate use of the period, 1935–44), nine adequate for five to twenty-five years, but fourteen—among them manganese, mercury, tungsten, tin and antimony—in which we have no natural supply,[16] or a reserve of less than five years.

Another comprehensive study, that of the Army and Navy Munitions Board, has listed, as of 1946, fifty-three "strategic" or "critical" raw materials—that is, raw materials which are essential to the waging of modern war—for which there are no substitutes or synthetics and for which there are not adequate sources in the continental United States.[17]

Some of these "scarce" minerals offer no great problem; nickel, for instance, is available in great quantities across the border in Canada, but our quartz comes from Brazil, sapphires and rubies (for instrument, clock, and timekeeping jewels and bearings) from India, manila fibers from the Philippines, palm oil from Africa, industrial diamonds from Belgium, the United Kingdom and the Union of South Africa. Our full needs in most of these vital materials, found in insufficient quantities in the United States itself, can be supplied by other Western Hemisphere nations—notably Canada, which is rich in minerals, and Mexico. There is always, however, a problem in securing raw materials *not* under our own sovereignty. Other suppliers—in some cases, the only suppliers (India as a source of kyanite, shellac and aluminum silicate, for instance) lie halfway round the world. Manganese offers a special postwar case. In 1947 we were importing considerable quantities of manganese from *Russia*, which could, and presumably might, at any time, cut off our supply. Large reserves of this metal are available but undeveloped in Brazil, and the war and postwar breakdown, and general inadequacy, of the railroads in Africa and India shut off our normal supplies from these areas. Chrome also was being imported from Russia.

In aggregate, the U.S. raw-material position—in availability, size and development of domestic resources and easy access to foreign resources—is good, unexcelled and probably unequaled (except perhaps in potential and undeveloped reserves) by any other nation. But there has been considerable diminution of our reserves and a tremendous increase in demand, and our general material position is not as strong as it was before the great maw of modern war and the needs of industrial technology embraced practically all the known elements of earth. Most important, the rate of discovery of minerals in the United States has decreased rapidly in the last twenty years.

In summary, the population, power development, industrial facilities, transportation networks and raw-material resources of the United States make it an economic giant of the world, its strengths greater, its weaknesses fewer, than those of any other power.

But no fair picture of our postwar economic position can be painted without some further discussion of our weaknesses, and particularly without describing the effects of the technological revolution in war and the influence of the new implements of war upon our industrial and raw-material position.

In effect, all that we have so far said is that the United States is in an unrivaled position to fight the last war.

But our industrial facilities and raw-material resources are today inadequate to produce the new weapons which are changing the face of war.

The 139-ton B-36, for example, is being constructed in a "model" war-built Fort Worth plant (designed to build an earlier plane, the B-32 Liberator) which is far too small for economical production of the giant plane. The B-36, which is the world's largest combat aircraft, has to be slewed into a "cater-cornered" position in the final stages of assembly, for its wings are longer than the factory is wide. The tail assembly is also higher than the roof trusses and projects between the trusses up into the vaulted roof areas. It is a nice problem in judgment to move this plane, and even to work on it, in a factory already outmoded after only five years of life.

But the size and layouts of factories are the least of the problems created by the new technology. Some of our machine tools are obsolete; new ones are required for manufacturing processes peculiar to the new weapons. The landing gear of the B-36, for instance, an unprecedented engineering and manufacturing job, required (in its original design, since modified) a machine of which only one was available in the United States.

General George C. Kenney in a talk on October 1, 1947, to the Army Ordnance Association, stressed other difficulties of the new technology: "I assure you those simple riveting jobs [of World War II] won't do in the modern fighter or bomber, whose surfaces have to be not only really true airfoil sections to a tolerance of plus or minus three thousandths, but have to be as smooth as polished glass. We can gain fifteen miles an hour on a jet fighter by a smooth paint job over the normal polished aluminum surface, but when the continual flexing of the wings puts a few cracks in the paint we lost twenty-five miles an hour. So far we haven't been able to develop a paint that doesn't crack. . . . Our instruments that were satisfactory for 400 or even 500 miles an hour are too crude for modern speeds. . . . In the armaments field it looks as though we have got to start all over again. Our bombs are all obsolete for the new high-speed aircraft. . . ."

The advent of jet engines has modified the whole aircraft engineering picture in the United States. The "old-line" established engine companies, makers of reciprocating engines, Pratt and Whitney, and Wright, and the newer liquid-cooled-engine manufacturer, Allison (a subsidiary of General Motors), must make what is at best an abrupt change-over to a type of manufacturing with specialized and vastly different problems, techniques and skills.

The demand, born of the jet and missile age, for new types of propellants is also taxing to the limit the American firms that make these fuels and somewhat obscure chemicals. Many of the jets use different types of fuel. Some of the newest airplane engines use kerosene or other fuels not produced ordinarily in the quantities required in war, and no standardization of fuel, even for the new planes, much less for guided missiles, has yet been accomplished. Liquid oxygen to fuel the V-2 rockets that have been fired experimentally in small numbers at the White Sands, New Mexico, proving grounds has had to be brought all the way from the New York area, and had we been firing thousands of these rockets operationally, the facilities for manufacturing liquid oxygen, hitherto servicing only limited commercial fields, would have had to be tremendously expanded.

Some other propellants, particularly the new chemical combinations that will power the long-range rockets, will probably have little commercial application but will be in major military demand. Many of these chemicals are dangerously volatile and explosive; there must be all sorts of safety factors in their manufacture.

These problems, in turn, create a greater problem. After World War I it became fashionable (though not altogether correct) to indict the "merchants of death"—the munitions-makers in each country, who, in time of peace, it was said, fostered war and in time of war made huge profits. This sweeping stricture may have been applicable (though with many reservations) to the nineteenth century and to the vanished age that ended with World War I. But total war, it quickly became apparent, demanded far more than a segment of a nation's industry; it was impossible to sort out and separate the "munitions-makers" from the bulk of industry, for every factory, every machine tool was harnessed to victory.[18]

Is the reverse process now true? Must there arise again a specialized, perhaps government-supported section of industry devoted solely or largely in peace to turning out the tools of war? Certainly the aircraft industry, with limited commercial orders, is for the present largely dependent upon military orders for its continued existence, and the new manufacturers of reaction engines, rocket powder and certain chemicals would seem to find a market chiefly in the military field.

But perhaps the most serious of our economic deficiencies which the new technology has exposed is our lack of certain raw materials which meant little commercially or militarily a decade ago but which have tremendous new-found importance in the jet and atomic age. The list of strategic or critical raw materials, compiled by the Munitions Board (see Appendix), has lengthened steadily in the last three years as the impact of the new technology was felt in metallurgy and a thousand other sciences.

Three of these materials of new and great importance are columbium or columbite, cobalt and uranium. Columbium (derived from columbite) has been discovered to be essential as an alloy in the manufacture of steels which will resist the high temperatures produced by jet engines. Relatively great quantities are required if satisfactory engines in large numbers are to be produced. Yet we have none within our borders, and the nearest supply is Nigeria, West Africa.

Cobalt is another such "scarce" mineral. Long used for hardening steel, it has always been in commercial and military demand. However, the production of "stellite" gun barrels during the war—a hard, wear-resistant barrel made of a cobalt-chromium-tungsten alloy—created a new military demand, and now the advent of the jet engine has created another potential demand which may tax all the world's supply sources. The United States is almost wholly dependent upon African sources.

Uranium, the raw material of the atomic bomb, is, of course, of even greater importance. It is found in nature in the form of carnotite and pitchblende, from which it must be extracted. "Patches" of these minerals are fairly frequent throughout the world, but rarely in exploitable amounts. Thorium, found in monazite sands and other deposits, is important to the atomic bomb—but only when used "in association *with* uranium."[19] Uranium itself is the magic metal, the indispensable element of the atomic bomb and atomic power.

Since the invention of the atomic bomb a great world-wide "treasure hunt" for uranium ores has been under way, but its results are in the "Secret" category; the little that is known can be considered indicative only.

In this country, available information indicates our only major sources of uranium ore are in Arizona, Colorado and Utah, where carnotite is found impregnated in sandstone.[20] Some 59,269 pounds of uranium[21] were extracted from the carnotite mined in these states in 1939. The American carnotite deposits are, however, of low grade, and extraction is a difficult problem.

Pitchblende deposits are known to exist in Northern Canada and in the Belgian Congo,[22] which probably has the largest known deposit in the world. A small deposit exists at Joachimsthal in Bohemia (Czechoslovakia) and another in Saxony; some "tailings" come from the South African gold mines, and Russia is known to have some deposits of either carnotite or pitchblende at various places within her borders, notably in Turkestan. India and Madagascar also have some small deposits. Various countries, including the Scandinavian, are believed to be working on the difficult problem of extracting tiny amounts of uranium from oil shales.

Rich thorium deposits are found in Brazil and India, less important ones in the United States, Ceylon and the Netherlands East Indies. Undoubtedly, these sparse deposits will be supplemented in the near future—if, indeed, this has not already occurred—by new discoveries. One of the great tragic epics of our time is the world-wide race for uranium.

In this race the United States, for the moment, is probably comfortably ahead. The sources of uranium which are *accessible* to us but *not* to Russia probably account for the bulk of the world's *known* reserves. The adjective *known* must be stressed; we do not know, and probably the Russians don't either, the extent of uranium reserves inside Russia. Today, the Russians probably have enough of the mineral to build a *very few* atomic bombs, but they will have more tomorrow. Moreover by far the greater part of the present known reserves lies *outside* the continental United States and outside the Western Hemisphere; the United States is plainly *dependent* on *foreign* sources.

The United States, though a "have" nation in its general mineral position, is, therefore, a "have not" nation insofar as domestic availability of certain highly important minerals is concerned. Our former position of virtual self-sufficiency and unequaled industrial facilities has also been weakened by the impact of the technological revolution.

There are, too, other weaknesses in the American economic position which must receive bare mention. One, which is as of yet *potential* rather than of actual significance, is the marked and almost dangerous production decline in the aircraft and shipbuilding industries. This was a natural consequence of the postwar era, especially following the wartime period of overproduction, and hence has no long-term significance, unless the decline in output (which means reduction in size) is carried to the danger point. The danger point is reached when the discharge and scattering to other occupations of skilled and indispensable technical and managerial employees occurs—and thus, the specialized "know-how" of an industry is lost.

Another actual weakness is our present deficiency born in part from shortsighted draft policies during the war, in part the product of American educational inadequacies—in properly trained scientific and engineering personnel. (See the next chapter.)

Another and more serious weakness in the economic position of the nation is the "boom-and bust" pattern into which capitalist economies have so far fitted. Needless to say, no economic position can be strong in the shadow of millions of unemployed or with hunger stalking a land of plenty, and the marked inflationary trends in the United States since the war, our enormous public debt, large budget, rising prices and high taxes seem to indicate the danger of a consequential "deflation" and depression. In the past the instability of the American economy—particularly the sudden and violent swings from the height of prosperity to the extreme of depression—has been a dangerous weakness. Unemployment and reduction of production not only reduces our "wealth-producing capacity" but affects adversely our domestic political stability and our international relations. The active revolutionary policy of the Communists would exploit to the full any future depression, and if it should be comparable in scope to the great depression of the Thirties, rioting, bloodshed and serious trouble, which would definitely affect the strength of our international position, would probably result. But even if this should come, the future of free enterprise can find solace from Stacy May's diagnoses of the past; whenever "there have been big fluctuations in production with strong upward trends followed by downward spirals, the successive peaks have been higher and higher and the downward spirals, though sharp, have not gone down to the levels of the peaks preceding them."

"Economy of force," a sound military principle, has not yet been fully applied to our economy or national resources. As Brooks Adams wrote, "the national characteristic [of the United States] is waste," and waste is no longer possible with safety in a land which already is exhausting some of its raw materials and which has expanded from sea to sea. Waste in every field and every aspect of life is a weakness of the American economic position.

Despite these "soft spots," the economic position of the United States today compares favorably with any nation of the earth. Only in two respects—*rate* of industrial growth and in unexploited sources of raw materials—do we compare unfavorably with any nation.

From 1920 *up to* World War II Soviet Russia's rate of industrial growth was greater than our own,[23] though she started, of course, from a far lower productive base. A larger percentage of the Soviet national income was put into industrial capital equipment than ever before in history. With World War II, the phenomenal growth of American industry during that period, and the simultaneous destruction of large areas of Soviet industry (notably the Ukraine, center of Soviet heavy industry, which is still incompletely restored), Russia's rate of industrial growth in comparison to our own has slowed down.

But Russia today has subordinated nearly all other tasks to expansion of her industrial facilities, particularly her heavy industries. The old Communist tenet, payment according to need, has been modified; incentives are offered to individual workers for greater production; the piecework system—scorned and largely outlawed by labor unions in the United States—is part and parcel of Russian economy.

Her fourth Five-Year Plan, launched in 1946, stresses heavy industries at the expense of consumers' goods, and the announced goals, and the statements of Soviet leaders themselves, show that military considerations are the major factor in the plan. The avowed Russian objective in their drive toward more complete industrialization is to "overtake and surpass the advanced capitalist countries technically and economically." That goal is essentially military in character, but stresses long-term military preparedness, rather than short-term. It emphasizes steel, coal, transportation, machine tools and the other basic industries essential to a great industrial economy in peace or in war. Its eventual long-term aim, of overtaking and surpassing the capitalist economies, is realistic in that no time deadline has yet been set, publicly at least, for this Gargantuan feat.

Russia's first postwar Five-Year Plan contemplates by 1950 a 43 per cent increase in total output of the basic industries as compared to 1945, a 62 per cent increase above 1940. Reduced to concrete and relative terms, however, this Soviet expansion, even if successfully carried out, seems no great threat to the United States. The 1950 goal of Soviet economy is the production of 25.4 million tons of steel, some 6,000,000 tons *less* than we produced in *1913*, and only 42 per cent of our production of more than 60 million tons in 1946. The Russians *hope* to mine 250,000,000 tons of coal in 1950, a 51 per cent increase as compared to their production in 1940, but only 40 per cent of the U.S. production in 1944. In electric power, the Soviet goal for 1950 is 82 billion kilowatt-hours, as compared to our production of 228,189,000,000,[24] kilowatt-hours in 1944. It is clear that even if Russian industrial expansion continues at the prewar rate, which is very unlikely judging by the goals of the fourth Five-Year Plan, it will be a long time, indeed, before the United States' lead is overcome. For there are several major Russian economic weaknesses which tend to handicap and hold back the Soviet peoples in their struggle for power.

One is the extensive system of controls and the autocratic authoritarianism which governs economic life in the Soviet Union, coupled with a bureaucracy of fear in which most men "pass the buck." Another is the very lack of consumers' goods which the Kremlin has persistently and consistently denied to its patient people; for the good laborer, real incentive—in the sense of ability to purchase material rewards—is largely lacking. Another grave weakness is the peculiar climatic susceptibility of Soviet agriculture to great droughts, and the weakness of the Russian transportation system, which handicaps the distribution of food from places of surplus to areas of scarcity. Famine has been a periodic part of Russian life for generations.

But the greatest handicap, in this technological age, is Russia's deficiency in technical man power—not in the scientific branches, but in the general mechanical aptitude and technical ability of her people, in shop foremen, in boss machinists, in practical construction engineers, in machinists, toolmakers, mechanics and the skills of the twentieth century.[25] This weakness needs to be stressed, for it seems to be one characteristic of the people. Intensive mechanical training and extensive industrialization over the period of the last two decades do not appear to have increased materially the natural aptitude of the Russian people for machines. Russia is still to a large extent a rural, an agrarian and a peasant economy, rather than an urban and an industrialized one. In maintenance, upkeep and construction of machines—and particularly in mass-production techniques (which must depend essentially upon skilled workmen)— the Russians still appear to be more a nation of peasants than an industrialized people. If this weakness is inherent (which some keen observers doubt) and hence not easily remedied by training, it may fatally handicap Russia's ambitious attempts to overtake and surpass the capitalist powers.

In any case, Ernest G. Ropes, former chief of the Commerce Department's Russian section and for years a student of Soviet economy, is unquestionably correct when he estimates that Russia will not have the industrial capacity to fight the United States for at least twenty-five years, possibly fifty. They just "don't have the stuff now."[26]

But Russia and the United States, though incomparably the greatest—in present output and future potential—are not the only industrial nations in the world. France, with important coal and iron-ore resources and steel mills which produced 4,400,000 metric tons in 1946, is an important factor in Europe's economy. England, though weakened by war and troubles, is today second to Russia, the greatest industrial nation of Europe, and her steel production of 13,100,000 tons in 1946, her excellent shipbuilding yards and her machine-tool and precision industries, as well as her aircraft plants, are major in peace or war. Even the smaller nations have economic importance in the struggle for power. Sweden's rich iron ore, her important Bofors munitions works and the high quality of her products, and Switzerland's precision manufactures of watches, instruments and tools and her advanced development of the gas turbine endow both these states with an industrial and techno-logical significance which transcends their size. Poland's coal and Belgium's and Luxembourg's steel are highly important to Europe; so are the grain fields of Eastern Europe.

But Germany, divided, broken and conquered, Germany is still the economic prize of Europe. Her industrial output today is small and disparate, but the potential that endowed her with power—an industrious, inventive, technological people; important coal and potash deposits; extensive industrialization, particularly marked in the chemical industry, machine tools and steel—is still hers. Many of her factories have been destroyed, but when reparations dismantling is completed—if it ever is—those that are left will be more than adequate in number to produce goods roughly equal to the total volume produced in Germany in 1936. And, most important, the coal mines and many of the great steel mills and factory complexes of the Ruhr are still being worked, or are operable. Germany, not actually, but potentially, still has the blood of empire in her veins; industrially, she has what Russia lacks; economically, her capabilities and resources make her a power in the future of Europe.

But the tense is the future, not the present, and even then—so complete is the political wreck of the Third Reich, so awful the moral disintegration of its people, so heavy the physical damage, so inferior in population numbers to its giant neighbor to the East—even then, a quarter century hence, Germany's military-economic greatness seems dependent upon liaison with another nation or nations—with Russia or the West.

The United States in 1948—leading exponent of "free enterprise," chief example of the capitalist system—stands unchallenged and unchallengeable on an economic pinnacle rarely reached in the history of nations. It is not an unassailable pinnacle; it is not a position without weaknesses, relative and absolute. And economic strength, it must be forever emphasized, represents, *not* military *strength*, but military *potential*; time is required to convert one into the other. Yet the American economic position is so strong, particularly in the military sense, that only time, the unchecked spread of our own weaknesses or the full realization of the vast potential of undeveloped Russia can overthrow it.

NOTES—Chapter IV

1. *The Decline of the West*, by Oswald Spengler, English Edition, Volume II, Alfred A. Knopf, Inc. Page 420.
2. *America's Economic Supremacy*, by Brooks Adams, Harper & Brothers.
3. But see Chapter V for some of the psychological weaknesses.
4. U.S. population, 145,000,000 in 1947, a predicted 160,000,000 in 1970 as compared to Russia's 190,000,000 in 1947 and predicted 250,000,000 in 1970.
5. See also Chapter I.
6. See also Appendices I and II.
7. United States commercial air transport—900 operational planes; 600 additional on order or option; 271,000 route miles.

Russian commercial air transport—87,000 miles (approx., 1944).

U.S. railroad mileage—229,000

British railroad mileage—20,000

Russian railroad mileage—59,000-66,000

U.S. motor vehicles—31,010,000

British motor vehicles—2,484,000

USSR. motor vehicles—801,000

8. Maritime policy has been under consideration and review since the war by a distinguished non-partisan committee, composed of men unassociated with the shipping industry. See Chapter VIII.

9. Another 12,360,000 tons or 1,297 ships, many of them obsolescent and worthless, were laid up and rusting away in "ships graveyards" from the Hudson to Puget Sound. Twenty-five more ships of 365,000 tons were under conversion. New shipbuilding was small—twenty-six ships in the first ten months of 1947, as compared to 588 ships in Britain in the first eight months of the same year. The United States has most of the world's tankers, but a notable scarcity of passenger liners. This was largely due to our wartime concentration upon tankers, cargo ships and transports, most of the latter ill adapted, even after conversion, to the peacetime carrying trade.

10. J. M. Letiche, Council on Foreign Relations.

11. From an article by Jim Roe in the September 1947 issue of *Successful Farming*.

12. "How Strong is America?" by Robert S. Bird, the New York *Herald Tribune*, September 14, 1947.

13. I have drawn upon Mr. Hotchkiss' article and particularly Mr. Stacy May's reports prepared for the Council for this mineral survey. Both these studies have also drawn upon basic data provided by the U. S. Geological Survey and the Bureau of Mines, summarized in an article by Elmer Pehrson in *Mining and Metallurgy* for April 1945. Another important article dealing with minerals is E. Willard Miller's "Some Aspects of the United States Mineral Self-Sufficiency" in *Economic Geography*, April 1947. A report, *Mineral Position of the United States*, a joint estimate of the U. S. Geological Survey and the Bureau of Mines, which was published in November 1947, is the latest "Bible" on the subject.

14. For an excellent study of our oil problem, see *Foreign Oil and American Security*, by Bernard Brodie, Yale Institute of International Studies.

15. See Appendix V.

16. By "natural supply" is meant supply in the ground. Importation and stock-piling of some of these scarce strategic materials (discussed in Section II) are being resorted to to compensate for our lack of natural supplies.

17. For complete list, see Appendix VI, taken from *Raw Materials in War and Peace*, Department of Social Sciences, U. S. Military Academy. Page 160.

18. The proximity, or VT, fuze, a war development, is a good example. *New Weapons for Air Warfare*, edited by Joseph C. Boyce, one of the volumes of the official wartime history of the Office of Scientific Research and Development (Atlantic, Little-Brown), states on page 172: ". . . the Central Laboratory at Silver Spring was the nerve center of a vast, country-wide activity. Five major plants were rolling out some 70,000 VT fuzes a day—millions of tiny radio sets designed to 'play' for a few moments. Feeding these assembly plants . . . were a host of more than 2,000 interlocking suppliers and subsuppliers. . . . It is reported that 75 per cent of the plastics-molding facilities in the United States were engaged in supplying the various plastic components for the fuze."

19. Document under discussion by the Atomic Energy Committee of the United States compiled by the U. S. Mission to the United Nations, page 19. June–September 1947.

20. See *Essential Information on Atomic Energy*, Special Committee on Atomic Energy, U. S. Senate, U. S. Government Printing Office. Page 16.

21. But it must be remembered that the fissionable material of the atomic bomb—U-235—or plutonium—represents less than 1 per cent of this amount.

22. In 1942, the Congo produced 590 tons of uranium metal. *The Absolute Weapon*, by Bernard Brodie, Harcourt, Brace & Company. Page 54. In 1947, according to estimates in a Belgian newspaper, the Congo shipped 9,666 tons of uranium ore, most of it to the United States and Britain (*New York Times*, January 4, 1948). Of this total, according to the newspaper, the United States got 3,650 tons, Britain, 2,600 tons. These figures, however, as well as those

of Mr. Brodie, are open to some question. All that is certain is that the Belgian Congo produces most of the world's uranium ore and that all, or most of it, is going to the United States.

23. "At the close of World War I, the Soviet Union, defeated on the field of battle, the economic order destroyed, her armies facing a hostile world, and hunger stalking the land, reached a low level of economic activity. Steel production fell from a prewar [pre-World War I] level of 5 per cent of world output to a low of 2 per cent in the years following the war. The recovery since 1929 has been rapid and remarkable until it is now approximately 20 per cent of world output. Likewise, coal production fell from a prewar level of 30 million tons to a low of 7 million tons in 1920 and has since then reached a level of 160 million tons. . . . The vast land area of Russia contains the raw-material elements of a potentially powerful industrial nation. The industrial possibilities are especially favorable in one respect because of the interior location increasing the safety factor against external attack" (but—my amplification—only against *surface* attack). "Postwar Russia and Her Mineral Deposits," by Walter H. Voskuil, *Journal of Land and Public Utility Economics*, Volume XXIII, No. 2, May 1947.

24. Russian statistics from "The Fourth Five-Year Plan," by Abram Bergson, in *Political Science Quarterly*, June 1947. This article gives a detailed and on the whole objective discussion of Soviet industrial progress. The great question mark of all such discussions, however, is the reliability of Soviet figures, which are always incomplete and very often misleading. U.S. statistics from *Statistical Abstract of the United States*, 1914 and 1946, *Minerals Year Book of 1945*, and the report of Secretary of the Interior Krug on the resources of the United States, the New York *Times*, October 19, 1947.

25. The mechanical and managerial inaptitude of the Russians has been repeatedly noted by Major General John Russell Deane (*A Strange Alliance*) and many other observers. Since the war, reports indicate that German factory machinery, removed to Russia for reparations, has been chosen in a haphazard manner. Parts of factories have been transferred but key machines left behind, and the transplanted factories are either producing minimal armaments or not at all.

26. Limited industrial capacity does not necessarily mean, of course, that Russia would not fight.

CHAPTER V

THE PSYCHOLOGICAL POSITION

There are only two powers in the world: the sword and the spirit. In the long run, the sword is always defeated by the spirit.

NAPOLEON I

THE "puzzling dualism" of American foreign policy—the most "lofty and generous professions of idealism"[1] sometimes coupled with crass manifestations of materialism—has long been the despair of foreign interpreters.

Their perplexity, however, can be matched, if not excelled, by the psychologist or student who attempts to explain this phenomenon by plumbing the mysteries of the human spirit. For the American mind, if there be such a collective genre—is a complex cross section of countermotivations; the national thinking is rarely lucid and is usually contradictory—a strange mixture of pragmatism, wishful thinking and wistful idealism.

The trends and attitudes that result are hence diffuse and diverse, as diffuse and diverse as the polyglot peoples of America. It is, therefore, impossible for any one man or group of men to interpret them with full fidelity; the best that can be hoped for is to paint a canvas of the national mood.

But despite its impressionism, it is important that this canvas be painted. For Napoleon and other great captains of history have repeatedly emphasized that "the moral is to the physical as three to one," and in this age of political and economic conflict which may lead to military strife, the attitudes of the civilian populations, first target in another war of the atomic bomb, assume almost climactic importance.

We have dealt in previous chapters with the relative power position of the United States in political, military and economic terms, and the insistent emphasis of the facts is clear:

The strength of the United States, expressed in these terms, is today superior to that of any other nation on earth.

But wars have been won by a song,[2] and civilizations have perished by an idea; no fortress guarded only by physical force is invulnerable to assault if the mind and the spirit be weak.

And there are today, amidst other attitudes of vigor and of strength, some disturbing trends and tendencies of weakness.

What are the American attitudes, and how have we changed?[3]

We are, first, a fairly homogenous people, who, despite disparate origins and the lack of a real mental common denominator, respond in moments of crisis with an emotional "realism" and intuitive logic which, so far, have been a source of strength.

But as a people we have lost—not all of us, but probably the majority of us—some of the pioneer virtues that made us great, those qualities of individual initiative, self-reliance, great physical courage, rugged honesty and determined faith which subdued a wilderness and conquered a continent. There are still, of course, major exceptions to this stricture; the heritage of past tradition does not die out in a generation. The oil riggers, the engineers, the geologists, the airmen and the traders who are still extending the horizons of our world into the primitive frontier regions of the earth, the gang boss, the businessman, the labor leader—many of these retain in different guise the ancient qualities.

But as a nation, we who used to scorn government, to regard the best government as the least government, we who were our own leaders have come to feel an extreme dependence upon government, to yearn for leaders, to shirk responsibility.

Make no mistake; we have not turned to the collectivism and autocracy of the East and probably shall never do so; yet there are among us too many who believe that the government owes every man a living, or even that man exists for the state, instead of the state for man. There are too few Jeffersonians today, too many who pay only lip service to democracy. The warm, personalized and responsive leadership of the past has too often given way to bureaucratic management and slick manipulation. We tend toward government by propaganda instead of government by fact.

Politically, socially, economically, the psychological trend is marked; as Americans we accept today without comment, indeed, without national concern, encroachments of government upon the political and personal freedom of the individual which would never have been tolerated in this country a quarter century ago. Legally and constitutionally we have shifted far, as Professor Edward S. Corwin has written, from a "constitution of rights and of checks and balances to a constitution of powers," and mentally, to quote Maynard Krueger, "Americans have assumed the dangerous tendency of thinking of a super-state as the solution to our problems."

This trend is natural, perhaps inevitable. The nation's "flaming youth" has ended and many of us have put behind us the excitements and adventures of liberty to sit by the warm hearth of security. The growth of "octopus government" with its greater and greater concentration of power and the dependence of the body politic upon that government is also a natural consequence of economic and political change. It has been accompanied and paralleled by a similar centralization of business and labor power, and indeed of social organization. These changes reflect the nation's altered circumstances from expansion to surfeit, from the days when development of a continent was the main concern of our peoples to the days when distribution of the products of a powerful industrial establishment is the problem. It reflects the transformation from an agrarian to an industrial economy, the great change from ruralization to urbanization. It is, perhaps, an inevitable change, but the psychological consequences of it have been considerable.

Accompanying this trend has been a growth of realism. In one sense, the pragmatic, this development has been beneficial rather than harmful, for a practical common-sense view of the world we live in was the great need of many Americans.

Our political leaders, our educational institutions, our geographical position and our cultural heritage helped to create of our youth a "lost generation" after World War I, a generation taught to believe that that war would end war. Materialism, which found its roots in the rich soil of American physical achievement, was for a time rampant. Those Americans—and there were many—who cared little for accumulating wealth and acquiring physical possessions turned to a sort of intellectual and spiritual and personalized isolationism. In the words of Dr. Harold D. Lasswell, the expectations of "no more war" led the individual to conceive of himself as free to continue pursuit of his *personal scheme of values* with little or no regard for the *collective* task of building a genuinely effective world community, or preparing against war. We turned to dollars, to art, to science, to religion, but gave scant thought to the practical art of government or the business of maintaining peace. When the depression came the demand for collective action was concentrated upon social security, upon domestic economic policy—not international political policy. We looked inward, not outward; we lived, indeed, in a world of dreams.

As a result of these diverse trends—materialism, personalized isolationism, impractical idealism—our youth looked for escape mechanisms as the irrevocable facts of conflict reared their ugly heads in the Thirties: pledges never to fight in any war; distortion of history; ivory-tower wishful thinking; political isolationism. If the world was not to be what our dreams indicated it ought to be, we would have none of it. World War II, therefore, came as a tremendous shock to American youth.[4]

The individual adjustments made to this shock were many and painful.[5] The national adjustment has taken several general forms. Our people are much more realistic; the public demand for American participation in the affairs of the world and in an effective international organization is far greater than it was after World War I. This change still is incomplete, however; we still assume a negative attitude of regret that our easy dreams of a bright new world could not be realized and have as yet failed to substitute a positive comprehension of the world of today. The majority of Americans now profess to believe, as history teaches us, that conflict is a part of life and that another war is probable, though they still hold wistfully, with hopeful optimism, to *some* of the wishful thinking of the past.[6]

These changes toward greater realism are in part good. We have climbed down off our pedestal into the arena of life. But the substitution of realism for romanticism is salutary only if it does not breed cynicism, disillusionment, amorality and selfishness—an ultra-materialism. Yet there are some signs of this insidious growth. The wartime emphasis upon force, the depravity of the enemy, the waste and impersonality of a military machine in action, the too prevalent Army philosophy of "gold-bricking," of "empire-building," of "getting mine while the getting's good," all had their effect. The doctrine of expediency extolled during the war; the total nature of that war; our bombardment of civilian populations, culminating with our use of the atomic bomb, all had the tendency of justifying the means, of inducing an amoral attitude.

These complementary trends, towards pragmatism, a new growth of materialism, and greater dependence upon government, are really an outer expression of an inner lack; fundamentally the American people have abandoned some of their faith in our ideal; there is an unease about our institutions, a lack of firm resolve about our purposes; we look toward ulterior direction to guide us to security.

These psychological changes have manifested themselves during and since the war in several specific ways.

First and most important from the military point of view was the moral failure of so many of our men during the war. Few, indeed, did the actual fighting; few, indeed, were the real leaders—the men of initiative and moral, as well as physical, courage; the great bulk were followers, neutrals with guns in their hands. Americans like to gloss over or conceal our weaknesses, but we did not have, in the bulk, the stomach for fighting or the heart for combat possessed by our enemies, or possessed, for that matter, by many of the Russians. Some of our finest units were outstanding exceptions to these strictures, but not the bulk of our armed forces. Enemy intelligence reports and our own secret training documents repeatedly emphasized the lack of *esprit de corps* in the American infantry; the enemy was as little impressed with the spirit of our fighting man power as he was much impressed with our mass of equipment.

The inculcation during the war of millions of Americans with the glorious irresponsibility of military life—their lives regulated, ordered and directed in neat patterns, with "security" assured and the hard processes of thinking too often reduced to a minimum—impressed many of our men, even though they griped at restrictions. There was a wartime hatred for the petty tyrannies of the military, but beneath the surface there is today a "strong latent demand" on the part of veterans for executive centralization in government, for the protective paternalistic system which they found in the services during the war. The fact of victory, at the same time, blinded many Americans to our weaknesses as revealed during the war, led to a strong "revitalized nationalism" and a "superiority attitude" or a contempt (toward France in particular) for those nations whose progress was expressed in the intangible form of culture rather than in the useful shape of plumbing. It is, indeed, paradoxical that to many of our men, but never to those who saw the concentration camps, the neatness, beauty and cleanliness of the German towns and the industry of the German people made a far greater appeal than the less earthly virtues of our allies.

With a surge of nationalism—which expresses itself sometimes in the feeling that "America ought to rule the world"; "we must hold on to everything we got"—has gone a new respect for our top military leaders and high civilian executives, which complements the latent demand for greater centralization of federal authority, and which has expressed itself in the form of political booms— "Eisenhower for President"; "MacArthur for President"; "Marshall for President." However, our population has shown no corresponding gain in respect for representative government or the courts. Put in the words of Dr. Lasswell, all these experiences and attitudes, our increasing dependence upon leadership, our nationalism, etc., which have helped to create the "strong latent demand for executive centralization in governments . . . may well lead to an open demand in the event of any general crisis."

These manifestations and these trends are tempered, however, by what Percy Bidwell[7] has well called the "underlying vein of idealism" in the American people. A British editor in *The Economist* has declared of the United States with some truth that "no nation is more firmly on the side of the angels in the long run." And the American idealism of today is a far more hardheaded idealism than the irrational cloud-gazing of the early Twenties. There are, however, two dangers, even in this "modernized idealism." For included in the ranks of the idealists are two esoteric cliques. The one might be called the "world-governmenters"—those whose whole ideals rest on outward forms, on immediate results, on the millennium tomorrow, on world union now, on nice plans and patterns of earthly parliaments, on abrogation of the veto power in the United Nations. The other might be called the fanaticists of democracy—those who would thrust democracy, like a dose of medicine, down the throat of the world—the professional minority-lovers and power-haters, those who would spread democracy even at the expense of one of democracy's first tenets, the self-determination of peoples.

These "residual idealists" differ, fortunately, from the more wide-awake Americans who have their eyes on the clouds but their feet on the ground. Yet these "splinter groups" deserve mention for, extremists as they are, they may wholly unwittingly ally themselves with extremists of quite different persuasion.

There is no doubt that since the war the military influence in American government has been increasing, no doubt but that the trend toward greater centralization of federal power has been increasing, no doubt but that our nationalism is, if not rampant, at least feverish. Our unilateral Pacific-islands policy, the lone-hand MacArthur administration in Japan, our occasional by-passing of the United Nations, the increasing "crisis psychology" of the nation and the prevalence of war talk—above all, the growing American tendency to find solutions for complex problems in physical strength or military force[8]—are perhaps natural consequences of our psychological attitudes.

But these attitudes, if strengthened, could have potentialities of far greater significance. For though isolationism is geographically dead, it is politically alive, dressed up in the new styles of postwar America. It still professes an aversion to foreign wars and still expresses revulsion for the nasty mess of the world by withdrawal attitudes, but it is essentially today economic rather than political or military isolationism, and it is isolationism coupled with and verging on frank imperialism. The people of America have heard its voice increasingly in the past two years—"let's stop wasting the substance of the country by all these loans; not one dollar more for foreigners, but all the money in the world for our armed forces." A logical and dangerous link is that between isolationism and militarism, which spells imperialism, perhaps in the form of a new crusade—"manifest destiny," or in the new and more polite lingo of the age—"The American Century."

To such a cause, on such a band wagon, idealists of any ilk would seem strange fellow travelers, yet the two "splinter groups" just described—the "world-governmenters," and the "democracy fanatics"—might well find themselves imperceptibly and perhaps unconsciously allied with any movement which promised world-wide extension of American power. For even from the idealists, perhaps chiefly from some of the idealists, has come the talk of a "preventive war," a war to prevent the use of the atomic bomb against this nation, a war to world government by way of conquest, if world government by way of negotiation proves impossible.

Thus, the strange and complex currents of American thought and feeling may meet and merge seemingly irreconcilable elements into a common stream. Where these crosscurrents may lead us tomorrow no man today can predict; potentialities, particularly in the intangible field of mass psychology, are far from realities.

But today this is clear: The American people are more dependent upon strong centralized government, more influenced by military opinion, more desirous of strong leadership than ever before. But they are, at the same time, far more realistic than in any prior epoch; they have come out of their ivory tower but they are still looking toward the stars. They lack a flaming cause, a flaming spirit, but they still retain a friendly sense of brotherhood, a hope for a better world, and an intuitive common sense which has helped them before in time of trouble. And as a psychological as well as an economic buttress, the United States still possesses what other nations have destroyed, a great (economic) middle class, which, with its innate but sound conservatism, has a natural repugnance for extremes.

What all this means to the world and its future depends not only upon what we do about our attitudes, but upon how other nations interpret those attitudes.

To the Russians we are painted, by Kremlin tactics, as the chief bulwark of decadent capitalism, as a warmongering country, as an imperialist, expansionist nation. But to many neutrals, far more impressed with our economic strength than with our profession of ideals, we do not appear lily-white. They remember our past history; of withdrawal—from the League of Nations; of imperialism —in Latin America and against Spain. They recollect our undependability, our "blow-hot-blow-cold" attitudes, product of those mismated forces, idealism and materialism, isolationism and world-consciousness. They listen to the charges of "hypocrisy" leveled against us by Soviet propaganda and accept, with some reservations because of the obvious political and economic imperfections of our democracy, our professions of liberty, equality, fraternity. And they saw in many Americans who came to their countries during the war only rude, feckless, uncouth fellows, representative of the materialistic barbarism of the New World.

Our first use of the atomic bomb has cost us dearly in all areas of the earth where human life is held of worth and ideals and morality have meaning. Our inventiveness and industrial ability are admired, but the lip service we too often pay to morality is deplored. The liberals of the world recall, as Paul P. Ashley of Seattle has put it (somewhat too strongly):

Since the time of the first Hague conference the over-all policy of the United States has been opposed to limitations upon destructive instrumentalities. We defended the use of dumdum bullets when many nations were willing to outlaw them. We stood for unlimited bombing and for use of gas when other nations advocated an international edict against them. Now, without warning, we have hurled atomic death upon women and children.[9]

We do not, therefore, I think, hold the moral leadership of the world, at least in the same degree that we did in the Wilsonian days of the "fourteen points" and the "self-determination of peoples." For the "fourteen points" we substituted the utter negation of "unconditional surrender"; we were, at the war's end, a leading exponent of the horrible art of total war, and now we offer a materialistic leadership, too often only sugar-coated with morality, to the world.

Yet it is precisely in the moral field, the psychological field, that Russia is appealing to the deluded and the depressed. Communism's appeal to the multitudes is as a blood-red banner streaming from the battlements of heaven; it promises the brotherhood of man. False though its promises are, we cannot counter them beneath a simple standard of the status quo.

The psychological attitudes[10] of the Russian peoples, unfortunately, have less influence upon the course of history than that of the American. For the collective Russian mind is an instrument to be played upon by Communist propaganda; the "iron curtain" is no idle oratorical phrase, but a real barrier to international understanding. The Russian people believe *en masse* what the Kremlin wants them to believe, but the cold-eyed, hardheaded members of the Politburo carefully build the party line upon a close understanding of Slavic interests and Russian historical traditions—the nationalism, amounting at times to chauvinism, of the moujik, and the omniscience—an indispensable fable throughout Russian history—of the great paternal leader. They have overlarded these fundamental attitudes with new ones of Communist origin—higher standards of living for all, a workers' world, an international band of brothers—but these appeals, except for the first, have far more meaning to the fanatics of the party than to the average Russian.

We may try to "reach" the Russian people, to break through the iron curtain that separates them from the world, but the results, if any, will be meager and slow, for the mind of Russia is a prisoner of the Kremlin. It is really, therefore, the psychological attitudes of the men in the Kremlin, the members of the Politburo, in which we are interested. Not that we are likely to change them; the purposes and goals of the *present* rulers of Russia are fixed, absolute and definite; they will not be altered. The leaders of the Communist party, in fact the great majority of party members, are complete prisoners of their own fixations; their minds are closed to outside arguments, appeals or ideas. The "security" of Russia, which probably means, judging from their own words, the eventual overthrow of capitalist governments, the conquest of the monopoly of power and the communization of the world, is still their aim and is likely (though not certain) to remain the aim of future *Communist* leaders. But this does not mean that the methods they will follow are fixed and immutable; on the contrary, as the shifts in the party line have shown, they are flexible and constantly changing. The members of the Politburo are ruthless realists; they respect power and purpose, but power without purpose confuses them, and purpose without power is an object of contempt. We must always remember that dictatorships shield and protect and insulate the dictator; this is always the danger of autocracy; the dictator's delusions of grandeur lead him astray. Napoleon's conversations with Caulaincourt, Hitler's assertions that the British would never fight for Poland, bear historical testimony to the danger. And, more pertinent, the erroneous reports to the Kremlin about Finland's political "weaknesses" and the underground "strength" of the Communist party there led to the Russian military reverses in the "Winter War" of 1939-40.

The conclusions are obvious; our policies and our intentions and our aims must be as clear as crystal to the Politburo.

Many of the rest of the peoples of the earth, particularly those of Western Europe, hope for bread and fear war; they are torn by factionalisms and doubt; most of them have lent support to greater governmental powers; few of them are fully resigned to the lesser roles in world affairs which they are destined to play. The old order no longer is the rampart of their spirit; there is a restless striving for change; the yeast of ferment is working in the mind of the world. But food comes first to most, politics second; the peoples are groping for security in an insecure world.

In such an arena there now goes on the crowning struggle of our age—the battle for the minds of men.

Such, then, is the American position viewed against the background of the world. The United States has strengths, great strengths, but no longer the unequivocal spiritual power of our past.

Notes—Chapter V

1. From an address by Percy W. Bidwell of the Council on Foreign Relations at Chatham House, London, July 9, 1946. Published under the title, "Ideals in American Foreign Policy," in *International Affairs* (London), October 1946.

2. "Wars have been won by a song." Figuratively, of course, not literally.

3. I have drawn in this chapter upon the able discussion of Dr. Harold D. Lasswell before the Council on Foreign Relations and upon studies of, and a discussion with, Dr. Rensis Likert, Director of the Survey Research Center of the University of Michigan. Drs. Lasswell and Likert were kind enough to criticize this chapter. It is unnecessary to add, however, that the interpretation here expressed is mine, and Drs. Lasswell and Likert are in no way responsible for the conclusions expressed in this chapter. See also *Men Against Fire* (Morrow), in which the author, S. L. A. Marshall, revolts against a materialistic concept of battle, describes some of our spiritual weaknesses, and rightly stresses the importance of morale.

4. The war was a shock not alone, of course, for the reasons stated; the effects of our domestic culture and the overprotective nature of much of the American social structure contributed.

5. Many men could not make the readjustments necessitated by war; psychiatric cases were numbered in the hundreds of thousands.

6. The American belief in the probability of another war is reflected in various public-opinion polls, and some 60 to 75 per cent of Americans believe that Russia is *not* trying to co-operate with the rest of the world, and that the chances of a peaceful settlement are not good.

7. See Note 1.

8. But ". . . the bullet [as Fuller puts it] is no answer to an idea. . . ."

Armaments and History, by Major General J. F. C. Fuller, Scribner's. Page 96.

9. Mr. Ashley forgot the Washington Naval Conference, sponsored by this country, which led to an era of naval limitations. But he also forgot to mention that the United States never ratified the Geneva Protocol of 1925 outlawing the use of biological agents (and poison gas) in war. Neither did we ratify, as he points out, the Hague declaration of 1899 outlawing "dumdum" (expanding) bullets.

10. For an excellent discussion of this subject, see the article by "X" in *Foreign Affairs*, July 1947.

CHAPTER VI

SUMMARY

"He hath no power that hath no power to use."

P. J. BAILEY, *Festus: A Visit*

THE implacable facts of power, marshaled in the preceding chapters, stress the tremendous strength of the United States. The war, the technological revolution and the unparalleled industrialization of our nation—plus the fortunate accidents of climate, geography and resources—have combined to form in the Western Hemisphere a power center unprecedented in *absolute* strength in the history of the world.

The destruction by military force of the great power concentrations in Western Europe and the Western Pacific, the decline of the British Empire and the political fragmentation process of the past half century which has broken down empires and fractionalized kingdoms has resulted in the creation of a bi-polar world, with both of the world's great power groupings outside Europe. Two super-states—America and Russia—cast their shadows across the earth. Great Britain, a great power but not comparable in potential to the two giants, nevertheless is of major importance strategically and geographically, as an island land mass flanking the coast of Europe, and, through her dominions, as a world-wide fraternal association of nations. France and Italy, Japan and China, but particularly Germany and the resources of the Ruhr, are pawns of power in the conflict already joined.

The conflict must be faced; it cannot be ignored. It should not be looked at solely or primarily in military terms, for it may not culminate in shooting war, but there is no doubt that there is conflict between Russia, exponent of the collectivism of the East, and the United States, champion of the free society of the West. In this struggle for political power and domination the United States holds a strong position, but the so-called "heartland" of Eurasia is controlled by the Soviets, and Russia's geographical position casts a long shadow across Western Europe and Northeastern Asia.

Superimposed upon the political revolution which was the product of the war is the technological revolution, product of science. The new face of war presents a frightening visage, though many of the intercontinental and transpolar instruments are as yet potential. But the atomic bomb, long-range missiles, new-type submarines, biological agents, new gases and other devices have completely altered tactics and have given the offense such a tremendous advantage over the defense that our strategic concepts have been changed and the security of all nations more greatly imperiled than ever before.

In this race for military supremacy, the United States today has definite advantages—by far the world's greatest navy, many times the size of our prewar fleets; an air force second to none in quality and not much inferior to Russia's in quantity; an army better equipped than any other; the atomic bomb (with annual production, however, still probably very limited); better long-range planes than any other nation; a good start in the development of new weapons. Russia has the great advantage of mass in area and population and the largest army in the world.

Economically the United States towers as a giant among pygmies. By 1950, the Soviet Union, if it achieves the goals of its first postwar Five-Year Plan, may be able to produce some 25,400,000 tons of steel, less than the United States produced in 1913. In developed raw materials and agriculture we are as close to self-sufficiency as any nation of comparable size ever has been. But the new technology demands ever new materials, and many of them vital to military or industrial power—uranium ore, cobalt, columbium—lie far beyond our borders.

Psychologically, spiritually, the position of the United States presents certain weaknesses. We are not an extremist nation, and our people have intuitive common sense, but there has been a growing trend toward dependence upon strong centralized government and upon military force and a reduction of individual initiative. We have no flaming cause. Communism presents an appeal, false though it be, to the depressed and the deluded. We cannot answer it solely with dollars or under the standard of the status quo.

In sum and in balance, the strengths and weaknesses of the American power position in the postwar world add up to a net preponderance of *relative* power unequaled in the world today. The United States has had greatness thrust upon her. There is no other nation—not even Russia—comparable in power to our own. Russia's rate of industrial expansion was faster than our own in the prewar years and may be so again, and her rapidly growing population is larger than our own, but it will be many years before Soviet power can hope to equal that of the United States. Yet Russia's geographical position, our own weaknesses and the virulent appeal of communism tend somewhat to balance our advantages.

And the mere existence of a "bi-polar" world is historically dangerous. History has given us ominous precedents for today:

Our present situation is formidable indeed. A survey of the historical landscape in the light of our existing knowledge shows that, up to date, history has repeated itself about twenty times in producing human societies of the species to which our Western society belongs, and it also shows that, with the possible exception of our own, all these representatives of the species of society called civilizations are already dead or moribund.[1]

NOTE—Chapter VI

1. Arnold Toynbee, in the *New York Times Sunday Magazine*, "Does History Repeat Itself?" September 21, 1947.

SECTION II

THE MEANING OF THE FACTS

STRATEGY REVISED—THE FUTURE DEFENSE OF AMERICA

You can't alter facts by filming them over with dead romances.

JOHN DRINKWATER

CHAPTER VII

STRATEGY REVISED

This preference of the good man for dying on his own soil instead of abroad is a serious handicap to the democratic state.

SPYKMAN[1]

A BRITISH statesman of the nineteenth century once remarked testily that if the military men were given their head they would—so great was their cautious passion for security—seek bases on the Moon to protect the Earth against Mars.

But the sarcastic humor of a generation ago is the distressing truth of today. Interstellar warfare is not yet even a remote possibility, but intercontinental warfare, or hemispheric warfare, will be technically feasible tomorrow. Strategically the world is, or soon will be, one world; the great ocean barriers and ice masses which have moated the continents, canalized the routes of trade and dominated military calculations are no longer effective ramparts. The compartmentalized strategy of the past—national, continental, hemispheric—is superseded by the grand strategy of the world.

This is not to say that distance has lost all its meaning; it has not. But the technological revolution described in the previous chapters makes a real "security" policy almost as apocryphal as the famous story about Winston Churchill and the angel Gabriel.

The great war Prime Minister of Britain stood, the story goes, in the throngs before the pearly gates on Judgment Day awaiting the awesome summons. Near him were his arch-opponents of life— Adolph Hitler and Joseph Stalin. Gabriel spied the three men of history in the throng and in a voice like a trumpet summoned them before him.

"Now, boys," he said, "before you are judged I shall give each one of you a final wish, and it will come true. Adolph, what do you want?"

Hitler stepped up, extended his arm in the Nazi salute and said: "I wish that Russia might be forever and totally destroyed."

There was a dull rumble in the distance and Gabriel turned to Stalin: "Well, Joe?" he asked against the distant background of a heavenly choir chanting the triumphant tones of the "Internationale."

Stalin was concise: "I wish that Germany might be forever and totally destroyed."

Another dull rumble, and it was Churchill's turn.

"Winston, what about you?"

Churchill paused, took the big black stogy out of his mouth, and said: "Do you mean to tell me that those two wishes actually came true?"

"Why, certainly," said Gabriel. "Both Russia and Germany have been blotted from the map of the world."

Churchill's face lighted up in his famous smile and he gave the V-for-Victory sign:

"Oh, well then," he said, "make mine brandy and soda." Churchill had found security for England at last.

Today only some such omnipotent act can provide real strategic security for any nation in a world that is physically one but politically, economically and psychologically two. The great and essential meaning of the facts of power, summarized in the preceding section of this book, is simple; there are no longer any "world islands" or remote continents. Seas and terrain barriers which for centuries have restricted the conquests of the past have little meaning in the age of the airplane and less in the age of the guided missile.

This does not mean that "defense," in a limited sense, is impossible. The United States, we have seen, has great power, greater power today than any other nation—tremendous industrial strength, and mechanically resourceful and technically ingenious people. The ancient lesson of military history is that of balance; the preponderance of the offense is cyclically overcome by the defense, and vice versa.

Yet no examination of modern weapons and their potentialities can comfort us in a purely defensive concept. Maginot Line spiritual, mental or physical, are dangerous and expensive; no defenses ever have been erected by man that have not been breached or by-passed. The world of the second half of the twentieth century is not a world which lends itself easily to physical isolationism. We have seen that politically and economically, as well as strategically, the United States is and must remain a world power; we cannot shut ourselves up behind such ramparts as we could erect and expect either security or prosperity.

"Defense" as a major policy, either military or political, must be discarded.

What of "defense" in its narrower meaning, what of military "defense," of fleets of fighter planes, radar warning stations, etc., etc., to mitigate, to lessen or to deny enemy attacks upon us?

Charting a future military policy for America immediately breaks down into two problems, the immediate and the remote.

Today and in the immediate future until the increasing ranges of aircraft make *two-way* transoceanic or transpolar raids possible and until Russia builds up a stock pile of atomic bombs, the *reasonable* security of the continental United States can be pretty well guaranteed against physical assault. The strategic importance of a plane with range sufficient to cross the oceans or the pole and *return* to base is major, particularly today when we are the sole possessor of the atomic bomb. Great bombing planes are not, like missiles, expendable. The Japanese Kamikazes were expendable, and there will be expendable piloted planes in great numbers in any future war. But the Kamikazes were essentially short-range, one-man planes. Bombers, capable of transatlantic ranges, are, *today* too valuable (with their highly trained crews) and too scarce to risk all of them, or even a majority of them, in one-way suicide raids, particularly if those bombers do *not* carry the atomic bomb. A nation planning today, before two-way planes or intercontinental missiles are available, an all-out attack upon another nation across the seas would hesitate a long time, indeed, even if it possessed the atomic bomb, before sending out all or a large part of its bomber fleet on a suicide mission. If that single mission did not force immediate capitulation of the enemy the ultimate consequences to the aggressor, with no sizable reserve force to draw upon, might be defeat or "suicide." No nation is likely to enter lightly, therefore, upon one-way intercontinental raids as long as the instrument of those raids must be the modern complex heavy bomber. Theoretically, therefore, although the bombardment of this country from Russia or vice versa is possible today, it is not a really feasible military operation and offers little danger—indeed virtually none, as long as Russia does not have the atomic bomb.[2] There is today no imminent danger. Our superiority at sea and in the air may not be able to prevent all attack but can fend off *serious* attack for the next four or five or even fifteen years until supersonic intercontinental missiles are developed.

But the problem of tactical defense grows progressively more complex as the technological revolution in war comes to its climax. Defense against a 300-mile-an-hour bomber which travels in level flight at maximum altitudes of 40,000 feet above the earth is infinitely simple, for instance, as compared to defense against a 3,500-mile-an-hour V-2, arching in a parabolic curve sixty to 100 miles into the air. The maximum rate of fire of present machine guns is about 1,200 or 1,500 rounds per minute, or one round every one twentieth of a second; the maximum muzzle velocity is about 3,400 foot-seconds, the distance between bullets 170 feet. A 600-mile-an-hour plane moves forty-four feet in one twentieth of a second, "so that it might pass untouched across a directed stream of such bullets."[3]

During the war some 2,000 V-2's crossed the English coast, and more than 1,200 crashed in London, landing and exploding before they could be heard, usually before they were seen. Not one was intercepted; there was no way of intercepting them. Nor is there any way today. These missiles are limited in range today; tomorrow they will have transoceanic capabilities. Instruments and weapons are being devised—powerful tracking radar, "beam-riding" defensive missiles—which give promise that eventually even some of the 3,500-mile-an-hour ionospheric rockets can be intercepted. But interception alone is not enough. The interception must be at the right point, and if the offensive missile carries an atomic warhead, as future missiles will, the defensive missile must be able to detonate that warhead many miles in the sky and far beyond our shores.

The huge problem of tracking and intercepting supersonic missiles is, therefore, clear, but the corollary problem is equally important. Because of the immense destructiveness of the atomic bomb or atomic warheads, a partial defense will no longer be adequate. During the war, it used to be reckoned by our Air Forces that an effective air defense was one which was able to exact average losses of from ten to twenty per cent from raiding planes. Such losses, implying as they did the complete destruction of the original attacking force in a week or so (if daily raids were made), were regarded as prohibitive and crippling by all powers; only the United States, with its immense aircraft production, could and did sustain such losses, but then only for brief periods. Though it was clear that the old adage—"some bombers always get through"—was valid, nevertheless the possibility of a reasonably effective air defense (if the industrial resources behind that defense were adequate) was also proved. Such a reasonably effective defense is possible today.

But tomorrow attrition losses of ten or twenty or fifty per cent will not be enough. For the damage done by an atomic bomb is so disproportionate to the cost of doing that damage that any nation that decides to use them might willingly suffer losses of 90 per cent or more in its attacking force of planes or missiles in the expectation of placing ten per cent or less of its bombs on targets.

This is the modern mathematical equation of horror, and it puts the problem of tactical defense against supersonic missiles with atomic warheads, or against completely submerged, high-speed missile-firing submarines, in its simplest, its most terrible and its most impossible terms. A defensive system capable of exacting even twenty-five or fifty per cent losses against attacking planes or missiles would entail:

1. A girdle of radar warning systems and communication networks around our coasts from the Canadian Arctic to Latin-American jungles.

2. A system of distant advanced bases—weather stations, radar stations, fighter bases—on islands halfway across the world.

3. Hundreds of mobile (or ship and plane) bases, constantly on patrol, similarly equipped with radio, radar and weather instruments.

4. Scores of rocket launchers, on ship, on shore and at advanced bases, for interceptor missiles.

5. Hundreds of anti-submarine craft.

Such a system would cost initially hundreds of millions—probably billions—of dollars, plus other millions for annual upkeep, and could, at best, mitigate, not completely prevent, a missile-atomic attack. Dependence upon it *alone* would mean not only the certainty of frightful casualties in our bombed cities but would insure our eventual defeat. For defense, no matter how perfect, has never yet won a war, and never will.

This does not mean that all defensive measures are obsolete. They are *not*. The difference between victory or defeat in the next war may be measured by the number of atomic-warhead missiles that "get through" a defensive screen; certainly a defensive system must be able to soften or "cushion" an enemy attack and above all to warn of one.

Despite the technical difficulties and financial expense of establishing such a static system, the problem is not completely hopeless. Louis Ridenour in an article, "There Is No Defense," in *One World or None*, estimates that 250 separate radar installations, requiring an operating crew of 50,000 men and costing $375,000,000, would be required to provide an adequate warning system against missiles and aircraft for the continental United States. This is "obviously not a prohibitively large undertaking,"[4] as Ansley Coale comments, and even the addition of the other elements of a reasonably good defensive system, if that system were kept in proper balance, need not be prohibitive. This author agrees emphatically with an officer of our armed services who must be anonymous:

I view with considerable alarm the growing acceptance [he writes] of the theory that security lies in offensive measures, and in offensive measures *alone*. . . . I believe that in all military planning we must provide the *minimum* defensive measures . . . early warning facilities, interceptor forces, and . . . ancillary means of defense against air attack . . . (possibly) manned only on a skeleton basis with major dependence placed upon emergency manning by reserves or civilians. . . .

The lessons of history teach us, however, that initial *defensive* efforts—particularly against surprise attack—rarely are very effective, and at best a defensive system is negative; the offensive always has held the key to victory.

But in the atomic age, in the age of tomorrow when the Atlantic can be spanned in an hour, the mounting of an offensive cannot consume weeks or months or years as in past wars. If, in that interval, we are relying solely upon the defense while we muster our offensive powers, if, in that interval, the enemy is slowly pulverizing our cities while we are powerless to reach him, we shall be defeated before our vast potential is ever harnessed.

This means clearly that defense today is in great measure attack and that that attack must be, strategically, a national reflex action, the instinctive and swift protective gesture of one exposed to danger. There can be no delay to muster forces, to summon up men, to mobilize ships or planes. The first strategic priority today is *not mobilization potential* or the gradual development of mass forces (though both, under certain circumstances and in later phases of any war, might be necessary), but *readiness potential*; i.e., the creation of a force in being ready for instant action at the drop of a hat. The best answer to atomic bombs falling in our cities, the best answer to guided missiles from across the seas streaking through our skies, the best answer to submerged submarines off our coasts is instant, swift and deadly retaliation in kind, bigger and better retaliation.

It may be argued that "bigger and better retaliation" or defense by attack is a pretty poor kind of "security," and so it is; this chapter was premised on the assumption, which will become a postulate in the military tomorrow, that no complete physical security is possible in the atomic age. But defense by attack is the only military alternative to obliteration in an atomic war. It may be argued, too, that retaliation in kind will not be possible in an atomic war, that there will be nothing left to retaliate with if we await attack. But this is a counsel of despair, and, given a reasonable *defensive* system plus a strong, alert, well-dispersed *offensive* mobile force, it is false counsel. The predictions of "atomic Pearl Harbors," of 40,000,000 dead in a night are possibilities, yes; but just that, and then only if we fail to heed the military lessons of this age.

Those lessons, to reiterate, are: first, defense by attack; which means the creation of a highly mobile, instantly ready offensive force;[5] and second, the maintenance of a "cushion" defensive system, able to mitigate somewhat the force of an enemy's attack.

These needs may appear to be conflicting and they can be so, but they are not mutually exclusive; they can be reconciled. But proper reconciliation requires application of that old military principle known as "economy of force," or judgment. We have seen that offensive strength is the ultimate hope for victory and is, indeed, a deterrent to attack. The greater part of our effort, measured in man power and defense dollars, should go therefore toward creation and maintenance of the offensive force in being which must be the basis of our whole structure of defense.

The efforts expended upon offense and defense must bear a logical proportional relation to each other, and money and man-power expenditures must be flexible to vary with technological possibilities. It is probable, for instance, that deadly anti-aircraft missiles of great accuracy will be available long before supersonic transoceanic missiles are developed. For an interval, three or four years from now, the defense may gain in power, vis-à-vis the modern bomber, and we would be foolish indeed not to exploit that advantage to the full. Flexibility, an acute sense of timing and a clear understanding of the technological timetable of possibilities are important elements of any sound arms program.

The speed and range of modern attack, both of which have dictated the pre-eminence of the offensive and the necessity of creating and maintaining an *instantly ready*, *highly mobile*, and *thoroughly trained* offensive force, also influence basically other of our defense concepts. If we are to have warning of attack in the years ahead when the oceans are reduced to ditches, we must reach out far beyond our shores. And if we are to attack any enemy with maximum efficiency we must also have springboards or bases far beyond our shores. For accuracy is a function of range, and the shorter the range (other things being equal) the greater the accuracy. So, too, is bomb tonnage dropped. The shorter the range the greater the number of plane sorties that can be made and, therefore, the greater the tonnage of bombs dropped. This will not be, however, in the missile and atomic age, as important a factor as it is in the era, still with us, of the piloted plane.

The technological revolution in war and the changed strategic concepts which it has forced upon us have therefore posed to the democratic United States—a nation which only forty years ago was inward-looking, isolationist, complacent, peace-loving—two revolutionary concepts. We must reverse fundamentally our traditional military policy which has sufficed for more than a century; we must gear our plans to an *offensive*, not a defensive, policy, and in the interest of defense as well as of offense we, traditionally a self-styled non-imperialist nation, must reach out far beyond our borders to secure positions in readiness.

For the plain and simple facts of our age are that for the first time since the days of the Indian wars the United States will soon have "live" frontiers.

A "live" frontier is a potentially hostile frontier, a frontier over which decisive attack upon a nation may come. For generations Europe and Asia have been seamed by "live" frontiers; forts and huge armies lined the national borders, ready to ward off sudden attack. But our traditional friendship with Canada, the seas that surround us, and our dominating power position in the Western Hemisphere spared us the unrelaxing rigors of a perpetual "On Guard." We, the fortunate nation, had no "live" frontiers.

But the atomic-missile age has created a new geography of terror. Today, we are just beginning to delineate our "live" frontiers; tomorrow, they will be well defined.

They are all about us. The "air ocean" knows no terrain impediments; the only barrier in the sky is weather, and missiles are an "all-weather air force." Aviation has by no means "licked" weather; it is still the greatest barrier to successful air operations. But radar bomb sights and new navigational procedures now make possible military operations of considerable efficiency (but far from the "bomb-in-a-pickle-barrel" standard) in overcasts and under weather conditions considered "impossible" five or six years ago. The three-dimensional nature of the "air ocean" makes possible air assault from any direction; the sweeping frontiers of the air are, therefore, the ramparts we watch. But the seas, too, once broad moats that girdled and protected our land, have become "live" frontiers. The wartime development of the world's first true submersibles with their ability to remain "invisible" for long periods, the evolution of the gas turbine and atomic power for marine engines, with resultant major increases in surface and subsurface speeds and endurance, and the arming of submarines with planes and missiles and atomic bombs will make them formidable strategic weapons.

To seek and find submerged submarines in the waters of the broad oceans with the means now at our disposal or those that can be immediately foreseen would be like looking for the proverbial needle in a very large haystack. We must include the oceans, once our sure shields, among our "live" frontiers of tomorrow.

Practically, it is possible to define these "live" frontiers with even more precision.

The shortest distances between most of the land mass of Eurasia and most of the land mass of North America are over the Pole. These are not, and probably never will be, important commercial routes; first, because principal communication routes usually lie between the centers of mass populations, and the peoples of both hemispheres are concentrated most thickly along the seaboards in the temperate latitudes; and second, because planes and missiles are the only transport vehicles able to negotiate the Polar routes, and their payload or capacity is very limited as compared to ships. Moreover planes cannot carry bulk cargoes, such as coal or grain, and bulk cargoes form a large percentage of the total trade between nations.

The Arctic airspace, therefore, is not likely to become laced with vapor trails in our lifetime, and even its *present*, though not its *potential*, military importance has been exaggerated. Today, neither the Russians nor ourselves can exert major pressure across the Arctic regions,[6] and many problems of cold-weather flying, cold-weather maintenance, airfields, navigational aids, etc., must be solved before we can. But tomorrow, when long-range missiles have been developed, will tell a different tale.

The importance of the Arctic air frontier, therefore, is not commercial and it is not logistic; in case of another war, we are not likely to deliver our major supplies by air over the Pole. But it is a frontier subject to sudden and surprise assault; if intercontinental or hemispheric war comes to the world, missiles (and bombing planes) will probably follow, other things being equal, the shortest courses to objectives, since accuracy (and payload) are functions of distance. And distances between certain important population centers and industrial foci in North America and in the USSR and Northern Europe are shorter over the Arctic regions than across the seas.

From the geographical center of the United States—Latitude 40 degrees N., Longitude 100 degrees W. (a point about midway between Denver and Kansas City)—a 5,000-nautical-mile[7] circle would touch the Black Sea, intersect Lake Baikal and would include in its area Moscow, Kharkov, Sverdlovsk, and part of Manchuria. From Alaska or other Arctic areas, the distances are, of course, much less—2,373 nautical miles, for instance, from Point Barrow,

Alaska, to Murmansk across the polar ice; 815 nautical miles to Northern Norway from Iceland. From the North Pole as a center, a circle of 3,500-miles radius would include all of Russia and all of the northern part of the United States, as far south as Sacramento, Kansas City and Washington. Vladivostok is only 3,400 miles from Fairbanks, Alaska; San Francisco lies about 3,120 miles from Anadyr, and Murmansk is some 4,200 miles from Pittsburgh over the polar icecap.

At one point, the Bering Strait, the great land mass of Eurasia is only forty-seven miles from Alaska, and in the strait a Russian island is less than three miles from one of our own. This proximity, and indeed, the relative shortness of the polar air routes, has been the basis for many casual and ill-informed remarks about the easy "vulnerability" of Alaska and our Aleutian Islands to possible attack from Russia. But the tremendous and well-night insuperable communications, transportation and weather difficulties of this region—particularly of Eastern Siberia, but indeed of all the Arctic—are given too little weight. Russian soldiers, Russian planes or even Russian ships might reach Alaska, but the difficulties of supply would minimize their threat. And, of course, if a Russian land army ever tried to "invade" the United States from Alaska as a base, it would defeat itself in the tangled wildernesses of the North; its remnants might reach Seattle, but not as an army.

The importance of Alaska and of the Arctic is not therefore as a land, or ice, bridge between continents, but as a short great-circle route for planes and missiles. The Arctic frontier is the one which abuts most closely upon Russia, the other "super-state" in this bi-polar world, and it is one most directly threatened (potentially, not today) by a sudden *débouchement* from its empty cold of the modern "cavalry of the skies"—the robot rocket, the supersonic plane, the air-borne soldier.

But the land masses along the Arctic frontier are not only potential bulwarks against such a surprise attack (in the form of bases for warning and detection stations, airfields, intercepting missile launchers), but have perhaps even more major importance to our *sea frontiers*. For these land masses—Alaska, Greenland, Iceland, etc.—*flank* the established great-circle sea-air routes across the oceans, and it is along these routes and through these oceans that the submarines of tomorrow must move, and it is by these sea routes that the United States must maintain her principal channels of communication with Europe and with Asia.

The commercial and strategic importance of these sea routes cannot be overestimated. If they are cut we have, indeed, lost the "struggle for the world," for only across these sea frontiers can the full measure of American economic, cultural and *military* strength be exerted, only across the seas can we maintain communication with Western Europe and Eastern Asia. The Arctic is a "tender" frontier, one to be eternally guarded, but the sea frontiers have far more enduring importance; only across them can we extend all forms of American strength to the Eastern Hemisphere. Which means, in terms of war, that if sudden swift missile and plane attacks, perhaps via the Arctic, did not quickly determine the outcome, then victory would sooner or later go to that nation which controlled the Atlantic and Pacific sea frontiers.

Southward, the United States possesses no "live" frontiers of comparable importance to those to north, east and west. But the Panama Canal, our principal arterial sea gate between our sea frontiers, demands a new scope of protection, and the vast mass of islands and jungled lands to the south could provide base space and launching areas for secret and hidden installations of a potential enemy.

The vulnerability of the Panama Canal to atomic attack is, indeed, forcing new strategic conceptions. "By way of Cape Horn" may again become a familiar sea routing of the latter half of the twentieth century. The airplane and the bomb have shifted Britain's Mediterranean "life line" around the Cape of Good Hope; ours may henceforth lie around Cape Horn. Various expedients are being considered to lessen the canal's vulnerability. The most important, of course, will be the extension of the ring of circling defense bases eastward to the outermost reaches of the Caribbean and in war to the Azores; westward to the Galápagos; southward and northward into the jungles of Central and South America. Political difficulties with Panama and other Central American states which came to a head in late 1947 when Panama refused to ratify a treaty granting us the continued use of bases on her soil may complicate the problem of Canal defense. But a new canal—either a complete new sea-level canal or another lock canal through Panama, or revival of the older dream, a Nicaraguan canal—should have rapid consideration. The strategic implications of a destroyed canal are, however, less serious to contemplate today, when the United States possesses a "two-ocean navy" (a fleet in each ocean superior to any possible combination of naval powers), than two decades ago, when our naval superiority could be insured only by concentrating in one ocean the fleets of both oceans.

Our new strategic perspective in the atomic age, therefore, must be three-dimensional and circumferential; we have "live" frontiers all about us.

The new-found vulnerability of these frontiers as well as a clear understanding of the timetable of technological possibilities and the capabilities and limitations of the new weapons dictates the necessity of bases—or base areas, or positions—beyond our own continental limits.

We have seen that the continental United States is becoming more and more, as the range of weapons increases, the main base for all our military operations. But we have also seen that it is more vital than ever in the atomic age to make the United States a "secure" base, in other words to protect that base insofar as possible against decisive attack. That cannot be done without bases overseas. As other chapters have emphasized, we have not yet reached, in our technological timetable, the era of intercontinental war. Any war involving the United States and an overseas power which occurred before 1955 or 1960 would have to be what our Air Force leaders describe as an "intermediate base" war. In other words, even if our planes operated from the main base, the continental United States, they could not reach the enemy without use of an "intermediate" or overseas advanced base at which to refuel, bomb-up, etc. In time, as ranges increased such an advanced base might gradually be reduced in operating importance, but even so advanced bases would —and will, as long as piloted planes are flying—continue to serve much the same function as that provided by Iwo Jima during the war. Iwo, bitterly and bloodily won, nevertheless paid for itself a hundred times during our bombing attacks against Japan. It was an "intermediate base"; the B-29's were based on Guam and Saipan, far to the south, but Iwo furnished weather reports, navigational guidance and a haven, on the run back, for "cripples" or planes low in gas.

The idea of operating from home bases, without the burden of establishing and maintaining advanced and intermediate bases, would be welcomed by every Air Force officer, if it could be realized without paying too prohibitive a price. From the inherent characteristics of the airplane as developed during the last forty years, however, it appears probable that the price of such a method of operation will continue to be extremely high in the measurable future. Even if aircraft had attained the range necessary to launch bombing attacks from a distance of 6,000 to 8,000 miles, it would be likely to remain much more economical in matériel, and therefore more efficient, to operate from nearer bases, wherever they could be obtained. . . .[8]

Intermediate or advanced bases, therefore, will always have major importance, if only because the shorter the range the greater the accuracy and the more the payload, but in the immediate future—say, between now and 1960—they are of absolutely vital importance if we are to be able to project one of the greatest elements of our strength, land-based air power, overseas.

The changing concepts of modern war have altered somewhat the characteristics of a desirable base. Geographical position is still of the first importance. But the old distinction between land, sea and air bases has largely vanished; military force is now "triphibious" and interdependent. The atomic bomb has emphasized in a desirable base the importance of dispersion and the availability of cover. This means space and preferably a rocky, mountainous, wooded area where protection for important installations can be provided by tunneling into the hills and where camouflage and concealment are possible. It also means, for naval vessels, an anchorage of wide and spacious proportions with more than one entrance. Pearl Harbor with its single narrow entrance and congested berthing facilities would not be a healthy place for any navy if an atomic bomb were dropped there. This premium upon dispersion must also affect air and ground; it means wide scattering of parked planes; it means several air strips instead of one, and numerous maintenance facilities. Ground installations and bivouacs ought to be far apart and well dug in.

These considerations definitely stress the importance, in an advanced base, of space. Small islands will continue to have their utility in the atomic age, but not as major bases. Tiny flat atolls, such as some of those in the Pacific, are unsuitable because of their low elevation above the sea for underground installations, and their restricted land area would facilitate destruction or neutralization of most of the facilities on the atoll by one atomic bomb, set to detonate close above the ground in an air burst, or dropped in the water close to the atoll. Major island bases, therefore, ought to be developed on medium to large islands, preferably mountainous and heavily wooded, like the Philippines, Okinawa, or Guam. Continental bases would ordinarily have no such arbitrary natural space restrictions as island bases, but even on continents the same dispersion rule must apply, for there are only two rules of thumb in "answer" to the atomic bomb—dispersion and digging.

The new-found strategic mobility of navies, stemming from the development of the "floating base system" during the war, and the increasing strategic mobility of air forces, resulting from greater range, tracked landing gear, etc., reduces somewhat the need for an extensive, widespread system of great base installations. Land bases with tremendous installations for servicing and repair are fixed targets for atomic bombs, and in the distant future an enemy will be able to "zero in" his rocket launchers upon such points well before war, and might cripple them in one blast. Some great land installations with all the complicated paraphernalia for maintaining a great mixed force are, of course, necessary, but the expense of modern maintenance and servicing equipment and the new-found need for putting much of it underground and widely dispersed will make many such bases prohibitively expensive, not only in money, but in man power.

Fortunately only a few such advanced bases—which are really not so much "intermediate" bases as main operating bases—are needed. Other types of subsidiary outlying installations are, however, essential. Particularly important is a widespread network of weather stations, radio stations, radar warning and relaying stations, auxiliary air strips, and installations for launching defensive and offensive missiles.

Fortunately again, this network need not be as extensive as was once thought, for mobile bases can do excellent substitute service, for some purposes better service, than fixed land bases. Weather reporting, radio relays, radar warning—even missile launching—can be done as well or better from ships than from land, with the added vantage that the ships are not a fixed point in space, and hence not so susceptible to swift neutralization. Ships can, of course, be sunk, and by many means short of an atomic explosion, but their future safety is in dispersion, which means numbers; in speed, and in the case of submarines, "invisibility." They possess inherent advantages over fixed land bases because of their mobility. They are not limited in space as most land bases are; the oceans are the only frame for their dispersion. For all these reasons—and another one, the importance of bringing your fire power as close as possible to the enemy —the major function of the Navy of tomorrow will almost certainly be the provision of bases in the hundreds, bases to supplement and extend our limited land installations, bases from which American sea-air-missile power, even American land power, can be projected, weather-reporting bases, radar picket boats, missile ships, offensive and defensive guardians of the sea frontiers, and even (in a more limited arena) of the Arctic frontier.[9]

Floating bases will, in time, be supplemented, to a more limited degree, by flying bases. Planes already have acted in weather-reporting capacities, as control stations for other planes, and as radar relay bases; in time, the scientists predict, satellite missiles endlessly circling the earth, equipped with telemetering devices to transmit the robot-collected data back to the surface, will be useful for weather forecasting and missile control.

Such a system of far-flung bases, fixed and mobile, have an over-all strategic importance in the atomic age that far transcends their individual utility. As William Liscum Borden has emphasized in *There Will Be No Time*,[10] such a system of bases might well become, when hostilities started, "military magnets" which would attract to themselves an enemy's missiles and atomic bombs, thus saving our cities and industrial areas the full force of atomic attack. Mr. Borden believes that no enemy could possibly afford to ignore our military installations, that those, rather than urban centers, would have to be the first target of an atomic attack. This theory correctly evaluates the strategic importance of bases; if this nation were well prepared with an atomic stock pile and the carriers to deliver the explosives to enemy targets, those carriers and those stock piles would have to be wiped out first if an enemy were to escape the "retaliation in kind" which might negative the results of the attack he had made.

Mr. Borden's thesis, however, cannot bring blind comfort to the "Home Front." For it is founded on an overestimation, at least in the immediate future, of the number of atomic bombs available; there will be too few of them certainly for the next five to twenty years to use them prodigally against fleets and advanced bases. Moreover, our experience of air war and total war leads to the conclusion that war, no matter how started, will probably be extended from military to civilian and industrial targets; indeed, this is so much the lesson of our time that it is idle to try to differentiate between the types of targets. For any enemy knows that our industrial superiority, if a war lasts a long time, will give this country its greatest advantage; if his lightning blows at our military installations did not succeed and our industry was left untouched he would be doomed to defeat. Industrial complexes are integral parts of modern cities, but so, too, in many instances, are actual military installations—the Brooklyn Navy Yard and Floyd Bennett Field in New York, for instance.[11] Finally, Mr. Borden's overoptimistic argument falls by the wayside, for sooner or later, the United States, we have seen, is almost certain to become a main operating base; and even if an enemy should aim his first attack at our military installations many of them would be on our own continental soil, and in many cases in areas in such close proximity to big cities that the two targets would be virtually synonymous.

Advanced bases, fixed and mobile, cannot, therefore, be regarded as a sure shield for "Home Front" defense; far from it. But they certainly possess major strategic importance, for no enemy can ignore their threat to his own military installations and to his own "Home Front." Their increased strategic importance in the atomic age emphasizes, however, the necessity for a reasonable geographical dispersion of these bases; numbers, as well as location, are now important, if solely to preclude the possibility of the neutralization or elimination of all our bases in one sudden attack. In the case of mobile bases—ships and planes—it is obvious that dispersion, rather than concentration, of our fleets of the sea and sky is vital; never again should our navies or our air forces be crowded into two or three or four ports or concentrated on a few fields; they must be widely scattered.

Despite the growing utilization of ships and planes as reporting or relaying stations and bases, an irreducible minimum of land bases always will be required, for ships and planes and men must always turn at last to the land.

Where, beyond the U.S. limits, are such bases needed?

Base positions should be dictated by strategic considerations and availability; they should be geographically cited to protect our "live" frontiers offensively as well as defensively.

What are our grand strategic conceptions in this bi-polar world? What must we do for our own protection as well as the world's good?

We have fought in two great wars to prevent the domination of Europe by any one nation. The present facts of power indicate the eventual danger to us of any such domination in the future. Neither Western Europe nor Eastern Asia can, with safety to us, be allowed to come under the sway of any one nation, or any two allied nations. This is not so much because the *present* industrial power of all Eurasia exceeds our own; it might on paper and in theory, but in practice our far better integrated economy could probably more than hold its own today. But if Eurasia, with all its coastal "fringe-lands," came under one domination, the *ultimate* potential of this vast population—1,700,000,000 people as compared to 276,000,000 in the Western Hemisphere—would be far larger than our own.

This potential could not, and would not, of course, be harnessed immediately. Soviet Russia is the only nation today that even seems to threaten such domination; yet a Communist extension of power to the Atlantic and to the South China Sea would meet with far more than passive resistance, and even when the yoke had been fixed, millions of dissenters would try to remove it. Yet it remains true that no nation which ever has been under Communist domi-nance for any length of time has escaped from its servitude, *except with outside help*. Communist domination of Eurasia, if we allowed it to become complete, might in time ultimately spread to Africa. It would lead to the grand-scale "encirclement" of our continental island and the isolation of the Western Hemisphere, inferior in population and resources to the Communist-dominated lands of the Eastern Hemisphere.

Single-nation domination—Soviet or German or Soviet-German domination—of Western Europe and/or Eastern Asia would almost certainly signal the start of another war, the dreaded intercontinen-tal war, for it is to be doubted if the New World could or would passively accept such a conquest and allow Russia or any other nation unlimited time for ideological, political or military consolidation of its gains.

Our first and fundamental strategic purpose in the modern bipolar world is, therefore, prevention of the extension of Communist influence or for that matter the influence of any one power to the Atlantic. Secondarily, the prevention of the extension of such single-nation influence to the East and South China seas. From a military point of view it is fortunate that it is the "fringelands," or coastal littorals, of Europe and Asia that are important to us and not the great central land mass, or "heartland." For our great elements of military strength and of military superiority vis-à-vis Soviet Russia are at sea and in the air, and in the development of the amphibious and air-borne techniques which were indispensable to victory in World War II. The coastal regions of both continents are within reach of our sea-air-amphibious power, and will in time be within reach of our air-borne power.

Maintenance of the political integrity of the "fringelands" of Europe and Asia is not now, and is not basically, of course, a military problem (its political implications will be discussed in the last section), but military strength looms behind political discussions, and that strength must have a fulcrum from which to act.

The most important fulcrum, or base, or position, on land from the point of view of the United States in a bi-polar world and from the point of view of the United States in the atomic age is the United Kingdom. For the United Kingdom lies close to Western Europe, squarely athwart the traditional lines of communication to that continent, and the full autonomy and political integrity of the independent nations of Western Europe are more important to the United States in the immediate future (but not necessarily in the distant future) than are the autonomy and integrity of Eastern Asia. This is because Western Europe is far more completely developed, industrially, culturally and even psychologically than Eastern Asia; it is more homogeneous, more modern; its immediate potential in military terms is far higher, despite a smaller population, than that of Eastern Asia. Communism might well expand into Eastern Asia, might, indeed, "dominate" some of that vast area, but its doctrines—superficially appealing to the starving, the hungry, the oppressed, the graft-ridden, the illiterate, the down-trodden peoples of Asia—could have no continuing or valid appeal unless, after ideological conquest, the same disease that nurtured communism was cured by communism. And this is clearly beyond the powers of Russian communism today; if Eastern Asia, with its teeming millions, its perennial famines, its ignorance and poverty and disease, its primitive network of communications and its embryo industry, is to be re-formed, reconstituted, revitalized it will require generations. Peasants and landholders heretofore have been "natural" enemies of communism; it has had its greatest successes in urban and industrialized societies; even in Russia one of Bolshevism's greatest struggles was against the kulaks. Yet Europe is urban and industrialized; Asia is largely agrarian. Europe is more compact; its capsule size, its high degree of literacy and industrialization make it at once vulnerable to ideology and more powerful in organization. In Asia, communism, facing the stubborn, weary, fatalism of the East, might well stuff its head into a feather pillow. Bred on the old traditions, the ancient religions, the customs of countless centuries, the millions of Asia might embrace, swallow and digest communism as they have digested so many ideologies before.

From the *military* point of view China and Eastern Asia are less vulnerable to Soviet conquest than Western Europe. The space of Asia is immense, that of Europe small; the communications of Asia virtually non-existent, those of Europe well developed; the terrain of Western Europe provides easy access to conquering hordes, that of Eastern Asia is more difficult. The Siberian communication and transportation system and the nexus of industry the Soviets have so far established east of Lake Baikal are capable of supporting an army of perhaps 1,000,000 to 2,000,000 men, but far greater Soviet military power can be exerted to the west than to the east.

From the short-term point of view therefore a conquered Europe is of more concern to us than a conquered Asia, since its *potential* can be far more quickly and more easily realized. England, *point d'appui* (maneuvering point) and guardian of a continent, is the most important *potential* American "advanced base" in the world.

Western Europe can be conquered, of course, prior to and without the conquest of Britain, but a conquered Britain is essential to the final consolidation of the conquests of the West. An unconquered Britain would always be a threat to the conqueror (as in the last war). As long as Britain was available as a base for the application of American military power, Europe would be, in effect, unconquered.

Britain is not, of course, and need not and cannot be in time of peace, an actual base for American military power; but our peace-time diplomacy should insure our access to that "position-in-readiness"[12] if war should come. But Britain's vulnerability in the atomic age has been noted; no island lying close to a continental land mass can in these days of the plane and the guided missile be a really secure base for military power. Britain's size, however, and her terrain meet the necessary requisites for a modern base, but her high degree of industrialization are both a help and a hindrance—a help, since the British base is theoretically capable of maintaining any form of military power; a hindrance, since urban and industrial concentrations in the atomic age are dangerous, and her large population must be fed from without the island.

The problems and dangers inherent in the use of Britain as a main base were well illustrated by our pre-D-Day experiences in the last war; the difficulties, horrors and bloodshed would be tremendously aggravated and multiplied in the atomic-missile age.

For all these reasons, our "positions-in-readiness" should not stop with Britain; our frontier is not on the Channel or the Dover Straits, but on the Adriatic and the Baltic, from Trieste to Stettin. These countries, west of the Trieste-Stettin line, like Britain need not and cannot be actual military peacetime bases for the United States, though Trieste, Austria and Germany may long be garrisoned by American forces. They are rather *potential* bases, beachheads for a continent if shooting war should come, political beachheads in this time of pseudo-peace.

It is difficult and not within the scope of this chapter to differentiate in detail between the countries of Western Europe, or to attempt to classify them by strategic importance. In terrain and in potential, Germany occupies a dominant position. The great northern plain between the Baltic and the Carpathians (and the western ranges of the Sudeten and Harz mountains) has always been the traditional route of land conquest from east to west and vice versa, and Germany's industrial position and her industrious people give her great potential strength. France and the Low Countries are a window upon England and a gateway into Europe; their raw materials and industries, their shipping and their ports are of major strategic consequences. Spain guards a gateway into the Mediterranean, and Italy dominates the central portion of that landlocked sea, and flanks Greece. Italy, too, has great cultural and psychological significance as a cradle of Western culture and the Christian religion.

There are other "beachheads" or "positions-of-readiness" in Europe which the United States should endeavor to preserve and strengthen, though none of them have the dominating importance of Western Europe. Greece and Turkey are two of them—the one important to the other and both to the whole, because of their geographical juxtaposition, their strategical domination of the Dardanelles gateway, and their influence upon Mediterranean strategy and upon the Italian and Near Eastern positions. Although the Mediterranean "life line" is not vital to Britain or to the United States, as the last war showed, its utilization would ease immeasurably the strains of any war. The Mediterranean itself projects deep into the Eurasian land mass and offers a highly important "field of development" for sea-air power. Our "positions-in-readiness" in that area ought to include virtually the entire southern coast of the Mediterranean, to provide "defense in depth" which Greece and Turkey lack, an alternate line of defense if those two countries should be overrun, and sites for air and missile bases.

The proper solution of the Palestinian problem, which contains in its blood-drenched contemporary history the seeds of a "holy war," is of high importance to this concept of a North African "barrier" position, for North Africa is the land of the Arabs, and a sullen, rebellious, hostile population would weaken any "position-in-readiness." The Arab League, a somewhat tenuous ideological organization of Moslems with its main basis of power in Egypt, enlists the loyalties of Arabs from the Persian Gulf to Casablanca.[13] Though its member peoples are backward and industrially impotent, the Abd-el-Krim rebellion in North Africa, which occupied the energies of French or Spanish troops for five years, demonstrates the dangerous potentialities of a jehad or "holy war."

Palestine and Egypt have hitherto been the main sources of British power in the Near East-Suez area, now to be replaced primarily by the Sudan, Kenya and other Africa bases, secondarily by Cyprus. British withdrawal must not mean, however, a dangerous power vacuum to be filled by the strongest near power or by civil wars.

Palestine is a geographic "backstop" to Turkey; it would be an essential communication and supply zone if Turkey were invaded by Russia, and as such, political and civil stability there are essential.

Iran and the nearby countries, with their wealth of oil and the access they provide to warm-water seas, are also potential "positions-in-readiness." They offer geographical positions closer to some of Russia's vital industrial areas than does any point in Western Europe, and their oil resources are highly important to Britain's economic and military position.

Those same resources are also important to the United States; that is one reason why major private and governmental support has been given to the construction of a trans-Arabian pipe line. In the viewpoint of American defense authorities, the depleted domestic American reserves, supplemented by the fields in Venezuela, ought to be conserved as much as possible for utilization in case of emergency. They would like to see the rich Middle Eastern fields assume the burden of supplying to Europe much of the oil that the "old world" now gets from this hemisphere, thus reducing the demand upon domestic wells.

The Near and Middle East is also a crossroads of, and gateway to, three continents, and its lands dominate the Suez Canal, the Eastern Mediterranean, the Red Sea and the Persian Gulf. It is a geographic, military and ethnic barrier against Soviet southward expansion. In the next few years of instability, pending the complete re-establishment of British power in Africa, the exploitation of additional sources of oil elsewhere and the development of longer-range planes and missiles, this area has *great* strategic significance, but ultimately less so than Western Europe.

In the Far East, our "positions-in-readiness" must be China, south of the Great Wall, and Japan. Manchuria and Korea were sacrificed on the altar of expediency at Yalta; they have been, strategically, in the Russian sphere of influence ever since that conference, and postwar Communist successes, military and political, in those areas have only served to confirm a *fait accompli*. Nevertheless the Shantung peninsula and the coastal littoral of China have strategic significance to our world role. We cannot allow any one power, other than China, to control all the coast of Eastern Asia if we are to remain a Western Pacific power.

Nearer home Canada, because of its importance to the Arctic

"frontier," and northern South America, because of its importance to the Panama Canal, are vital in our politico-military strategy. Both differ somewhat from the other "positions-in-readiness" in that politico-military agreements and the regional arrangements permitted under Article 52 of the United Nations Charter permit actual development: in Canada of radar and weather stations, airfields and cold-weather testing facilities;[14] in Latin America actual maintenance of base positions.[15] The "Permanent Joint Board on Defense" of Canada and the United States have had a "meeting of minds"— and hearts—which is making possible the transformation of a Canadian "position-in-readiness" into actual base sites. These are as yet limited chiefly to meteorological and radar stations, but certain areas may be suitable for airfield development. Latin America is linked with the United States in the regional Western Hemisphere pact of Rio de Janeiro, and military liaison is maintained by the Inter-American Defense Board.

The creation of a system of "positions-in-readiness," such as that described, implies the world-wide application of the famous Dale Carnegie formula for winning friends and influencing people. "Positions-in-readiness," in the sense used in this book, mean friends and allies; in peacetime, we must use political, economic and psychological methods to win and hold friends and allies, who can provide wartime "positions."

But, in addition to these "positions-in-readiness," or friendly areas which we might be able to use in time of *war*, we require, of course, actual military bases, occupied, maintained and developed in time of *peace* by our armed forces.

In the Pacific, our base position is more favorable than in the Atlantic.[16] The Hawaiian Islands, a hub of Pacific communications, are at present our main Pacific base, but if they are to remain so with safety in the atomic age the congested facilities now concentrated on the island of Oahu must soon be dispersed and spread out to the other islands and new anchorages and repair facilities found for the Fleet. The Marianas complex, Guam, Saipan and Tinian, with outposts to the North on Iwo Jima, are also major installations and because of their geographical location in the Western Pacific may well replace Hawaii as our principal operational base. Another major base area of growing importance to both Pacific and Arctic strategy will be Alaska and the Aleutians.[17] In the extreme Western

Pacific the Philippines and/or Okinawa are our principal bases. The former has two disadvantages. The maintenance of bases in a country at least nominally independent, and amidst a population none too reliable politically, causes continuing "headaches." Our troubles in the Philippines since V-J Day—shootings, frictions, sabotage, wire cuttings, and wholesale pilferage of military supplies —have been major. Because of these and other difficulties, the Philippines, which were originally scheduled to be our main base in the Western Pacific, have now assumed a secondary position, and Okinawa has at least temporarily replaced the Philippines in importance. However, Okinawa is in the typhoon belt (the southern Philippines are not), and it is Japanese territory; to utilize it permanently we shall have to rend it from Japan by the peace treaty, which might not sit well with our past professions of "no aggrandizement." But the geographic position of Okinawa is more strategic than that of the Philippines, since Okinawa is nearer to that portion of the Asiatic coast from which danger might come.

Our Atlantic base position is less satisfactory, particularly as far as distant advanced bases are concerned, than our Pacific position. "Close in" to our shores we are well off; the Canal Zone is protected by the fringing islands of the Caribbean with bases at Guantánamo, San Juan, Trinidad, etc.; and Bermuda and Newfoundland-Labrador give offshore protection to our Atlantic seaboard to east and northeast. Of these bases, Newfoundland, Puerto Rico and the Canal Zone are the main ones. We have, however, no actual bases in the Atlantic favorably placed in relation to the coast of Western Europe. The Azores, important in the past two wars, would again have compelling significance in a future war as a weather, radar, and anti-submarine base. The much-discussed base at Dakar is of little importance, so long as we retain the right to use a base in Brazil, and so long as the North African "barrier" is in non-enemy hands.

Our real weakness in the Atlantic is to the north. By agreement, and after negotiation, our forces have been withdrawn from Iceland, and although our military aircraft retain transit rights until 1953, these are almost of academic importance; we have no effective base in Iceland. We still retain weather and radar stations and air strips in Greenland,[18] and it is highly important to the distant (not the immediate) future that our base rights there be preserved.

In the Atlantic, therefore, in addition to the bases we already maintain, we need, as a minimum, long-term security requirement, the *right*, in case of hostilities, to use Iceland and the Azores. As a minimum requirement we must make certain that no hostile or potentially hostile power ever uses Iceland as a base, for that island is, in the words of Haushofer, "a pistol permanently pointed at England, America and Canada." Agreements which will permit us to retain our bases on Greenland—some of them perhaps under Danish management, all of them, if necessary, in co-operation with the Danes—ought to be reached, and they must be followed in time by agreements which will permit us to expand our facilities there. For Greenland, as the last war showed, occupies an important position in Arctic strategy, and as ranges increase and polar war becomes more possible, Greenland's vastness and geographical position will lend it added importance.

However, in the case of Greenland, in the case of Okinawa—indeed, in the case of all bases where political considerations and military strategy conflict—we must be exceedingly careful not to let our search for military security nullify our political aims. A brusque policy in Greenland might turn Denmark and much of Scandinavian sentiment against us, with a consequent blow to our aims in Western Europe. Similarly the ruthless severance from Japan—without adequate consideration of the Japanese point of view—of Okinawa and the Ryukyus would certainly breed in the future irreconcilable irredentism in Japan. We have already made this mistake, the mistake of "seeking bases on the Moon from which to repel an attack from Mars," in the case of the Japanese mandated islands. Many of these islands are strategically of little moment, yet we insisted bluntly in the United Nations Assembly that they be placed under the strategic trusteeship of the United States, in other words under our *de facto* domination. Such tactics have a psychological as well as political disadvantage; they expose us to the same charge of imperialism which we profess to oppose.

Our strategic requirements in bases must, therefore, be balanced carefully against possible political liabilities. In any case overseas bases ought to be kept to a minimum consistent with our security; we should permanently retain and garrison only those which are necessary to reduce the effectiveness of enemy attacks against the United States or are essential for our own counteroffensive operations in the *early* stages of hostilities. Judged by this yardstick, Iceland-Greenland, Newfoundland-Labrador, the Azores and the Caribbean islands, and in the Pacific, the Hawaiian Islands, the Marianas-Bonins, the Aleutians and the Ryukyus (Okinawa) appear to be most important.

In addition to the *positive* base needs of the United States we have certain *negative* requirements. In other words there are areas of the world—Norwegian-owned Spitzbergen[19] and Jan Mayen land in the Arctic, for instance—which we do not require for bases for our own use but which we would not like to see used by Russia as bases. Indeed, a good many of our so-called base requirements could be met negatively if we could be assured that certain areas of the world could not be used by any enemy in case of war.

The base needs of the United States therefore must be solved by a nice balance of military and political factors. We are fortunate in the bases we possess; they are on the whole well sited for defense and offense. We are somewhat weak in two areas—particularly in the Eastern Atlantic and the Northeastern Arctic—but if we can retain our "positions-in-readiness" or friends and allies in the British Isles and in Western Europe this weakness is more than compensated.

The United States' strategic position in a bi-polar world has one inestimable advantage, vis-à-vis Soviet Russia. We have actual military bases and "positions-in-readiness" across the seas in some cases close to Soviet territory, and Russia has no such comparable positions in the Western Hemisphere.

Our new concept of strategy must be global; it must be conscious of the three-dimensional nature of modern war and of the new-found importance of the polar regions. We have "live" frontiers. Yet in studying our geographic position, which is still one of great strength, and in preparing our bases overseas, we must be ever mindful of the principles of "economy of force."

Extensive systems of base installations "eat up" men and money; we cannot be strong everywhere. We must remember, too, that bases are only fulcrums for the exercise of military power; without that power to be exerted from them and to tie them together into a strong system, they are individually a liability. "Positions-in-readiness," which this chapter has interpreted to mean friends and

allies, should, however, be extensive and far-flung. The more friends
we have in the world the better. But our friends are, strategically,
of varying degrees of importance. Of fundamental importance is
Britain and her empire, particularly Canada.

Notes—Chapter VII

1. *America's Strategy in World Politics*, by Nicholas John Spykman, Harcourt, Brace & Company. Page 27.

2. The importance and feasibility of "one-way combat" is stoutly argued in an article of the same name by Colonel Dale O. Smith, in the Fall 1947 number of the *Air University Quarterly*. Colonel Smith predicates his arguments upon use of the atomic bomb in such "suicide" missions. "One-way combat," he writes, "will quickly expend our bomber force if the war is not soon brought to a decision. The chances, however, of assuring a lightning victory are so great that it would be shortsighted indeed to hoard our bomber force at home until that doubtful time arrived when we would have bases near enough to make conventional round-trip missions. Add to this the crushing consequences of the enemy attacking us by one-way flights and we have no alternative but to accept this concept." This view is important but not by any means conclusive; it seems to the author more likely that "one-way combat" will be employed as a tactic, perhaps of desperation (as were the Kamikazes), sometime after a war starts, rather than in its very first stages, *unless* one side terrifically outnumbers the other in bombers and bombs. The development of plane ranges and of guided missiles will, in any case, make this concept an unnecessary one after a couple of decades or less.

3. From a talk by General George C. Kenney, United States Air Force, to the Army Ordnance Association, October 1, 1947.

4. *The Problem of Reducing Vulnerability to Atomic Bombs*, by Ansley J. Coale, Princeton University Press.

5. The desirable composition and nature of this offensive force will be discussed in subsequent chapters.

6. The Russians have a head start in polar navigation and arctic technological experience, and they have developed a Northern Sea Route along their Arctic coast. Icebreakers, some of the newest of which were sent to Russia by the United States during the war, air reconnaissance, and very careful weather and ice "prognosis" are essential to the successful utilization of this route during the brief summer "season." This route is administered by a typically powerful Soviet bureaucracy, "Glavsevmorput" (Administration of the Northern Sea Route), the main purpose of which seems to be the exploitation of the hitherto largely undeveloped wealth locked up in the tundra and the frozen northlands along the 18,750-mile Russian Arctic frontier. These summer ice trips, and the other work of "Glavsevmorput," have, of course, an ancillary and important military value. The United States, however, apparently is catching up, particularly in the technique of air operations in polar regions. The Forty-sixth Reconnaissance Squadron of the Air Force

had logged more than 1,000,000 miles of Arctic flying by the fall of 1947, had discovered two new magnetic poles, had flown frequently over the Pole, had mastered many of the secrets of Arctic flying (though not all, by any means, of Arctic maintenance) and had mapped an extensive area.

7. The nautical mile—roughly 2,000 yards, equal to about 1.15 land or statute miles—has been adopted as the standard measurement of air, as well as sea, navigation.

8. From "Mobility in the Next War," an article by Colonel Clifford J. Heflin, *Air University Quarterly*, Fall 1947.

9. For a discussion of the base problem, see *There Will Be No Time*, by William Liscum Borden, Macmillan, and *Bases Overseas*, by George Weller, Harcourt, Brace & Company.

10. Ibid., Borden.

11. The eleven naval shipyards in the United States are, for instance, all located in or near great cities, and probably would have to be, since they are, in the words of the Navy, "highly integrated industrial establishments, which, taken together, cover some 9,853 acres of land . . . [with] 4,150 buildings . . . 55 miles of berthing space and fifty-three dry docks." These shipyards are essential to the maintenance of the fleet, yet they in turn subcontract and depend upon a nexus of civilian industry.

12. The term "position-in-readiness" is used in this chapter, not in the ordinary tactical military sense, but as a graphic expression to denote a geographic area under the sovereignty of a friendly or allied power, which we might hope to use for military purposes in time of war. In other words a *potential* rather than an *actual* base.

13. But the member states of the Arab League are: Egypt, Saudi Arabia, Iraq, Yemen, Transjordan, Syria and Lebanon.

14. A string of weather stations across Northern Canada is being established. Fort Churchill on Hudson Bay is a cold-weather test station whose facilities the Canadians have shared with the United States. A string of ferrying bases for fighting planes was established across Northern Canada during the war and can be developed.

15. An air base in Brazil used during the war is still open to our use, under a ten-year agreement expiring in 1956. We maintained, until recently, anti-aircraft positions and other bases in Panama and have the right to use the Galápagos Islands and other bases.

16. For a list of our principal world bases, see Appendix VII.

17. Military installations in the Alaska-Aleutian area include:

Navy—Kodiak, Adak, Fairbanks, Sand Bay, Dutch Harbor, Attu

Army and Air Force—
    Fort Richardson and Elmendorf Air Base, Anchorage
    Ladd Field and Mile 26 Field, Fairbanks
    Fort Glenn and Fort Glenn Air Base, Umnak
    Fort Raymond, Seward
    Fort Randall and Fort Randall Air Base, Cold Bay

Nome Air Base (Mark Field)
Whittier
Fort Mears
Fort Greeley, Skagway
Naknek Air Base
Yakutat
Big Delta Airfield
Annette
Adak Air Base
Galena Airfield
McGrath Airfield
Nenana Airfield
Northway Airfield
Tanacross Airfield
Amchitka Air Base
Casco Cove Airfield, Attu
Shemya Air Base, Shemya

Amchitka and Shemya are two of the four fields in Alaska—the others are at Fairbanks and Anchorage—capable of handling and servicing planes as big as B-29's and B-50's. The new Mile 26 airfield in the Fairbanks area, still incomplete, will be able to handle the bigger B-36's. Many of the others listed are inactive, or virtually so. Alaska's principal air and army installations are at Fairbanks and Anchorage, with Adak and Dutch Harbor important in the Aleutians.

18. Negotiations with Denmark about retention of base rights in Greenland have been protracted and somewhat difficult. Suggestions that Greenland be bought by the United States have been made. Such a suggestion has aroused some indignation among the Danish people, however, to whom the Eskimos of Greenland are as children, and to whom Greenland represents the glorious period of Danish history. The negotiations, therefore, are bound to be delicate, particularly since the agreement which now permits us to retain bases there can be terminated by either party on twelve months' notice. The United States, during the German occupation of Denmark, received in an agreement of April 9, 1941, the right to construct and operate military bases in Greenland, and at the time (and reiterated since by the inclusion of Greenland in the Rio de Janeiro definition of the "Western Hemisphere"), this agreement was construed as a logical development of the Monroe Doctrine. But the wartime agreement was to remain in effect only until danger to the peace and security of the North American continent had passed, and it was further provided that consultations looking toward termination or modification were to be held, after which the agreement could be terminated at either party's pleasure within twelve months. The consultations have been started. In addition to its strategic importance, Greenland's cryolite mine at Ivigtut is one of the most important sources of this mineral—used in aluminum.

19. Spitzbergen lies squarely on a great-circle air route between the United States and the USSR; it dominates the entrance to the Barents Sea and to the

ice-free ports of Murmansk, Archangel and Petsamo. The USSR asked Norway in a series of discussions in 1944-45-46 for joint sovereignty and administration over the archipelago. But the Treaty of Paris of 1920 prohibited the use of Spitzbergen for military purposes, and the nine allied signatories ostensibly had to be consulted before modification. Norway, however, at first appeared amenable to the Soviet suggestion, but later—undoubtedly under pressure from other of the allied signatories of the Paris treaty, which included Sweden, France, Britain and the United States—said that no agreement could be reached without the signatories' approval, and finally indicated diplomatically that she preferred the status quo of sole Norwegian sovereignty. This may be another of the many issues ultimately to be referred to the UN.

CHAPTER VIII

TACTICS REVISED—ROLES AND MISSIONS—ORGANIZATION

Set thine house in order.

Isaiah, XXXVIII, I

WHEN is an air force not an air force?

This conundrum is not chaff from a radio quiz show but an inevitable resultant of the technological revolution in war which has produced guided missiles and the atomic bomb.

Tactics is the science of the proper utilization of weapons; it must necessarily define the type of military organization built around those weapons. Unlike strategy, the principles of which are immutable (though the applications differ), tactics, being built upon weapons, is in constant flux. Today the technological revolution which has revolutionized weapons has also revolutionized tactics, and sequentially, the organization, training and administration of armies, navies and air forces are in the throes of complete change, of which we have seen only the first faint beginnings. So sweeping is this change that even the designations—armies, navies and air forces—are in jeopardy.

Is, for instance, a "pilotless" missile fired from the ground a weapon of air power or of ground power; is it a "plane" or a "projectile"; does it belong tactically to the air force or to the field artillery? What of air-borne troops; are they part of air power or of ground power? Amphibious tanks—who shall develop and operate them—are they properly the responsibility of the navy or the army?

The military lexicon is too limited to fill the needs of modern war. The simple shield and spear have been replaced by a multiplicity of gadgets, many of them used with common catholicism on the sea, in the air and on the ground. Armed man has been forced back upon an encyclopedia of awkward terminology: "anti-aircraft guided missiles battalion"; "air-to-ground"; "ground-to-ground"; "magnetic air-borne detectors," etc., etc.

This jargon is really military semantics; it represents a linguistic attempt to clarify, but at the same time to escape the inevitable, the indivisibility of military force. The true meaning, tactically, of the technological revolution and of total war is just this: it has forced a "shotgun marriage" or rather an atomic-bomb marriage, of all the fighting services, and a grudging but growing recognition that military force is indivisible and that all forms of it are interdependent, not independent.

There is no solution, however, in oversimplification, no solution in saying: "Well, put them all in the same uniform and it will work out."

For there will always be need for the military specialist; no one man or group of men will be able to maintain and fire all the new missiles. An airplane pilot cannot also be a submarine commander; the air-borne foot soldier will have his hands full with the peculiar specialities of his calling without attempting to become a seaman. Indeed, modern war multiplies the need for military specialists, instead of merely adding new requirements. And that phrase, *multiplication* of force, which is General Eisenhower's phrase, is the key to the new tactics—*multiplication* of fire power, *multiplication* of all forms of force.

This revision of tactics and the consequential inevitable merging of sea, air and ground power, with revolutionary changes in the weapons each uses, have created a major problem in organization and concept. Who does what?

This problem has been answered legislatively in the United States, and for a time administratively and tactically, by the passage of the miscalled "unification" or "merger" law, Public Law 253, the National Security Act of 1947, which took effect in September 1947. This law split the old two-department system of the armed forces, dear to American tradition, into three departments, adding the new Department of Air Force created as an independent unit, ironically, at the very time when the interdependence, not the independence, of the services was marked, and in a period when planes, per se, may be superseded by guided missiles. But it accomplished more permanently useful service: it put all three departments—Army, Navy and Air—under a "super" Secretary of Defense, empowered to co-ordinate them and to formulate common policies and a common budget. It provided for the co-ordination of military with foreign policy and for the mobilization of the total resources of the nation in war.

Perhaps even more important, it established, partially by legislation and partially by executive order, the roles and missions of the armed services. It tried to answer, in other words, the question, "Who does what?"—the question that was the real issue behind the months of wrangling and dispute and backbiting that led at long last to 1947's revised defense organization.

The answer it evolved—in no sense the final answer, for tactics and hence organization, administrative as well as tactical, change with weapons—will nevertheless "freeze" our military organization for some years. The roles and missions of the services, the assignment of specific tasks to specific services, was made on functional rather than physical lines, and is on the whole sound militarily, even though expensive in dollars and probably conducive to some unnecessary duplication in practice. The unification law rejected the oversimplified and dangerous solution of assigning everything that flies through the air (except artillery shells or projectiles) to the Air Force, everything that floats to the Navy, and everything that is needed for ground fighting to the Army. Such an assignment of "roles and missions," deceptively attractive in outline, is nevertheless perilous, for it is not really an assignment of roles and missions at all, but an arbitrary division of weapons, regardless of functions or responsibilities, by their physical form.

The solution accepted, at least for the immediate future, does attempt to assign roles and missions, though in general terms. The armed forces as a whole have been given the responsibility of maintaining the security of the United States by timely and effective military action, and the Joint Chiefs of Staff provide strategic direction for the armed forces. The Navy, for instance, retains its own air force, flown not alone from carrier decks but from land bases when needed, for the primary purpose of controlling the seas. Anti-submarine warfare and long-range patrolling, a primary function of the Navy in the last war, remains a primary function of the Navy today, and the Navy retains one of the principal weapons needed, the plane, to perform this function (or role or mission). This does not mean that the Air Force is excluded from over-water reconnaissance or anti-submarine missions; its planes will be used if needed and if assigned by the Joint Chiefs of Staff, but the Navy is expected to provide the majority of the forces necessary for these missions and to have operational command over all forces so engaged. The Air Force, on the other hand, has as its primary function air fighting, the strategic bombardment of the enemy, and the air defense of the country, and as long-range strategic bombardment missiles, ground-to-ground, are developed, they will almost certainly be utilized by the Air Force to take over the roles formerly filled by big bombers. Nor are these missions exclusive. The primary responsibility for the air defense of the country, for instance, rests with the Joint Chiefs of Staff, which has assigned to the Air Force the function of providing the means for co-ordination of air defense among all services. Practically, air defense would have to comprise a vast complex of men and equipment furnished by all the services and by civilians. All suitable and available naval planes, for instance; all army anti-aircraft; naval anti-aircraft aboard ships in port; and radar and civilian warning systems would have to be used. But the Air Force, as the service with primary interest, would co-ordinate and operationally command these combined efforts.

This functional definition of service responsibilities, though inherently sound, is not complete and cannot be complete or fixed, since weapons, tactics and organization change with time. It is easy to say, for instance, that long-range ground-to-ground guided missiles ought to be the responsibility of the Air Force, but where does "long-range" start? The field artillery of the Army has revised upwards its range concepts and is now thinking in terms of 100-mile missiles as artillery weapons.

The development of new weapons useful to all three fighting services is tending to erase the formerly distinct definitions of *functions*. Strategic bombardment by an air force is in a greatly expanded sense, for instance, "blockade" of an enemy country, since it reduces the enemy's strength by behind-the-lines *attrition*, as naval blockade does less directly.[1] On the other hand navies in the future may have as one of their principal functions not only control of the seas but strategic bombardment of enemy cities, with ship-launched missiles and planes. And the ground forces with their anti-aircraft weapons must obviously participate in the air defense of an area.

Functional definitions of service responsibilities are not, therefore, easily established in the atomic age, and they will tend to become more and more blurred as weapons develop.

It is clear, however, in this age of tactical flux when no one can foresee what tomorrow holds, that a functional definition with all its imperfections is better than a physical one. It would be a profound mistake, as the so-called "unification" act recognized, to limit *arbitrarily* any service in the development and operational use of any weapon which it might need. In eras of great change it is sound wisdom to permit the fullest possible flexibility for technical and tactical development, even at the risk of unnecessary duplication; otherwise the full potentialities of each service will not be developed. This flexibility and autonomy must never, however, become extremism; the three services require over-all guidance and direction lest the resources of the United States be strained and stupid duplication occur.

The "unification act" attempted rather broad definitions of functional responsibilities, which will guide our services in the important years ahead. The Army is to be "organized, trained, and equipped primarily for prompt and sustained combat incident to operations on land." The Navy's function is "prompt and sustained combat incident to operations at sea," including "naval reconnaissance, anti-submarine warfare, and protection of shipping." The Marine Corps, part of the Navy, is to be "organized, trained and equipped to provide fleet marine forces of combined arms, together with supporting air components, for service with the fleet in the seizure or defense of advanced naval bases and for the conduct of such land operations as may be essential to the prosecution of a naval campaign." The development of amphibious techniques is its specialty. The Air Force is to be prepared for "prompt and sustained offensive and defensive air operations."

These definitions do provide wide latitude for tactical development and organizational flexibility. They support the sound principle of "unity of command"—or of giving the organization ordered to do a specific job all the tools it needs to do that job, instead of dividing the responsibility and the tools. Specifically, this means that in anti-submarine warfare, for instance, both ships and planes will be designed and built and their crews prepared and trained for that primary purpose; the Navy will control and direct *all* anti-submarine operations, instead of dividing the tools and the responsibilities between the Navy with its ships, and the Air Force, with its planes, even though Air Force units may be employed in this work.

The "unification act," therefore, is, in general, sound, but it cannot be expected to eliminate tactical or organizational problems; indeed, it should be viewed merely as an evolutionary step, not as the final solution. Functional ambiguities will increase, rather than decrease, as the new weapons become operable; interservice frictions may develop, and changes will be necessary.

What is most essential in this transition period is full flexibility for the development of the maximum combat potential of all services, and a firm and wise central authority over and above all three services. This central authority has now been provided in the person of the new "super" Secretary of Defense. His is the great and grave responsibility of holding the organizational reins, with which he must lightly check and direct but rarely curb. The indivisibility of military force must be his guiding principle. He must permit flexibility but check unnecessary duplication; he must continuously balance one weapon and one service against another and determine in the interests of the country which deserves what share of the defense dollar.

But the National Security Act of 1947 did considerably more than create a new department of armed force and a "super" Secretary to "exercise general direction, authority and control" over the three services.

It established, or gave legislative validation to, a number of new agencies, all of them designed to integrate military policy with foreign policy and to "harness" all of the national powers in case of war to one goal, military victory. These are commendable and necessary measures, a frank organizational realignment to the modern concept of total war, and an effort to increase our combat efficiency. But the act as passed, though it recognizes the principle of civilian supremacy over our military forces, does create, or lend legislative sanction to, several agencies or offices that, by their composition and makeup, tend to weaken civilian authority.

First, and foremost, the act *increases* from *two* to *four* the number of secretaries devoted to military affairs in the Federal Government. The so-called subsecretaries of Army, Navy, and Air Force, though not designated as cabinet members, are not specifically disqualified as such, and they draw the same pay as the "super" Secretary of Defense. At the will of any President, therefore, all four of these service secretaries could serve in the Cabinet, thus disproportionately increasing the military influence.

The act also creates a "National Security Council" "to advise the President with respect to the integration of domestic, foreign and military policies relating to the national security." This Council, which could become a highly important policy-forming body, or "super-Cabinet," would also ordinarily have, with the four armed-forces secretaries as members, a disproportionately large representation from the military departments.[2]

The National Security Act, instead of creating a single chief of staff or military head for all the armed forces, perpetuated the wartime Joint Chiefs of Staff, composed of the Chief of Staff of the Army and Air Force, the Chief of Naval Operations, and the Chief of Staff to the President (in the language of the act, "if there be one").[3] But the 1947 act sanctioned the creation of a Joint Staff of "not to exceed 100 officers" under the Joint Chiefs of Staff, to be headed by a director, and to "perform such duties as may be directed by the Joint Chiefs of Staff." This joint staff was originally modeled by some of our Army planners in the close image of the Greater German General Staff to supplement and uphold the centralized authority of a single chief of staff over all the armed services. A powerful staff of such a nature would unquestionably have increased tremendously the influence of the military in government, but the Joint Staff, now provided for, if *restricted to the frame of 1947's legislation*, has no such dangers. But in the interests of civilian control, restriction to the size and duties outlined in the legislation is important.

The Joint Chiefs of Staff (subject to the direction of the President and Secretary of Defense) has a broad multiplicity of military duties, including the formulation of policies for joint training of our armed forces in time of peace. But the most important are the preparation of strategic war plans, in time of peace, and the strategic or general over-all direction of our military operations in time of war. It has been objected that the Joint Chiefs of Staff waged war "by committee and compromise" during World War II and suffered from the lack of a single authoritative head. There is no doubt, administratively, that a single head is better than three or four, and that quicker decisions can be expected from a single over-all commander, and deadlocks can be avoided. But the history of past wars shows clearly the tremendous dangers of a single authoritarian military commander. Great military powers, unchecked or untempered, tend to weaken judgment; inevitably the megalomania of power sooner or later affects strategic decisions. "Power tends to corrupt, and absolute power corrupts absolutely," as Lord Acton said.

Inevitably, "war by committee" has its inefficiencies and may at times be productive of delays (though a strong President or Secretary of Defense can resolve many deadlocks), but sounder judgments can be expected in the long run, on the high strategic level, from a group than from one man. Our democratic system, military as well as political, has been built on checks and balances; some of these in the age of total war must be sacrificed to greater efficiency, but many must be retained, not only for the sake of democracy but for the sake of ultimate rather than immediate military success.

Hitler's rages and military aberrations, which became more and more pronounced with conquest and victory, are a graphic example of the dangers of one-man military control. Harold Nicolson, in *The Congress of Vienna*,[4] gives another and unforgettable illustration of a megalomaniac of another century, Napoleon, during his return with Caulaincourt in a frowsy sledge from the disastrous Russian campaign:

During all those days and nights Napoleon talked and talked. Feverishly he talked about his former glories and his future plans. Three hundred and thirty thousand men of the *Grande Armée* lay hummocked in snow upon the plains of Russia, but he talked only of further armies, further campaigns, and further victories. His voice at times was almost jubilant; at other moments it would rise or fall into the scream or snarl of hatred. One name alone (since as a rule he was mild about his enemies) would rouse these paroxysms of rancour. That name was England. The insatiable enemy, who had defied him all these years, who had defied him even when she stood alone. England! England! England!—as the postillions lashed their tottering horses and the great red box slid and lurched across the snow.

It can be argued that the American system precludes the development of a Hitler or a Napoleon, and this, fortunately, is probably true, but Napoleonic or Hitlerian concepts—i.e., one-man military control—can, nevertheless, be a danger. And in a democratic system built upon checks and balances, those checks and balances must, for safety, be maintained.

The Joint Chiefs of Staff, therefore, is soundly organized as a committee of military peers, rather than as a staff dominated by one military man.[5]

Antithetically, the precise opposite is true in the field. A committee for planning and directing grand strategy or the whole war effort of a nation, but a single military commander of all arms and services for execution and operation in each *theater* or potential *theater* of war is sound military practice. "Unified command" in actual operational theaters is a basic requirement for success in battle; wars can be won without it, but the strains and difficulties are immensely eased if one man, with a combined staff from all arms and services, directs the operations of each major segment of the national effort. The United States has learned this lesson from bitter experience in World War II, and the postwar world has been divided into operational theaters with one military commander in each theater responsible for the operations of all forces in that theater.

Theater responsibilities and theater boundaries are not, like service roles and missions, easy to define or limit without ambiguity and overlapping, and they must, of course, change with a changing world situation. One theater, the United States, now the "zone of the interior," but in time fated to become the main operating base for our armed forces and likely target of enemy missile and plane attack, offers a greater problem in command unity than any other. A single unified command for the defense of the United States, or a unified *air* defense, or at least a system of fine co-ordination which will integrate into the defense "grid" all available facilities of all services and of the civilian Home Front, will someday become essential. Should a unified command, or at least a unified air defense command, for the United States be created, or should there be four great American quadrants of defense each under separate command, or two halves? There is considerable urgency in this problem—for the Northwestern sector of the United States probably could be raided today by long-range C-54 or B-29 type planes based in Siberia or Kamchatka. Continuous and persistent bombing with present planes and from such bases would be impossible but even one atomic raid might be disastrous. The circumferential nature of our "live" frontiers and the shrinking nature of the missile-age geography lend validity to the arguments for one unified command, which might in time provide the framework for an air defense command for all of North America. Yet such a command on the Home Front would inevitably acquire enormous power, perhaps unbalancing power, in time of war or emergency. It might tend, too, to assume some of the prerogatives of operating forces and offensive commands and to absorb defensively, as the Sea Frontier and Naval District commanders tended to do during World War II, strength that could better be employed offensively. Despite its danger to democracy—only part of the danger of enormously expanded and centralized military power that democracy must face in any future war—a unified Home Front *air defense* command probably must be faced in the atomic age. The commander of such an area, like all theater commanders, must be firmly subject, of course, to the orders of the Joint Chiefs of Staff and the President.

Such are some of the broader organizational problems which the revolution in tactics precipitated by the technological revolution in weapons has created.

There remains the broad and overreaching problem of the *kind* of military force we need, its composition and tactical organization.

Size, organization and composition must, of course, vary with technological development and with the world politico-military situation. *Absolute* preparedness is impossible; *relative* preparedness is sound. No firm and permanent prescription can be devised, but some elucidation of principles and of the balance of forces required is possible.

We have seen in previous chapters that our "live" frontiers are the seas and the air, and that the offense is so far outstripping the defense that today to defend is to attack.[6] Backbone of a sound atomic-age defense policy must be a highly mobile, instantly ready force trained for swift *offensive* action overseas. Since such a force can move against any enemy only through the *air* or by *sea*, and since serious attack can come to this country only through the *air* or by *sea*, the core of any such offensive force, and the principal strength of any purely defensive measures we may take, should be built around air and sea power. For control, or at least superiority, in the air and at sea, while not insuring complete protection for our land, would insure heavy attack upon the enemy and would automatically fix the geographic location of any major land campaigns, if they developed, overseas, and not on our continental soil.

There are other arguments for strong air and sea power as the core of our military policy. Ships and planes are, fortunately, in the American military tradition. More fundamentally even than land power, they are wedded to the factory, and utilization of these arms therefore exploits our natural advantages. In the immediate future prior to the development of ocean-crossing missiles and transpolar planes and the stock-piling of atomic bombs by other powers, control of the sea and the air means relative security for the United States. In the age of intercontinental war not even this degree of relative security can be promised, but since retaliation-in-kind or defense-by-attack is the only possibility if mass weapons of destruction are used, air and sea power must have high priority. If the atomic bomb, biological agents and other mass killers are *not* used, it is nevertheless true that the first way in which we can reach the enemy is by air and by sea, and air and sea superiority and a long period of preparation will be essential before any major land campaigns can develop. In other words, if the war of the future is won *quickly* it will be won primarily through the *air* by weapons launched from across the seas or by weapons launched from ship bases; if it is *not* won quickly great *air* and *sea* superiority will nevertheless be essential to win it ultimately by *ground* campaigns.

The weapon with the longest range, the weapon which can reach the enemy first today, the weapon which is, indeed, our first purely military "line of defense" is air power—planes today, missiles tomorrow. The weapon which can project the bases for air or missile power to any place on the seven seas and to the vicinity of the coastal "fringelands" of two continents, the weapon with range and mobility second only to that of air power, the weapon which must be used to control the vital sea frontiers, is sea power.

The United States Air Force, comprising the strategic bomber force with its "seven-league" boots, and, in time to come, intercontinental missiles; and the United States Navy, comprising its own ship-based air power and the weapons needed to assault enemy coasts and to control the seas, must, therefore, have A1 priority and the highest proportion of the defense dollar, particularly in the distant tomorrow.

This does not mean, of course, that ground troops have no place in our postwar military scheme; no sound security organization is ever complete without them. "The doughboy with his rifle," as a general has commented, "will always be a valuable fellow to have around, as he is capable of doing many things in peace and war which a bomb or a battleship cannot do."

The trend—even in the past war (except in Russia and China, where mass numbers still took the place of technology and big factories)—has been toward smaller, more mobile and more highly equipped ground armies. Our actual fighting forces often were smaller in numbers than the enemy they opposed, but vastly superior in fire power. In a war of tomorrow this trend probably will be accentuated. If weapons of mass destruction *are* utilized, their tremendous destructiveness may reduce the role of the ground forces to that of a "mopping-up" and occupation function. If weapons of mass destruction are *not* employed, larger numbers of combat ground troops would be needed. In either case, the numbers of actual fighting men, as compared to prior wars, are likely to decrease, but the need for great numbers of men will be re-emphasized, not so much for actual combat on the ground, but to manufacture, transport and supply technical and mechanized equipment for the relative few who do the fighting.

It will be forever true, however, that war, like every other occupation of men, is based fundamentally upon the land, and future wars may start in the air but end in the mud. The final validification of victory is occupation and consolidation of enemy territory, and this can never be accomplished without ground troops. It is conceivable, of course, when the age of intercontinental missiles arrives, that sudden terrific assault through the air could decide a war within a matter of days, and that the victor would relinquish any idea of occupation or consolidation of the territory of the vanquished.[7] In such a case ground troops, except for anti-aircraft, missile-launching and ancillary purposes, would be useless.

But no one now living can predict with certainty the nature of a future struggle, and it would be foolhardy, indeed, to risk the safety of the nation by gambling entirely upon "pushbutton" war[8] and by failing to provide at least a necessary minimum of the old and tried implements of warfare. The problem, in other words, is that faced so frequently in the past history of warfare, when a new technique or new weapon seems to make obsolescent the familiar, the tested and the tried. A British committee, reporting years ago on a controversy of that day—the future of the battleship—put the situation neatly: "The advocates of the extreme air view would wish this country to build no capital ships (other powers still continuing to build them). If their theories turn out well founded, we have wasted money; if ill founded, we would, in putting them to the test, have lost the Empire."

A mobile field force of ground troops must, therefore, have a place in our plans even in the missile age. But it may be that we shall not need again in *war* a mass army comparable in size to our 6,000,-000-man army[9] of the past war, and certainly there is no need for maintenance of such an army in time of *peace*.

The long-term objective of this ground army is simple; it must become the first and the greatest air-borne army of the world There are tremendous limitations on the present equipment for air-borne and air-transportable troops, but given time they can be, at least to a degree, overcome. Air-borne troops are a part and parcel of the native American military tradition; yet since the war we have made little progress except on paper. Air-borne techniques will never progress until as much time, thought and money are expended on them as upon the development of amphibious techniques. The objective must be to make possible the use of considerable numbers of troops against distant targets (transoceanic targets) on D-Day or soon thereafter, and these troops must be fully equipped with field artillery, recoilless guns, and light tanks of great fire power. This is totally impossible now, but may not be impossible tomorrow, if energies are unlimited and funds are made available. Aircraft limitations are at present major, as we have seen in Chapter III, but most of the Air Force talent since the war has gone into designing combat planes, not air transports or cargo ships. The utilization of atomic bombs and the eventual replacement of large numbers of bombers by missiles will release an enormous amount of air lift for air transport or air-borne work, and will ease somewhat the strain upon the aircraft factories of America. The development of air-borne strategy and air-borne techniques should have high priority as a long-term goal.

In the immediate future before the development of transoceanic missiles a mobile field force, whether or not air transported will have relatively greater importance than in the distant future. This is particularly true as long as we are dependent upon "intermediate" (or advanced) bases, for only from those bases would our planes have the range necessary to reach deep into the Eurasian "heartland." For this same reason, the Navy, and particularly its aircraft carriers, will continue to be a highly important first line of defense. Until bombers with transoceanic ranges, which can operate from this country, are available the floating bases of the Navy may launch some of the first blows against any enemy.

For the next decade, at least, and probably much longer, the same techniques employed toward the close of World War II, modified by available new weapons, may be valid in conflict. "Positions-in-readiness" would be utilized or advanced bases would be seized after naval bombardment from guns and rockets, under cover of carrier-based planes, by Marines and soldiers wading ashore from amphibious vehicles. Air-borne troops would be used, but the limitations of the plane would prohibit the transport of mass forces by air over *long* distances. In this next decade, therefore, a mobile field force has particularly emphatic importance, and even when the full-fledged intercontinental missile is produced, mobile field forces, transported by plane, submarine or ship, may have to be used to seize enemy missile-launching sites, to perform suicide missions of destruction against enemy atomic-bomb plants, to seize advanced bases or to blast an entrenched enemy out of underground positions.

The ground army of tomorow, both in the immediate and the distant future, has many other roles and missions besides creating and maintaining a mobile field force. It must provide garrisons and police troops for Germany, Japan and other occupied territories until such time as those garrisons can be withdrawn. It must provide static defense forces to protect the overseas bases of air power and sea power. It must provide anti-aircraft troops, radar specialists, military police and anti-sabotage units, etc., to help defend these bases and the continental United States. It must provide men for such missile-launching functions as may be assigned to the ground arms (primarily anti-aircraft and field-artillery functions). It must provide the cadre of supply and communication troops which are essential to all military efforts. It must provide a school system for the proper training of our officers in the techniques of future war.[10] It must provide at least a training cadre and a nucleus of experienced officers and men to form the skeletal structure of a far larger ground force—perhaps a very large field force, which would be required if we went to war in the *next decade*; which would be required in the *distant future* if mass weapons of destruction were *not* used; or which would be required if those mass weapons did *not* secure quickly a *definite decision*. (See Chapter XIII.)

A fourth element of national security, and a fourth kind of force needed in the atomic age, is a merchant marine of the sea and of the sky to transport and support our armed forces. In the immediate future our excess of war-built ships, many of them rusting away at "ships' graveyards" along our coasts, are adequate to fill our needs, but as these reserves wear out and become obsolescent, replacements must be provided. For planes will never (in the foreseeable future) replace surface ships in the transport of bulk cargo. Some forty-four cargo ships of standard size, manned by perhaps 5,000 men or less can transport 100,000 tons of cargo each month from San Francisco to Australia. To do the same job in the air 10,000 four-engined C-87 planes would be required, manned, serviced, and maintained by 120,000 men—plus eighty-nine seagoing tankers to provide gas for the planes. A balanced merchant fleet of 1,000 to 1,100 operating vessels is required to provide the proper nucleus for wartime expansion, and these must be fast, modern vessels—passenger liners, easily converted to transports, combination passenger-cargo ships, cargo vessels, tankers and specialized types. The war left us with an excess of slow and inefficient cargo vessels and troopers, but with few passenger ships. A presidential commission has recommended a $600,000,000 four-year construction program for forty-six "high-quality" passenger ships, including two 50,000-ton transatlantic liners, the largest ever projected for this country. A building program for high-speed cargo vessels and tankers also was recommended. The large liners may not be necessary; certainly they will prove difficult to operate profitably, for American shipping costs are higher than those of any other nation, and American seamen do not take easily to "personal service." But a passenger-ship construction program is important, and the suggested four-year program must be extended into a regular annual replacement program which will prevent the obsolescence of our merchant marine. A healthy air-transport industry, numbering at least 500 to 1,000 commercial transport planes (plus military transports plus air cargo ships) is also essential. The latter form of transport, the plane, would, indeed, have transcendent importance in a short, quick war of missile "Blitzkrieg." For in such a war the immediate objectives of both sides, if the very first missile and atomic attacks did not bring decision, would be seizure of vital advanced bases, strengthening of "positions-in-readiness" and, if necessary, actual troop seizure of enemy missile-launchers or atomic stock piles. Speed and surprise would be the primary requirements for such operations, and air transport would be the necessary vehicle. If a swift decision were not reached, large numbers of ground troops would probably be needed and sea transport would become vital.

All these considerations fairly well limit and define the nature and composition of our postwar military forces. The core of these forces must be offensive in nature; first—heavy strategic bombers of the Air Force, later transoceanic guided missiles; second—naval vessels, at present aircraft carriers and their supporting types; later, submarines and other missile-launching or plane-carrying types; third—small mobile ground forces, trained for and capable of transportation by air or sea, and experienced in both amphibious and air-borne techniques; fourth—a "merchant marine" of the sea and the sky to transport and support our armed forces.

This offensive force must, however, be integrated with and dependent upon static, or fixed, forces or special defensive forces. Our occupation or policing forces in Germany, Japan, Austria and Korea, though too small in most instances for really effective defense and completely inadequate for effective offense, are nevertheless stabilizing forces of great political and psychological importance. These forces should not and need not be large; the smaller the better, so long as police duties can be fulfilled. Their function is political; their very presence, token evidence of the immense power and prestige of the United States, is a deterrent not only to rearmament and recalcitrance on the part of our former foes but to aggression by Russia or other powers. These forces could probably be overrun quickly, but any nation that attempted it would have to face the certain consequences of war, something that would not be true if our troops were not present. Our occupation troops are the military outposts of America and stand guard on the "frontiers" of U.S. influence; they must, therefore, have high priorities in men and money, which will vie, in this occupation period, with the needs of the mobile offensive force. A nice balance of needs, therefore, must be accomplished in this transitional period, but as soon as possible major emphasis must be put upon the establishment and maintenance in this country and at our main bases overseas of an instantly ready, highly trained "strategic reserve"— air, sea and land—organized and equipped on offensive lines. It goes, of course, without saying that when and if a United Nations police force or any other sound type of international military force is established our peacetime forces must be large enough to meet our share of the obligations formulated by the Security Council.

This offensive force need not be large, but it must be highly trained, superlatively equipped and instantly ready. The general lines its organization should follow already have been defined[11] by the services in their postwar organization charts, but there must be revisions in size, emphasis and weapons as conditions change. In 1948 some unbalance in allocations of defense dollars and service man power definitely exists; greater emphasis ought to be put upon offensive air power, somewhat less upon the Navy. This assertion must be qualified immediately. Far from being outmoded in the atomic age, navies have a continuing validity. In the period immediately ahead before guided missiles and transoceanic bombers are developed the Navy may be the nation's first striking force. And for the indefinite future ships, not aircraft, will carry the lifeblood of international trade and navies will be needed to protect the world's merchant fleets. But air power flown from ships, and particularly from land bases, is today and tomorrow a dominant arm. Today, in all the services, too much man power is dissipated in overhead and unnecessary command installations; a lot of it is wasted in small "empires" which the American organizational mind—particularly the military mind—tends to create.

The United States Air Force should have between 400 and 1,000 operational heavy bombers (in instant readiness) in its strategic command; in 1948, they number between 300 and 400. Too small a portion of the man power assigned to the Air Force is earmarked for this command. It is a sad commentary on the American propensity for overorganization that with an air force numbering 325,-000 officers and men in the fall of 1947 only some 37,445 were assigned the most vital offensive arm, the strategic air command. In considerable measure this weakness is temporary; it has taken more than two years for the armed forces to recover their strength after the hasty postwar demobilization. In 1948, "the Air Force is still picking itself up off the floor," still facing an immense job in organization and training. Nevertheless, there is wastage of man power in the air arm. The Air Force, partly because it has had to appeal to political pressure to achieve its military peerage, is—in 1948—too "political"; as a young and forward-looking arm it should be far more free of "empire-building" and "rank-consciousness" than it is. It must whittle off its "excess fat" and allocate more of its strength to its offensive arm, but even internal reform within the Air Force is insufficient, for too small a portion of the total (peacetime) military man power of the nation is assigned to the Air Force. Our offensive air striking power must be at least doubled.

The Navy (and the Marine Corps) can reduce with safety its over-all man power; it does not need more than 250,000 to 350,000 officers and men, plus 60,000 to 75,000 Marines. Six to eight carriers each in the Atlantic and Pacific, supported by one or two battleships or anti-aircraft ships and an ancillary number of cruisers, destroyers, submarines, etc., with amphibious "lift" for perhaps one to two divisions and a nuclear force for anti-submarine operations, is ample operating naval strength for the immediate future.

The Army, with perhaps 170,000 men in the continental United States, has only a fraction of this number organized in combat units. Large numbers are required for supply, overhead and training duties, but elimination of some unnecessary activities and careful organization could produce many more men for a combat strategic reserve, without any over-all increase in Army strength. In any case, initially one to three divisions (plus two Marine divisions), and eventually, when occupation of the ex-enemy countries has been completed, three to six Army divisions ought to be ready in this country for a strategic reserve.

The tactical organization of these land, sea and air forces already is changing in detail, as indicated in Chapter III, to conform with the changing weapons of war. The heavy bomber is still the basis

of the offensive strength of air power, but it is possible that as
bombers grow in size and range, they must depend more upon
speed and their individual armament than upon formation flying
for their protection.

Even before the war ended, the air-to-air rocket, with tremendous
bursting power, was threatening to break up "tight" air formations.
Tomorrow, until the supersonic bomber appears in the skies, powerful anti-aircraft missiles may force tactics of dispersion, of individual attack, rather than of mass attack. This trend is re-enforced by
the atomic bomb; only one, two or three planes are now needed to
attack each objective, instead of the massed air fleets of World War
II. The principal tactical objective of the attackers in atomic bombing will be to *insure* the delivery against the objective of the atomic
bomb itself. This concept alone is forcing a revolution in tactics
and in bombing. Misses and near-misses are now no longer tolerable;
the atomic bomb *must* be delivered to the right target. To this end,
the plane that is actually carrying the bomb will undoubtedly be
accompanied by others to act as decoys or dummies. Atomic bombs
are too expensive to waste, and the number intercepted therefore
must be reduced to a minimum; this strategic consideration must
affect tactics. In time these tactics of evasion and dispersion and
subtlety will doubtlessly make use of drone planes, controlled from
one or more mother ships; either one of the drones or a piloted
plane might carry the bomb.

Air refueling from great flying "tankers" may in time become
operationally feasible—and if so, the range of nearly all bombers
will be extended to worldwide limits. Such a development would
demand a corresponding development in air logistics. Refueling
in flight would also solve the problem of fighter protection for
long-range bombers. But such a development is still some distance off.

Today, the tactical problem of protection for the big bomber—
though it may become an academic problem as supersonic speeds
and long-range missiles are developed—is, and will remain, for some
years, a major one. Altitude (very high or very low) and speed and
dispersion, particularly the latter two, seem the only possible protection against radar-directed anti-aircraft. Against hostile fighters a
parasite fighter with folding wings and no landing gear to be carried
in a bomber's bomb bay is being developed.[12] Long-range escort
fighters will probably provide a better answer, although great tech-

nical problems, magnified by the high fuel consumption of jet engines, intervene.

Bombing with conventional bombs—a type of attack that may possibly continue to be of major importance in any future war, particularly in any which might develop in the near future—would have to continue to utilize the tactics of mass attack rather than of individual assault. However, even in this type of assault, the close-packed bomber formations of the past may yield to the individual, split-second saturation type of raids which the British used during the war.

As bombers become larger in size the tactical organization of the squadron and the group will probably change; there may be fewer planes in each squadron, with the ultimate, the flying battleship, organized as a single individual unit.

As missiles become operational weapons new tactical organizations must be formed to handle them. The Air Force already has formed one such experimental and still tentative "outfit," the First Experimental Guided Missiles Group, composed of men with wings on their chests who never get off the ground but fire robots at distant targets. The formation of this guided-missile group may forecast the doom of the piloted plane; General H. H. Arnold predicted that World War II was the last war of the pilots. But there seems room for major doubt about any such conclusion. When the long-range guided missile has been developed it may, indeed, supersede the piloted bomber for all area bombardment, but precision bombing of small objectives will still be within the pilot's province. So, too, will photo reconnaissance, anti-submarine warfare, close support of ground armies, if any is needed, air transport and air interceptor work. The pilot still seems to have a long lease on life. Even when the guided-missile age is fully developed, the men with wings on their chests will still be seeking the "wild blue yonder."

Naval tactics are centered around the aircraft carrier, which in time, will launch long-range heavy bombers. Carriers, however, may become mother ships for drones, and as large missile-launching ships are developed, they may replace the carrier as the principal surface ship. The advent of high-speed true submersibles, missile-launching and plane-carrying, will force a corresponding development of anti-submarine types. Indeed, one of the major functions of tomorrow's Navy will be to establish a "picket line" across the wide oceans of radar-warning and sonar-warning ships to detect plane, missile or submarine approach toward our continent.

No longer can we think of navies in the terms of Nelson's day or of Jellicoe's time. No longer do fleets oppose merely fleets. A modern navy must be prepared to meet enemy air forces, to assist in the containment or destruction of enemy forces on the ground, and to carry the war to the heart of an enemy by missile or plane bombardment or other means. The carrier task group, in World War II, the principal tactical grouping of our fleet, still retains tremendous strategic mobility, self-sufficiency and striking power; tomorrow, with jet planes and atomic bombs and guided missiles, a new form of naval striking force may do much to extend the long arm of American power to the "fringelands" of the world, and even deep into the continental land masses.

The new naval power may comprise "missile groups," "warning groups" and other tactical units little known to naval war. Of major importance to a nation like our own which pins its military policy upon its ability to extend its strength across the seas will be the construction of effective anti-submarine ships and planes. The new submarines can be an important addition to our great sea power, but to any other nation, weak in sea power, they offer a powerful weapon of attrition against us. The development of submarine and anti-submarine tactics and techniques will, therefore, be a major role of the future fleet. The atomic bomb and other modern weapons will force tactical changes in naval cruising and battle formations, and particularly in fleet-anchorage dispositions. There will be safety in numbers and distance; the problem will be to develop concentrated anti-aircraft and missile fire from widely dispersed ships.

On land, the division is still the standard tactical unit, and the postwar trend until now has been to increase the division in size and self-sufficiency, and particularly in fire power and mobility. The 1948 American infantry division possesses three times the fire power of the World War II division. Gradually, under the spur of new development and as larger planes and transport vehicles are built, the specialized types of divisions—armored, infantry, airborne—may tend to merge into one, a trend that already is pronounced in infantry and armored divisions. Armor is now an integral part of both type divisions. The old prewar tactical fallacy, so stubbornly adhered to by much of the American Army during the war, that tanks should never be fought with tanks, has now been abandoned, and it is recognized that the best anti-tank gun is a tank. Our divisional structure, however, still tends toward bulk, and many of the redundant and unnecessary administrative personnel and equipment which the American Army has come to consider necessary to battle must be sloughed off in the interests of the new mobility and the new readiness. It seems likely, too, if air transportability and amphibious techniques, particularly the transport of troops in planes and submarines, are to be developed as fully as they must be, that the regiment is too large a tactical unit. Regimental combat teams of the types which spearheaded all our operations during the war are bulky; in the future even smaller units— battalion teams,[13] specially equipped for each particular mission— probably must form the tactical backbone of our offensive field force. A variable number of these battalions could be assigned to a division for administration and supply.

The ground forces, like the sea and air forces, must develop new technicians and specialists and form new tactical units to handle the new weapons. Like the Air Force, the Army also has formed its first missile "outfit," the First Anti-aircraft Guided Missiles Battalion, which so far has participated in the firing of the German V-2's at White Sands, New Mexico, and is studying specifically the operational utilization by ground troops of anti-aircraft missiles. Numerous problems have been encountered in the organizational birth pangs of this battalion. There is a special need for officers with an electronics background and the more than 700 men assigned to the battalion by its initial tables of organization must be "monkey-wrench conscious," but at the same time ought to have at least a high-school education and a high intelligence rating.

All of these changes will tend to erase the formerly distinct differentiations between the Army's arms and services. Just as armor and infantry are tending to merge, so, too, are armor and field artillery. Guns on self-propelled mounts, with armored shields, are in reality one form of tank, or a tank is one form of a mobile gun; the artificial distinctions between them are disappearing. In the ground army, too, the indivisibility of military force has inexorable technological support.

The tactics of ground forces, modified to the atomic and missile age, present a seeming paradox of dispersion and concentration. These forces must concentrate for maximum offensive effectiveness but must disperse for maximum defensive protection. The need for protective dispersion is particularly marked in amphibious operations; a closely cluttered beachhead, piled high with supplies and congested by a constant stream of amphibious vehicles, would provide a favorable target for an atomic bomb. The key to dispersion for defense, concentration for offense is not simple; mobility and communications and digging in appear to be the only answers. The communications network of any ground force will grow in importance and complexity, because upon it will depend fundamentally the ability to disperse and the ability to concentrate.

Tactically and organizationally the trend of the armed forces today is plain; many of them—certainly the striking core of them —must become sooner or later "weaponeers," capable of operating a considerable variety of modern arms, of utilizing not so much their individual biceps but the collective fire power of their monstrous weapons. This puts a somewhat greater premium upon intelligence as a major military requirement than in the past; physical courage and hardihood and endurance are still important, particularly in submarine crews, air crews and air-borne ground troops, but mental capacity of an increasingly high order will be necessary in the armed forces of tomorrow.

It would be, however, a dangerous oversimplification to contend that tomorrow's tactical developments will make war fully a "push-button" art. There is no doubt that it will tend to become more and more mechanistic, but there is every indication that conventional armed forces, much as we now know them, will play a dominant role at least for the next decade, that ground troops, fighting ships and piloted planes will still be among the principal pawns of war for at least an additional one or two decades, and that full "push-button" war,[14] if it ever comes, will always be planned, directed and controlled by man, and possibly complemented by more conventional arms.

The machine therefore has by no means eliminated man.

But the compelling conclusions of the organizational and tactical changes forced by the atomic age are clear. Modern emphasis, as a previous chapter has indicated, must be primarily upon combat readiness—a force in being—not upon mobilization potential. That force, offensive in character, must have air, sea and land components, but air—the plane and the missile—must have first priority, with the navy second, but with the army—a highly trained air-borne army—by no means neglected. Organizational problems and tactical problems have not been solved by the so-called "unification" act, and there will be an inevitable tendency to blur over service lines and to merge service functions as new weapons are developed.

The indivisibility of military force and the multiplication of that force by new weapons is a military postulate of the atomic age.

Notes—Chapter VIII

1. This comparison of strategic air bombardment with naval blockade is, of course, somewhat figurative. An Air Force officer comments:

"It is believed that strategic bombardment can be referred to as 'internal blockade' and compared with naval blockade only when it is applied against internal transportation. True strategic bombardment is the progressive destruction and dislocation of an enemy's economy to the point where he is no longer able to wage war, through direct bombardment of a carefully selected series of vital target systems."

2. The Secretary of State, the President, and the chairman of a National Security Resources Board (the latter created by the act for the purpose of co-ordinating military, industrial and civilian mobilization) ordinarily complete the membershp of the National Security Council. The President, who presides, can, however, call in other heads of departments, etc., from time to time as he desires. Normally the four service secretaries would, however, outnumber considerably the representation from purely civilian agencies, and at all times the Secretary of State would be one as opposed to four. Of course, the purpose of this act is to prevent such *opposition* which, too often, has crippled the effectiveness of foreign or military policy in the past. Practically the danger exists, although it is entirely potential, that unity of position may be obtained by triumph of the military viewpoint.

3. Admiral of the Fleet William D. Leahy has been the first and so far the sole occupant of that office, which exists by virtue of presidential authority. Future presidents could, if they desired, dispense with the office.

4. *The Congress of Vienna*, by Harold G. Nicolson, Harcourt, Brace & Company, New York, 1946. Page 6.

5. It has been necessary to defend, at some length, the present strategic direction of our armed services by a committee, for the Joint Chiefs of Staff is a kingpin in our defense structure. Undoubtedly from time to time unwise

attempts will be made to alter it fundamentally in concept and organization.

6. "To defend is to attack" does not imply, of course, "preventive" or imperialist war. Section III discusses this. It must be qualified, too, as Chapters VII and VIII have qualified it. The defense cannot be completely forgotten.

7. Perhaps occupation might be foregone by a victor because of the danger to his own forces of radioactivity or plagues induced by biological warfare.

8. Bernard Brodie gives the problem of so-called "pushbutton" war a negative emphasis in a footnote to *Foreign Oil and American Security*, by Bernard Brodie, Yale Institute of International Studies, Memorandum Number Twenty-three, page 2: ". . . a war in which atomic bombs are used from the outset in substantial numbers must necessarily be of short duration, at least in its decisive phases"; but he would not recommend that military policy be based *exclusively* on that premise.

In other words, Mr. Brodie, in common with the world's military planners, is very wisely hedging and trying to cover all bets.

9. To the nearly 6,000,000-man army of the past war was added a 2,500,000-man air force—total 8,500,000 in the U. S. Army. Of this number only a relatively small proportion represented *combat* ground troops.

10. The school systems of all services, expensive in money and man power, are nevertheless one of the most important peacetime activities of our armed forces. These systems, particularly good in the Army ground forces, are credited by many officers as one of the principal reasons for our victory in World War II. They provided that indispensable cadre of highly trained officers and men which leavened with military "know-how" the whole mass of our forces.

11. For details of U.S. military organization see Appendix VIII.

12. This parasite fighter has been designed for the B-36, but if carried, would, of course, largely nullify the usefulness of that particular bomber as a bomber, in other words would reduce materially its range and bomb capacity. This would probably mean the utilization of a bomber purely as a mother ship for a parasite fighter, which would be expected to protect two or more bombers. This is obviously a wasteful procedure and one without too much promise.

13. The peacetime organization of the Marine Corps is built around the battalion team.

14. The popular picture of full "pushbutton war" is that of a duel to the death between two nations utilizing intercontinental missiles with atomic warheads against each other's cities and industries.

CHAPTER IX

INTELLIGENCE—OVERT AND COVERT

. . . what enables the wise sovereign and the good general to strike and conquer, and achieve things beyond the reach of ordinary men, is foreknowledge.

SUN TZU, *On the Art of War*

E. PHILLIPS OPPENHEIM, Sax Rohmer, beautiful ladies, codes and ciphers, torture, daring and death—such are the traditional recipes and ingredients for the fictional story about spies and spying.

But the greatest spy thrillers of the past are but pale reflections of present actuality. Truth is not only stranger than fiction; it outdoes fiction. Nothing Oppenheim dreamed can equal the amazing adventures and unsurpassed hardihood of the French underground. The Canadian spy ring was composed of modern human beings, not shadowy figments of the imagination. The great victory of Midway was fundamentally due to "foreknowledge," which Sun Tzu considered 2,500 years ago so essential to any good general; the Japanese intentions, strengths, and dispositions were known to the American forces before the battle because the enemy's code had been "broken."

"Magic"—the wartime system of collecting and "breaking" codes —also gave us a major advantage in the land fighting against Germany in World War II's last phases. Psychological and occasionally physical torture, as well as adroit questioning, helped elicit valuable intelligence from prisoners of war; where that failed an injection of sodium pentothal, the so-called "Truth Serum," sometimes worked, and when that failed, a system of microphones hidden in prisoner-of-war barracks collected and recorded information given by the unwitting.

World War II started with a famous espionage contretemps, the exact but huge effects of which upon the course of the war it is even yet impossible to assess; it ended with another famous achievement, which helped bring about the German collapse in Italy.

In the former, two British agents, one of them director of all agents in Germany, were "lured" and "kidnapped" on November 9, 1939, near Venloo on the Dutch frontier and disappeared in Nazi Germany. The immediate result, five months before Germany smashed into the Low Countries and France, was the elimination of the entire British espionage ring in the Reich.[1] The tables were turned at the war's end, when Allen Dulles, head of the Office of Strategic Services in Switzerland, through his contacts with the German underground, was instrumental in arranging the surrender of the German armies in Italy and thus in hastening the final enemy collapse.[2]

Modern intelligence, therefore, transcends fiction. In World War II it was, with all its romantic and dirty details, a vital tool of war, and an essential part of national preparedness. In the age of air power, in the guided-missile age where an atomic Pearl Harbor can mean complete destruction and absolute defeat, in the age of supersonic speeds, warning—that is, intelligence—is vital. It may be too much to expect any intelligence agency in the years to come to give exact warning of impending military attack,[3] but if the nation is to survive, the United States must maintain an intelligence service capable of anticipating crisis and of analyzing the nature of the crisis and the strength of the enemy. Without such strategic warning, without the "foreknowledge" more indispensable than ever to the split-second judgments necessary in the twentieth century, the finest military forces will be helpless. A sound intelligence service is, next to diplomacy and the foreign services, our true "first line of defense." Our military forces can act rationally only after our intelligence network has functioned, and then only as a result of the facts collected by that network.

Intelligence is therefore of supreme importance in the atomic age. But a proper intelligence system, necessarily working in a secrecy which even Congress (as a body) cannot penetrate, knowing, in wartime, no moral or legal or monetary checks or restraints, and restricted in peacetime only by money and government policies, is an institution of tremendous power, with great potentialities for good or evil. It must utilize all men and all methods; it is amoral and cynical; it traffics with traitors and heroes; it bribes and corrupts; it kidnaps; sometimes, in war, it kills; it holds the power of life and death; it utilizes the grandest and the lowest passions; harnesses in the same team the loftiest patriotism and the basest cupidity; it justifies the means by the ends. Such an organization, of tremendous importance and terrible power, must obviously be blueprinted with care and maintained in a framework flexible enough to permit its efficient functioning, but not broad enough to develop as a danger to the democracy it must serve.

To most Americans the idea of an espionage system—a spy system—is abhorrent, at least in time of peace. The Office of Strategic Services and the adventures and accomplishments of its agents did much to "sell" the public on the wartime necessity of espionage, yet there is still a native repugnance to the permanent establishment of a peacetime system. It smacks too much of duplicity and hypocrisy and poses hidden dangers to the social system. It implies an "unfairness" foreign to the American mind, and some details of any intelligence system unquestionably are a "dirty business."

Yet one of our early heroes, Nathan Hale, was a spy. And war has proven the absolute indispensability of an organized system of fact-collection and fact-analysis. We learned this lesson with difficulty; Pearl Harbor wrote in letters of blood the necessity of such a centralized system. But not until World War II was well advanced did the Office of Strategic Services, despite opposition and handicap, try to provide that over-all and centralized intelligence agency which this country had heretofore lacked. Even after the establishment of OSS (Office of Strategic Services), there were major flaws, as was to be expected of any agency so quickly built; a world-wide intelligence service requires time for development. Much balderdash has been written about the "brilliance" of the work of OSS; some of it *was* brilliant—particularly in Switzerland and some of the work in China and Southeast Asia—but much of it was inefficient, some of it was stupid, and for a considerable part of the war we were dependent upon the British for much of our secret information. Not even the OSS provided the single integrated "clearinghouse" which had been contemplated and hoped for, largely because the opposition of the old-line agencies hamstrung it. Foreign intelligence agencies in their dealings with the United States found themselves confused by a multiplicity of intelligence services—OSS; the Army's G-2 (Intelligence branch of the General Staff); the Navy's ONI (Office of Naval Intelligence); A-2 (Air Intelligence); FBI (Federal Bureau of Investigation), etc. In many instances, these duplications resulted not only in inefficiency and embarrassment but in confusion and in aid to the enemy.

OSS itself grew out of the obvious need for a centralized over-all agency; its very failures emphasized the desirable nature of our postwar intelligence organization.

Intelligence is of two general types—*strategic or general* information, which is fully as important in peace as in war, and *tactical* (combat) or localized or specific information, which usually has wartime application only. Sometimes localized or specific information is of such importance—notably the first use of the atomic bomb, or the existence of the new German Sixth SS Panzer Army formed shortly before the 1944 Battle of the Bulge—that it affects the whole general picture and therefore assumes strategic significance. And always the local or specific must be fitted into the general.

Tactical intelligence, or *combat* intelligence as it is sometimes called, is a primary function of every echelon of military command in wartime. The commander of a regiment, the commander of a naval vessel, the commander of an advanced base must know the enemy capabilities in general and specifically in relation to his command. The chief implement of tactical intelligence is neither espionage nor the quieter methods of strategic intelligence. Tactical intelligence is often gained by *fighting* for information; on land, patrols and reconnaissance are its methods; in the air and at sea, photography and reconnaissance. Our tactical or combat intelligence has not always been good; it was, with exceptions, bad shortly before the Battle of the Bulge during World War II, and it was woefully wrong in some of our Pacific estimates. The failures were due to a variety of causes. There was no proper liaison, link or coordination between the intelligence officers of various echelons of command; disparate estimates tended to confuse rather than clarify. The tactical intelligence estimates tended too often to become exercises in semantics; the estimating officer in outlining the enemy "capabilities" tried to cover all possibilities and therefore rarely arrived at any precise conclusion. There was a superabundance of useless information passed on, up and down, the chain of command,

and too little attempt was made to separate the wheat from the chaff. Jealousies and frictions played their divisive roles. There had been little proper intelligence training prior to the war. The function was traditionally underemphasized in rank and importance; until just before World War II the G-2, or Intelligence, deputy of the War Department General Staff was the only one of the principal deputies who was not a general. Our ground patrols and reconnaissance were pushed with too little vigor; even at sea late in the war, our battle-seasoned Third Fleet under Admiral "Bull" Halsey failed, during the Battle for Leyte Gulf, to detect the passage of a portion of the Japanese Fleet through San Bernardino Strait, north of Samar.

Too often, therefore, our tactical or combat intelligence knew, in the words of one intelligence officer, "the whereabouts of every *bistro* and compliant Fräulein near the front, but had not spotted enemy mortar emplacements or concentrations of his reserves."

Remedial measures to rectify the services' past neglect of intelligence have been taken since the war, and service intelligence schools have been created; intelligence officers have now been dignified with new rank and authority; intelligence "careers" have been made possible and the whole system methodized. But peacetime backsliding can undo all the wartime good unless continued emphasis is put upon the collection and analysis of combat information.

Far more important, however, in the atomic age than combat or tactical intelligence is general, or strategic, intelligence, which is of major importance in peace or war. Strategic intelligence is not only the relation of the specific to the general but is the building up, the creation, out of a vast amount of disparate and localized and specific information, of an intelligible and *correct* over-all picture of importance to the *national* security.

This means, first of all, a system of collating all pertinent information from all sources, a group to evaluate it and analyze it expertly, and a method for distributing the assembled picture rapidly to using and acting agencies.

The wartime OSS was the first attempt at such a system; following the war a Central Intelligence *Group* to serve much the same functions was created by executive order. This group was legitimatized by law, its purposes defined and its name changed to Central Intelligence *Agency* by 1947's "unification" act. The new agency headed by a director, is neither a creature of, nor subordinate to, the armed forces, but answers to the National Security Council (of which the President is chairman and the Secretary of State a member). The CIA (Central Intelligence Agency) is specifically empowered to correlate, evaluate and disseminate "intelligence relating to the national security" and to perform such other duties as the National Security Council may direct. The agency, it was hoped, would represent the first really integrated intelligence service in the country's history; it would not supersede the older intelligence agencies, but it would help to co-ordinate them and prevent dangerous duplication.

These hopes, alas, have fallen to some extent on barren ground. The central agency has been beset from its beginnings with frictions, internal and external, and particularly by the natural resentment of the older agencies, a resentment always pronounced in Washington, a city obsessed with the struggle for power. A bitter behind-the-scenes fight between some of these older agencies, particularly the Army G-2 and the CIA, has been waged, with the nation's security the ostensible issue, but personal power and service prestige the real one.

The fight has centered chiefly about the powers to be accorded to the CIA. There has been no disagreement about its correlation, evaluation and dissemination functions, but there has been much disagreement about the CIA's proper role in the *collection* of information.

Some ninety per cent of intelligence information, it has been estimated, is "overt" or derived from open sources—newspapers, radio broadcasts, industrial and agricultural statistics, corporation reports, etc., etc. Only about ten per cent of it, but sometimes a vital ten per cent, is derived from "covert," or clandestine, or secret sources, spies, "broken" codes, stolen documents, etc. The chief "fight" has been about the centralization and control of "covert" sources of information under CIA; the Army G-2 in particular objected to transferring its chain of agents to CIA control. In effect the chief issues have been twofold: should the CIA collect information as well as analyze it; should the CIA have a dominant voice in co-ordinating all intelligence activities?

Under existing "unification" legislation the CIA itself has not been granted specific power to undertake either function, although the National Security Council, under which the CIA operates, has broad authority to assign functions. Since the war executive decision has resulted in establishing under CIA control a single espionage agency; the agents of the Army, the only service which maintained any real spy chain, have ostensibly at least been disbanded or transferred to the CIA. For the time being "Magic," or the monitoring and breaking of foreign codes, remains under Army G-2 and Navy ONI, and so efficient are these organizations that no changes are indicated.[4] The CIA is starting, with the aid of other government departments, a master filing system and "Who's Who" catalogue of personalities, indispensable to the correct evaluation of world information. It has also taken over from the Federal Communications Commission the monitoring of foreign broadcasts.

These are sound functions for a Central Intelligence Agency, and one to which no reasonable objections ought to be made. Yet sharp exception has been taken by some "old intelligence hands"—most of them those who wear, or once wore, khaki—to the concentration of all covert collection of information in the CIA. Other critics, who want a sort of rugged individualism for each of our intelligence services, don't like the thought of "co-ordination" by any "super" agency. Yet both principles are sound.

Consider the first—the centralized espionage system. There is no doubt that duplicate or triplicate *cells* of a spy ring are invaluable, but duplicate spy rings, each under separate authority and control, are dangerous not only to each member of the ring but to the national interests. They can too easily "get their signals crossed" and work *against* each other. That small percentage of pertinent secret information which is actually collected by agents must be collected, if it is to be done efficiently, by a high-level agency and under a single directing authority; there cannot be numerous agencies, each mysteriously going its own secret ways, each "holding out" on the others. This has actually occurred in our own government. During the first year of the centralized agency the older intelligence services "held out" on the new agency; they did *not* communicate to it all essential information.

It has been objected that such a centralized system would deprive the older services of the ability to secure information especially pertinent to them. This objection is not valid. There is ample room in the new system, which is not vastly different from the British system, for all agencies. The "spy-ring" portion would be under control and direction of the CIA, but might draw some of its skilled and specialized personnel from the armed forces. Naval attachés and fleet intelligence officers would continue to collect naval intelligence information—data about fleets, ships, etc., and ONI would continue to evaluate it; military attachés would collect data about armies and G-2 would evaluate it, and A-2 would collect and evaluate pertinent air data. Each intelligence service would specialize in the *overt* collection of specialized information pertinent to its functions. CIA by operating all spy rings would not only increase efficiency but would save the official and overt arms of our government from possible embarrassment.

It has been offered as an objection by those who ought to know better that a single spy ring, centrally directed, lends itself to detection; if one agent is caught, it is held, the whole ring may be uncovered. A Venloo incident is, of course, possible, but one of the British agents captured at Venloo had no business on, or near, the Dutch-German frontier; as a director he should have stayed out of the field. No single field agent in any spy ring ever knows the identity of all or even a majority of most of the other agents. He may know those in his "cell," but he will know nothing of other "cells"; yet each of these cells is directed by the controlling agency toward specific goals. "Double agents"—that is, men who actually or ostensibly work for both sides—are an important part of any spy system. Obviously the control of such agents—many of them slippery customers, most of them in possession of information perhaps of great, perhaps of questionable value—cannot be managed by half a dozen masters; a single authority is imperative.

The arguments for a single central control of all espionage agents seem, therefore, conclusive, and the new Central Intelligence Agency is the logical organization to manage this form of secret intelligence. Some observers are inclined, however, to doubt the wisdom of having secret intelligence evaluated by the same body which is responsible for its collection. "Human enthusiasm is such," remarks one keen observer, "that it is difficult for me to believe that secret intelligence will be objectively evaluated by its collectors." In other words, some fear a predisposition to bias toward CIA's own reports, and a tendency to favor the data collected by secret agents, simply because they are CIA-managed secret agents, at the expense of other data perhaps openly collected. This does not seem a valid objection.

If it were, it could be applied equally well to the collection and evaluation of intelligence by G-2, ONI, etc., for each of these agencies in the past made its own analyses, and, despite the postwar creation of CIA, will undoubtedly continue to do so in the future. Moreover, the collection of secret intelligence is the responsibility of a division of CIA which is entirely separate from, as it ought to be, the evaluation and analysis section. In other words, CIA's own information goes into the general pot along with all other information fed in to it by a hundred agencies, and if mistakes are made in interpreting it they will be due more to failures of the analytical mind than to the administrative and operating organization outlined here. Indeed, if anything, control of the collection of secret information by the CIA ought to help, not hinder, correct analysis by the CIA, for that agency would be in possession of all the facts necessary to evaluate the reporting agent, something that would not be true if that agent was under the Army or Navy.

It seems clear, therefore, that the answer to the first great question raised about the CIA's functions—should it collect information as well as evaluate it?—must be an emphatic affirmative.

Nor can the second question—should the CIA have a dominant voice in co-ordinating all intelligence activities?—be answered in any other way. If we are to have order instead of chaos in our intelligence picture, the National Security Council must delegate to the CIA authority to prevent unnecessary duplication and dangerous competition. This does not mean a blank check for the CIA; it should have no unlimited powers, and it will not, if the National Security Council, as it should, retains its authority to pass upon policy and to assign functions. But the CIA must have some general co-ordinating authority, which, it goes without saying, must always be exercised with tact and discretion.

That such intelligence problems are written about in 1948 is good evidence that they have not been finally resolved. It is, of course, true that the birth pangs of the CIA are probably over; the "unification" act of 1947 should do much to smooth its way, and pending amplifying legislation, if approved, will define CIA's functions so clearly and give it so broad a grant of power that much of its external opposition will crumble.

But even in 1948 dangerous duplication of intelligence collection still continues. New agencies sprout like mushrooms; one of the latest is the intelligence service of the Atomic Energy Commission; and the State Department's intelligence branch has expanded greatly, partly owing to opportunism and the vigor of its director, partly owing to failure to receive adequate information from other sources. Naval and military attachés still fancy themselves as Von Papens and Boy-eds who will be too clever to be caught. The fetish of secrecy and "oversecurity," always a potential danger in intelligence work, has doomed too much important information to the dark recesses of government safes, where it is of no use to anyone. In volume and quality our foreign intelligence reports have fallen off markedly since the war; friction still continues between our intelligence agencies and within the CIA itself, and "empire builders" have constructed neat little personal kingdoms.

The unsatisfactory state of the nation's intelligence system has been reflected since the war in a series of intelligence "disasters" which can be recorded but not described, and in a number of Graustarkian events and ludicrous mistakes. It is necessary to mention only one of the latter here: on August 21, 1947, a State Department background report gave an unflattering picture of M. de Gaulle, and then predicted—two months before a sweeping swing toward de Gaulle in the French municipal elections—that his chances for a "comeback are considered slight."

All of these faults and failures are cause for deep concern, for time is safety in the atomic age, and it takes time—much time—to build a good world intelligence service.

The chief problem of intelligence—indeed, the chief problem of the world—is not blueprints, but man himself; in other words, personnel. The collection and evaluation of intelligence requires a vast number of specialists of all types, as well as those rare "generalists" who *can* see the woods despite the trees. Intelligence requires the intuitive mind and also the mind with an immense capacity for taking pains.

Probably much of the major information necessary to the waging of war, any war, lies today in Washington pigeonholes; the problem is finding it, cataloguing it, collating it, and finally evaluating it fairly and correctly; this calls for both reportorial and statistical ability. The chief failures of intelligence in the past have not been in collection, have not been a scarcity of facts, but have been failures of analysis and evaluation. To take a broad mass of data and to paint out of it an impressionistic but still accurate picture requires a very particular kind of mind. There is, of course, great need in the intelligence field for the "narrow specialist"—the expert on Voodoo rites, or the atomic physicist—but his specialized knowledge must be used by, and put at the disposal of, the seer who gazes into the world's crystal ball; never must the reverse be true.

Uncertainties of tenure, uncertainty, indeed, about the nation's determination to maintain an adequate intelligence organization in peacetime, small salaries, and lack of incentive in government work have robbed our intelligence services of many of their best wartime brains. There are still some exceedingly able men in the work attracted by its peculiar pleasures—its aura of mystery, its sense of knowing more than the average man, its analytical challenge, its sense of power—but there are also too many mediocrities, too many chair warmers. Above all we must guard against subjective prejudicial interpretations and the "freezing" of our analytical processes in a preconceived bent; this is always the danger of bureaucracy, and if the intelligence services ever become bureaucracies we are, indeed, lost. What is needed, therefore, is a cadre of long-term, stable, efficient and high-caliber intelligence officers and a periodic infusion of young, new blood, vigorous, argumentative and equally able.

Many of both long-term and short-term personnel should be experts in a particular field, but an irreducible minimum, perhaps ten per cent, ought to be well grounded in the social sciences, have a long view of history and logical, objective, analytical minds. The experts must include industrialists and statisticians and, particularly in the atomic age, scientists, professors, and research and foundation representatives. Some scientists must be attached to our embassies abroad to keep abreast of research in the world's laboratories. The need for skilled linguists requires little stressing, but the specialized training of these linguists in the technical verbiage of military or scientific language should be emphasized. Important, too, to a keen intelligence service, particularly to a high-echelon one like the CIA, which deals with strategic intelligence, are the opinion-sampling techniques developed by so many of our domestic poll organizations. Some of our experts in sampling public opinion should be a part of the CIA organization, their talents devoted to a scientific sampling of the morale of foreign powers.[5]

Presiding over all these varied talents, many of them necessarily "prima donnas," must be a director of unusual talents, capable above all of handling people, able to analyze objectively and determined to devote his life to a career of intelligence. The director of the CIA must make intelligence his life and love; there have been since the war far too many episodic changes in the top control for efficiency.

There are other guideposts to an effective intelligence system.[6] The Central Intelligence Agency must be empowered to select and train its own men. Its personnel must have a passion for anonymity, but its director must blend this desirable intelligence characteristic with a recognition of the fact that the political existence and well-being of an agency under the American form of government is dependent upon a J. Edgar Hoover-type sales appeal to Congress and the people.

The CIA must receive its funds directly from Congress and indirectly also from the older services—Army, Navy, Air and State. Careful co-ordination of intelligence with planning is vital; to this end, the director of the CIA must know the nation's general war plans, must thoroughly understand the national objective, and he must work closely with the Joint Chiefs of Staff; otherwise his organization will operate inefficiently and with a lot of waste motion which might be fatal to effectiveness. The CIA's internal subdivision ought to be simplified; the two independent collecting divisions, "operations" and "special operations" (formerly called "overt" and "covert"), might well be combined in one general division of "operations" or "collection." The other principal branches should be analysis and evaluation; dissemination and presentation; and administration. For simplicity and ease of overseas operations, where quick access to codes and communications with Washington is essential, chief agents may wish at times, to operate under the theoretical administrative "cover" of our "Embassy" or legation in each country, though actually the CIA personnel would be independent. The primary principle of espionage, that a collecting "ring" ought to be controlled from outside a country, still holds good; the German ring, for instance, might be controlled from Switzerland as it was during the war.

Security and secrecy are imperative; the CIA, and the service agencies, must have the right to choose, pick, hire and fire without publicity; indeed, without trial. Above all, the information funneled to the CIA must be all-inclusive; we must not lose a war because some piece of vital information, lying in a government safe, was not sent to the CIA because the particular holding agency was not "on the team."

There is one other caution, which is well expressed in the words of an experienced intelligence officer:

Intelligence in wartime requires rather different techniques from intelligence in peacetime. In time of war, in dealing with an enemy or those friendly to your enemy, there is a justification for the use of ruthless methods which I would hardly favor in time of peace. If one's activities are uncovered in wartime, that is too bad, but there are no serious political repercussions. In time of peace, however, one must be far more careful and more subtle. One should not take the long risks or act on impulse as one has to do in time of war. Secret intelligence in peacetime should be a long-range affair, methodically and carefully built up with every emphasis on security and with an avoidance of the slap-dash, cloak-and-dagger methods which may be justified in time of war.

Time and care and caution are, in other words, the three pillars upon which the edifice of a satisfactory national intelligence service must be erected.

Such are the difficult requirements for an adequate atomic-age intelligence service. It must be alert, fast, keen—more so than any other agency of government. It must operate in secrecy, and it *must*, despite our past qualms and residual prejudices, receive the full support of the American people and of Congress.

But we must, too, safeguard our processes of government and we must clothe this new agency in the habiliments of democracy. Certain checks and balances are essential.

First of all, the CIA must have, in the words of Allen Dulles, "no axe to grind, no policy to justify." It must not be a policy-making organization, though it must be kept closely attuned to policy.

Second, it must have no authority over civilians; the unification law provides that it shall have "no police, subpoena, law-enforcement powers or internal-security functions"; this law must be observed. The Federal Bureau of Investigation is properly charged with the *domestic* task of counterespionage and anti-subversive activities. This does not mean, of course, that the CIA and the service intelligence agencies should be entirely excluded from countersubversive and counterintelligence functions. Overseas, all intelligence agencies must participate in such activities, but they should be co-ordinated, where co-ordination is required, by the CIA. In this country, the CIA and the service agencies must limit their counterespionage and anti-subversive activities to their own organizations and to the armed services; the FBI must be in charge of all activities in connection with civilians, though its reports and files must be open to the CIA.

Third, the CIA director and much of his personnel ought, if possible, to be civilians. Military personnel are rarely suited by training for the collection or evaluation of strategic or national intelligence; some will be needed, but they must be men of particular talents; and they must rid themselves of departmental, or service, loyalties and acquire a higher loyalty to the national good. Above all, they ought to be strictly subordinate to the civilian director. The director should be a man of broad knowledge and intellectual attainments, thoroughly in accord with democracy, but with a fine sense of tact and a political "know-how" which would enable him to "get along" with the older and entrenched services and in the wilds of Washington.[7]

Fourth, the National Security Council should closely control and examine the operations of the CIA, both to guard against unwarranted assumptions of power and to insure efficiency. This control ought to be checked, examined and supervised by a special congressional subcommittee, chosen for its wisdom and discretion.

It has been necessary to emphasize somewhat these safeguards, for any intelligence agency of the scope of the CIA will, per se, arrogate to itself immense power, all the more so since its operations must necessarily be secret. Any tendency to broaden and expand its powers too greatly must be checked, unless absolute need for greater grants is proven. A proposed bill to amplify the intelligence provisions of the unification act would, for instance, endow the CIA with powers for "purchase, maintenance, operation, repair and hire of passenger motor vehicles and aircraft, and vessels of all kinds" and would enable the director to expend funds "without regard to the provisions of law and regulations." These are broad and dangerous grants, the second probably necessary in the interests of secrecy, the first seemingly redundant and wastefully expensive as written, and possibly unnecessarily grandiose.

The CIA must be supplemented in its secret work by other branches of government. The Federal Bureau of Investigation is an agency which, in the scheme of war, is in many ways of comparable importance to the CIA. It is charged with internal security in the United States, or domestic counterespionage and anti-subversive activities. These are obviously tremendous tasks in an age when communism is utilizing the termitic tactics of treason to undermine the edifice of government. But the FBI, an excellent police agency, still has much to learn about counterespionage. Its wartime capture of the saboteurs landed on our coasts inflated its reputation as a security organization without good cause, for in nearly every case the FBI was first informed of the presence, actual or impending, of the saboteurs by citizens or by other government intelligence agencies. Counterespionage, countersabotage, and anti-subversion are delicate and specialized roles. They call, when captures are made, for less publicity than J. Edgar Hoover usually gives them; they demand a degree of training and a skill of touch that transcends even the skillful police work of the past.

The FBI, a jealous and sacrosanct organization, has great power chiefly by virtue of its secret files and the personality and political "know-how" of its chief. Taught to combat criminals, the FBI sometimes has utilized its anti-criminal methods in anti-subversive and counterespionage work—a process that is not always efficient and may be dangerous to democracy. Great restraint is necessary in the use of the power entrusted to the FBI; that organization, too, should be subject to the close scrutiny of a congressional committee or mass hysteria may force it into undemocratic, unnecessary and un-American methods. This does not mean, however, that Communists and all other potential traitors ought not to be watched and identified and tabbed and ticketed. They must be, for the Communist party forms a potential "fifth column" of considerable danger. But the methods by which this is done are all-important; the FBI must develop a greater deftness and a greater sensibility for democratic processes than it has sometimes shown. There has been, in the postwar period, some tendency on the part of the FBI to "expose" alleged Communists, quietly, of course, by producing for their superiors "records" of rumors, anonymous reports, and other uncheckable "data." Countersubversive work often requires the utilization of such material, but the FBI, used to stool pigeons and criminal investigations, has been too prone on occasions to prop up its non-criminal cases with the weak reeds of coincidence and rumor. This is dangerous, distasteful and, above all, inefficient, for such an "investigation" in no sense exhausts the proper possibilities of counterespionage or countersubversive work. We want no "thought police" or political suppression in this country, but a better investigative procedure, more skill and more deftness.

The FBI must work, too, in close teamwork, better teamwork than it has sometimes shown, with the armed services and particularly with the CIA, for many of the "leads" to espionage rings and anti-subversive activities in this country come from overseas, where they must be collected and developed by the CIA.

Our domestic security often has not been good. There are not, and need not be, many secrets, but those ought to be real secrets.

The FBI, like the CIA, must not be stunted in growth, in development or in funds. For the country's future safety depends, in major measure, first, upon the collection and proper evaluation of facts, open and secret, about foreign powers, and, second, upon checkmating foreign agents who attempt to collect secret information about us. Intelligence is an important game, a dangerous game, indeed, a dirty game; it must be held in bounds, for "eternal vigilance is the price of freedom." We may not like it, but we must support it; there is no other choice. In the atomic age, information, facts, warnings are vital; without them we perish.

Notes—Chapter IX

1. These agents, who the British supposed had died under torture, were found in good health in the dreaded Moabit prison of the Gestapo in Berlin after the German collapse. Presumably they had yielded to torture and had told all, the only fate that is worse than death to an espionage agent. The British to this day have remained discreetly and embarrassedly silent about the "Venloo incident."

2. See *Germany's Underground*, by Allen Welsh Dulles, Macmillan. Mr. Dulles' book deals with the plot against Hitler but reveals the excellence of the sources of our information in Germany and explains the reasons back of our later Italian success.

3. Warning should have been available before Pearl Harbor, for the essential information was available; it was not properly processed and analyzed.

4. The future importance of "Magic" or code breaking in intelligence work is open to some question. It seems probable that encoding and enciphering devices now in use will make code breaking virtually impossible, or so difficult, that codes can be changed far faster than they can be broken. The importance of "Magic" in the last war cannot, however, be overestimated, and the United States starts the postwar era with a major lead in encoding devices and in code-breaking techniques.

5. The Strategic Bombing Survey reports and other war documents showed the way in which this might be done, even in wartime.

6. See *The Future of American Secret Intelligence*, by Dr. George S. Pettee, Infantry Journal Press.

7. All three directors so far have been military—one lieutenant general, two rear admirals.

CHAPTER X

RESEARCH AND DEVELOPMENT

Science, the endless frontier . . .
                        DR. VANNEVAR BUSH[1]

TO A materialistic culture, like the American, conditioned to regard inventors like Edison and Morse as modern Olympians, and accustomed to measure success in terms of washing machines, vacuum cleaners, labor-saving devices and technical and production achievements, it is not necessary to preach "science, the endless frontier."

The value of the scientist to the armed forces and the impact of technology upon war, graphically illustrated by the ruins of Hiroshima, have been so forcibly impressed upon the public consciousness in World War II that "sales persuasiveness" is something of a redundant precedent to a discussion of research and development.

Even a casual reading of the preceding chapters of this book, particularly Chapter III, should convince the doubting that in coming decades the race will not always be to the swift nor the battle to the strong. The struggle of the laboratories, the battle of the proving grounds and test stands, the conflict of the drafting rooms may well decide *today* the wars of tomorrow. For modern weapons, though still finite in range and destructiveness, have so vastly extended their scope and power that a relatively slight qualitative advantage by either side—in missile range, for instance—might well mean the difference between victory and defeat.

The struggle for *qualitative* superiority in armaments is therefore more intensified in this age than in any prior epoch in history.

This has been implicitly accepted by the general public, though with some complacency. Our development of the atomic bomb, the marvels of radar and our invention and perfection of the proximity fuse have blinded too many Americans to our own past failures in research and development. The atomic bomb, it is too easy to forget, represented chiefly a triumph of American organizational talent and production know-how; the scientific synthesis which had to precede the engineering and development work was in large measure the product of the minds of foreign-born scientists. In nearly every field of the application of science to the battlefield— that is, in research and development applied to weapons and equipment—the Germans, in the last war, were well ahead of us.[2] They should, of course, have been, for the Nazi state harnessed its energies to the preparations for war long before our nation awoke from its daydreams of eternal peace.

The Nazi accomplishments and our own demonstrated to the world the fundamental importance of science—of research, basic and applied, and of development—to military strength. The scientist, the engineer and the soldier are a modern triumvirate of national strength; in the atomic age a vigorous and well-directed weapons research and development program is vital to the national safety.

But the importance of time has not been so well understood. Basic research knows few short cuts; time is its one indispensable factor. Long before the predevelopmental weapons stage is reached hundreds of scientists and technicians must spend thousands of painstaking hours in laboratories proving, or disproving, some abstruse theory that may change the lives of us all. Time, in research, is victory.

That is why basic research with its time-consuming methods of trial and error, theory and analysis, must receive major and high priority in peace. In war applied research and development must take precedence, but in peace the broadest possible scale of inquiry is essential.

For no one knows today where tomorrow's researches may lead. The "rain makers"—not the old medicine men of the past, but physicists, who have seeded moisture-laden clouds with dry ice pellets—may even hold the key to future control of weather in their laboratories. If the experiments now being undertaken can "make" rain, a way may be found to "eat up" fog, or to eliminate the "icing up" of airplanes.

Still another graphic example of the fundamental importance

to the military art of basic research was given in 1947 by the announcement of the Sperry Gyroscope Company and the American Museum of Natural History that the common drone fly may provide a vital clue to the proper guidance of missiles. An investigation of the fly would seem to have no relation to war, but the museum, with the aid of motion pictures of the fly in flight taken at the rate of 3,000 a second, demonstrated that the fly maintains its equilibrium by a set of vibrating balancers, called *halteres*, under its wings. The Sperry company, which has been trying to develop a virtually frictionless gyroscope as a main element of the guidance system necessary for long-range supersonic missiles, seized upon this finding as a possible way out of its difficulties. The mechanics of a fly's wings may show the way to manufacture of a gyroscope with no real bearing surfaces.

While a research program, both basic and applied, has received generally enthusiastic support, the means and methods of organizing and maintaining such a sound program are not so well understood; indeed, the armed services themselves have displayed, even in the postwar period, a singular lack of comprehension of some of the basic needs of sound research.

Any technical program is, of course, fundamentally dependent for its success upon its participating personnel. Today, the United States is suffering in its military research and development program from the short-term mistakes of the war years when the draft took with catholic action the scientist and the engineer, the student and the technician. Scientific education, particularly graduate education, virtually was suspended in many major institutions during the war; we, alone of the major combatants, made this mistake. The result today is clear: in the war years the normal anticipated increase in the number of American scientists was halved.

Dr. Vannevar Bush, in *Science, the Endless Frontier*,[3] has estimated that:

The deficit of science and technology students who, but for the war, would have received bachelor's degrees is about 150,000. It is estimated that the deficit of those obtaining advanced degrees in these fields will amount in 1955 to about 17,000—for it takes at least six years from college entry to achieve a doctor's degree or its equivalent in science or engineering.

A long-term and perhaps more basic error which has had, and is still having, its effect upon quality (rather than quantity) of personnel has its roots in our educational system. Unlike the European system, our own provides no real synthesis of the technologies (and certainly none of the humanities and the technologies). A man can graduate from an American university as a good engineer, or as a good scientist, but rarely is he both; rarely do we produce engineers who understand the terms of science and view their designing problems in the wide frame of science's new horizons; rarely do we produce scientists able to reduce the general to the specific, capable of translating scientific possibilities into engineering tangibles.

Another personnel weakness, a quantitative weakness, stems in part from the increased demand, born of the technological age, for scientists and technicians in universities and in government and industrial laboratories. Our universities do not have capacities, facilities or funds to provide scientifically and technically trained personnel in the numbers needed in the modern age, and not until greatly increased private and government support is extended to such universities will they be able to answer our needs.

A fourth personnel weakness, again quantitative but an artificially induced one born of bad administrative practices, has developed since the war, and it must be laid squarely at the doors of the Army and Navy. Postwar cuts in funds for the armed forces—inevitable, necessary and desirable—at first threatened to slash the moneys directly appropriated for research and development. The importance of both basic and applied research had, however, been so tremendously impressed upon service and civilian mentality during the war that the moneys to be expended for research have not been greatly reduced; indeed, some scientists regard the current basic research appropriations (as distinguished from funds for applied research and development) as a glut on the market—too much for available skilled personnel to exploit properly. But the contracts the Navy, for instance, has made with universities and other institutions for fundamental work in various fields must be administered and supervised and co-ordinated with other contracts by the Navy

Department, and liaison must be maintained with the contracting institutions by the Navy Department. However, the financial cuts made—while scarcely affecting the contractual research moneys—have been applied "across the board" and without consideration of their ultimate effects on the personnel administering and supervising the contracts. If, for instance, the Navy was forced to accept a ten per cent over-all cut in man power, civilian and/or military, ten per cent of the personnel in the Office of Naval Research were lopped off. Though the powers-that-be in the government apparently have not yet awakened to its full significance, this represents a most shortsighted policy. The personnel cut reducing the administrative and supervisory group makes impossible that close direction which prevents unnecessary research duplication. This and other cuts—in travel allowances, telephone and telegraph expenses, etc.—have virtually eliminated in some contracts actual physical liaison between the contracting institution and the parent government agency, with an inevitable bad effect upon the morale and teamwork of both. This "penny pinching" is obviously wasteful and inefficient; it results in getting perhaps $12,000,000 worth of results out of $20,000,000 worth of research contracts.

A final personnel weakness is psychological and administrative and can be overcome only by wise adjustments. Many scientists, essentially rugged individualists, at least in their fields, are loath to work in government service under the harness of civil-service restrictions and the security regulations of the armed services. Others who can accommodate themselves to these bureaucratic conventions find it impossible psychologically or mentally to "get along" with the military mind. To some extent these difficulties have been outweighed by the relatively high pay scales with which desired technicians and scientists are being tempted to enter government service; many of the salaries and corollary inducements, such as government housing, now being offered, are considerably higher in range than those offered in academic institutions. Too often, however, these materialistic temptations have brought into government ranks, not the foremost scientists and technicians, but those who seek security. This is not, of course, a universal truism; there are many able technical men in government service. The problem will be to keep them happy and contented and yet still scientifically eager, alert and ambitious.

Such are some of the personnel weaknesses which today affect and hamper the development of a postwar weapons research and development program.

That program, organizationally, has been built upon three principal pillars.

The first pillar is a complex structure of staff and administrative agencies and research facilities within each of the three service departments—Army, Navy, and Air. The Army has established a Research and Development Group, under a general staff division, its duty to co-ordinate and correlate all military research and development within, or sponsored by, the Army. Atomic energy and special weapons boards or groups have been established. The Navy has the Office of Naval Research which is concerned primarily with basic research; each of the Navy Department's matériel bureaus has sponsored an extensive applied research and development program, and, as in the Army, officers of high rank in charge of guided missiles, special weapons and atomic energy have been appointed. The Air Force, with a slightly different organization, has a chief of special weapons and a director of research and development under the deputy chief of staff for matériel, in addition to a guided-missiles section under the deputy chief of staff for operations—a definite indication that, in Air Force opinion, guided missiles are moving out of the laboratory and proving ground into active operational use. In addition to these administrative and staff agencies each service has greatly increased its investment during the war and postwar era in laboratories, test centers, development centers and proving grounds. Wind tunnels, ballistic ranges, prodigious calculating machines, chemical, electrical and physics laboratories, some of them with the finest equipment in the world, are working hard on applied research, design and development, testing and proving. The recent improvement of these physical facilities has been major; the Naval Ordnance Laboratory at White Oak, Maryland; the naval missile test and development center at Inyokern, California; the considerable expansion of the Army's laboratories at the Chemical Center at Edgewood Arsenal, Maryland, and the Aberdeen Proving Ground, Maryland, are typical. These laboratories and development centers handle many conceivable types of problem, even some only remotely applicable to the military art; for instance, in the engineering laboratories at Fort Belvoir, Virginia, the largest synthetic crystal of its kind in the world for use in infrared ray work has been grown.[4]

The service installations are supplemented and aided by other government laboratories and facilities, notably those of the Atomic Energy Commission, and the NACA (National Advisory Committee for Aeronautics), with its wind tunnels, shops and testing grounds. A total of some forty different governmental research agencies are in operation.

The second pillar of our postwar research and development organization is extradepartmental, the Research and Development Board, an outgrowth of the "preunification" Joint Research and Development Board. The Research and Development Board is an integral part of what is now called imposingly the "National Military Establishment," which is simply the catch-all phrase applied in the so-called merger legislation of 1947 to all three of our service departments, the "super" Secretary of Defense, and all the numerous agencies and boards under him. The Research and Development Board is composed of the civilian-scientific chairman, and two representatives each from the Army, Navy and Air Force. The board's function is to advise and aid the Secretary of Defense in the formulation and proper co-ordination of "a complete and integrated program of research and development for military purposes," to formulate research policy involving agencies outside the National Military Establishment, and—a new and important role for the scientist—"to consider the interaction of research and development and strategy, and to advise the Joint Chiefs of Staff in connection therewith."

These are broad and imposing duties which involve tremendous responsibilities and establish the board, at least in theory, as a kingpin in the research and development field. It is premature to predict whether theory will be borne out in practice, for service administrators have a habit of playing the cards close to their chests and of nullifying by polite inaction directives with which they do not agree. But the experience of the preunification Joint Research and Development Board indicated clearly that there is a large interservice area where the board can function to prevent unnecessary duplication and to insure proper co-ordination of effort. There are also important extraservice duties for the board to perform—particularly the marshaling of scientific talent and the intermediary duties of service liaison with the civilian, scientific and technical world.

The success or failure of the Research and Development Board, like so many other activities of government, is going to depend fundamentally upon the personality of its chairman. The present board has a majority of service members and is answerable to the Secretary of Defense and, therefore, does not possess the favorable autonomous position of the wartime Office of Scientific Research and Development, whose chief reported directly to the President. The function of the board is, of course, somewhat different from that of the OSRD; nevertheless if it is to avoid becoming simply a "mouthpiece" for the services, the civilian chairman and the civilian scientists selected to head its committees or panels must preserve an independence of thought and action not always found in government bodies. The chairman, particularly, must be forceful and strong and yet, of course, tactful; he must "get along" with the services but he must not be dominated by them.

The Research and Development Board should be particularly useful—as its predecessor, the Joint Research and Development Board, was—in reducing unnecessary service duplication and in blueprinting carefully thought-out programs for the large-scale installations needed to prosecute properly the new research. Two of these gigantic projects already are well mapped. A tremendous wind-tunnel program for Army, Navy, Air Force and the National Advisory Committee on Aeronautics has been planned to provide the needed subsonic, transsonic and supersonic tunnels for development of the new planes and guided missiles. The overlapping and duplicating programs of the various interested agencies—formerly ridiculously expensive and unnecessary—have been reconciled and pared down to a reasonable plan. Even so, the ultimate cost of such a program, for wind tunnels and ancillary laboratories and test facilities, will probably exceed half a billion dollars. Another great project in which the Research and Development Board will play a major role is in the provision of adequate proving and test facilities for guided missiles. During and after the war many new service facilities, like Topsy, "jest growed," and there was temporarily considerable unnecessary duplication. Much of this, chiefly due to the efforts of the JRDB and its present successor, has been eliminated, and the services generally are using each other's test facilities co-operatively. But a new long-range test center where guided missiles can be fired and observed for hundreds or perhaps thousands of miles must be established, probably either in the Central Pacific or in Southern California. There is some disposition to consider this and similar test centers or proving grounds as "national" institutions, and the suggestion has been made that the Research and Development Board should operate such test centers. But the board was not organized as an administrative and operating agency, and in the interests of efficiency it is probably preferable to have some one service administer each proving ground, but for the clear and unbiased benefit of all. Careful supervision of the construction and maintenance of test and development centers by the RDB is, however, essential, for hundreds of millions of dollars already have been poured into these facilities, and probably another half billion will have to be expended for the new long-range center and additions to existing facilities *before* a single long-range guided missile is ready for mass production.

The third pillar of a sound military research and development program is a "National Science Foundation." A bill creating such an organization was passed by Congress in 1947 but was vetoed by the President because of what he considered the unsatisfactory administrative nature of the projected organization. The Foundation remains, however, of major importance to the nation's future military welfare, and the quicker it is established the sooner we may expect to compensate for our postwar shortages of scientists and technicians. The proposed National Science Foundation would, in effect, provide government subsidies to promote general basic research, "long-range" military research and scientific education. The demands in all of these fields are now greater than the capacity of private agencies to meet them; government aid is inevitable.

What is proposed is a national federal foundation, supported by government funds, administered by a director, but controlled in effect by a scientific "board of directors" who would make policy. The foundation, it has been estimated, would require an annual budget increasing from about $33,500,000 in its first year of operation to some $122,500,000 in its fifth year of life. The foundation would not operate any laboratories itself, but would sponsor with its appropriated funds general basic research in many fields—notably in medicine, the natural sciences and national defense—by grants-in-aid to research institutions. The national defense research would have the invaluable asset of being civilian-initiated and civilian-directed, as the highly successful OSRD efforts were during the war. The National Science Foundation in this and its general fields would thus prove an admirable supplement to the Research and Development Board, with its more restricted scope. The foundation could be expected in time to sponsor basic research projects which until now have been sponsored by the services (the Navy in particular), because no other government sponsoring agency possessed the requisite funds. It would work, of course, with service representation in its military division and in close liaison with the Research and Development Board and the services. One of the foundation's divisions would "support and supervise the grant of scholarships and three hundred graduate fellowships per year."

Such a National Science Foundation would thus be a powerful factor in the scientific "health" of the nation; it would in time help to remedy the personnel weaknesses, quantitative and qualitative, from which we are now suffering, and it would provide a powerful *independent* stimulus to service tactical thought and to weapons development. It would remove the major share of federal sponsorship of basic or pure research from the hands of the services, where it now is, to the hands of a civilian expert group, where it properly belongs. It is, therefore, an essential third pillar in the edifice of research security.

But it is equally clear that the tremendous postwar significance of research and development as a factor of national strength which has compelled extensive federal support of science has certain dangerous implications to our body politic, unless the federal intervention is carefully circumscribed and administered.

The great emphasis on military research and on *applicational* research can subvert science. The research contracts with private institutions and the extensive development of a network of government facilities all geared to the same end, bigger and better weapons, can minimize scientific progress in the non-military fields and might, indeed, build up a vast "vested interest" scientific empire, plainly dependent for its existence on military appropriations and hence tending to support, even to an unnecessarily large degree, those appropriations. Similarly, the projected subsidization of scientific education, coupled with other governmental educational "subsidies" poured into the colleges by Army and Navy Reserve Officers' Training programs, grants for agricultural research and the universal military training act (if passed) would make the government the largest "customer" of the colleges and universities of the nation, with all the dangers to curricula and educational freedom that implies. The emphasis on secrecy in government contracts, which hampers developmental work by overcompartmentalization and security restrictions upon the documents dealing with a project, is another danger. When scientific papers cannot be freely published, and when scientific interchange is curbed, as it is today, scientific growth is handicapped.

These are real dangers and not lightly to be ignored. Nor is it easy to meet them and at the same time to provide the indispensable minimum of federal subsidization of research essential to our national welfare. There are, however, several principles that can guide us.

First, the federal expenditures—particularly the armed-services expenditures for physical installations for research and development —ought to be complementary to *private* research and development and not competitive. They should also be restricted in physical scope and capital expenditures to the minimum consistent with efficient performance.

Second, the Research and Development Board must include a proper blend of civilian-scientific and military thought. It should not be subservient to the armed forces if it is to perform any useful function.

Third, federal subsidization of the physical sciences alone offers some long-term educational dangers, unless some comparable emphasis is devoted to strengthening our understanding of the social sciences. Because the social sciences deal with imponderables and hence are often controversial and inexact, there has been considerable hesitancy to include them within the scope of the National Science Foundation's projected program, lest ideological prejudices imperil the whole effort. This may be a sound objection, but somehow, in some way, whether it stems from government or not, we must emphasize the teachings of the humanities in our schools and encourage an understanding of society and social controls. The American culture is already in too many ways too materialistic and too physical; we must control the inventions of science or be destroyed by them.

Fourth, a National Science Foundation, under clear-cut civilian control and scientific direction, is perhaps the most important pillar of our whole postwar research edifice, primarily because of the dangers and difficulties already noted. It must have a broad view of the welfare and liberties of the people as its primary aim; it must sponsor basic research, and it must cling to that independence of concept and thought which is the keystone of any democratic educational system. Because its blueprint meets all these aims and insures a civilian guidance to basic research and scientific education, it is of major importance that the projected foundation be established and assigned funds with which to operate within the 1948 calendar year. There well may be differences about its administrative organization or the scope of its work, but there are ten basic principles which must govern it: It should:

1. Be independent of the armed services.

2. Receive its funds, in major part, directly from Congress, in minor part by transfers from the armed services.

3. Be empowered to enter into contracts with industry and academic institutions, and to administer these contracts with a minimum of red tape.

4. Be governed and administered by a policy-making board of non-governmental civilian scientists and technicians and educators, with a director under them to implement these policies.

5. Limit its activities to well-defined areas and its organization to a small number of divisions.

6. Devote a major percentage of its attention and funds to fundamental or basic research.

7. Avoid restrictive policies on the free exchange of information.

8. Work through private facilities—industry and the colleges—and not establish laboratories or facilities of its own.

9. Leave internal control of "policy, personnel, and the method and scope of the research" contracted for to the private institutions. "This is of the utmost importance."[5]

10. Have "stability of funds" over a long-term period, so that long-range research projects can be properly planned. Five- or six-year authorization measures, similar to authorization bills for naval building programs, ought to be legislated by Congress.

Under such a system and with wise direction, research and development in its broadest fields and in its narrower (but still tremendous) application to the military art can flourish without undue danger to our democratic system.

As Colonel Leslie E. Simon writes in his book, *German Research in World War II*:[6]

In peace, of all times, the wise government will foster research, especially long-range research, to build up its funds of knowledge and to prepare for the evil day when it will again have to live on its fat while doing considerable development and little research. Better yet a strong research policy may contribute to forestalling or preventing the evil day.

NOTES—Chapter X

1. *Science, the Endless Frontier,* by Dr. Vannevar Bush, U. S. Government Printing Office, Washington, D.C., 1945.

2. The Germans, strangely enough, while excelling in basic and applied research and excellent in design, were often poorly organized for actual development. For the Reich's strengths and weaknesses in research and development see a study by Colonel Leslie E. Simon, *German Research in World War II*, John Wiley & Sons, New York, 1947.

3. Dr. Vannevar Bush, *Science, The Endless Frontier,* Page 3.

4. This great synthetic crystal at Fort Belvoir was grown with the guidance and help of a German scientist, expert in this abstruse art, one of many brought to this country after the war in "Operation Paper Clip." This use of the former enemy by our government has been condemned by many of our own thin-skinned scientific men, some of whom have absolutely refused to work with the Germans. This attitude, motivated in part by professional jealousy, in part by ideological prejudices, is however, unrealistic, for the Germans filled a blank space in our knowledge—particularly in rocketry. Their major usefulness is drawing to an end, since they have been "milked dry" of their knowledge and experience, but their employment has paid the nation major dividends. Not to have utilized all available talent would have been to handicap the nation in a crucial technological era. It is noteworthy that the Russians are using far more German scientists and technicians than we are, particularly in the development of atomic energy and in submarine design, though we got the pick of the rocket scientists.

5. Dr. Vannevar Bush, *Science, The Endless Frontier.* Page 27.

6. Colonel Leslie E. Simon, *German Research in World War II.* Page 206.

CHAPTER XI

ECONOMIC MOBILIZATION

. . . battles are only a sort of public verification of mastery gained during "peace."

WILLIAM JAMES

THE big factories rather than the big battalions *were* the principal architects of victory in World War II.

The big factories rather than the big battalions *are* among the *primary* bulwarks of our military strength in this era of non-shooting war.

And the big factories rather than the big battalions *may* be the principal architects of victory in another war.

Industrial mobilization—the preparation and organization and indoctrination of American industry in time of peace for wartime duties—is still, therefore, a major element of a sound security program. But in concept, scope and time factor it differs fundamentally from the industrial mobilization of World War I, and even World War II.

In the era of total war it is no longer sufficient to think in terms of *industrial* mobilization; the term is too limited. The revised concept is *economic* mobilization, which includes as one of many items industrial preparedness. The national mobilization of man power on the home front as well as for the armed forces, price controls and rationing, export and import controls, agricultural mobilization, financial preparedness, plans for economic warfare against any enemy, industrial preparedness, stock-piling of scarce raw materials —all these are now included in the scope of the new concepts.

Thirty-five basic elements, functions and controls are involved in the modern concept of economic mobilization. They include:

1. Allocations
2. Civilian Protection
3. Communications
4. Conservation
5. Demobilization and Reconversion Planning
6. Facilities
7. Food and Agriculture
8. Foreign Economic Relations
9. Fuel
10. Housing
11. Intelligence
12. Legal and Legislative Basis for Economic Mobilization
13. Man Power
14. Materials
15. Morale
16. Over-all Co-ordination
17. Personnel for Staffing the War Organization
18. Power
19. Price Control
20. Priorities
21. Procurement and Procurement Co-ordination
22. Profit Control
23. Public Health
24. Public Opinion
25. Public Works
26. Rationing
27. Requirements—Civilian
28. Requirements—Foreign Claimant
29. Requirements—Military
30. Research and Statistics (the factual basis for policy and administrative action)
31. Security
32. Technological Progress
33. Transportation
34. Wage Control
35. War Finance

The frame of reference, in other words, includes nearly all of the elements of national strength. Economic mobilization contemplates the development in war of our maximum economic potential.

But the time factor, too, has changed. It is no longer adequate to think of industrial or economic mobilization in terms of a blueprint to be implemented at the start of crisis. Long-range air power, the atomic bomb and guided missiles have transferred the emphasis on the economic front as well as in the armed services from mobilization potential to readiness potential. The term economic *mobilization* presents, therefore, something of a study in contradictions; it must be interpreted as *including* economic *readiness*.

William Liscum Borden in his book, *There Will Be No Time*, argues effectively for economic *readiness* rather than economic *mobilization*, and stresses the obvious—that a strong military posture, an offensive posture, reduces the atomic threat to our cities and industries.

But his thesis goes much too far when, in emphasizing economic readiness, he virtually dismisses as useless economic mobilization. The "wartime weapon," he writes, "which the atomic bomb renders obsolete is not navies; it is cities and industry."[1]

Now, there is no doubt that the cities of the world huddle under a threat of death and destruction in the atomic age unparalleled in the life of man. There is no doubt that dispersion and decentralization—i.e., de-urbanization (see the next chapter)—would be the ideal answer to the clouds of warning that darken urban civilization. But to dismiss the possibility of utilizing the great energies of our urban centers and of our industry *after* war starts is dangerous dogma, which is dependent for its validity upon a prophecy which no man can make with certainty—the prophecy that the next war will be won or lost in the first few days, long before our factories could be mobilized for maximum output. Now this prediction may turn out to be true, but if it does not and we are not prepared to mobilize economically, we shall lose the war.

There will be few, therefore, who will agree with the conclusion implicit in Mr. Borden's book, that economic mobilization in the atomic age is worthless.

It is, to the contrary, more vital than ever before. Plans for economic mobilization are of tremendous importance to a democracy, particularly in the atomic age, when time may mean victory, for a democracy rarely strikes the first blow in war. In order to make sure that our advantage in vitality and dynamism is not destroyed at the very start of war, we must have time-saving plans.

The modern problem of *industrial* mobilization is to achieve a nice balance between economic readiness and economic mobilization, and in giving new emphasis to the former, to avoid insofar as possible dislocation to our economy and the further extension of federal controls which preparations for war always mean in time of peace.

It is clear that the timetable of technological development will affect the relative emphasis to be placed on "readiness" and on "mobilization." In the next decade or so, while the conventional weapons that won World War II are still in the ascendancy, we can still count heavily upon mobilizing the nation economically *after* war comes. But when intercontinental missiles come to the world we must put more emphasis upon economic readiness *prior* to the outbreak of war and less upon economic potential to be realized after war comes.

First, and most important, we must recognize and stress that we cannot achieve *complete* economic readiness, in other words we cannot fully mobilize the nation economically in time of peace, without becoming a "garrison state" economically (and probably politically and psychologically) and without eventual bankruptcy.

But there are measures which can be taken with political and economic safety which will promote our military effectiveness.

The economic *readiness* measures, which also, of course, aid economic *mobilization*, are several; some of them, however, pose major problems to a nation never heretofore used to "live" frontiers.

1. There must be an immediate formulation of our peacetime military requirements, in production terms, for long-term periods. Because of the changing technology of war and the inconstant factor of world politics, this formulation cannot be constant or forever fixed. But it can be programmed for a three- to five-year period.

This industrial "five-year" plan must take account of strategic and tactical changes caused by technological developments. In our first five-year plan, for instance, major emphasis ought to be given to heavy bombardment airplanes, but in our second five-year plan, the development of anti-aircraft weapons and of short or medium-range missiles might well shift production emphasis to anti-aircraft missiles and naval rocket-launching ships. Building programs of this nature have long been a familiar part of naval authorization bills, but Air Force and Army equipment always have been provided during peacetime on a wasteful, hand-to-mouth annual basis. It is vitally important to intelligent planning and production that three- to five-year authorization programs for *all* military equipment be initiated.

2. The long-term formulation, or blueprinting, of peacetime military requirements must be accompanied by a fixed annual production of munitions of all kinds. Economic readiness must imply a stock of modern weapons on hand and ready for use and a steady and continuing production of a definite annual quantity of the latest weapons. The amounts to be produced must be based on a progressive replacement program to prevent the obsolescence of our military equipment. Planes are outmoded rather rapidly; perhaps twenty to twenty-five per cent of our operating and active reserve planes ought to be replaced annually. Ships normally have a somewhat longer life; a ten per cent annual replacement program for naval material would seem adequate. Army equipment must also be replaced on an annual percentage basis, to be estimated as a function of the useful "life" of individual items. Rockets and rocket launchers might become obsolescent quickly and require 100 per cent replacement in any three- to five-year program, but rifles and small arms might continue to be useful in their present form for twenty years.

3. A three- or five-year production plan plus an annual production output implies, of course, certain corollary measures—the production and availability of sufficient machine tools, factory space, agricultural output, raw materials, etc. Since the amounts produced under any economic-*readiness* plan—though they must be far greater than any prior American peacetime munitions program—would be only a fraction of the potential contemplated by an economic-*mobilization* plan, these items should offer no serious technical or production problem in peacetime.

Economic mobilization is inherently a far more abstruse, intangible and difficult problem than economic readiness, for the latter, though highly important, is only a part of the former. Our past experience with industrial-mobilization plans showed they suffered from some major defects. They were primarily detailed blueprints, which were probably basically sound in organization and in many policies and procedures, but were too narrow in scope and lacking in vision. They failed completely to present a realistic picture of our military requirements and were somewhat too inflexible to permit quick change. The industrial-mobilization plan of pre-World War II had little relation, in its estimates of needs, to the military realities of the war as they actually developed, or to our ability to produce munitions. Some authorities believe that military stubbornness in adhering to the plan's greatly understated estimates of requirements cost the country six months to a year of time in developing our production potential to the maximum.

There were other blind spots in the prewar plan, but it is probably true that if the President had adhered in 1939 or 1940 to the basic skeletal organization blueprinted by the plan, our transition from peace to war in World War II would have been smoother.

The requirements for sound economic mobilization in the future —i.e., for planning and developing means and methods of harnessing as rapidly as possible the total economic strength of the nation to the cause of victory—are many and complex.

1. The A1 priority is the detailed integration of economic-mobilization planning with strategic planning. This always has been hampered by the ultra secrecy of those officers who are charged with the duties of preparing war plans and the traditional reluctance of the military mind to share official secrets with civilians. Yet no realistic economic-mobilization plan can be made, for that matter no reasonable strategic plan can be made, unless both are made together. For instance, in the postwar period "A-3," or the officer charged with development of war plans for the Air Staff, has predicated certain air operations some weeks or months after the outbreak of a future war upon an aircraft-production schedule which bears no relation to actuality. In other words, the strategic planners have assumed the production in a given period of numbers of aircraft which our industrial planners say it would be impossible to produce in any such period. This Alice-in-Wonderland mentality has long befogged the economic-mobilization picture. The first and fundamental requirement in economic mobilization, therefore, is a wedding between economic planning and strategic planning, between requirements and production.

2. "It is better to plan too big than too little," in the words of Stacy May. All the resources of national power must be tapped in any future war; a mobilization plan that, like the last war's plan, is restricted in scope and vision is worse than no plan at all.

3. *Military* economic mobilization is only one phase of the total problem of economic mobilization. A National Service Act controlling and directing the allocation of labor may, for instance, be a fundamental requirement in the next war. Civilian economic mobilization is fully as important as plans and policies designed to provide equipment, food, etc., for the armed forces. Too much emphasis on munitions production at the expense of shelter or protective equipment for the "home front"[2] might cost us the next war.

4. Civilian, not military, control must guide economic mobilization in war and *in peace*. This does not mean the exclusion of the military from economic mobilization; no plan that does not include the military and give great weight to their programs, policies and opinions will work. The military must have a big voice in the "what, when and where" of the program; the civilian must decide "how." In the strictest sense economic mobilization is the product of civilian and military teamwork. But in the final analysis the civilian must predominate. This is not only because of the primary importance of the home front in any future war and the great importance of meeting at least minimum civilian needs, but also because the civilian by training and knowledge is better equipped to cope with economic and industrial problems than a military man. Civilian authority must be dominant in this, above all other, fields of war preparation, because economic readiness and economic mobilization touch at least the periphery of every phase of national life, and democracy is built upon the fundamental principle of civilian supremacy. Donald M. Nelson, head of the War Production Board, in his book, *Arsenal of Democracy*,[3] stresses this great lesson of World War II: "The lesson taught by these recent war years is clear: our whole economic and social system will be imperiled if it is controlled by the military men."

5. Any economic-mobilization plan must be as flexible as possible and must provide the greatest possible autonomy, in plans and execution, for industry, labor, agriculture, etc. The fewer controls the better, but, given total and atomic war, controls are bound to be many. They must be effective, and they must be flexible, and there must be a certain degree of centralization of authority. But under this centralized authority responsibility should be delegated and operations decentralized to the fullest possible extent. Dr. Albert

Speer, the production genius of the Nazi regime, is a living witness of the mistake of overcentralization of authority in bureaucracy. Until he took power, German industry was muscle-bound by red tape; he revivified it, fortunately too late. Decentralization and flexibility mean, it should be needless to say, competitive, privately owned industries rather than government-run or government-subsidized industries. It has been suggested that the aircraft industry ought to be subsidized. But there should be no subsidy other than the military budget; we must provide funds to procure enough military aircraft, but the industry itself must be privately owned. This is a "must" for any sound economic mobilization.

6. The total-requirements program for any economic-mobilization plan must be reconciled carefully under civilian direction with the available national resources. This "matching" of total requirements against total resources must be detailed and periodic, for technological developments will create constantly changing requirements in raw materials.

7. Any sound economic-mobilization plan must consider the national welfare *in peace* and in war. Past plans or the execution of them have been geared too much to the single concept of military victory, without sufficient consideration of "winning the peace." If we strip ourselves completely of our resources, military victory may have little meaning.

Such are some of the general principles which must govern the development of a sound economic-mobilization plan.

There are many policies which must be implemented to carry these principles into execution.

In addition to the factories constantly producing war materials in peacetime to implement our *economic-readiness* program there must be a minimum number of government-owned "stand-by" plants, either idle or devoted to other purposes in peacetime, but instantly ready to commence military production at the start of crisis. These plants and others must have machine tools. Such a program already has been implemented in part by congressional action, and there are now available to the Air Force, for instance, some nine "stand-by" factories and facilities and 40,000 machine tools in storage, ready for future use.

Still another way of minimizing the time between crisis and maximum output—which was, in World War II, more than two years after our entry into the war despite the preparatory period from 1939 to 1941—is by allocation of "educational" and service orders to factories not ordinarily engaged in peacetime military production, but certain to be utilized when war comes. This technique involves the placing of orders, in some cases fairly large ones, with widely distributed firms as new equipment and new weapons are devised. Such orders tend to "iron out" the production "bugs" and to accustom the firm to the peculiar problems of producing the latest-type equipment.

Another technique, new to this era, is the production with each service order of detailed blueprints in duplicate, triplicate, or in any numbers required, for use by plants other than the parent plant in case of war. This technique is particularly important in the case of planes or missiles and could save many months' time. The Martin company, for instance, would be required, if it received an order for 100 new planes of a type needed in mass production if war should come during that plane's anticipated lifetime, to produce also enough blueprints to enable other firms to build the plane. This technique implies, of course, a fixed percentage of increase in cost for each service order—from $5,000,000 to perhaps $25,000,000 for blueprints alone, blueprints which might never be used. This seems wasteful but is actually one of the "insurance" penalties we must pay to win time in the age when time is life.

A similar but more restricted technique can be applied to new machine tools. A certain additional number of these might be purchased by the government with each service order. Mass-production machine tools often differ not only in numbers but in type from those used for the normal small orders of peacetime. No contractor, therefore, could possibly absorb the expense of purchasing mass-production machine tools unless he received mass orders, which he would probably never receive in peacetime. The alternative is for the government to pay the extra amount needed to purchase these tools; in other words to pay higher prices for each individual airplane.

Stock-piling of essential raw materials and commodities of which we have an insufficient supply is now an accepted government policy. The so-called "strategic" raw materials vital to war must be accumulated by the government in time of peace. A detailed program, well started since World War II, has been worked out by the Munitions Board of the National Military Establishment and implemented by Treasury buying. The complexities of this program, however, are major, since government buying, particularly of scarce raw materials, can affect national and international economies and can cause artificial scarcities. Moreover, some raw materials have limited storage lives; certain stock piles must be renewed periodically. Asbestos, normally stored in burlap bags, can become contaminated and virtually useless by rotting and deterioration of the bags. Iodine in storage can become contaminated or large losses can occur through sublimation. Tin must be stored in heated warehouses. Special packaging is required for quinine. Rubber deteriorates rapidly under improper storage conditions. Some stock piles have a life of only one year; that is, they must be "rotated" or renewed every year; some others have life cycles of two to ten years.[4]

Stock-piling also presents major domestic and international political problems, as well as technical and economic ones. For stock-piling must dovetail with conservation practices; for instance, it is certainly to our interest to tap new sources of foreign oil and foreign minerals and to conserve reasonably our own domestic resources. But the search for minerals requires a capital risk which private companies can scarcely be expected to undertake unless assured of government interest and some government support. Our whole economy and our whole future depend on a continuous flow of resources, and the material resources of the country have been somewhat depleted. The exploitation of foreign sources is, therefore, vital. Prospectors must have some support from the State Department, something which they have not always received in the past. The "confidence factor" in business risk plays a major part in development, and there can be no "confidence" in foreign investments without some government interest. For the foreseeable future the United States will be exporting more than it can possibly import. This trade differential cannot be balanced, and hence world economic dislocation will result, unless imports are increased or U.S. capital is exported; in other words, unless American investments are made abroad. But today the biggest deterrent to such investments is the lack of "confidence"—of fear that the investment will not be properly protected. U.S. investments abroad, particularly in the form of capital investments for development of new raw-material sources, must be supported and encouraged by our government.

In view of the nation's, and the world's depleted mineral resources, stock-piling and conservation measures represent one of the most important elements of a sound economic-mobilization plan. It has been estimated officially that $2,100,000,000 would be required over a five- or six-year period for purchasing and stock-piling scarce minerals or commodities. Of this amount $300,000,000 would be provided by transfer of surplus property to the nation's strategic stock piles. Of the balance of $1,800,000,000, Congress has appropriated in the first three postwar fiscal years only $275,000,000, a dangerously small proportion of our needs. Moreover, the economic isolationists and "America-firsters" in Congress forced the insertion in the latest stock-piling legislation of a "Buy American" clause which virtually forces the purchase in this country of raw materials whenever they are available (even if dangerously depleted), thus defeating the intent of the legislation, which was to build up our over-all reserves.[5]

Stock-piling and conservation are too important to be political footballs.

United States has never had a long-range mineral policy. . . . United States has been the most wasteful nation in the world in its mineral exploitation. Since we have frequently destroyed the best we must conserve what still remains, which implies a working conservation policy which has as its basis the most efficient production and utilization of minerals which can be employed to meet present-day demands. . . . We have developed an almost unlimited demand for minerals. If we are to supply the needs of our country a sound over-all mineral policy is a necessity.[6]

The development of a sound mineral policy and of a stock-piling and conservation policy is an extremely complex problem. Recently, for instance, we have been importing the bulk of our manganese from Russia, obviously not a desirable long-term political or military policy. But if we are to provide alternative sources, we must consider the political and financial and military practicability and desirability of: (1) providing capital, probably government capital on Brazil's terms, for the exploitation of Brazilian sources of manganese; (2) providing a loan, either by government, private capital or some other agency like the Export-Import Bank, for the rehabilitation of the railroads in Africa and India, so that manganese normally drawn from these areas could be transported to seaports.

No general rule, except one, can be formulated to cover all stock-piling and conservation measures, for each specific item and each specific case presents vastly different problems. The one rule is that all such measures must be under civilian control (though military advice must, of course, be available), and all programs must be shaped and fashioned with the aid of civilian advisory committees (for each commodity) formed from the leading experts of both production and consumer industries. This is basic, for stock-piling and conservation affect the nation's entire economy and the civilian's interests. The civilian expert, moreover, is better equipped by virtue of his specialized knowledge to direct such a program, and *civilian*, instead of *military*, direction would assure greater public acceptance.

Economic mobilization must also arrange for combined or co-ordinated procurement to prevent competitive orders or unnecessary duplications by the services or by civilian agencies.

It must study the best means of reducing the vulnerability of our factories and transportation networks to the atomic bomb, and it must continue the dispersion and underground-facilities studies (discussed in the next chapter) already started by the Munitions Board.

Proper economic mobilization must take account, sooner or later, of the problem of conserving, perhaps of monopolizing, our technical "know-how." Until recently technical processes and production "know-how" at which Americans excel have been virtually free for the asking to any foreigners; even today we are teaching many Russians processes which they could not learn elsewhere. This technical knowledge is the warp and woof of our military strength; it is, indeed, shortsighted to permit its "export" without some equivalent exchange. Some export controls on materiels exist, but so far slight attention has been given by the government to the export of technical knowledge. We must avoid lowering a complete "American iron curtain," but U.S. firms are entitled to some guidance from the Department of Commerce and the State Department when they are confronted with requests to train foreigners in their factories, and the State Department, in turn, might well consider such requests on a reciprocal basis.

Finally, the education of the services, particularly of the air services, to sound principles of economic mobilization and the revision of their staff and administrative economic-mobilization organizations are imperative. Too much lip service and too little action have been given in the postwar period to economic mobilization, and the air services, at least, have been jealous of too much civilian influence. Military equipment and particularly military aircraft must be designed with more thought to mass production; in 1947, Wright Field and the Air Materiel Command in evaluating new designs were assigning only fifty points out of 1,000 to the producibility of the design. As a result aircraft like the giant B-36 could not be mass-produced in major quantities without unnecessarily great expenditures and frightening delays. In the case of the B-36 it has been estimated officially that $120,000,000 for redesigning, re-engineering, tooling, etc., and three years' time would be required to *prepare* to produce this plane at the rate of 100 a month. Even more important is the growth of military "vested interest" in the planning of economic mobilization. H. H. Rosenheim, former director of the Industrial Preparedness Staff of the Air Materiel Command, testified in late 1947 before the President's Air Policy Commission that:

. . . not a single industrial advisory committee has been created by the Air Force for the tremendous job of mobilizing one third of this nation's industrial capacity [the estimated amount needed to support our air forces in war], nor is one single representative of industry now on duty in a responsible capacity either at Air Force Headquarters or at the Command responsible for industrial mobilization—Air Materiel Command at Wright Field. Instead, progress has been brought to a standstill by volume assignment of numerous non-industrial officer personnel whose record and attitude is one of industry exclusion and who have steadfastly rejected the lessons of the pre-World War II period when militarization of industrial preparedness created basic and enduring shortcomings in the nation's air defense structure.

As Mr. Rosenheim pointed out, sound economic mobilization can be planned only by maximum utilization of industrial and other civilian experts, and the Air Force and the Army and Navy must utilize industry advisory committees and civilian or reserve-officer experts to the maximum.

Such are some of the multifold principles, policies and problems of economic mobilization. Unfortunately the principles represent an ideal not easily achieved; unfortunately, too, some of our military leaders lend lip service, but little else, to these principles.

There are today three major agencies which deal with economic readiness and economic mobilization.

The "superagency" which may possibly perform in the next war the functions of the War Production Board, the War Manpower Commission and other government agencies of the last war is the new National Security Resources Board, which is essentially a non-military board. This board, headed by a civilian chairman, utilizes during peace "to the maximum extent" the facilities of other departments and agencies of government, and in peacetime may therefore remain chiefly a "shadow" agency or skeletal structure. It is charged specifically with advising the President "concerning the co-ordination of military, industrial, and civilian mobilization." Its duties, theoretically at least, include planning for the *civilian* aspects of industrial mobilization and co-ordination of all economic-mobilization matters *outside* the National Military Establishment.

As such, it must enlist the planning aid of industry, labor, agriculture and the public; indeed, the National Security Resources Board might well charge the representatives of these segments of national life with primary responsibility for development of detailed plans for the administration of various programs involved in economic mobilization.

The National Security Resources Board, judging from its legislative fiat, is essentially a peacetime planning board, with advisory powers. Yet it was envisaged, in the minds of the men who helped to establish it, as a skeletal planning agency in peacetime which could well be expanded in wartime into the superagencies of the last war, such as the Office of War Mobilization, the War Production Board, War Manpower Commission, etc. There is no certainty, however, that it would so serve as a skeletal structure for wartime expansion; indeed, one of its peacetime jobs is to determine the best type of wartime organization, and in any case the political philosophy and administrative bent of the then wartime President would determine, as it did in the last war, the type of organization that would evolve.

The Munitions Board, second of the great economic mobilization agencies and outgrowth of the former Joint Army and Navy Munitions Board, is composed of a civilian chairman and an assistant secretary or undersecretary from each of the three service departments. Its duties include the co-ordination, *"within the National Military Establishment,"* of industrial matters, including "procurement, production and distribution" (in peace and in war), and planning for the *"military* aspects of industrial mobilization."

The Industrial College of the Armed Forces aids, and co-operates with, the other two agencies and teaches the theory and practice of economic mobilization to Army, Navy and Air Force students. It has been instrumental in working out the details of an economic-mobilization plan, but its greatest usefulness lies in "selling" economic mobilization to armed services not yet fully convinced of its practical utility. Each service also maintains as part of its staff or administrative organization various offices having to do with industrial mobilization.

This organization seems good in theory but is open to several great dangers in practice. Since the National Security Resources Board is to some extent a *"shadow"* and planning organization in peacetime, the *Munitions Board may tend to become the dominant agency* in economic mobilization. The functions of the two somewhat overlap, responsibilities seem to be split, and there is ample room in the legislation establishing them for basic conflict. The National Security Resources Board, which is *outside* the National Military Establishment, got its first lease on life with the passage of the National Security Act of 1947, whereas the Munitions Board, a *part* of the National Military Establishment, had a long history of wartime and prewar service, in the form of the Joint Army and Navy Munitions Board. These facts handicapped the National Security Resources Board in its initial assertion of authority, and a tendency of Army officials to side, in 1947, with the Munitions Board at the expense of the NSRB also helped to reduce the latter's authority. These differences have, however, been reconciled, at least partially and temporarily, but danger of a split still exists when a new presidential administration takes office. Indeed, the great danger to sound economic mobilization is conflict in peace and in

war between military and civilian for economic control. Such a
conflict between the old Army and Navy Munitions Board and the
War Production Board characterized much of our economic war
effort in World War II. Though Donald Nelson eventually won
this battle, military influence was in some phases of it dangerously
dominant. The creation of the new agencies has not completely
eliminated this danger, although a recent executive order, defining
the functions of these agencies if endorsed by future Presidents,
seems to give the overriding authority to the National Security
Resources Board.

There is no doubt that the National Security Resources Board,
not the Munitions Board, should be in charge of the formulation of
an over-all economic-mobilization plan, since such a plan transcends
the military services. The Munitions Board has a major job to do
in preparing and keeping up to date a clear statement of military
requirements, plotted against the estimated time (after Mobilization
Day) that they will be needed; it has also the difficult task of co-
ordinating procurement and production among the armed services.
The larger job of reconciling military and civilian requirements,
and of determining how both can best be met, belongs to the
National Security Resources Board. The Resources Board may well
find that, in the interests of flexibility, it will be unwise to spell out
economic mobilization in too great detail. A specific catalog of our
basic resources, such as available raw-material reserves, productive
capacities, transportation facilities, etc., is the first essential; if the
estimated military and civilian requirements exceed these resources
the plan obviously must be changed. A general organizational
pattern to cover the economic administration of a war also can be
developed. But the fundamental requisite for a successful plan is
a clear statement of estimated military requirements keyed to
strategic and mobilization plans; the National Security Resources
Board must insist upon the compilation of such a statement by the
Munitions Board, and upon its periodic revision.

A second major element of economic-mobilization planning is
the preparation of statutes and enabling legislation, such as price-
control laws, contractual legislation, etc., "packaged," considered
and the t's crossed and i's dotted, ready "on the shelf" for enact-
ment at start of war or emergency. The National Security Resources Board may find that one of its important functions is the

gradual preparation of this legislation. Congress might even be asked to approve these laws, with an "if and when" safeguard, in peacetime, and then all of them could be implemented quickly when war came. This process, though advocated by our high military planners, may be too precise and too detailed; time changes might invalidate many of the laws, and prepassage by Congress might carry with it certain dangers to democracy. But a general draft of necessary mobilization legislation certainly can and must be prepared in peacetime.

The National Security Resources Board, the Munitions Board, and the Industrial College of the Armed Forces are merely the top-drawer mobilization agencies; they can blueprint an economic-mobilization plan in broad organizational strokes and can lay down basic principles and policies. But the actual executing agencies (in peacetime) are the services themselves, and the efficiency of economic mobilization depends fundamentally upon how well the services adhere to basic principles. The Army, particularly Army Ordnance, which is the real "father" of modern industrial mobilization, has learned its lesson well, and the surface navy also has learned through bitter experience. Both are well organized to take advantage of the talent and ability of industry through the Army (or American) Ordnance Association and the Navy Industrial Association. But the U. S. Air Force in particular and the Navy's air arm have lent chiefly lip service to economic mobilization. In staff work and administration, economic mobilization has been relegated to a subordinate agency of current procurement—a profound mistake, and the "pilot" psychology of the flying services, which considers a "hot" plane as the first requirement, has given far too little attention to producibility.

There is a final and major weakness, and that is the public apathy about the importance of economic mobilization, not only as a weapon of military victory, but to the lives of each of us. Our economic strength won World War II; it remains the greatest element of our strength today. Yet the speed and range of modern weapons can reduce the importance of this potential unless we create a plan to utilize it as rapidly as possible. In other words we must reduce the more than two years it took us, after Pearl Harbor, to reach maximum production. We must fulfill, as a former Army officer has written, three basic conditions if we are to hope for victory in any future war:

"(1) An intelligence organization that can bring us warning of impending aggression.

"(2) A degree of national realism that will permit us to start all-out mobilization when such warning is received.

"(3) Ability to mobilize our resources in an absolute minimum of time."

These conditions for a reasonable security can be met only with public support. Public support can be enlisted for economic mobilization, not only by a proper public-relations policy which will keep the planning and its importance actively before the public, but by full and energetic participation in economic planning by qualified representatives of industry, labor, agriculture and the public chosen for their ability and their public influence.

Economic mobilization is an undramatic, dry-as-dust subject, little considered by the average citizen. But it must have public interest and public support, for it holds the key to future victory, and it can affect more basically than any other security measure the lives and liberties of all of us.

Notes—Chapter XI

1. *There Will Be No Time*; *The Revolution in Strategy*, by William Liscum Borden, the Macmillan Company, New York, Page 110.

2. The term "home front" is deliberately used in this and other chapters as a simplification of the more correct term, "civilian economy." It is recognized that the next war might possibly be fought in the continental United States and that it would thus be difficult to distinguish between the military "front" and the "home front" or between military economy and civilian economy. The two, in any case, are so interrelated and interlocked in modern war that it is difficult, if not impossible, to differentiate between them.

3. *The Arsenal of Democracy*, by Donald M. Nelson, Harcourt, Brace & Company, New York.

4. See *Raw Materials in War and Peace*, Associates in International Relations, Department of Social Sciences, United States Military Academy Printing Office, West Point, 1947. See also Appendix VI.

5. Ibid., pages 134 and 135: "Unfortunately, the influence of powerful pressure groups was strong enough to prevent the elimination of the 'Buy American' clause which vitiated the 1939 Act and which now reappears in Public Act 520. That clause in effect prevents the addition to the nation's over-all reserves (including stocks held above ground by government and private

industry) of a single ounce of the wanted materials unless specific stock-piling purchases from domestic producers are determined to be 'inconsistent with the public interest' or unreasonable in cost. In effect, the 'Buy American' clause places the burden of proof on the government whenever it desires to buy abroad a single ounce of scarce material for its stock piles so long as it is available in any quantity, however small, from domestic producers. Obviously, no such state of affairs could continue if the nation's citizenry understood the situation. Until it does understand, ignorance and complacency must continue to stand in the way of our taking out this minimum insurance of national security."

6. "Some Aspects of the United States Mineral Self-Sufficiency," by E. Willard Miller, *Economic Geography*, April 1947. Pages 83 and 84.

CHAPTER XII

DISPERSION AND DECENTRALIZATION
—UNDERGROUND SITES

"Dig, Son, Dig!"[1]

MODERN man, wrote Norman Cousins, is obsolete.

This grim commentary upon the atomic age has particular applicability to the crowning manifestation of modern man's society —his cities. The clustered buildings and congested areas of our great cities are natural "area" targets of immense vulnerability for all the mass killers of the age—atom bombs, guided missiles, radioactive dusts, gases and biological agents. No possible program of defense can protect our cities completely against one, much less all, of these mass methods of destruction. Only a strong offense— military forces of great strength instantly ready to strike an aggressor with missiles, atomic bombs and mass killers—may possibly discourage the use of such weapons against us, or, if used, may attract some of the attacks away from our cities to our military installations.

Yet the national responsibility for optimum atomic-age security cannot rest with the provision of such an offensive force. Failure to protect our cities, our people, our industries, our transportation and communication systems and our government as fully as possible against mass attack would invite attack. And if 40,000,000 Americans were to be killed overnight in a sudden atomic attack, as some scientists have predicted, the effectiveness of our own military retaliation would be of small consequence to a prostrate America, and "victory," even if achieved, would also spell defeat.

"Passive"[2] defensive measures for the home front are, therefore, of far greater importance in the atomic age than they were in

World War II, when they enabled both sides to withstand bombardments unprecedented in the history of war.[3]

There are five major types of "targets" on the home front, the vulnerability of which to atomic bombs and other mass agents of destruction must be reduced as much as possible. These are: cities; people; industries and power plants; transportation and communication systems, and government. Many of these "targets" overlap and coincide; Washington, for instance, a great city, houses hundreds of thousands of people; is the site of our national government; is an important communications and (less important) transportation center; and contains some industry. Some measures taken to protect one target automatically, therefore, help to protect other types of targets, but some defensive measures, most efficacious for some purposes—evacuation, for instance—would, if injudiciously accomplished, handicap the nation's war effort. In general, there are only two methods that promise a passive defensive answer to the atomic bomb—dispersion and digging.

Consider, first, the problem of our cities. There are some 200 cities in the United States with populations of more than 50,000 persons. A modest "guestimate" of the cost of decentralizing these urban areas, and of breaking them up into dispersed towns of no more than 50,000 persons each, is about $300,000,000,000. Such "de-urbanization" would mean, of course, a basic change in our entire social, economic and political system; the enormous implications of it stagger the imagination. To be executed effectively such a plan would require the endowment of government with powers of compulsion so enormous that the "garrison state" would no longer be a figure of speech. The political, economic and psychological problems of such a measure are so major that forced and compulsory de-urbanization can safely be termed "impossible," at least in peacetime.

But there are measures short of this Draconian step which can promote a gradual decentralization, while avoiding the social revolution implicit in de-urbanization. Many cities, for instance, have adopted forward-looking city-planning projects. Proper slum-clearance programs, zoning laws to restrict the numbers of apartment houses or businesses in a given area; establishments of suburban "green belts" with peripheral housing developments as girdles of extra space around our cities; new urban arterial highways—all these plans, already initiated in many cities, tend to disperse and decentralize. Such programs should be aided and expedited by federal funds.

Other intra-urban measures that would materially reduce a town's vulnerability have been emphasized by the Strategic Bombing Survey in its report of the atomic bombing of Hiroshima and Nagasaki. In most American cities frame-, brick-and-mortar- and stucco-type constructions predominate; yet the survey found that earthquake-type construction—steel girders and concrete—was the only type that met fairly satisfactorily the blast of the atomic bomb. Such construction can be provided at an estimated 15 per cent increase in cost. City building codes can, and should, be changed to require this type of construction on all future building in those urban areas most densely populated by business and homes.

Decentralization of city administrative, hospital, police and fire-fighting facilities is also possible and highly important, the Strategic Bombing Survey found. In Japan the atomic bombs destroyed most of these facilities in the two cities bombed because they were all clustered in the centers of the cities. Most city government departments are centrally located in congested areas; most hospitals and most fire stations are similarly located. A gradual program to disperse and decentralize these facilities and to duplicate and disperse the power stations upon which they in turn depend could be carried out over a ten-year period without excessive costs. Such dispersion would be socially useful and economically helpful[4] and, if atomic bombs were ever employed, would prevent the administrative crippling of a city and would localize damages and reduce casualties.

Cities—for their own self-protection, and also for the protection of military targets—*must* rid themselves, as far as possible, of the military installations that have grown up in many of them. These installations make a city a doubly inviting military target and enable the enemy to "kill two birds with one stone"—wreaking havoc alike upon both military and home front. Dispersion insofar as possible of the military installations to other non-urban areas would at once render those installations more safe than they could possibly be in the heart of a city and would at the same time tend to divert the enemy's attacks from the cities to the military installations. In Washington, for instance, the Navy Yard manufactures not only many of the Navy's guns but numerous items of confidential ordnance equipment important to all the services. In New York, the Navy Yard, vital for ship repair and overhaul, is compressed in the most congested heart of the city. Even military airfields, like New York's Floyd Bennett, are within the limits of many great cities. To remove all of these installations beyond urban areas is economically impossible and not feasible from the point of view of industrial support and maintenance, communications and transportation, but some of them can be removed, and a government program for such transference ought to be undertaken.

The cities of America must also band together for mutual interurban help and protection if their vulnerability in the atomic age is to be reduced materially. Atomic catastrophe, for instance, can mean fires so great that the fire department of one city would be helpless to cope with them. The fire-fighting apparatus of Newark, Paterson, Garden City, White Plains, and of surrounding communities as far away as Albany and Philadelphia might be needed, if an atomic bomb were to be dropped on New York. But today many of these pumping engines would be helpless, for there is no standard gauge for fire-hydrant outlets in the United States; hose lines, couplings and connections are of many different sizes. A program of standardization in this and numerous other items should be initiated.

Gradual decentralization is thus not only practical; it has the validity of economic approval. Tremendous cities are today uneconomical. The reasons which once compelled urban concentration are no longer valid, with arterial express highways and other improvements in communications and transportation. Urban living could be cheaper, healthier and more efficient if the great cities were "spread out."

But cities are only shells; the life that pulses in their veins is human. The peoples of America—their bodies, their minds, their hearts—are the most important targets of the atomic bomb. Mass casualties, numbered in the scores of millions, would almost certainly mean defeat and would make military "victory," even if achieved, an exercise in semantics.

Dispersion and digging are the only adequate means of passive protection for human beings in the atomic age. There is no safety in numbers today; indeed numbers invite attack. But complete peacetime dispersion of big city populations to small units is, we have seen, impossible. However, plans for extensive wartime or immediate prewar evacuation—possibly compulsory evacuation—of all *non-essential* urban dwellers are not only possible but imperative. Evacuation was utilized during World War II; it can be developed to a far higher degree now in time of peace. It would require government support—perhaps the conversion of existing unused Army barracks for shelter for the evacuated, perhaps the construction of new quarters. It would require intricate transportation and train scheduling to avoid interference with military movements. It would involve detailed planning and considerable expense. But evacuation plans for every major American city are an atomic-age "must."

Gradual dispersion of population in peacetime can be encouraged by government-sponsored economic and social measures. The trend toward urbanization in this country—a product of the industrial age—can and must be reversed. Many large businesses, attempting to avoid the congestion and expense of the great cities and seeking lower-cost areas and new labor markets, have chosen small towns or even semirural sites for their new postwar building projects, and this "flight of the factories" tends to some extent to draw population after it. No "back-to-the-farm" movement is, however, discernible today; the trend is still in the other direction. American agriculture does not really need more workers, and we must avoid simply transferring our slums from cities to poverty-stricken rural areas. Stringent city zoning laws, limitations on city relief rolls, and, no matter how reluctantly, immigration regulations must be invoked. Many immigrants, probably most, tend to settle in cities; entry conditions may have to be modified to require their settlement in towns under a certain size or in rural areas. The present influx into New York City of Puerto Ricans, who are citizens of the United States and upon whom no immigration checks are possible, ought to be restricted by city authorities, or by special federal or state action, if municipal laws prove inadequate. The concentration in crowded, congested, disease-ridden slums of hundreds of thousands of poverty-stricken peoples, many of them depressed and ill, adds immeasurably to the vulnerability of New York or of any city in the age of the atomic bomb and of biological warfare. Plagues started in such focal points of infection would spread like wildfire, and congested, depressed hordes of the foreign-born, speaking no English, strangers in their own cities, are panic centers—a danger to themselves and to all their city neighbors. Elimination of these depressed, congested areas is vital, but this cannot be accomplished if a continuous influx of new arrivals presses always into the cities' gates. There are definite dangers to democracy in attempting to dam up or restrict the free settlement of any citizen or even of any immigrant, yet, in the interests of the whole, zoning and health laws and other local ordinances should be invoked, tightened, broadened and enforced to prohibit undue concentration of population and to encourage dispersion.

As the Strategic Bombing Survey has recommended, a program of experimental personnel shelters should be started immediately. Shelters at Hiroshima and Nagasaki—even those directly beneath the bomb's bursting point—protected their occupants efficiently against blast, heat and radioactivity. It would be far more difficult, indeed quite impossible, to provide 100 per cent protection against gas, radioactive dusts and biological poisons, but filtering and air-conditioning apparatus, proper sanitation and decontamination measures, and construction of the proper type of shelters would certainly greatly reduce casualties, and those that did occur could be more adequately cared for by the decentralized system of hospitals which the new cities of America must provide. Tests of various types of underground structures already have been started under the supervision of the Army engineers and private contractors. A far more extensive experimental program is needed, to be followed in time by the actual erection in the principal American cities of a system of shelters, which, for optimum efficiency, could also double in peacetime as garages, business centers or other socially useful projects. The minimization of human casualties on the vulnerable home front, horrible enough no matter what is done if mass killers are ever used, must be one of the primary aims of any postwar security policy. For in our system of government people make war and peace, people make policy, and if the will of a people is broken a war can be lost.

The protection of populations must also contemplate the protection of the water supplies of a people. Some urban watersheds are peculiarly vulnerable to contamination, and biological warfare poses tremendous threats. New water-supply systems should be studied and purification systems devised.

Finally, peoples can—and must—learn to protect themselves. The basis of this self-protection must be organization and training. All of the municipal, state and federal agencies which normally have to do with public utilities and public welfare—water supply, gas and electricity, sewerage, garbage disposal, hospitals, welfare and relief, transportation, Red Cross, etc., etc.—must be tied together in one co-ordinated and integrated civilian home-front defense scheme. The military must have a part in such organization, for military order and discipline will be essential if catastrophe should come, in police work, fire fighting, etc., and because in certain areas martial law might be esssential. Above all, the steadying quality of discipline—military discipline—is essential to quell panic, the panic which might result, not solely from atomic catastrophe itself, but from fear of impending attack. The dominating pattern of home-front municipal defense must, however, be civilian; not only because democracy requires it, but because soldiers are not trained to run cities, collect garbage, or conduct the manifold housekeeping duties of emergency.

The reduction of the vulnerability of our factories, industrial areas and power plants to atomic bombing, missile attack and mass agents of destruction is vital to economic mobilization, as a previous chapter has stressed. Again, the only foreseeable passive defense is dispersion and digging.

Actually, a considerable degree of natural economic industrial dispersion already has been accomplished in the United States. It is fashionable to speak in somewhat contemptuous terms of the "vulnerable concentration" of the "vital" segment of our industry in the northeastern part of the United States. But this is an over-simplification which gives a fallacious picture of a concentration more apparent than real. The northeastern section of the United States is an enormous region—one-fifth the size of all of Europe; it could not possibly be blanketed by atomic bombs. In 1939 it was true that of an industrial plant valued at about $39,558,000,000, more than 70 per cent was located in the New England, Middle Atlantic and East North Central States. However, in the war years of 1940–45 we added the stupendous total of $25,158,000,000 in plant facilities, and of this amount probably less than 50 per cent was built in the same regions. Noteworthy was the growth of the West South Central States as an industrial region. Industrialists have reported, moreover, in the postwar era the spontaneous tendency of industry to "drift away" from large urban centers; the avowed policy of some large firms like Procter & Gamble and General Motors is to choose relatively small cities as sites for the establishment of new plants. There has occurred, therefore, and is occurring, a natural tendency toward industrial dispersion. This must be encouraged, fostered and promoted by government; industries with military contracts—particularly the new plants that may have to be built to supply the new weapons and equipment—must be required, as part of those contracts, to build in small cities or rural areas of the government's own choosing.

These contracts for new facilities might also require the construction of several relatively small duplicate installations rather than single large ones. Each of these new installations must be provided with its own sources of emergency power, its own stock pile of materials and supplies, and each should be made as self-sufficient as possible.

Decentralization of industry, which also means decentralization of cities, can be encourage by (1) fostering the migration of industries from the centers of cities to their peripheries; and (2) by establishing new manufacturing plants in the heart of rural areas. The latter, exemplified by the transference of New England cotton mills to North Carolina, is the most useful and valuable method—both economically and militarily.

Some manufacturing plants—notably those that are vital, like Oak Ridge and the Hanford Engineering Works—both keystones of the atomic-bomb project, must in time be duplicated elsewhere, and/or put partially underground.

There are many misconceptions about underground plants, which a study of the German subsurface factories does not support. Workers can quickly become accustomed, despite initial psychological opposition, to such plants; indeed, in time of atomic war, labor would eagerly seek employment where there was protection. Efficiency can be fully as high in a well laid out plant beneath the surface as in a surface plant.[5] The great handicap to the erection of such factories is cost of capital construction; they are initially very expensive, and private industry cannot be expected to meet this expense. Again, government must lead the way by gradual but definite development and construction of a few underground factories for our most vital military requirements. Any wholesale placing of our industry underground may be physically and economically impossible, and probably even an extensive program, unless an international crisis develops, is politically impossible. But pilot underground plants can be constructed now and the problems of their operation solved. Some facilities *must* be underground; our stock piles of atomic bombs or of fissionable material, obviously of vital importance, are, for instance, already protected in underground installations in the New Mexico mountains and elsewhere. Other similar facilities must also be "dug in." The extensive cavern systems of the country and the large number of abandoned mine workings lend themselves naturally to storage and industrial utilization, but there is one grave handicap—the remoteness of most of the most usable caverns from adequate transportation networks.

Neither dispersion nor underground installations are adequate if only a single factory and its machine tools are dispersed or dug in. For no single factory is self-sufficient under our present economic scheme. To make it so, or to build up a self-sufficient economic nexus of factories, nodal industrial areas in great numbers, scattered widely around the country, must be established—each self-sufficient, each internally connected by its own communication and transportation system. Vital factories, sited perhaps underground or widely scattered, must alter our normal economic pattern of subcontracting, for each such key factory must learn to manufacture the whole article, and/or it must retain on hand great stock piles of subassemblies. Stock piles of material adequate for a certain period after war should start must also be scattered across the country—each near or in its using factory. This, too, is vital to adequate economic mobilization—dispersion of the stock piles of raw materials which the nation needs to utilize its industrial potential to the maximum.

Finally, our power system must be restudied and our power-distribution system made less vulnerable to interruption than it is today. Too many industries and too many cities are dependent mainly upon one source of power; a single bomb might darken them and stop the wheels of life. Great dam and power sources like Boulder Dam, TVA, and the Columbia River require not only extensive active protection, but whatever passive protection can be provided by duplication of generators, distribution systems, etc. New dams and power projects must be erected, portable generators for emergency use developed, and a flexible means of "tying-in" the country in a national power pattern arranged. All of these efforts require government leadership and government encouragement; none of them need to be done suddenly and abruptly and "all-at-once," but all of them should be started on a modest scale in the near future.

Transportation and communication systems cannot be put underground, but both of them are naturally dispersed in this vast continent of ours. German transportation, with a far smaller and more congested network than our own, was bombed repeatedly until the war's end, yet functioned until almost the last months. Because of the peculiar intricacy of our economic and industrial system—built upon a far-flung pattern of subcontracting, with a master plant drawing perhaps from 2,000 subplants—the dispersed and underground factory system previously outlined could not hope to function indefinitely without communications and transportation to knit it together. Our own systems, though not nearly as vulnerable as those of Europe or of Russia, have certain dangerous choke points and bottlenecks—St. Louis and Chicago for the railroads, for instance; Washington, in the telephone and telegraph system—which, if bombed and destroyed, would complicate and embarrass and delay the entire system. The Panama Canal, important for intercoastal shipping, the Sault Sainte Marie Canal, with its iron-ore traffic, and other points are transportation bottlenecks which must now be restudied in the light of possible atomic warfare. How can traffic be rerouted around them, what other switch points or alternate lines or routes can be developed, contrived or built? This problem is primarily a transportation study; not until such a study is completed thoroughly can the railroads and other means of transportation be encouraged, if necessary with government grants, to construct any essential new routes.

The telephone companies in particular must restudy their switchboard problems; long-distance trunk lines now funnel through a few focal points which, if damaged, could cripple much of our telephonic communication system. Alternate switchboard systems must be established, and some government agency, perhaps the Army Signal Corps, must be given the peacetime job of preparing an emergency radio communication system for the nation.

Commercial radio broadcasting offers a special and difficult case.

Voice broadcasts might be, in an emergency, the only way of communicating with millions of American people, and the broadcasting system would be invaluable to transmit directives, warnings, etc., and above all, if properly used, as an anti-panic medium. To protect broadcasting centers, some thought should be given soon to preparation of one or more underground radio headquarters, similar to the one used by the British Broadcasting Corporation in London during World War II. The sources of radio's power must be protected, and since nation-wide broadcasting utilizes land wires extensively, these vital cables must be duplicated. It is not too soon, either, for radio to formulate a code and standards of its own for utilization in emergency. Radio, more easily than any other medium, can spread panic—or calm hysteria. So tremendous might be the effects of an excited nation-wide radio description of the atomic bombing of New York, for instance, that some form of control or censorship over radio broadcasting may be essential in the event of another war. Better still, a self-imposed and voluntary censorship by commentators and radio stations ought to be prearranged; excitable and hysterical descriptions barred, reliance put insofar as possible upon a calm recital of the truth without spicing it with drama, and a code for broadcasting written which would emphasize calmness and restraint and assurance in delivery and would inculcate all radio speakers and commentators with a sober appreciation of their national responsibilities in the atomic age.

Other mass mediums of public information, such as the newspapers, ought also to evolve their own "codes of conduct" in case of an atomic war or mass catastrophe. Their arrangements must necessarily include plans to continue publishing by emergency or stand-by means despite disaster. News, accurate calm news, is the best antidote to rumor, and rumor and fear will be the nation's greatest psychological enemies when another war comes.

Perhaps the most vulnerable single target on the home front for mass-destruction weapons is government—federal government. More today than ever before the administrative, political and military nerve center of the nation is Washington. All the principal leaders of government, all the major departments of government, most of the files and communications of government are concentrated there. This is a profound mistake in the atomic age. Norman Cousins should have written that Washington, not modern man, is obsolete. Washington must both disperse and dig. Agencies of government that must be clustered together must prepare in peace underground shelters of great strength, protected by all the devices known to the defense. Important officials must be scattered throughout the nation; essential files must be duplicated and distributed; perhaps someday even Congress must arrange to "convene" and to vote from widely scattered parts of the country. Most essential in time will be some bill to provide for an emergency succession to the presidency; all those now named as successors might die in atomic war. The problem of military command—less important because in the services there is always a well-recognized chain of command—must, however, be clarified and a solution decided upon prior to catastrophe.

Such are some of the measures of "dispersion" and "digging" which the nation must prepare on its home front if we are to have a reasonable chance of victory without crippling casualties or lethal damage in any atomic war. These measures need not be accomplished immediately, nor need tremendous expenditures be authorized, *as yet*, to implement them. Every effort should be made to accomplish our major purposes—the decentralization of population and of industry—by encouraging natural trends or by creating those trends. What is vital is that a *start*—an integrated, reasoned *start*—be made on all these and other measures of passive defense immediately, not only to eliminate the confusion of haste if war should come, but to serve notice on any aggressive nation that the United States is determined to "keep its powder dry." What is equally important is that all such measures for home-front passive defense should be under civilian control; purely military measures must be coordinated with this civilian control, but the dominant voice must be civilian. For the implication of such measures as those suggested is totalitarian; out of them, no matter how modestly applied, could gallop a man on horseback; out of them could grow the "garrison state" which is the great specter of the atomic age.

Little has been done in the postwar era about these problems on the home front. New York State has organized on a very modest scale a State War Disaster Military Corps; other states have made some halfhearted beginnings. But there has been no national direction. A War Department board has made a study of the subject and as a result has urged further study and the creation of a part-civilian agency to undertake further investigations. But that report lay dormant for months, and no provision was made in the so-called "unification" act of 1947 for any civilian defense board; no agency now set up is competent to handle these problems. A great and glaring omission in the National Defense Establishment and the agencies that co-operate with it is the lack of such a board. Legislation should be authorized immediately to create a civilian defense board or home-front board with a civilian as chairman, a predominantly civilian membership but military liaison members. This board should be on the same level with, and should have powers comparable to, the National Security Resources Board, with which it must be closely co-ordinated. The civilian defense board must work in team with the military, but civilian authority must be supreme in peace and war; we must not succumb, under the pleas of emergency, to national martial law.

These, then, are some of the principal measures which government should take *now*:

1. Establishment of a civilian defense board.
2. Formulation of service contract policies which will provide for dispersion of new manufacturing plants.
3. Relocation, where possible beyond city limits, of service facilities—navy yards, airfields, etc.—now located in cities.
4. Revision by municipalities of building codes, zoning laws, city plans, etc., to provide for greater decentralization of cities and greater protection to buildings and administrative facilities.
5. Preparation by municipalities and states, with the aid of the Federal Government, of disaster aid and emergency relief measures, evacuation plans, etc.
6. Creation of semimilitary forces specifically organized and trained for home-front disaster duties.
7. Construction of a number of experimental underground personnel shelters.
8. Construction of a number of experimental underground plants for manufacturing and storing purposes.
9. Elimination, insofar as possible, of our power-communications and transportation bottlenecks.
10. Decentralization of Washington.

The reduction of the home front's vulnerability insofar as possible is the fundamental requirement of our present age; yet no real passive defense measures have been undertaken by our government. Zola's *J'Accuse* will echo down the political corridors of time, and our leaders will be more guilty than Chamberlain and the men of Munich if they do not today foresee and prepare for tomorrow.

NOTES—Chapter XII

1. Brigadier General Robert Wood Johnson, in article of same title, January-February 1947 *Army Ordnance.*

2. The word "passive" is used in this chapter as it was throughout World War II to denote civilian defense measures—such as shelter building, evacuation, etc.—as distinguished from *active* defensive measures undertaken by the military—i.e., anti-aircraft guns, etc.

3. Two key sources which have been consulted in writing this chapter are: *The Problem of Reducing Vulnerability to Atomic Bombs*, by Ansley J. Coale, Princeton University Press, and *The Effects of the Atomic Bomb upon Hiroshima and Nagasaki*, U. S. Strategic Bombing Survey, U. S. Government Printing Office.

4. Economists estimate the per-capita cost of municipal services in cities, fire fighting, police protection, etc., rises steadily after a certain size has been reached.

5. *Foreign Logistical Organizations and Methods—A Report for the Secretary of the Army*, by an Army board headed by Major General C. F. Robinson, states on page 149: ". . . The Germans . . . proceeded to the point where most authorities believed that it was practical to place any type of industry underground. . . . Production underground could generally be maintained at the same standards and costs as above ground. There were no adverse effects on workers. The initial costs of underground plants were, however, except in rare cases, in excess and often greatly in excess of those for comparable plants on the surface. Maintenance and operating costs were on the other hand favorable and sometimes less than above ground. . . . The German experience indicated that it was better to build a few large centralized underground factories, especially designed for the specific product in question, and as self-contained as possible, than to scatter production in a large number of small dispersed or underground units. . . . While the underground plants themselves were not effectively damaged by bombing, the lines of communication leading to and from the plants were disrupted and in many cases knocked out by persistent re-attack, thus slowing down or completely stopping production. . . ." (Published in limited copies for official use by the Army Department).

CHAPTER XIII

MAN, THE CENTRAL PROBLEM

Man is the measure of all things.
PROTAGORAS

ARMS and the man, I sing. . . ." So wrote Vergil two thousand years ago, but today, as then, the order of his listing should have been reversed. For man—personnel—is the basis of military force and the creator and executive agent of total war. Weapons without men are even more meaningless today than men without weapons.

Men always have been the indispensable common denominator of war and of preparations for war. But as weapons and equipment have developed, man-power requirements have changed in quantity and quality.

In the dawn of the human age *Pithecanthropus erectus* won his battles by superior strength and agility. Both qualities have their place today, but modern man wins or loses by superior intellect and superior heart and, collectively, by superior direction. The brawn of *Pithecanthropus erectus* is no longer the decisive factor, as it was in the world's beginning; the brain is the qualitative determinant of battle.

Quantitatively, massed man still counts, but again his collective strength is more a product of his collective brain and his industrial brawn than of his battlefield numbers. Massed man—Cannon-Fodder Man—still influences battles, but his day as a decisive factor is also done.

Nor is it any longer adequate to think merely in terms of "arms and the man." Men in factories, men in laboratories, men at type-writers and filing cabinets, men in intelligence organizations, men in home-front defense duties—all these, in modern concepts, are men under arms. For total war means total man power, and the preparations for total war require a total blueprint.

The first and most fundamental personnel postulate of our age, therefore, is that the nation's man-power requirements must be viewed as a whole, not as unrelated problems. It is useless to talk of the number of men needed for the Army, for the Navy, for the Air Force, useless to demand "universal military training" without first relating the needs of the armed forces to the needs of diplomacy, research, intelligence, industry, agriculture and the thousand and one other activities of peace and war that also require men. National strength is not and never has been solely armed force; a narrow concept of man-power needs, viewed solely, or even primarily, in military terms can today mean defeat.

This principle is so vital that its *wartime* application in the form of a National Service Act, distributing and allocating man power to the armed forces, industry, research, etc., etc., is probably inevitable in another war. Such a War Man-Power Act, or National Service Act, should be part of our economic-mobilization legislation (to take effect at the start of war or emergency) and should be administered by the National Security Resources Board, established by 1947's "unification" legislation (or by the board's wartime successor). Such compulsion is distasteful and dangerous and can be made somewhat more palatable only by utilizing labor to help plan a labor draft and by coupling a labor draft with a strict limitation on war profits. These measures require, however, a neat balance and extreme care in phrasing and application, for too much compulsion and too little incentive always has tended in the history of man to reduce efficiency and to undermine democracy.

Man-power allocation in wartime cannot stop, however, with quantitative allocations. There must be very careful qualitative allocation, not only by skills and talents, but also by personalities. What the Army belatedly has been trying to do since the war (and as yet with inadequate success)—"putting the personal into personnel," fitting round pegs into round holes—is of fundamental importance to all users of man power. Civilian industry and the research laboratories long have understood the importance of qualitative and personality placement, but one of the weakest branches of the services always has been personnel. The reason is clear. Military, particularly Army, thinking has been geared to the concept of mass; it is hard to displace Cannon-Fodder Man with Qualitative Man. But the need is proven; the ground forces, generally built in the past on the basis of quantitative rather than qualitative man, recognized in

World War II that the fighting ability of their divisions was being seriously impaired by the priorities on qualitative man accorded to the Air Forces and the Navy. Today, missile battalions are becoming integral operating units of all forces, including the ground forces, and the quality of the men they now need is considerably higher in intelligence and in specialized knowledge than the average "dough-foot" who fought World War II. More and more the science of war and the society of peace demand a careful estimation of an individ-ual's abilities and the matching of his specific abilities to a specific task.

It is not adequate, however, to think of qualitative and quantita-tive placements or allocations of man power only after shooting war starts. This is also a peacetime problem, for peacetime mistakes can vitiate all wartime plans and controls. If, for instance, we do not educate and properly place enough scientists in peacetime, our research and development program will suffer and our weapons and equipment may lag behind an enemy's. If there are not enough men of specialized and broad knowledge, if there are not enough analysts available for our intelligence services, we may never receive the warning which is indispensable to modern survival. If industry or diplomacy or other branches of national power fail to meet their man-power requirements in peace, we may lose tomorrow's war before it starts.

The emphatic need of a national man-power survey and a national man-power program in *peacetime* is, therefore, indicated. No such survey or program, in terms of national security, has yet been made; the nearest thing to it was the report, *A Program for National Security*, of the President's Advisory Commission on Universal Training, headed by Dr. Karl T. Compton. This report, however, concerned itself primarily with the needs of the military services; it studied and discussed only cursorily the needs of diplomacy, research and development, industry, etc. A more comprehensive study should be undertaken immediately by the National Security Resources Board with the aid of government departments, and anticipated man-power needs should be projected ahead, insofar as it is scientifically possible to do so, for ten, twenty or more years. Plans and programs should then be formulated intended to foster and encourage—in peacetime chiefly by voluntary methods and governmental inducements—the recruitment of men in proper numbers and with proper qualifications for armed services, industry, etc. Such a program would complement and supplement the services' educational programs and the broader educational aims of the projected National Science Foundation. The fundamental aim must be to see our man-power problem whole, in peace and in war; heretofore it has been viewed, from a national-security viewpoint, almost entirely in the narrow frame of military needs.

Once this principle has been understood, and only then, is it possible to discuss intelligently the specialized man-power needs of the armed forces, which in peace are a minor fraction, in war a major fraction, of our total national man-power pool.

What are those needs?

The first requirement is men for occupation duties. Our forces occupying ex-enemy countries, except in certain specialized circumstances, need not and should not be large. These forces are police and stabilizing forces, *not* combat forces. We could not possibly make them large enough in peacetime to obviate all risks of their being overrun in case of war, and to attempt to keep them large would be to negate the purpose for which they exist. Large funds that would otherwise go to economic reconstruction would be required for their maintenance, and large bodies of idle troops are a drain upon the country they represent and the country they occupy, and potentially a source of trouble and friction. The smaller the better, therefore, should be the rule for our occupying troops, commensurate, of course, with their proper functioning as police and stabilizing forces.

In addition to occupation duties, there are two other major functions, and a host of ancillary duties, which our regular armed forces must fulfill. Men are required to garrison our overseas bases, and our main "base" here at home, and to provide a "strategic reserve." Overseas bases need not be heavily garrisoned in time of peace with the exception of a few key points, but the garrisons must be alert, well trained and ready. The major bulk of our combat strength, deployed at home and/or at overseas bases, must be organized in our "strategic reserve"—ground, sea and air—in mobile, operating forces, ready for instant action. Upon this strategic reserve and its instant readiness rests the main burden of the nation's military security; the success or failure of the policy of "defense-by-offense" depends upon it.

The ancillary duties which the regular armed forces must perform in time of peace are those of supply, training and administration. Cadres of well-trained regulars must form the backbone of our reserve forces and must provide the skilled instructors required for training the reserves. Large numbers of regulars, as well as reserves, must themselves be trained; the service school systems, so essential a part of any military system worth its name, ought to be filled to capacity in peacetime. A large part of our military man power must perform the vital duties of supply, and a considerable force is required for the administrative structure of the armed forces—a force considerably larger than the peacetime size of the forces warrants in order to permit orderly wartime expansion.

Such are the peacetime duties of the armed forces. When and if war comes, these peacetime forces must be capable of expansion. If the war should end in hours or days after devastating missile-atomic bombardments, the wartime man-power needs of the armed services would not differ substantially from their peacetime needs. But there is, as we have seen in previous chapters, no certainty that a future war will be short, and if it is measured in months or years, the armed services must expand tremendously. In such a case, the whole man power of the nation would be utilized, either on the home front or in the services, and quantitative and qualitative allocation of man power would have to be made on a national basis in accordance with a prewar blueprint. But the core of the expansion of the services would be the reserve forces, or "civilian components" —the so-called "part-time" soldiers, sailors and airmen who in peacetime serve in the National Guard or reserves of one of the armed forces. These forces, trained one drill night a week, and with two weeks' field duty every year, would require considerable additional training, after emergency came, to fit them for combat. Nevertheless, their peacetime training, *if efficiently conducted*, would materially lessen the time required to prepare them for combat, and these units, with a cadre of regulars, would provide the skeleton of expansibility, the framework for putting 8,000,000 or 10,000,000 or 12,000,000 Americans into uniform if the need dictated.

Such, then, are the military man-power needs of the nation—a relatively small permanent full-time force, highly trained and instantly ready, capable of immediate offensive action when war starts and of gradual expansion with the aid of semitrained reserves to very large mass forces.

In addition to these purely military needs, there is an ancillary need of semimilitary character of tremendous importance. The home front, as the previous chapter has indicated, could be, in a future war, the decisive front. If great casualties weakened the people's will, or if panic swept the cities of America, the cry of "peace at any price" might force any government's hand. So great are the potential disasters of the atomic age, so huge the potential emergencies, that any effective home-front civilian defense organization must be stiffened by a thread of discipline and must have in its framework at least a cadre of military personnel. This home defense military force must be prepared for air-raid warning service, auxiliary police duties, auxiliary fire-fighting, emergency first-aid, anti-paratroop and anti-sabotage duties, and, above all, for control of riots and panic and, if necessary, for the duties of martial law.

There should be no mistake about these functions. No *military* defense force can, or should, if our democracy is to endure, assume major responsibility for *civilian* defense. Civilian defense is a civilian function, civilians must help to provide their own defense in any atomic struggle. If the military attempted the entire, or even the major, job, not only would the nation be militarized, but the military would find its energies concentrated in purely passive defensive tasks. Civilians should be more competent than the military to plan and execute municipal and interurban defensive measures, which, to be effective, must enlist scores of agencies, private, city, state, federal, the Red Cross, water supply, electrical power, etc., etc. The role of the military in this field should not be a dominant one, but a *strongly supporting* one.

Given these military man-power needs of the nation, how can they best be met?

There have been throughout history only two major methods of recruiting military man power, the voluntary and the compulsory. Both systems have produced qualitatively good armies—and poor ones; the quantitative mass armies have nearly always been the product of compulsion. Navies and air forces, more specialized than ground armies, usually have produced the finest forces by voluntary recruitment and have depended, even when they expanded to mass size, far more fully than the ground forces upon the voluntary system. Men usually fight best (if leadership and other factors are equal) when they fight voluntarily, not because of compulsion. But volunteer systems generally do not produce mass armies of great size; large military forces can be raised by this method, but 8,000,000-man armies, like that mobilized by the United States in World War II, are invariably the product of compulsion. Purely volunteer methods have grave disadvantages in wartime; the best and finest blood of the nation tends to be drained out upon the battlefields, while the cowards and the slackers remain at home. Many volunteer for the armed services who would serve the nation more effectively in industry, laboratories or elsewhere.

It is clear, therefore, that the draft—or compulsion—ought to govern the raising of man power for the armed forces in any future war or emergency. But immediate qualifications must be made. The draft must never again be applied as it was in World War II. Future wartime draft legislation ought to be considered, and its provisions carefully approved, without any of the politics of passion or the spur of haste, in peacetime before emergency comes. A wartime draft act for the armed forces ought to be made part of the broader National Service or War Man-Power legislation, which in turn must be, part of the nation's economic-mobilization legislation. Automatic provisions in the legislation should start the draft functioning upon approval of Congress when emergency arises, even prior to war. But the military draft must be keyed closely to the whole national war man-power system. To make certain that the nation's man power is being utilized to best *long-term* as well as short-term advantage, and for the good of the whole war effort rather than for the narrower good of the services, the draft ought to be administered by an agency functioning under the National Security Resources Board, or its wartime successor, fundamentally a civilian agency. Such a measure would provide mass armed forces, if they were needed, in another war.

But what about peacetime; how should service needs be met in this present era of "armed neutrality"? The answer is to be found quite clearly in the type and character of the regular armed forces we require, in the functions they must perform—both described in this and previous chapters—and in our own past experiences. The emphasis, we have seen, in our future military policy must be upon readiness potential rather than upon mobilization potential. The war of tomorrow may be won or lost by the military force in being at the time war starts. Various authorities have warned that if atomic war comes it might end in complete victory or defeat within a few hours, days, weeks or months (depending upon the authority). General of the Army Dwight D. Eisenhower told the President's Advisory Commission on Universal Training that (in the words of the commission report) "the decision in a future conflict would be determined by our ability to act and react in the first sixty days." Whether or not we agree with the predictions of quick victory or defeat, it is clear that unless we are *ready*, unless readiness potential is emphasized, we shall never be able to *mobilize*, even if we have emphasized mobilization potential.

If we are to emphasize readiness potential, if we are to produce and train a highly mobile, instantly ready force capable of swift and terrible retaliation against any attack, it is clear that that force must be composed of long-term volunteer, professional troops. Today, so great is the technical burden of knowledge to be learned by the soldier (and even more so by the airman and seaman) that it is almost axiomatic that no military force can be a good military force that is a part-time force or a quick-turnover force. Long-term application—and interested, not compelled, application—is essential to master the problems of modern military tactics and to build up that basic doctrine of military knowledge and "know-how" which none but the keen, intelligent professional can develop. The National Guard and other part-time "civilian components," despite all the will in the world, cannot possibly develop this competence on a part-time basis; they cannot possibly be ready for effective combat action on M-Day (Mobilization Day). Nor can the peacetime drafted man, unwilling timeserver, give the *élan* or the interest essential to the peacetime tasks of the services—occupation, garrison duty, training. Fresh in our memory are our postwar experiences with the callow, short-term, hastily trained volunteer, induced into service by the G.I. bill of rights, and with the reluctant drafted man. Both proved themselves equally unsuited to the hard task of peacetime occupation duties, of peacetime garrisons, or of peacetime professional preparation for war.

Our regular forces in peacetime must be highly trained, instantly ready, long-term professional troops. Their morale and their philosophy must be that of the professional soldier, who does not serve for pay alone, but for the love of it, the glory of it, the service of it; they must be men who take pride in the uniform, a quality that

lies at the very root of military efficiency and one that is too rare
in the modern services. We must have our own Gurkhas, our own
Tommy Atkinses, who can accustom themselves to severe duty,
occasional skirmishing, and intermittent casualties in time of *peace*
—in fact as part of the *price* of peace—without the persecution
complex or hero psychosis of the drafted or civilian soldier, and
without arousing international crises or fear of war. Voluntary
recruitment is the best basis for a long-term force of regulars; the
finest troops in history have been volunteer, long-term professionals.
Today's emphasis *must* be on quality, rather than upon Cannon-
Fodder Man.

The man-power needs of the regular military services ought,
therefore, to be met by the draft in war, by voluntary recruitment
in peace. But the reserve components of the armed forces and the
home front also require, in the atomic age, militarily trained man
power. How are these needs to be met?

These man-power needs of the reserve forces and the home front
are to be answered, in the official service view—a view endorsed
unanimously by the President's Advisory Commission on Universal
Training—by the projected plan for universal military training.
This training, compulsory for every boy physically fit (and modified, the commission recommended, for those who are not), would
be the "apex," in the commission's view, of a sound pyramid of
national defense, but the base of that pyramid would be other
requirements—strategic mobile striking force, regular services, a
sound intelligence system, economic mobilization, etc., previously
discussed. Under the plan, all lads between eighteen and twenty
would be compulsorily inducted, for *training*, *not service*, into a
special training corps. They would be subject to a special discipli-
nary code, would wear special identifying insignia and would not
be liable for *service* in this country or overseas. The youths would
serve six months in the regular training cadres—an annual estimated
432,000 of them under the Army, 232,000 under the Navy and
Marines, 186,000 under the Air Force—and upon completion of
this basic six-months course they would be given the choice of a
number of options, one of which each youth must choose. These
options are intended to provide the *equivalent* of an additional six
months of training. They include continuation of training for a
second six-months period; enlistment in one of the regular services;

entrance into a service academy; enlistment, probably for a three-year period, in the National Guard or one of the Organized Reserve components; the entry into ROTC at one of our colleges, etc.

Such training and such a system, it is argued, would meet the needs of the reserve components of the services and, by encouraging enlistments in the armed forces, might also help fill the man-power needs of the regular services. If the reserves could be assured of a definite source of man power in peacetime, men already given basic training, they would be more ready for combat when war came, and more ready for home defense duties. These are the essential military arguments for the universal military training system now projected.

Whether or not they are sound arguments can be determined only by a consideration of the type of training intended and the organizations into which the man power thus provided is to be funneled. For the method of recruitment is only one problem of man power; the others of co-equal importance are training and organization.

Universal military training, as now programmed, is *basic military* training. The inductees would be taught the school of the soldier, discipline, military courtesy, service ranks and nomenclature, service methods, personal hygiene, the care of personal equipment and weapons, etc. The trainee would be put in good physical condition; he would learn how to care for himself in the field, and he would learn how to handle and operate, at least in rudimentary form, most of the weapons the Army uses, up to and including tanks. In the Air Force, the trainee would learn organization, military discipline, the rudiments of "ground school" training, etc. The Navy would carry the trainee through "boot camp," might give him a touch of sea duty and accustom him to the basic duties of shipboard life. But UMT is primarily intended as a source of mass man power for the ground forces. In his Army six months the young man would receive "small unit" training; that is, he would be taught how units up to and including a platoon and company in size are organized, and how they operate and maneuver; and he would experience one battalion problem during his six-months course. He would learn little, if anything, about riot duty; he would not be taught the specialized jobs of home-front forces, but he would receive a fairly complete, but rudimentary, training in military fundamentals. His training, because of the time limitation, would have to be a "once over lightly," and some of it, because of the rapid changes now occurring in military technology, would probably be obsolescent in five years.

Upon completion of their basic six months the trainees would exercise their options. Some would continue a second six-months training. Some would enlist in the regular services. Some 218,000, it is estimated, would enlist in the National Guard annually for a three-year period. Some would enter the reserve organizations. The efficient use of this man power would be dependent fundamentally upon its organization into military units and the character and function of the units formed.

UMT would undoubtedly stimulate somewhat the flow of recruits into the regular services, but probably in insufficient numbers to affect materially the man-power problem of the professional forces. For a very considerable training cadre would have to be supplied by the regular services to train an average of 850,000 youths annually. The total number of persons needed to supervise, administer and give this training has been estimated at 230,000—military and civilian, Army, Air Force and Navy, of which about 185,000 would be military personnel. The annual flow of recruits from the UMT camps into the regular forces would probably not even compensate for the regular personnel needed to train the UMT lads; in other words, UMT would do nothing to add to the readiness potential of the regular services.

The flow of recruits from UMT into the Guard and the reserves would be sizable. But these "civilian components," as now organized, suffer from grave handicaps which make it impossible for these forces to become, in fact rather than in theory, M-Day forces, or troops ready to fight on Mobilization Day. The National Guard and the reserves are "part-time" soldiers, sailors and airmen, and no such units can possibly master the intricate science of modern war.

The National Guard is a part state, part federal force, supported by both state and federal governments, dominated in peacetime chiefly by the states, but its training supervised, common standards prescribed, and most of its equipment provided by the Federal Government. In wartime the Guard is "federally-inducted" into the regular forces. The Organized Reserves on the other hand are federal forces in peace or war—inactive and subject only to intermittent, voluntary training in peacetime, active and part of the regular federal forces in war.

Friction and divided authority between the Guard and the Army and Air Force reserves and between the civilian components and the regulars hamper development. The Guard in particular, the reserves to a lesser extent (the Naval Reserve scarcely at all), are influenced in peacetime by politics. The partial state, partial federal control of the Guard is inefficient and administratively difficult, and state politics inevitably play a part in the appointment of some officers to high command. A number of National Guard divisions have been commanded even since the war by men with long political records but with no combat experience whatsoever in World War II, and in some cases with no federal service as general officers. Our experience in the war indicated that National Guard divisions sometimes required a longer wartime training period after induction than a new division built from "scratch." The Guard divisions had to be reorganized, new commanders appointed, unfit officers removed, sometimes new "non-coms" made before the real process of integrating and training could start. Many postwar reforms have been made in the Guard, it is true, and the influence of state politics has been reduced as compared to prewar days. But the "civilian components," as now organized and trained and given their present avowed mission, add nothing to the nation's *readiness* potential, even if plumped out to full strength by a flow of man power from UMT camps. Nor would these reserve forces, as now trained and organized, be of much aid in atomic disasters on the home front. Their avowed mission is, in any case, a military one; they are to become part of the regular forces on M-Day—theoretically ready (but not actually ready) for fighting or service outside the country on M-Day—not available for permanent home-front duties.

Universal military training as it is now conceived and planned is neither fish nor fowl nor good red herring. It dangerously over-emphasizes *mobilization* potential at the expense of *readiness* potential. It is not conscription for *service*, to supply men for the regular forces; the regulars may *suffer* in readiness because of it, not *gain*. It is not voluntary recruiting. In other words, UMT suffers from the disadvantages of compulsion without providing compulsion's major advantage—the supply of mass man power to the *regular* services.

What UMT does do is to supply half-trained mass man power to the *reserve* components of the services. Whether this will result in a reduction of the time required for this nation to mobilize its maximum man power, in case of need, is problematical; that will depend in turn on other factors—the efficiency of organization, the availability of weapons, the elimination of politics from the reserve components, proper leadership, etc. But it is clear that UMT as now conceived would add little or no strength to the nation at the *start* of any future emergency, for we must then depend upon the armed forces already in being—the regular, long-term, highly skilled professionals. If the next war should be fought and finished in the first few hours or days, as some prophets have indicated it might be, these regular forces would win or lose it; if it lasted weeks additional men from the reserve components might be mobilized, but probably few of them could "get into action"; if it lasted months, some newly mobilized units—air and naval and missile units and radar warning battalions—might be used, but only if it lasted more than a year could we hope to utilize the bulk of our reserve forces as they are now established.

The services' plans contemplate the mobilization of between 7,500,000 and 8,500,000 men within one year after M-Day, including the regulars already in service, the National Guard, reserves and UMT trainees. But it is completely optimistic and utterly unrealistic to assume that, at the maximum, more than a third of this force could be satisfactorily trained and ready for combat in this one-year period, so long as the present UMT and National Guard and reserve program is adhered to.

In effect, the present plans seem to "sell the regular services short"; emphasis is put upon the reserve components at the expense of readiness potential.

These then are the broad problems and major considerations involved in the recruitment and organization of men for the armed forces. But the use of the compulsory method in peacetime must be judged, not only against the yardstick of man power, but by other yardsticks.

There is distinct danger that UMT would create in our minds a psychological Maginot Line, the shadow of security without its substance. There is even more danger that too large a proportion of the military budget and much too large a proportion of our military energies would go to basic training and mobilization potential, far too little to readiness potential. The military utility of universal military training in the atomic age is open to considerable question. If we must use the principle of compulsion in peace-time, let us at least be realistic and reap its minimum benefits; let it be compulsion for *service* instead of for *training* only, and let the men it supplies re-enforce—and not reduce—the readiness potential of the regular forces.

There are other dangers. Compulsory military training in peace-time is in no sense a progressive step. Its proponents regard it as of spiritual and moral benefit to the nation, a unifying force. It might so develop. But what a teacher and what a cost! If we must revive the dying flame of national spirit by military means, then, indeed, we exchange our heritage of freedom for a mess of pottage. UMT, more than any other single measure, would extend the power and the influence of the military in American life. It offers no solution, no easement of the present tense international situation. It is not the American way. UMT as now contemplated offers dubious military benefits in return for *certain* social risks.

What, then, are the alternatives? For the regular forces, there is no better way in peacetime than voluntary recruitment. Those apostles of stagnation and prophets of doom who thought that the armed services would never be able to meet a fraction of their needs by voluntary methods have been confounded by postwar enlistment figures. We maintain today by far the largest volunteer forces in the world, and there is good prospect that we can continue to maintain forces of the requisite sizes if the proper methods are employed. The services have discovered since the war the appeal of inducements—monetary and otherwise—to the recruit, and they have learned the pulling power of American advertising. Yet recruiting techniques and advertising appeals have not always been well done. Eric Larrabee pointed out in *Harper's Magazine* in March 1947 that:

> The announced intention of the recruiting program is to enlist quality rather than mere numbers; the inducements being offered will tend to produce exactly the opposite result. . . .
> The Army is advertising that never before has it been such a soft touch, and it is getting the men to whom such a soft touch appeals.[1]

Better leadership, less "chicken" or unnecessary privileges of rank, far better administration of military justice, and improvement of all personnel relations, making personnel "personal," would promote recruiting and would also increase the efficiency of the armed forces. Renewed emphasis on career building in the services to foster long-term enlistments is another tactic which might be more successfully utilized than it has been. And one major basic advertising appeal, calculated to enlist the interests of the best red-blooded Americans and at the same time to bolster psychologically the sometimes faltering spirit of America, has been overlooked. Service, service to the nation, to fellow man, to Western society, service to country and to world, pride of service and pride of uniform, in other words a spiritual rather than a materialistic inducement to recruiting, might result gradually in magnificent returns.

There is still another means by which the man power of the regular forces could be supplemented, particularly those of the Army ground forces, the only service which has experienced major trouble in meeting its needs. The utilization of foreign legions, or of "language legions," is of renewed and particular importance to the United States with its new world role. There are many expatriates, many displaced persons, many willing volunteers from foreign lands who would gladly serve the United States Army in special units, either combat or supply. Some of our own native citizens who speak foreign tongues, such as the Puerto Ricans, could similarly be grouped in "language" battalions. There is an unreasoned prejudice against such groupings, but the performance of the Nisei battalions in World War II should have overcome it. Foreigners who served long and faithfully in the military uniform of the nation might be rewarded by citizenship; these recruits would unquestionably find more financial security than most of them could ever hope to find in their own homelands. All such units, if properly screened, organized, trained and led, would be useful adjuncts to a professional military force, and they could be so utilized and so geographically distributed that their national prejudices could have no effect upon their military service or upon our international relations.

For the "civilian components," voluntary recruiting also may serve to fill the ranks, at least partially. Much unnecessary hubbub about the numerical "weakness" of the National Guard and Organized Reserves has filled the press in these past two years, but it was natural that in the immediate postwar era, while demobilization and postwar reorganization was taking place, the Guard and Reserve components should be virtually non-existent. In 1947 new units were activated and the first throes of organization completed, but the Guard never had planned to reach its postwar strength of 723,000 until the 1950's. Today, it is still some distance from that figure, but already it has reached a strength which exceeds all its prior peacetime maximums, and the Reserves are also achieving new highs. Whether or not the Guard and the Reserves will be able to recruit, without compulsion, to their ambitious maximums seems questionable, though it is probable that the civilian components can recruit voluntarily a *large proportion* of their announced needs.

Man power was *not*, in any case, in 1948 the limiting factor in the size of the Guard or of the Reserves. Organizational problems were a greater handicap, but a long-term limitation—the number of armories and other training facilities available—was a more permanent and fundamental factor. The National Guard expects to reach a strength (by voluntary recruits) of 300,000 ground troops and 41,000 air personnel by June 30, 1949, but long before that strength is reached the nation's 1,400 state-owned armories will be "bursting at the seams." Some 1,500 more armories at a cost of some $600,000,000 will be essential if the Guard is to be increased to the stated goal of 723,000.

Nevertheless, the civilian components are weak, though not in numerical man power. As long as they are organized and trained as they are today, they will be "half-baked" military forces of limited usefulness to the home front. Immediate reorganization and reorientation of the civilian components should be initiated. It is wasteful and productive of friction to have two "reserves" as the Army and Air Force now do; the National Guard and the Organized Reserves might well be merged into one organization, under dominant federal control. Care must be exercised, however, in altering the traditional state role of the Guard to prevent too great a centralization of federal powers or to incur too great an expense.[2] The mission of this new combined reserve component or "National Reserve" must be changed; the "civilian components" must frankly acknowledge the obvious—that they cannot, with part-time training, be ready for combat duty anywhere in the world on M-Day. Some of these units, perhaps half of them, ought frankly to aim at readiness for combat with a field force three to nine months after M-Day; the other half might well alter its traditional mission as a field force and devote all its energies to increasing the "readiness potential" of the home front—to providing that cadre of militarily trained units needed to cope with atomic disaster. These troops should be trained in fire-fighting techniques, riot and panic control and other specialized tactics essential to this age.

Such a program would at least be spiced with atomic-age realism. But even so, it would not be enough to serve the full needs of the home front in the era of atomic war. Each state, to replace its federalized Guard unit, may well have to create a semimilitary "State War Disaster Corps" similar to New York's (composed, perhaps, of those physically unfit for military duties). This corps would supplement the work of the federal forces specially trained for Home-Front duties.

But in the atomic age we are, more than ever before in history, the "nation-in-arms." All ages and both sexes are exposed to the horrors of war. A proper Home-Front organization must frankly face this universality of conflict. Civilian defense must be organized somewhat as it was in World War II, on the precinct, district, county and even the block basis. Willing volunteers—and there were many who performed loyally the drab and unexciting duties of civilian defense in the United States in World War II—might initiate such a program gradually in peacetime, but in time of war participation would have to be compulsory. Volunteer spare-time training programs for all ages and both sexes should be initiated under the government's supervision in peacetime and could be expanded in scope by proper advertising techniques and, if necessary, by small monetary inducements. If a great body of civilians thus instructed and organized in air-raid warning service, panic prevention, fire fighting, first aid, rescue work, etc., were supplemented by uniformed, military cadres specifically trained for home defense duties, at least the nucleus of Home-Front preparedness would have been created. Later, if the voluntary response was not adequate, and if the need dictated it—but not until the steps previously outlined have been taken, or until plan and organization, function and purpose are far more clarified than they are today—some form of universal training and *service* for part-time Home-Front duties and for the reserve components may be needed. But until and unless such a plan and organization are produced, universal training would have little meaning.

For our first and major efforts must go into readiness potential, into assuring American superiority in the air, in missiles and at sea; nothing must be allowed to reduce that effort.

It is obvious from this discussion that a military man-power program is a major requirement. Today our service man-power estimates are a hodgepodge of confusion and "guestimates."

Each service and each branch of each service developed their postwar man-power requirements virtually in a vacuum. There was no real consultation, and certainly no meeting of minds, between the (former) War Department and the Navy Department prior to the Navy's announcement that its postwar man-power needs would total 552,000 men. Each service estimated its needs as high as it thought the traffic would bear. Some numerical estimates were deliberately pushed to large figures on the supposition that Congress would not provide funds for all the services asked for, and that if the needs were overestimated the services might get out of the pared budgets funds enough to support their actual needs. There has certainly been, so far, no real attempt to correlate the needs of all services, no attempt to assess and weigh the needs of the Navy against the needs of the Air Force, for instance. As a result the following astronomical requirements—which bear no considered relationship whatsoever to each other, or to the relative importance in the defense picture of the services concerned, or to over-all national man-power needs—were produced to guide our postwar military program:

Summary of personnel requirements of postwar military establishment—Regular Establishment and civilian reserve components:[3]

(Number of persons)

Service	Regular establishment	National Guard and Naval Organized Reserve	Organized Reserve Corps and Navy Volunteer Reserve Corps	Reserve Officers' Training Corps enrollment	Enrollment in service academies	Grand Total
War ...	1,070,000*	723,000	876,000	255,000	2,496	(Army & Air Force)
Navy ..	552,000	223,737	951,263	} 19,600	} 3,100	
Marines	108,200	44,000	188,250			
	1,730,200	990,737	2,015,513	274,600	5,596	5,016,646

* To be reduced to 875,000 (ground and air forces) upon completion of all occupation duties.

To this tremendous peacetime total of more than 5,000,000 regulars and part-time soldiers, sailors and airmen already *authorized* by Congress would be added—if UMT were implemented—another 185,500 permanent *military* personnel for UMT training cadre, and 850,000 youths in UMT camps each year. And all these men in uniform would, in turn, be supported by hundreds of thousands of civilian employees in Army, Navy, and Air departments.

These figures, of course, are goals or authorizations, not present actual strengths. Congress, for instance, has never provided enough funds for a Navy of 552,000 men, or for a Marine Corps of 108,200, and Congress is right; the man-power needs of these two services were set too high in relation to our total military requirements. But even the actual naval personnel strength in 1947, some 545,000 naval and Marine officers and men, is larger than the world situation dictates as necessary, whereas the Air Force man-power total, some 325,000 in 1947, is somewhat too small. The National Guard, and the reserve components of the Army and Navy, but not of the Air Force, also have been inflated to too high a figure. Their *authorized* strength could well be cut by one third to one half.

In sum, these figures, which represent the peacetime aims of the armed services, are prodigious, unprecedented, and out of balance, bear little relation to the realities of the atomic age and involve a burden in expense and in the diversion of productive man power to non-productive tasks which would tax in time the economy even of the United States.

One of the first tasks of the Secretary of Defense and the new National Military Establishment provided by 1947's "unification" legislation must be a restudy of these man-power requirements and service plans in the light of national needs. Secretary of Defense Forrestal has recognized the urgency of such co-ordinated planning. Prior to his assumption of office in 1947, there was no common defense planning; each service boosted its own needs. The process of co-ordination has started, but even today there is no integrated defense plan. Careful man-power (and matériel) priorities for the services and their various branches must be determined for three- to five-year periods, but these priorities must be flexible and subject to change as technological developments put greater or lesser accent on this or that service or branch or arm. Above all, the parts must be integrated with the whole, and the man-power needs of the

National Military Establishment must in turn be fitted into the nation's needs. Until this is done, until we have a reasonable statement of military and civilian man-power requirements, we can have no logical military program; until this is done we shall have a postwar defense policy that, like Topsy, "jest growed."

Once a sound program of man-power needs and requirements has been established, a sound program of training can be evolved. In many of its essentials the training program is, indeed, sound today. The service school system, mentioned elsewhere in these pages, is excellent, but there is some duplication and overlapping, and not enough common schooling and common service for Army, Navy and Air Force officers. Annapolis and West Point, contrary to so much loosely formed opinion, deserve well of the nation; the graduates of these institutions are the backbone of our officer corps which in turn is an indispensable element of national security. Both academies stress duty and country; West Point, in particular, tries to inculcate its graduates with that high sense of honor which should be the badge of every officer.

The services must, however, train their men for better leadership and for a higher degree of moral courage. Leadership, strong leadership, from top to bottom of all military components—particularly good junior leadership—is a crying need.

As D. W. Thompson wrote (in "Paraphrase of Euripides"):

Ten good soldiers, wisely led,
Will beat a hundred without a head.

Good leadership, in turn, implies better morale, and better morale is badly needed in all the fighting forces, and in the United States. We must develop a common sense of dedicated purpose, and we cannot do it by hopes of monetary rewards. The Army's appeal, in particular, has been based too much on the material, not enough on the moral. There is double danger in this process. The first badge of servitude in any nation is the development of a specially favored military class; our military pay today is already the highest in the world; special prerogatives and prerequisites make the military a definitely privileged group; yet more and more requests for increased service pay are being made. The second, and perhaps greater, danger is to the spirit of an Army built upon such a system of pecuniary rewards. We must find greater pride in uniform and pride in service than Americans have developed in the past.

A training and school system built upon such principles, and dedicated to forward-thinking, continual self-questioning and to a progressive study of the techniques of the next war, not of the last, can make the most out of the great potential strength of American man power. But it must be a system which recognizes and utilizes the worth of the individual; it must not be—in the personnel sense —mechanistic.

For man, even in the atomic age, is still the soul of the machine, and upon him—qualitative and quantitative man—around him, about him, must be built the whole edifice of national security.

Notes—Chapter XIII

1. "The Peacetime Army:—Warriors Need Not Apply," by Eric Larrabee, *Harper's Magazine*, March 1947.

2. Major General Ellard A. Walsh, president of the National Guard Association, an arch opponent of merger of the Guard and the Reserve, has estimated that if the Guard and Reserve were merged and maintained at present projected strengths, the expenditure of some $5,135,000,000 would be required for the construction of new armories and facilities, and the annual maintenance budget would total $2,695,875,000. But General Walsh's figures must be accepted with a grain of salt. He is right in stressing the high costs of the "civilian components," but if the strength of the Guard and the Reserve were cut down to a reasonable figure, there is not much doubt that a merger of the two organizations would result in eventual, though not immediate, economy and certainly in increased military efficiency.

3. *A Program for National Security, Report of the President's Advisory Commission on Universal Training*, U. S. Government Printing Office, Table I, page 445.

CHAPTER XIV

SUMMARY—THE MONETARY COSTS

Money is like muck, not good except it be spread.
BACON

FOR the first time in its history, the United States in the atomic-guided-missile age has "live" frontiers—the frontiers of the sea and the sky.

Long-range aircraft, supersonic missiles and new-type submarines make "defense," in the old sense, impossible. "Defense-by-offense," the maintenance in being in time of peace of a strong offensive mobile force, capable of instant and devastating retaliation against any attacker, must be the basis of our atomic-age military policy.

This force must be flexible in size, organization and composition, quick to adapt itself to the changing technology of war. In order of priority its constituent parts should include planes and guided missiles capable of carrying atomic explosives; submarines and plane-carrying and missile-launching naval vessels; and air-borne troops.

Since ranges of weapons are now approaching transoceanic and intercontinental distances, American strategy must be global in concept. Bases overseas for warning stations, airfields and rocket-launching sites will always be important; they will be particularly important in the next decade or so before weapon ranges achieve intercontinental distances and when any war that might develop would be an "intermediate base war."

Equally important are "positions-in-readiness" or friends and "allies" who would aid the United States in case of war and whose soil might serve as additional operating areas or base sites. The most important "positions-in-readiness" in the world are the British Isles and the nations of Western Europe; the American frontier today lies in the Sudeten hills and along the rocky shores of the

Adriatic. The Arctic "frontier"—because transpolar distances are the shortest routes between the Old World and the New—has major atomic-age importance, but the traditional sea lanes across the Atlantic and Pacific would be of vital significance if any future war should last long enough to require the mass transport of troops and munitions across the seas.

Active, professional, armed forces well organized under a single "super" Secretary of Defense must be the backbone of our future military organization; the emphasis must be on instant readiness—on "readiness potential" rather than on mobilization potential. But no military force today can be expected to provide even a degree of security unless it has sound and comprehensive knowledge of a potential enemy's capabilities. The "first line of defense," therefore, is an integrated world-wide intelligence service, which should be headed by a competent civilian and should have the authority to co-ordinate all intelligence services, as well as to manage all American "covert" or espionage systems. Second only to intelligence comes research and development, basic and applied. This, too, should be under civilian direction at the highest levels; it must be broad and as free as possible of restrictions.

Economic mobilization is still of great importance, though it must be modified to fit the new atomic-age concepts. Three- to five-year replacement programs for military weapons and equipment must be authorized; blueprints and machine tools for quick mass production in case of need must be purchased and provided in time of peace, and new equipment must be designed for mass production. The passive protection of the home front, insofar as it is possible in the atomic age, the provision of shelters, the organization of a civilian defense authority, limited decentralization and de-urbanization, the construction of "pilot" model underground factories, decentralization of government, and other measures which would limit damage, restrict casualties and reduce as far as possible the vulnerability of the home front to atomic attack must be undertaken.

Man—qualitative and quantitative man—is the key to all these measures; a sound military policy must plan comprehensive measures for the raising and allocation of man power on a *national* basis. A National Service Act for the nation's man power must be provided in another war, but programs for the most effective use of military, scientific and industrial man power must be formulated now. The service man-power programs, as now blueprinted, like Topsy "jest growed," and they bear little pragmatic relation to our actual military needs. The Navy is somewhat too large, the Air Force too small; until today, when the mechanism for co-ordinated planning and a unified military program has at last been provided, there has been no over-all, integrated military planning for the atomic age. Universal military training, as now projected, places too much emphasis on mobilization potential at the expense of readiness potential and promises to "eat up" too large a proportion of the defense dollar. Moreover, it would greatly extend the influence and strength of the military, a trend that must be closely watched and strictly curbed in the atomic age, when attempts to provide insurance against the ravages of total war might lead to the gradual formation of the "garrison state." This is the great danger of our age, the extension of military influence and control into all phases of the national life. We steer a difficult course between the Scylla of the "garrison state" and the Charybdis of military inefficiency. Yet the course can be followed without disaster. Military efficiency *must* be increased by the measures outlined in preceding chapters; the military *must* participate even in hitherto non-military fields, but there must be checks and balances upon their power; civilian authority *must* remain supreme.

The costs of any such national security program as that outlined will inevitably be large. The new technology is frighteningly expensive; the "garrison state" can easily become the "bankrupt state." A pilot model of a modern bomber now may cost $20,000,000 to $30,000,000; guided missiles with their intricate propulsion and guidance systems will be ten to a thousand times more costly than the shell which they will largely displace. The basic facilities for the development and testing of the new weapons—wind tunnels, proving grounds and laboratories—will require the expenditure of billions even *before* a single intercontinental supersonic weapon has been tested. The limited measures to reduce the vulnerability of the home front which have been advocated would require, in time, more billions, and the maintenance of an active, highly trained regular force, ready for instant action, will "eat up" perhaps five to ten billion dollars annually, more than our entire national budget of eighteen years ago.

The costs, actual and potential, of a reasonable security are staggering. America has had greatness thrust upon her. These costs are the burden of power. Yet they can become an impossible burden, unless expenditures are wisely planned. They are not so planned today.

For the 1948 fiscal year (ending July 1, 1948), the military services were budgeted some $11,256,000,000, or more than $77 for every man, woman and child in the United States. Yet our military pay and *maintenance* costs alone—exclusive of the costs for research and development, new equipment and new facilities—have by no means reached their postwar peak; UMT has not been implemented; the National Guard is still at a fraction of its planned strength, etc. A very conservative estimate by the President's Advisory Commission on Universal Training of the annual cost of UMT was $1,750,000,000 annually; other observers think direct and indirect costs of this program may eventually double this estimate. In addition to this expenditure, the National Guard, the same commission estimates, will cost the Federal Government $700,000,000 annually to *maintain* when it reaches its full postwar strength of 723,000 men, plus $65,000,000 annual expenditures by the states, plus $600,000,000 "capital investment" for the construction of necessary new armories and facilities. The Army's Organized Reserves, when fully organized, will cost $400,000,000 annually; the ROTC, National Science Foundation scholarships, etc., etc., more millions. The Atomic Energy Commission has stated that we must double our prior investment in atomic energy, and that we must expend approximately $2,000,000,000 for the commission budget *alone* in the course of the next four or five years in order to increase our output of fissionable material. The President's Air Policy Commission, which held extensive hearings in 1947, discovered real and potential weaknesses in our air strength, and urged the increase of that strength by additional annual appropriations of more than a billion dollars. A four-year construction program for the merchant marine, to cost $600,000,000, has been recommended, and a stockpiling plan for the acquisition of scarce raw materials, to cost $2,100,000,000 over a five- or six-year period, has been authorized. Thus, at least five billion, possibly six or seven billion, dollars would be *added* each year to the present military budget simply by UMT, the authorized National Guard and reserve programs, and other recommended measures. A 1947 recapitulation of the costs of maintaining all the components of the armed services at the strengths now projected reached a staggering total far higher than the present military budget; under these plans "national defense"—one item in the national budget—would cost, *in peacetime*, an average $15,000,-000,000 to $25,000,000,000 *annually*.

Yet only one authoritative voice, that of Secretary of the Army Royall, has been raised in warning against such grandiose and inchoate expenditures.

"We must realize," he told the President's Air Policy Commission, "that there is a dollar limit on what this country can spend for national defense. There is an absolute limit beyond which we cannot go without endangering the economic security of the country."

But his was a voice crying in the wilderness.

The implementation of *all* of these plans, unless imminent emergency threatens, is absurd, unnecessary and irrelevant. Some of the projected expenditures bear no relation to the realities of the atomic age and are definitely unnecessary; we should cut down or eliminate the unessential and use some of the funds thus saved for the "things left undone" that have been described in previous pages. The sizes of the regular Navy and of the National Guard and of the Organized Reserves have been established at much too high a level; the expensive luxury of UMT is certainly not a military "must" in its *present form*; and even the air services have set their sights too high. National safety does not lie in military strength alone, and certainly not in numbers; too large military expenditures might well divert the American dollar from more inportant tasks—aid to Europe, for example. A sound economy cannot be maintained beneath a crushing burden of taxation, particularly if a major part of that taxation must go in peacetime to non-productive military expenditures. Nor can the national morale be maintained if terrific taxation eliminates incentive. If we devote in peacetime too large a part of our man power and real wealth to preparations for war our standards of living will remain static or will decrease. A people whose hopes and plans for a better life have been frustrated cannot be a strong people; their morale will crack in time of crisis.

Yet even when these cautions are sounded America must reconcile itself to the financial burden of power. We must insist upon an economic and efficient defense, but the elimination of service "empires," the curtailment of grandiose military plans to realizable proportions, and the reduction of service expenses will not obviate the need for heavy military spending, as previous chapters have shown. For years to come, until and unless the international situation is far more stabilized than it is today, from one fifth to one third of the national budget may have to go to "keeping our powder dry." For such is the burden of power.

THE EFFECT OF THE FACTS

POLICY REVISED—THE COURSE
WE MUST FOLLOW

Facts, when combined with ideas, constitute the greatest force in the world.

CARL W. ACKERMAN

CHAPTER XV

THE UNITED STATES AND "TWO WORLDS"— A WORLD ORDER?—A PREVENTIVE WAR?— PRESERVATION OF THE WEST— THE NATURE OF TOMORROW

> This day we fashion destiny; our web of Fate we spin.
> WHITTIER

POLITICS is the art of the possible.

This is a useful definition and one that ought to be emblazoned on every American's political consciousness. For we tend in our thinking about international affairs to leap too easily over the chasm of the impossible into the millennium; we fashion nice political theories which have nothing to do with reality. We look, as a people, for permanency in a world forever changing; we want "solutions" and "settlements" of problems which by their nature can have no permanent settlement. We want things all black and white; we want to cross the t's and dot the i's of history—and to forget about its recurrent problems.

We are more realistic than we once were, but today we still are looking with sad nostalgia upon our postwar dreams, seeking a scapegoat and retreating into regret.

We are, even yet, incompletely aware of our great power and certainly only half prepared to shoulder the burdens of that power. We have been behaving in some ways in the past two years like cowering schoolboys passing a haunted house at midnight; our actions and attitudes—domestic and international—have not always expressed our strength and our pride in our institutions but have reflected an inner fear, an attitude compounded of hysteria and bravado. We throw stones at the windows of the haunted house and then run like hell.

This is scarcely the attitude of a great superpower, nor is it an attitude conducive to that stability, even though it be temporary, which we so devoutly desire. A change in American attitude, therefore, is basic to improvement of the international situation. Yet a change in attitude, in turn, must be predicated in part upon a clear understanding of the "art of the possible."

Previous sections of this book have faced frankly the nature of today's bi-polar world, have described the terrible range and destructiveness of the new weapons, have stressed the power of the United States, and have itemized the military measures we must take to achieve a reasonable degree of relative security.

What do these facts mean from a political point of view? What does the "art of the possible" permit?

There are four principal courses, any one of which we might, in theory, follow. These are: (1) isolationism; (2) a world order by agreement, with international atomic and other controls; (3) a world order by conquest; i.e., imperialism and the waging of a deliberate preventive war against Russia in the near future before she manufactures atomic bombs; (4) the middle road; the maintenance and utilization of our national power for international rehabilitation and world stability—the objective, a balance of power.

1. Isolationism.

The first of these courses, isolationism, cannot be fitted into the "art of the possible." We have seen in previous chapters that military or geographic isolationism is impossible in the atomic-guided-missile age. Isolationism today is simply escapism, retirement into a fool's paradise and "never-never" land.

An ideological offensive knows no barriers of distance; communism cannot be defeated by retreat. Nor are ocean barriers and ice masses sure ramparts against guided missiles and long-range planes. This nation, standing alone, or with the Western Hemisphere at its side, has such tremendous strength *today* that it could face with some assurance for a few years a Europe and even an Asia aligned beneath the standards of a single power.[1] But if, in time, anti-Communist forces were scattered and broken; if, in time, the potential of Europe and Asia was harnessed and developed to the

Kremlin's ends, we would be threatened physically and militarily and particularly ideologically as never before in our history. Yet we do not need to rest the case against isolationism on this one danger. Even if this danger did not exist, it is certain that we cannot serve the cause of Western civilization by shutting ourselves up in our hemisphere; we cannot promote any sort of world stability or improve our own security by creeping into bed and pulling a blanket over our heads. Our prosperity depends upon the world; we need the world as the world needs us.

Isolationism is no answer.

2. A World Order by Agreement.

The type of world order contemplated by many of our blueprint internationalists is not compatible with the "art of the possible." Men's minds and men's emotions are not yet adjusted to the elimination of national boundaries, to the vesting of supra-national powers in a world state. Such a development seems to me to be psychologically impossible today and, in any case, well beyond the limited dimensions of our political and social knowledge and of our organizing ability. The deliberate reduction of national military *strength* to a position inferior to the strength possessed by some overruling world order has been shown to be politically impossible by our postwar experiences. This "solution" begs the question of practical means and methods of achieving world order, and it begs the question of military *potential*, which will continue to be the inherent right of every nation, unless the world is to be deindustrialized and depopulated. Above all, as Bernard Brodie and Jacob Viner have pointed out, "we live in a world dominated by two giants, each of which is too strong, relative to the total power potential of the world, to be proper members of a world government."[2]

In a narrow legal sense [Viner comments],[3] sovereignty can easily be formally surrendered, but actual power is more difficult to surrender and can be effectively surrendered only to an agency still more powerful. In the present state of the world, such an agency with superior power not only does not exist but cannot be manufactured out of existing ingredients, even if the genuine will to do so existed, *unless that will goes to the extent of preparedness on the part of the United States and of Soviet Russia to dismember themselves. . . .*

This is to reduce the problem to absurdity. But there is another and even more compelling reason why a world order by agreement is impossible today.

A world state or world government must necessarily imply control by that government of weapons of mass destruction—the atomic bomb, biological agents, etc. But the physical and psychological difficulties of such control are so huge as to be insuperable unless based on mutual international confidence and trust, something that obviously does not exist today.

The Lilienthal-Acheson-State Department plan for the international control of atomic energy, which has been submitted to the United Nations, rejected by Russia and debated these many months, represents a carefully worked out mechanical-physical scheme of control and inspection. It is not a foolproof scheme; evasion would be possible, though difficult, under its terms. But it would involve considerable surrender of sovereignty and such free access to the soil of sovereign states by the international control and inspection authority that it does not come within the "art of the possible." This atomic-energy control plan would mean—if it was to be as physically foolproof as it could be made—planes controlled by an international authority flying over Russian (and U.S.) territory; international ownership of all atomic-energy plants, and free access of foreign inspectors to our own and Russian soil. Such Draconian measures would obviously rend Russia's iron curtain. In time, many observers are convinced, our plan for the international control of atomic energy would imply, if it was to be physically effective, the eventual doom of the present type of government in Russia, a government founded on political and psychological isolationism and on absolute control of information. No government is going to sign its own death warrant; the chances of Russian acceptance of the Lilienthal-Acheson plan seem, therefore, slight.

Even if such a plan were practical, however, it would by no means meet the problem of control. For there are many other mass killers beside the atomic bomb, and for some of them *no practical form of physical control can possibly be devised*. A modern bomber, with a 42,000-pound TNT bomb, is, in one sense, a weapon of mass destruction; are the nations going to agree to ban bombers? Or missiles? Or submarines? And if so, how will such international agreements be made foolproof and policed and enforced? For some of the new weapons, notably biological agents, *no scheme of control, no matter how extensive and inclusive, can possibly be established that would mean safety.* For biological agents are of tremendous importance to peacetime medicine as well as to wartime destruction; small, not large, installations produce them, and tiny laboratories, easily concealed, could quickly amass "weapons" adequate to kill a million people.

Even a cursory study, therefore, of the problem of control and inspection of mass weapons of destruction demonstrates that *the fundamental requirement is mutual confidence and trust.* We must have a sublime conviction of the good intentions of the other fellow, or no control scheme will work.

Since a satisfactory scheme for international control and inspection of all mass weapons of destruction is an essential part—at least initially—of any real world government, international faith and confidence is an essential to the establishment by agreement of any world state. Such an international attitude never has existed in world history; certainly it does not exist today. Perhaps it may exist in the distant tomorrows, but world-wide trust implies an abandonment of the quest for power and an educational process of centuries. It will not come in our time.

What of the possibilities of some scheme of world government, which would fall short of a blueprint paradise, would accept the impossibility of international control of all weapons and would content itself with a general "settlement" or agreement which would not involve the surrender of national sovereignty to a supra-state?

Perhaps the best answer to this is the United Nations itself, which is precisely—except for its continuing attempt to control uncontrollable weapons—this sort of an international organization. By the same token it is obviously an organization of considerable, though by no means absolute, futility. It is stymied on the same obstacle that would halt the progress of any other world order of this type—the difficulty of achieving a broad, workable and general settlement between Russia and the West. There well might be a very considerable easement of the present world tension; there might be peace treaties; there might even be a seeming settlement, but real settlement with the *present* rulers of Russia is impossible. For no settlement based on mutual trust and confidence, which is the only real type of settlement, is possible with a philosophy such as communism which justifies the means by the ends and which is based, not on confidence, but deceit.

It is conceivable that a Soviet-American settlement, not based on trust, but on a mutual respect for the so-called vital interests of each could be evolved. But the vital interests of each superpower, as we have seen, are virtually world-wide and therefore conflicting; moreover, any such settlement would perforce have to be an armed settlement, an uneasy truce, a watchful "on guard," not a real settlement or a real international order.

World order by agreement is no answer, save in our dreams.

3. World Order by Conquest—A Preventive War.

This course, no matter how described, is naked imperialism in new guise. It stems in part from fear, in part from exasperation, in part from reluctant conviction that since world order by agreement is impossible, we must achieve world order by force. Our motives are always sublimated, extolled; of course, we do not want to "rule" the world, the advocates of this course say. We want only an end of tension, a world brotherhood. But the loftiest motives are generally transmuted into baser and more material aims in a struggle for power, and world order by deliberate conquest would besmirch the United States with blood and dishonor. It would be, I think, fatal to the American ideal of government, fatal to democracy, fatal to our already diminished moral standing in the world to embark deliberately upon a preventive war against Russia. For we would be descending morally in such a case to that pernicious doctrine we have so long opposed—that the end justifies any means. After all, Hitler claimed that World War II was a "preventive" war on his part, but to the victims it was a war of aggression. The American people, moreover, never have fought a preventive war, and they are, in any case, war-weary today. Psychologically and morally this course does not lie within the "art of the possible."

But there are also compelling practical reasons against world order by conquest. This concept, first enunciated, ironically enough, by some atomic scientists and then espoused by some of our military men, implies a deliberate war against Russia in the next few years before she acquires a stock pile of atomic bombs. We are to prevent her from eventually attacking us with atomic bombs by first attacking her. In the past we have fought only when attacked; in the atomic age, it is argued, to wait for attack may be fatal. If Russia will not agree to adequate international control of atomic energy, this dilemma can be resolved, so the reasoning goes, only by attacking Russia. Such a course has been described as the only way to avert disaster and catastrophe.

The reasoning is specious and the conclusion dangerously false, because both are based implicitly on three fallacious premises.

The first is that an attack by Russia against us sometime in the future after she has built up a stock pile of atomic bombs is inevitable. This is a doctrine of frustration and a counsel of despair; an attack by Russia upon the United States with *physical* weapons within the foreseeable future is unlikely. There are numerous reasons for this; our superior power position and the head start that we have, not easily overtaken, in the atomic and research and development race, are major reasons against such a probability.

The second false premise is that such a preventive war against Russia, if waged in the next few years before Russia acquires atomic bombs or long-range weapons, could be won quickly and easily, primarily by atomic bombardment. This premise is based primarily upon an inaccurate estimate of the number of atomic bombs available to the United States, and an overoptimistic assessment of the ranges of our planes and missiles. In reality, as previous chapters have shown, our stock pile and production rate of atomic bombs are, in my opinion, very limited, *so limited that victory by atomic bombardment could not be assured* at any time prior to the date when Russia is likely to "get" her first bomb. We do not have now, and will not have in that period, any real guided missiles of sufficient range to reach Russian industrial areas from available bases, and our long-range planes would face very considerable opposition from great numbers of Russian day fighters. The Russian night fighters and anti-aircraft defense are weak, but so great is the area of Russia that certain industrial points deep in her territory could not be reached in a few hours of darkness. Bombing, with a few atomic and many conventional bombs, would not alone be likely to win a war against Russia in the near future; Western Europe, for instance, almost certainly would be overrun by Russian ground armies. Such a war would probably be long and exhausting, even though our eventual victory would be almost certain. In any case, the fruits of victory might well be dust and ashes.

For the third fallacious premise upon which the thesis of a preventive war is founded is that the result of such a war would be "stabilization," "enduring peace," "prosperity"—a world order of law and security, the brotherhood of man. Nothing could be further from the truth. Readers of these pages will have noted before now that I do not believe there is any such thing as a *"permanent* solution." Certainly it is true that war provides no general solution, but merely substitutes one problem, sometimes far more serious, for another. Another great war in the near future would produce problems far transcending even those we face today. For the world, particularly the Western world which we are trying to save, already is a morass of misery and of want as the result of two wars; the peoples are weary and morally and physically exhausted. Much of the middle group—the true liberals and the mild conservatives with whom lies the hope of the future—already has been liquidated by the inexorable pressure of recent events. A third great war in the near future, fought on Europe's soil and in Europe's skies, would probably eliminate for years to come the rampart of the middle way, and the resulting chaos and destruction would push the peoples of Europe to extremism. If another war should come to Europe soon, that continent, repository of so much of Western civilization's traditions, might be finished irretrievably. Certainly its battered survivors would turn to the alien doctrines of the ultra right or the extreme left. Thus would we have lost that for which we fought; our victory, in a preventive war, would have but hollow meaning.

The tragic myopia of those who urge this course is plain; you cannot defeat communism by the sword, for communism battens on war and chaos; it sickens and dies during stable and tranquil peace.

World order by conquest—a preventive war—is, therefore, no answer to the problem of tomorrow.

4. The Middle Road—A Balance of Power.

This course implies the full participation of the United States in *international* affairs combined with *national* security measures; it means the *maintenance* and *utilization*, multilaterally and unilaterally, of our *national* power for international rehabilitation and world stability.

This, the middle way, is the only course open to those who truly seek for a better tomorrow. It lies between the extremes of isolationism and imperialism; it rejects the cynical doctrine that the end justifies any means, but it also rejects as naïvely impractical the world-order-by-agreement schemes of the blueprint internationalalists. It is not only the best way; it is the *only* way, for the postwar period has provided ample evidence that the American people are not going to go "hog-wild" either on internationalism or isolationism; nor are they going to start a war in the near future. Practical internationalism, combined with national strength, is certainly within the "art of the possible." It represents practical politics; it is a "feet-in-the-mud-eyes-on-the-stars" approach.

But it offers no easy path, nor is it a course simple to define. It has none of the beautiful oversimplicity of a retreat into a "to-hell-with-you" isolationism; it cannot be blueprinted like the ideal world order; it has many of the difficulties but none of the drama of war. It offers no certain security and no sure goal; indeed, it is a policy of the calculated risk.

It implies a continuation indefinitely of the same kind of world that history always has known, a world of power politics and power centers, a world of tensions and conflicts, problems and difficulties, but a world, too, of hopes and aspirations, energies and achievements, a world of all kinds of peoples.

This course of practical internationalism combined with national strength requires the full and complete participation of the United States in international affairs. It means support of the United Nations and attempts to strengthen that organization, but vetoes, stalemates and frustrations cannot be allowed to hobble our influence; we must express it in words and deeds through the UN and other organs of international co-operation when possible, unilaterally when necessary. Morally and politically we must continue to strive for collective security, but practically and militarily we must recognize that national strength is still the primary determinant of international relations, and we must prepare for a perpetual "on guard."

This "middle" course cannot possibly be spelled out in tangible political terms to cover all eventualities; each specific case will have to be met on its merits. The guiding principles must be a determina-

tion to accept our world responsibilities, a clear understanding that
the world is geographically one and that the new weapons impose
a continuing threat to us all, a basic definition of our security needs,
a firm loyalty to humanitarianism, liberalism and freedom and an
unwavering opposition to extremism and totalitarianism of any type.
And these principles, to be effective, must, of course, be founded
upon strength, justice, firmness and wisdom.

More explicitly, these principles mean many things in the course
of the next few years.

They mean, first, a continuation of our efforts in the United
Nations, despite the discouraging difficulties and meager accomplishments of UN's first years. The United Nations has suffered from
tremendous handicaps. Not the least of these was the "overselling"
done by public officials and zealous but misguided blueprint
internationalists. We must discard the idea of the millennium
tomorrow, and we must consider the UN as a limited instrument—a step but only a step on the long, toilsome, difficult road
not to be traversed in our lifetime—toward a world order. We must
recognize, too, as Foreign Minister Evatt of Australia has noted, that
the UN has suffered greatly from an anomaly not of its own making;
it is an organization "set up to preserve world peace in a time when
peace has not been made."

The UN, therefore, when its growing pains are ended, may
develop into a more hopeful instrument for political action; in any
case, it must be supported as an evolutionary means, weak though
it be, toward a distant goal. The UN's non-political activities—
social, economic, cultural, humanitarian and statistical—should be
expanded and encouraged; these offer great opportunities for building the first foundations for real international co-operation.

But we must face squarely the failures of the UN and try to do
something about them, even though the prospects fall far short of
the perfect.

We cannot abolish war in the foreseeable future, but we can work
to avert it, and above all to limit its frightfulness. The armaments
discussions in the UN have stranded so far on one rock—the Russian
refusal to accept the Lilienthal-Acheson-State Department plan for
the international control of atomic energy. This is the best plan
that could be devised and a generous plan on the part of the United
States, but it has proved to be beyond the "art of the possible." A

new approach to weapons control ought, therefore, to be employed. A simple agreement, for instance, *not* to use biological agents in *war* might point the way to similar bans on other mass weapons. It can be objected and rightly that such agreements have no real strength without an international authority and an international inspection and control system, and we have seen that such a fool-proof system is impossible to devise. But the agreement to ban weapons is *per se* a sort of moral restraint, and above all, since each nation explicitly would be free to continue its development of such weapons though not free to use them unless first attacked (as in the case of gas, prior to World War II), the restraint of fear, of retaliation in kind, would be added to the force of a plighted word.

It is true that armaments limitation is clearly dependent upon international confidence and political stabilization, but the three go hand in hand; attempts to devise some satisfactory program of arms limitation can, if successful, *promote* political stabilization and confidence. Qualitative and quantitative limitations must, therefore, be explored thoroughly; a world-wide ban on conscription might be studied, or numerical limits established for national forces.

In blazing new trails of this sort, we must be careful, however, not to put the cart before the horse, not to disarm unilaterally prior to multilateral agreement, and not to expect dramatic results quickly. The "element of urgency," a result of the open diplomacy of the UN and of the postwar period, helps to lead the American people, always impatient for results immediately, "to expect a snappy comeback the same day, or at least the next day." But sound policy cannot be formulated that quickly. Moreover, our representatives will inevitably encounter difficulties if they "get too far behind or too far ahead of U.S. public opinion."

Our efforts toward armaments limitation ought to be pressed energetically, but the steps we take in the UN must be reasoned and carefully thought out; our representatives must not be subject to hysterical pressure, and a full and comprehensive public understanding of our aims and methods is therefore imperative.

But armaments limitation is a means to an end; the end is security, and the UN suffers from the fact that it has not the strength to provide security. Absolute security, we have seen, is an impossible chimera, but measures to stabilize the world and to increase relative security are possible. The UN's attempts to do so have, however, been buried in a welter of argumentation and stalemated by the veto power. No military forces have been made available to the UN by its member nations, and though no real permanent international army or police force ever was to be expected, it should be within the powers of even a strictly limited international agency to call upon its member states at need for *ad hoc* military contingents. The United Nations has not been able even to achieve this minimum goal, since any positive action of this sort can be, and in actuality has been, blocked by one of the five permanent members of the Security Council, namely Russia.

Some means for achieving collective political action despite the veto, and if necessary without Russia, and for setting up the mechanism of an *ad hoc* joint military force must, therefore, be established, if the United Nations is to serve any useful political purpose. No better means of doing this, considering the *de facto* stalemate and the present world situation, has been offered than the suggestion of Hamilton Fish Armstrong, editor of *Foreign Affairs*. Writing in *The New York Times Sunday Magazine* of September 14, 1947,[4] Mr. Armstrong suggested that, under the authority given in Article 51 of the United Nations Charter:

a group of United Nations members enter into a brief supplementary agreement—a sort of protocol or "optional clause" open to all —binding themselves to carry out the Charter obligation to resist armed attack.

This agreement [Mr. Armstrong wrote] would come into operation if two thirds of the signatories decided that collective action had become necessary under the Charter and if the Security Council failed to act.

Such a proposal, it has been objected, amounts *de facto*, if not legally, to an alliance, which could only be interpreted by Russia, if she did not sign the protocol, as a combination against her. In effect, the Armstrong proposal would promote a system of collective alliances, but, if Russia joined, they would be alliances aimed at no one, and the mechanism would thus be provided for some sort of collective accomplishment, unmarred by the veto. If Russia refused to join, which seems probable, this method would still have the great advantage of promoting the collective security of all other nations in the world, and at the same time it would further our own national security by tying friends and allies to us by compact.

If the "Armstrong plan" or other means (such as the "Little Assembly" program), designed to "strengthen" or change or promote the principles of the United Nations and to make it responsive to the will of the majority, should fail of adoption, our alternative program should include an outright Anglo-American alliance, broadened to include all other nations of the Western world and other anti-totalitarian states who wished to join.

It is high time we stopped boggling at the "specter" of alliances. The United States is a world power and wants to remain one. All world powers in the past have utilized alliances, both *for* and *against*. The Armstrong plan and the regional agreements expressly permitted to member nations by the United Nations Charter explicitly point the way to alliances (though by a sweeter name) as an instrument of collective security. If such a system of collective alliances can be entered upon within the framework of the United Nations, so much the better; if not, they should be established outside the framework of that organization.

This, it may be objected, is a strong step, and it is. It would result, its opponents will argue, in the clear division of the world into two camps. But this division already has occurred, and implementation of the Armstrong plan or the setting up of a system of alliances would merely be tacit recognition of an actual condition. Such a definitive step might, as one wise critic has said, "put an unwelcome strain upon the European governments that are trying to develop a middle-of-the-road policy"; it might make them stand up and "choose sides." But this strain is not of our making; it, too, already exists; the Communist parties in France, Italy and the West—with riots, strikes, bloodshed and marching men—have seen to that. If we equivocate we are lost; we *must* organize our friends and allies.

At the war's end, while there was still hope that bi-polar power would not necessarily imply bi-polar politics, such a frank move would have been undesirable, but we must now face the facts of life and recognize the existence of conflict between the world's two great super-states. Such a system of collective alliances ought not to be primarily *against* anything, except aggression; it ought to be *for* collective security. Such a move, more than any other one thing, would tend to stabilize the "front" against an expanding and aggressive Russia and lessen the possibility of war.

Such an evolution can be, and probably would be, called a return to the balance of power. And it would be that, though a balance of power in a beneficent sense, as described by Paul Scott Mowrer in the New York *Post* of September 17, 1947:

Balance of power . . . is the instinctive tendency of free nations to combine against that one or group among them that seems to be expanding so aggressively and exerting such domination as to endanger the liberties of all.

The balance of power has eventually defeated every would-be world conqueror since Roman times.

And such a balance of power would be so overwhelmingly strong that Russia would not dare, in the near future, to challenge it.

Such a development might also prove to be a progressive step toward a better world order. The dream of the World Federalists of "one world" is likely long to remain a dream, for reasons already explained, but closer political, military, and economic ties between the United States and the nations of the West would at least promote that Western federation which is the Federalists' first goal. A common citizenship and elimination of tariff barriers among the Western nations are distant goals—probably never to be achieved in our lifetime—but closer ties among the nations of the West for mutual interest and for mutual protection are possible and desirable attainments.

But we cannot confine ourselves to political moves or collective measures alone. As the world exists today, our own national power is still the major bulwark against aggression and the major factor in the history of tomorrow. We must use that power unequivocally and openly but firmly and justly. We cannot be mealy-mouthed or pussy-footed with communism or any other totalitarianism and still expect to exist a free and independent people.

This means firmness without provocation, and it means anticipating the possible moves of any aggressor. It means, too, slamming the barn door *before* the cows get out. We must, for instance, learn to cope with the subversive and the underhand methods of communism. A carefully arranged coup (aided by one of our own mistakes) led the way to the Communist domination of the Hungarian Government. The strikes, riots and unrest in Italy and France in 1947 were plainly dictated by Moscow; their minimum objective was the crippling of the government's political and economic power;

their maximum objective could be in the future the seizure of political power by armed force. The Communists, in 1947, were fighting a guerrilla warfare—economically, politically, psychologically and (in Greece) militarily—against legitimate governments and against stabilization. We cannot permit the illegal seizure of power by such methods. We must oppose "planned chaos." "Legitimate" national revolution by a majority of the people against decadent or corrupt or tyrannical government is one thing; we must never forget that the United States was born from revolution in blood and fire. But arranged Communist revolution by a minority controlled by Moscow is a bastard movement which in no sense represents the will of the people and leads, not to freedom, but to certain enslavement. We must not allow Turkey, Greece, Italy, Austria, France, Germany (particularly), the Low Countries or Scandinavia to be blackjacked into communism. For if Western Europe goes Communist, there will surely be war, sooner or later, and we shall be handicapped in winning it. We must, therefore, prevent this, and prevent it we can. A simple declaration, before emergency occurs, that the United States will not tolerate arranged illegal coups or sponsored civil wars, but will support with arms, if necessary, the legitimate government so attacked would probably suffice to blunt this Communist technique. We must be firm.

On the other hand, we must not be provocative. Our Turkish policy in reverse—if, for instance, Russia were supplying funds to rehabilitate Mexico's armed forces—would be considered by us extremely provocative. Provocation breeds fear, and there is no doubt that part of the virulence of Russian propaganda is a product of semihysterical fear—fear of attack by capitalist powers. Our intervention in Turkey, a country on Russia's doorstep, suffers from this drawback; it is understandably considered provocative by Russia and it induces fear. Moreover, it is questionable whether the means will accomplish the ends, whether the funds that we can reasonably provide for Turkey will really be of much use in strengthening her armed forces. This is not to write Turkey off. Unlike Mexico, Turkey *is* a strategic pawn in the game of the nations; unlike Mexico, a world war could erupt from Turkish soil. The Turkish position, controlling the entrance to the Black Sea, land bridge between Europe and the Middle East, is a vital one; if Turkey falls under Communist domination, Greece probably goes and parts of the Middle East. We cannot afford to stand by and see this happen. But methods must differ in different countries, and what might be provocation in Turkey, situated as she is on Russia's doorstep, is certainly not provocation in Greece, which is removed from Russian borders and is clearly the victim of Communist aggression. Turkey, unlike Western Europe, has little reason to fear internal coups; if her economy can be built up she need not fear the possibility of internal trouble in the future. Her threat is external armed aggression, and we must not invite that by provoking it. Our Turkish policy might, therefore, be revised, if further study should support these arguments, by limiting our dollar aid in the future chiefly to economic measures. The danger of armed external aggression could be met by the system of alliances previously proposed and/or by a unilateral declaration that we would oppose such aggression by force.

Nor can the Middle East be allowed to degenerate into a chaos of hatreds and slayings. The immediate future of that part of the world is not bright. The British are withdrawing, leaving behind them something of a power vacuum. The Russians may try to take Britain's place. The Palestine "solution" is not a solution; out of it may come months or years of blood and suffering. The United States must shoulder its responsibilities in the Middle East as well as in Europe and Asia, even though those responsibilities are heavy and onerous.

The so-called Marshall plan or European Recovery Program for economic aid to Europe is part and parcel of the active diplomacy we must sponsor if we are to uphold the cause of Western civilization. It is, primarily, a plan to "buy time"; we shall not save Europe with dollars alone, nor will trade alone suffice to lure Russia's satellites away from her. The economic determinist theory of history will not stand the test; dollars and pounds do not necessarily buy loyalties. But economic measures must go hand in hand with political measures. The Marshall plan is not an open-and-shut business deal; it cannot be viewed in the cold terms of profit and loss. Conservative bankers would hardly recommend it to widows and orphans. It involves risk, considerable risk; it may not work. But it is a hopeful plan. Already, there are signs of economic recovery in Western Europe—and trade between East (particularly Czechoslovakia and Poland) and West is commencing to flourish. The

Marshall Plan offers the only opportunity Western Europe will have to rehabilitate itself with our aid; it buys time and helps to promote political stability. It should not, in the words of Ambassador Lewis Douglas, be viewed as a "statistician's paradise." The problem we face is a social and humanitarian and moral problem, as well as a political and economic one; Europe must know it has our support and our aid. The alternative is not pleasant; it probably is chaos first and quite probably communism, or conceivably, fascism next.

In our preoccupation with Europe, particularly Western Europe, unquestionably the most important area in the world to us for the short-term future, we must never forget Asia. Asia, with its teeming millions and its potential wealth, may have a long-term importance transcending any other area of the earth; in any case our position and our interests today are world-wide; we cannot neglect any one area of the earth without danger. Between communism and Chiang Kai-shek there is but one choice; only if we decide to oppose communism in China can we hope to eliminate *some* of the corruption and inefficiency of the Central Government. Our shilly-shallying policy toward China must end. We must aid non-communist China with dollars and moral help and political declarations and military equipment, but wisely and sparingly, and with strictly limited means; Europe comes first, and, unless careful, we could easily empty our wealth into the bottomless pit of China. Nor must we expect reformation or rehabilitation of Asia in our time. There will be continuing corruption, continuing misery, famines, bloodshed and death; civil strife will wax and wane in Asia for decades to come.

Help of this scope to Asia and to Europe will clearly require a careful balancing of our resources against the needs; we must not exhaust ourselves. The military principle of "economy of force" is equally applicable to dollars.

In our efforts to stabilize and rehabilitate the world and to stop the spread of communism, we must not concentrate upon one evil and ignore the other. We should never forget the form of totalitarianism against which we so lately fought; the extremism of the right can become in the future as much of a menace as the extremism of the left. Indeed, it is paradoxical that the guerrilla warfare of the Communists against the Marshall plan and their violent attempts towards "planned chaos" may well result in a renaissance of the very forces we and they—so short a time ago—fought so hard to kill. We must keep a "weather eye" on Germany and Japan, and upon all movements in all countries that appear to reincarnate the spirit of Hitler.

We have cultivated the idle fancy in this country that we are democratizing the Germans and the Japanese. Nothing could be further from the truth. Democracy stems from a soil and a climate of freedom, in turn the product of struggle, growth and education; it blooms after long cultivation like a century plant. Too many of us seem to have forgotten the horrors of Belsen and the death march of Bataan, but our ex-enemies today are still our enemies under the skin, in most of what they stand for and believe in. In both Japan and Germany still exist many of the elements of totalitarianism; in both there smolders hatred of the United States, suppressed but yearning.

This does not mean that there cannot be, or will not be, any evolution in German or Japanese or, for that matter, Russian, attitudes, points of view or ethical or moral principles. Such changes do occur. But they take place slowly; we cannot expect by altering the Nazi textbooks to produce as a result a new and peace-loving generation overnight. Ethical and educational changes, on a national scope, require centuries for completion; we must encourage such changes, but we cannot depend upon a quick enemy about-face.

These ex-enemy states still have within them the seeds of future power; they can become forces for evil more easily than for good. The measures we take must, therefore, be uncompromising. Demilitarization must be long continued. No aviation should be allowed Germany or Japan; no armed forces (other than strong police forces) should be permitted either one. Control of the foreign affairs of Germany will have to be exercised for a considerable period by the occupying powers; in the case of Japan primarily by the United States. If a satisfactory agreement with Russia is not attainable, a merger of the Western zones of Germany and a return of a greater degree of self-government to these zones is mandatory. So, too, is a greater economic health; Germany cannot remain indefinitely the sick man of Europe hanging about our neck. But our occupation forces and policing garrisons, even if token, must long remain, not alone to check the recrudescence of German militarism and the almost certain growth of German irredentism but to stand guard against Communist aggression. An armaments inspection and control group to prevent or at least delay and hamper German rearmament must stay in the Reich for years to come. The Ruhr should be placed, at least temporarily, under control of an international condominium—the United States, the United Kingdom, France and the Low Countries. Japan, less dangerous to the world, and an island rather than a continental power, can be watched from outside her borders, but she, too, must be watched.

We must forever remember, too, as previous chapters have pointed out, that Russian strength for a long time to come will remain markedly inferior to that of the United States and that potential danger in the foreseeable future will come not from Russia alone, but from Russia *and allies*, particularly from an alliance between Russian mass and German technique; secondarily from an alliance between Russia and Japan.

It is for this reason, fundamentally, that we must be prepared to keep American troops in Europe, if necessary for years. Too many Americans have envisaged the signing of peace treaties and the evacuation of all troops of all powers from occupied territories as a "solution." It is true that such peace treaties might officially "end the war." But unless their clauses were very carefully drawn, and unless all sorts of safeguards were provided against a Communist coup or Communist seizure of power by devious means, the withdrawal of troops might well pave the way for a Communist extension of power.

It is this that we need to fear, an alliance between Russia and Communist-dominated nations beyond her borders. This already has occurred in Eastern Europe. It could occur in Western Europe if all troops were suddenly withdrawn from occupied areas and the resultingly weak state, without armed forces of its own, were subjected to sudden internal assaults from Communist enemies. The technique is clear. In Rumania, for instance, the withdrawal of Russian troops will have little meaning. The government, under pressure of the occupying Red Army, has been completely dominated by Communists, and most of the important political opposition has been wiped out. The Army has been purged; Soviet officers oversee its activities. A training school conducted by Russian officers has been established in Constanta. Russian soldiers have been demobilized by the thousands in Rumania and have settled with their families as "civilians" on Russian farms, particularly in the Dobruja, Banat and along the "elbow" of the Carpathians. The Russians and their Rumanian Communist followers control the police, the courts, the border guards, the customs, the militia—all of the military and semi-military forces of the nation. And, close at hand, in nearby Russia looms the mass of the Soviet Army.

Germany and Austria are not so geographically exposed as is Rumania, and their division into different occupation zones has prevented the Communist domination of these countries. But troop withdrawal, unless carefully hedged, could be followed by the extension of Communist influence into Western Germany and Southern and Western Austria by modifications of the same methods used so successfully in Eastern Europe. Russian "civilian" settlers would be left behind on the land. Factory "guards," Communist-dominated police forces, and a disciplined Communist party—all supplied with arms and help by Moscow—would provide strength for the seizure of complete power. If this were not enough, the Russians in the case of Germany would play their trump card, the Soviet-trained and equipped German Army, formed of German prisoners of war, and the Soviet-dominated Union of German officers. Unless some sort of an international police force, or a military force at the disposal of the central German government (the latter something we would want to avoid, in the interests of a demilitarized Germany) were available, it would be virtually impossible for the young state to withstand such pressures. The peace treaties, therefore, are filled with the most difficult complexities, but it will be well for the future of the United States and of the world if we reconcile ourselves to a long pull and do not impatiently push our leaders into hasty "solutions" which are no solutions. At all costs Germany must not again be allowed to threaten the peace of the world; at all costs a German-Russian rapprochement must be avoided; at all costs we must build up the power and stability of Western Europe while trying to avoid a permanent division of Europe into two camps.

All of this adds up to a dynamic and vital foreign policy. We must avoid the static and the defensive; we must try new ways and new methods; we must show an awareness of our new greatness, a knowledge that we are a *world* power.

The initiative and the vigor that once distinguished the American character must be revived and applied to the field of foreign policy. We are not helpless against the street-fighting tactics, the groin kick, the rabbit punch, the canard and the rumor; we can meet Fascists or Communists with the tactics of democracy and defeat them both, so long as we believe in our faith and work for it.

This means new methods. We might, for instance, as V. S. Makaroff has suggested, put into effect a policy of giving political sanctuary to deserters from the Soviet Army. There have been many such deserters since the war; according to one 1947 estimate from Germany ten per cent of the Soviet armed forces in the Eastern Zone had deserted. Our policy has been to return these men to Soviet authority, despite the fact that proved desertion in the Soviet Army is almost always punishable by death or at least by Siberian exile. Mr. Makaroff believes an announcement that the United States would resume, in accordance with its once traditional policy, the granting of asylum to deserters and political refugees from Russia would "stimulate a vast exodus from the Soviet Army." This assessment of what such a measure might accomplish is over-optimistic, and it is obvious that the granting of such asylum could become a two-edged sword, unless all refugees thus accepted were very carefully screened to prevent the harboring of undercover Communists, spies and saboteurs. But the suggestion at least represents original and practical thinking and a freshness and initiative of approach which too rarely characterizes American policy.

On the other hand, the "tooth-for-a-tooth" philosophy can be blindly carried to absurd extremes. Recent demands that all exports to Russia be stopped at once offer an example of the dangerous nature of such thinking. The United States has been importing considerable and much-needed amounts of manganese and chrome and platinum from Russia since the war, and part of the objective of the Marshall plan is to encourage the countries of Eastern and Western Europe to resume their prewar trade. By stopping all exports to Russia we might at one blow cut off our own supplies of raw materials and imperil the Marshall plan. Reciprocity is a good principle if not carried to extremes, but we must remember foreign policy rarely is sound when dictated by passion and prejudice.

Our new policy must avoid these two dangers. Above all we must recognize that modern diplomacy, like modern war, requires total methods. We shall not find an economic or a political or a psychological short cut to success; we must use and blend all methods —political, economic and psychological—backed up by military strength.

The world is two worlds; it does no good to refuse to accept that fact. We *must* consolidate our portion of it and try to make that portion as large and as powerful as possible. But our ultimate objective, even though it be decades or centuries away, must be one world, and we must constantly try to heal and patch and bind and to avoid the final hardening of Europe into two camps.

Above all, our new policy must "sell" the American ideal to the world. The Communists, chiefly through their "Cominform" (Communist Information Bureau), have set out to deliberately distort our motives and to defeat the European Recovery Program (the Marshall plan). They have had their greatest successes in the propaganda field, chiefly because the voice of America overseas is weak and hesitant and equivocal. Congress bears much of the responsibility for this; the postwar cuts in the State Department's information program did not help our cause. The failure of the State Department to consider domestic and world-wide public opinion sufficiently in the formulation of policy, and sometimes the heavy-handed methods of presenting our case to the world, are other faults. We do not need and should not have a government press service, but we do need, can well afford and must support a government information service which will present the American case overseas to foreign opinion. This must be done vigorously and extensively, for the war of words—the battle for the minds of men—is fully joined, and he who wins it conclusively will have little need of guns and armor, bombs and planes.

Such measures as these and such a vigorous and affirmative foreign policy must imply a change in the attitude of the American people. We have been, in a political and economic sense, introverts, concerned with our own affairs. We have not yet completed our psychological readjustment, a stupendous one, to a world of perpetual crises and of complex techno-scientific discoveries. This adjustment is essential to the future; it will have to be made whether we like it or not. A philosophical detachment, a thick skin and spiritual solace are essential to the man of tomorrow, for there is and can be no easy or immediate solution—if, indeed, any is ever evolved—to the problems which man himself has created.

The face of tomorrow is a bleak visage; we are embarked upon a "time of troubles." Political easements and adjustments are possible and probable; economic difficulties will wax and wane. But there remain the new weapons which man himself has created but for which man cannot devise foolproof, effective and inclusive physical controls. We have opened for all time the lid of Pandora's box of evils. We cannot now push the genii back into the box. We may not like it, but we must face it. Atomic bombs, biological agents and other weapons of mass destruction are now a permanent part of man's society; and no perfect *physical* system of control is possible for all these weapons.

We are thus living in the shadow of a slumbering volcano, yet with philosophical detachment and spiritual fortitude this need not mean a fear complex. This is not a new state for man, for death is always a part of life. Robert Louis Stevenson, in *Aes Triplex*, expressed this concept beautifully; his description fits well the world of tomorrow:

. . . although few things are spoken of with more fearful whisperings than this prospect of death, few have less influence on conduct under healthy circumstances. We have all heard of cities in South America built upon the side of fiery mountains, and how, even in this tremendous neighborhood, the inhabitants are not a jot more impressed by the solemnity of mortal conditions than if they were delving gardens in the greenest corner in England. There are serenades and suppers and much gallantry among the myrtles overhead and meanwhile the foundation shudders underfoot, the bowels of the mountain growl, and at any moment living ruin may leap sky-high into the moonlight and tumble man and his merrymaking in the dust.

How, then, will the history of tomorrow develop?

No man is seer or prophet; only general expectations can be suggested.

The short-term political outlook is far from all black. Even as this book goes to press, one acute crisis may have passed. Britain's coal and steel production is on the upgrade, and the breaking of the Communist-led strikes in France in late 1947—a defeat for Russia—may have marked one high tide of communism in Western Europe. No longer is democracy fighting on the defensive. A better balance of power in Europe is taking place slowly. Yet the struggle is by no means ended. Russia has lost "battles" in recent months but not the "war." Strikes and work stoppages contribute to chaos and to the defeat of the Marshall plan. And that is the avowed Communist goal.

Peace treaties may gradually be achieved, the occupied countries gradually evacuated of most of their occupation troops. Whether or not this occurs, a period of less strain and tension in international relations will come. But it will be temporary, and the new climate can beguile the American people into complacency. For unless and until communism as an international force changes its stripes, or unless and until Russian national power is broken or a strong stabilized balance of power set up in Western Europe to offset it, unless and until the potential of fascism is forever eliminated, there can be no basic change in the world situation. The Communists are fanatics; there is no *present* indication that they will abandon their proselytizing and aggressive philosophy. Russian power is likely to increase, rather than diminish, in the future, unless it is destroyed by war. The restoration of Western Europe is, therefore, essential to the world, yet the Communists are still doing their best to defeat such a restoration.

There appears to be in the immediate tomorrows no surcease from *basic* conflicts, although great easing of present *tensions* is possible, though not probable immediately. There is not, and there never has been, much probability of imminent war with Russia. The compelling reasons against a deliberate "preventive" war of our making already have been discussed in this chapter, and our own strength today is so great, vis-à-vis Russia, that the men in the Kremlin would not willingly risk war to gain ends which they hope, in any case, in time to achieve by other means.

Can they achieve those ends; is communization of Europe and the world probable? Nothing is impossible, and communism today is a virile force—aggressive, expanding. Much will depend upon the growth of Russian power relative to that of the Western nations in the next quarter, or half, century. Soviet power will inevitably increase, relative to our own, for in time the Russians will be producing atomic bombs and other weapons of mass destruction; their population is growing faster than our own; it is possible, though they start from a lower base, that their *rate* of industrial expansion will in future years exceed our own. As a totalitarian state Russia can, at any moment, earmark a far higher percentage of her production effort to war or any other specific purpose than we can do. The USSR does stand, therefore, to gain by time. But she starts far behind us in the struggle for power. She can really overtake and overbalance us only by ideological and political successes, only by the proselytizing methods of communism; if she can convert Western Europe to a system of satellite Russian states we shall, indeed, be undone. On the other hand, if Western Europe can be restored to strength, political integrity and independence, Russian power, despite increases, will be more than balanced by the forces of the West.

We must work, therefore, with full heart and effort to "contain" communism, and in particular to restore Western Europe's strength. We must work to postpone war, in the hope that the imponderables of history which no man can judge may completely alter the present situation in the decades ahead. The fervent Red apostles of revolution of today might conceivably, for instance, grow fat with the surfeit of their conquests, might in time become "non-practicing Communists." Stalin will die in the years to come; the "palace" struggle for succession may produce another "Trotsky split" which will weaken somewhat, no matter how little, the monolithic edifice of communism. Internal pressures in Russia, typified by the recent revaluation of the ruble, may force external policy changes. The potential enemy of a quarter century hence, indeed, may not be Russia at all; new forces may sweep the world. We must never forget the potential menace of fascism.

War, therefore, should be postponed. If despite our best efforts it should come, it must be limited; we should never be the first to use the new weapons of mass destruction. Does that mean we must "take" the first blow? It may well mean that, but that blow need not be of the crippling consequence now foreseen if the military and political safety measures outlined in this book are taken.

And, if our powder is kept dry and Western Europe's political integrity preserved, war with Russia, even a quarter century hence, should end in military victory for American arms, unless we made tremendous errors. Russia can be defeated; she has in some ways feet of clay. Indeed, we are, I think, in danger of overestimating her military strength today, just as we once underestimated it. If we must, we can defeat Russia today or a quarter century hence—*if* we keep our power dry and our spirit strong.

But we want *no* war; that we must make plain to the world. We must work specifically against war with Russia. There is no other war in sight.

But as we labor for peace we must remember the lessons of history; there is no perpetual peace; someday, somewhere, somehow, with someone, war probably will come again to the world. This has always been true in history. Tennessee Williams, the playwright, has epitomized, out of his own experience, the "vacuity of a life without struggle":

. . . the heart of man, his body and his brain, are forged in a white-hot furnace for the purpose of conflict. . . . Security is a kind of death, I think. . . .[5]

This is not to enshrine war, not to deny the validity of *relative* security. It is to state only a truism—that conflict is a part of life, though conflict does not *have* to mean a shooting war.

But today war—international war—can mean chaos. And so the face of tomorrow is the face of danger; we must anticipate a "time of troubles" while man learns to make peace with himself.

Notes—Chapter XV

1. No single nation in history ever has succeeded in dominating all of Europe, except briefly during a war; no single nation in history ever has controlled all of Asia.

2. "The Atomic Dilemma," by Bernard Brodie, *Annals of the American Academy of Political and Social Science*, January 1947.

3. "The Implications of the Atomic Bomb for International Relations," by Jacob Viner, *Proceedings of the American Philosophical Society*, Vol. 90, No. 1, January 29, 1946, page 56. Quoted by Brodie (see Note 2), page 35.

4. This article with another in the New York *Times* was subsequently expanded by Mr. Armstrong into a short book, *The Calculated Risk*, Macmillan.

5. Tennessee Williams, in an article, "A Streetcar Named Success," in the New York *Times* dramatic section, November 30, 1947.

CHAPTER XVI

SUMMARY—THE PRICE OF POWER

> Men at some time are masters of their fates:
> The fault, dear Brutus, is not in our stars,
> But in ourselves, that we are underlings.
>
> JULIUS CAESAR

THE United States is master of its fate and architect of the future.

We hold the power, if we but have the heart, to win the struggle of tomorrow. Upon us, more than upon any other nation of our times, depend the history of the next century and the fate or fortune of millions of the world's peoples. To us has been granted greatness, and the power and the glory. Favored by nature, bulwarked by the oceans, these United States have enjoyed a century and a half of expansion, progress, prosperity and freedom unparalleled in the record of man. Today, the veil of distance and the mist of space have been sundered by the plane; no longer do we dwell upon the fringes of history; the little colony on the edge of a wilderness that our forefathers dedicated to liberty has now become the center of the stage. We need the world, and the world certainly needs us:

> Nor sitting by his hearth at home,
> Doth man escape his appointed doom.[1]

To us has been passed the torch of Western civilization, the political birthright of Magna Charta, the cultural traditions of Greece and Rome and France and England, of Cervantes and Shakespeare, of Goethe and Milton. The lands of Europe from which our settlers came are old and weary, bowed and desolate; to us has been passed the torch. We may carry it high, or it may be dashed into the dust.

Ours is the future; upon us rest the responsibilities and the compulsions of power.

The responsibilities are heavy and the compulsions stern. The price of power is huge; it is not ease but toil, not peace but struggle, not wealth but taxes. The roadside of history is lined with the bones of civilizations that had become fat and slothful, careless and complacent, that had accepted the privileges of power but not its obligations. The obligations are many. For the face of tomorrow is the bleak face of danger—danger from without from the mechanistic robots that man himself has created, danger from within from the false gospel of demagogues and the plausible cant of the deluded.

This is the age of extremism—"spend enough money on defense and you will be saved"; "give labor full power and you will be saved"; the age of fascism and communism. The false prophets urge us to the right, to the left, to extremes. There is no salvation, they say, without: (a) return of the Garden of Eden to earth; or (b) a nation bristling like a hedgehog with armaments. The millennium or imperialism; disarmament or world conquest—so the alternatives are drawn.

There is no truth in these extremes; there is safety only in the middle way. A previous chapter has tried to sketch the international nature of the middle course we must take; it is a hard course; it promises no certain solutions, no quick millennium. But it avoids both the precipice of isolationism and the chasm of imperialism; it advances firmly and unequivocally against the obstacle of totalitarianism. Justice, freedom, dignity—these are the markers that must keep our feet upon the hard path of the middle way.

But it is not enough to have a foreign policy that avoids extremes. We must keep our feet upon a middle course domestically as well as internationally, for what we do domestically will inevitably affect our international policies.

We must have strength—actual and potential military strength—for without military strength, power in the world of today has no meaning. This book has tried to answer the question of what type and what amount of military strength we need; it has tried to show the way to the achievement of a reasonable security without becoming a "garrison state." It has attempted to describe the "defense" of the United States in an age when to defend is to attack, and it has tried to plot the general course our foreign policy should take in the years ahead.

To recapitulate: The United States today is the strongest potential military power on earth, and in many ways the strongest actual power. We have the world's greatest navy, the finest and one of the largest air forces and a long lead in the production of atomic bombs and other new weapons. We face no immediate military threat. Yet we cannot rest upon past laurels or prepare to fight the next war with the last war's weapons. Our present plans for "defense" are unco-ordinated, inchoate, and inordinately expensive, nor do they emphasize sufficiently the necessity in the atomic age of "readiness potential," of maintaining a highly trained, completely ready mobile force prepared to retaliate instantly and massively against any aggressor. That force must emphasize air power and guided missiles, aircraft carriers, missile-launching ships and submarines, and the most efficient air-borne army in the world. A "cushion" defensive system of radar warning stations, anti-aircraft and anti-missile emplacements, fighter defense and picket ships must complement our offensive force. We must have bases overseas to warn us of possible attack, to attract the blows of an enemy away from our great cities and to serve as springboards from which we can retaliate more effectively. The range of the new weapons emphasizes the necessity of bases and friends far from our shores. We must depart from the traditional American policy of no alliances, for the hope of at least temporary peace and certainly the future of America and of Western civilization depends upon consolidating the spirit and the resources of the nations friendly to us and to our way of life.

A world-wide efficient intelligence system, to give us warning of crisis, is of fundamental importance in this era of danger; it is, after a sound diplomacy, the first line of defense. An extensive, thorough and well-integrated research and development program for new weapons, an economic-mobilization plan calculated to harness in the least possible time the full resources of the nation to the cause of victory, a program of civilian defense for the home front, and a reasoned and well thought out plan for the raising and mobilization of the necessary man power—preferably, in peacetime, by voluntary methods—are other fundamental pillars in the edifice of a reasonable security. In all of these measures civilian authority must be the ultimate authority; the military must be strong but not all-powerful; they must have influence but they must not dictate.

There are three great dangers in the development of total preparations such as these for total war. The first is that we shall not go far enough, that in our complacence and our sloth we shall not appropriate enough funds; the second is that we shall go too far and that we shall thus become both the "bankrupt state" and the "garrison state"; and the third is that the funds appropriated may be improperly allocated, in other words that one service, or one arm, or one weapon will receive too large a proportion of the defense dollar, or that not enough will be made available for intelligence or for civilian defense, etc.

We need not, today—despite the jeremiads of the past two years—be much concerned with the first danger. The funds presently appropriated for defense are considerable. Some increase is definitely needed, but there is grave danger that projected expenditures may become far too large. Although the first danger is potential today, it could be actual tomorrow if Russia were to suspend her virulent accusations and threatening gestures and put on the suave mask of friendship. In such a case, the American people must forever remember that there is no known method of control for all mass weapons of destruction; the sword of Damocles, now and henceforth, is to hang over our heads, and if we sleep or grow forgetful the thread can snap. The American armed services must stay strong, or we perish.

But today, the third danger and the second are more threatening to our defense establishment and our democracy. The third—the improper allocation of defense funds—is a present product of past disunity; the unification act of last year and the new governing authority of a "super" Secretary of Defense may remedy it. But this is not certain. Service rivalries still exist; each service still beats the big drum for its needs. The Air Force lobby, the Navy lobby, the Army lobby are all powerful forces; each is thinking in terms of its own narrow interests. There is, I think, little likelihood that we shall neglect our air power; there is greater danger that we may dangerously subordinate the surface services which still have major validity in war, and even greater danger that we may subordinate or ignore passive or home-front defense. We are, too, *potential* victims of what Under Secretary of State Robert A. Lovett has called the "numbers racket." We are in danger of making a Maginot Line of numbers—numbers of planes, numbers of men, numbers of ships. Operating forces of all services are important and must be maintained at a figure considerably larger than in the past, but until the verge of war, more major emphasis should be put upon research and development and production rate and capacity. We are operating too many ships today; we may be in danger, if some of the present grandiose plans are implemented, of operating too many planes, maintaining too many men, tomorrow. Numbers alone may give us the illusion of security but probably not its substance. For maintenance in the armed services of great numbers of men, ships and planes in peacetime will eat up the bulk of the defense dollar; research and development, passive defense and production capacity may be stunted, and we may possess, when war starts, an obsolescent standing establishment. This must be avoided at all costs. "Readiness potential," however, is of primary importance in the atomic age, and numbers *are* an index of this potential; we need in the period ahead a larger army and navy and especially a much larger air force than ever before in our peacetime history. But neither military strength nor security can be achieved by numbers alone.

The second danger—the danger of appropriating too much for our armed forces—is a danger to democracy, rather than to the armed forces, and it, too, is an active danger today.

Secretary of the Army Royall has warned of the consequences to the economic security of the country of spending too much on our armed forces; there is, as he says, a "limit," and projected expenditures entailing annual outlays of perhaps $15,000,000,000 or more exceed a reasonable limit. But such spending has consequences even greater than the economic. Too great an expenditure on military strength will inevitably subtract from the European Recovery Program and the sums that *must* be provided to rehabilitate the world. Those appropriations must have first priority; for if we win the political, economic and psychological conflicts now joined we shall not have to fight a "shooting war" against Russia.

Excessive military expenditures also pose a definite danger to our democracy, economically and ideologically, as previous chapters have pointed out. It would be easy, in preparing for total war, to lose the very things we are trying to defend; we must hold the balance true. Excessive armaments appropriations can also promote an arms race and can sour the whole soil of international co-operation. Neither too little nor too much for the armed forces and a proper allocation of the defense dollar to the individual services, to research and development and to passive defense is basic to all our objectives—an efficient defense and reasonable security, rehabilitation of Western Europe, and perpetuation of the political system and way of life for which America stands.

We cannot contemplate, therefore, any immediate decrease in defense spending; we must insist upon an increase, but a reasonable one in no way measured by the astronomical yardsticks the services have advocated. We must insist, too, upon a reallocation of the defense dollar so that first things will come first.

But a proper defense of our way of life must mean more than guns and dollars. We can prepare for total war, even in the atomic age, without becoming a garrison state, we can achieve "defense-by-offense" without becoming an imperialist power, but we can do these things not with guns or dollars alone but with spirit, mind and heart.

The American people must grow to their new responsibilities of power. They can be political introverts no longer; the past is dead; the future reigns. Nor can we, with safety to our institutions or to the world, retain the adolescent instability which has characterized too many of our past policies. We must develop, as Dr. James T. Shotwell has put it: an international "sense of humor [which] is a sense of proportion, and proportion is the prime condition of justice."[2]

Americans must also develop a political awareness. There is no government without politics and no politics without government; if we want good government, we must study politics. Particularly must we resist the increasing power of the military in non-military fields, but if we want a good defense, we must also study the military. The American citizen has, as an obligation of citizenship, the imperative duty of an *active* interest in military affairs. The civilian must participate with the military in the task of security. Military *influence* in government must remain strong, for total war means total preparations, but military influence *must*—for the sake of our liberties and the efficiency of the military—remain secondary to civilian control.

Again the middle way is the best way. The military must be honored but not extolled, allowed to influence but not to dominate, have their place in government, but a place strictly circumscribed.

We must forever remember that the military mind thinks, even in democracies, in terms primarily of force; Marshal Lefebvre, of the Napoleonic era, well illustrates this dangerous mentality: "We have come to give you liberty and equality—but don't lose your heads about it; the first person who stirs without my permission will be shot."

Particularly must we cherish our bill of rights. There has been a dangerous tendency to gloss over its principles, to accept infractions, to condone loss of freedom. Censorship and secrecy, principally the products of military influence, have been more pronounced since the war than ever before in any peacetime period in our history. The nature of the new weapons and the tenseness of the world situation demand some secrecy, but again there must be compromise which will not infringe the basic freedoms. We must oppose the "octopus state"; we must not kowtow to government or pay obeisance to the military. A jealous determination to protect our individual liberties against the encroachments of government is essential to a healthy America.

All of this implies a new mental outlook, a new approach. We have been seeing Reds under every bed these past years; our sense of values has been confused by hysteria. We must have a renaissance of liberalism and of common sense. As Samuel Grafton put it in the New York *Post*:

The simple, corny and rather sordid question which each of us faces today is whether he is for democracy or just afraid of Russia. It makes a difference . . . if one is only afraid of Russia, one is on the defensive, and we learned a few years ago that defense will not win the war.[3]

Again we must seek the middle ground. We must be aware, without becoming hysterical; we must recognize danger without waving the flag of panic.

The plain truth is we do not need to be afraid of anyone. As Saul K. Padover has written:

The Russian challenge is indeed serious. Nothing is gained by minimizing it, or by suggesting that it is easy of solution. But there are ways and means of meeting it. . . . The heart of the question . . . is whether this country today has the will, the moral greatness and political wisdom to use its immense power for the good of all.[4]

This then is the great issue. Do we have the "will, the moral greatness and the political wisdom" to be masters of our fate and architects of the future?

I think we do, but the answer, if it is to be affirmative, must come from the strengthened spirit of the American people.

The nation, if it is to remain strong, must be integrated in a common purpose and devoted to a common ideal. Leaders of high heart and firm aim—servants of the people, not their masters—are essential to our future security in the dangerous tomorrow.

For we shall travel no easy road. The middle ground is never smooth, least so in the atomic age. The awful weapons man has created are now forever with us; we shall walk henceforth with their shadow across the sun.

The task ahead is hard; it requires common effort and individual sacrifice. The price of power is huge. But there is no alternative to the middle way.

Notes—Chapter XVI

1. Aeschylus.

2. *War as an Instrument of National Policy*, by James T. Shotwell, Harcourt, Brace & Company. Page 267.

3. "I'd Rather Be Right," by Samuel Grafton, the New York *Post*, December 4, 1947.

4. "The American Century?," by Saul K. Padover, *The American Scholar*; Winter, 1947-48.

BIBLIOGRAPHY

Brooks Adams, *America's Economic Supremacy*, Harper & Brothers, New York, 1947.

Hamilton Fish Armstrong, *The Calculated Risk*, Macmillan Company, New York, 1947.

Hamilton Fish Armstrong, *The Task—and Price—of World Leadership*, the Overbrook Press, Stamford, Conn., 1947.

Atomic Scientists of Chicago, Inc., *The Atomic Bomb*, 1946.

James Phinney Baxter, 3d, *Scientists Against Time*, Little, Brown & Company, Boston, 1946.

Herman Beukema, William M. Geer, and Associates, *Contemporary Foreign Governments*, Rinehart & Company, Inc., New York, 1946.

Percy W. Bidwell and Harold T. Tobin, *Mobilizing Civilian America*, Council on Foreign Relations, Inc., New York, 1940.

William Liscum Borden, *There Will Be No Time, The Revolution in Strategy*, Macmillan Company, New York, 1946.

James C. Boyce (editor), *New Weapons for Air Warfare*, Little, Brown & Company, Boston, 1947.

Bernard Brodie (editor), *The Absolute Weapon*, Harcourt, Brace & Company, New York, 1946.

———. *Foreign Oil and American Security*, Yale Institute of International Studies, Memorandum Number Twenty-Three, New Haven, 1947.

Lewis H. Brown, *A Report on Germany*, Farrar, Straus & Company, New York, 1947.

James Burnham, *The Struggle for the World*, John Day Company, New York, 1947.

Dr. Vannevar Bush, *Science the Endless Frontier*, U. S. Government Printing Office, Washington, 1945.

Ansley J. Coale, *The Problem of Reducing Vulnerability to Atomic Bombs*, Princeton University Press, 1947.

George B. Cressey, *Asia's Lands and Peoples*, Whittlesey House, McGraw-Hill, New York, 1944.

———. *The Basis of Soviet Strength*, Whittlesey House, McGraw-Hill, New York, 1945.

Kingsley Davis, *Population Trends and Policies in Latin America*, Office of Population Research, School of Public and International Affairs, Princeton University; reprinted from *Latin-American Studies, II, Some Economic Aspects of Postwar Inter-American Relations*, University of Texas, 1946.

Maj. Gen. John Russell Deane, *The Strange Alliance*, Viking Press, New York, 1947.

J. Frederick Dewhurst and Associates, *America's Needs and Resources*, Twentieth Century Fund, New York, 1947.

Allen Welsh Dulles, *Germany's Underground*, Macmillan Company, New York, 1947.

Louis Fischer, *The Great Challenge*, Duell, Sloan & Pearce, New York, 1946.

William T. R. Fox, *The Super-Powers*, Harcourt, Brace & Company, New York, 1944.

Maj. Gen. J. F. C. Fuller, *Armament and History*, Scribner's, New York, 1945.

Reginald Russell Gates, *Human Genetics*, Macmillan Company, New York, 1946.

James S. Gregory and D. W. Shave, *The USSR, A Geographical Survey*, George G. Harrap & Company, Ltd., London, 1944.

B. H. Liddell Hart, *Revolution in Warfare*, Yale University Press, New Haven, 1947.

Corliss Lamont, *The Peoples of the Soviet Union*, Harcourt, Brace & Company, New York, 1945.

C. K. Leith, *World Minerals and World Politics*, Whittlesey House, McGraw-Hill, New York, 1931.

C. K. Leith, J. W. Furniss, and Cleona Lewis, *World Minerals and World Peace*, Brookings Institution, Washington, 1943.

Willy Ley, *Rockets and Space Travel*, Viking Press, New York, 1947.

Frank Lorimer, *Population of the Soviet Union*, League of Nations, Geneva, 1946.

S. L. A. Marshall, *Men Against Fire*, the *Infantry Journal* and William Morrow & Company, New York, 1947.

Lynn Montross, *War Through the Ages*, Harper & Brothers, New York, 1944.

Sydney Morrell, *Spheres of Influence*, Duell, Sloan & Pearce, New York, 1946.

Samuel Eliot Morison, *The Battle of the Atlantic—History of United States Naval Operations in World War II*, Little, Brown & Company, Boston, 1947.

Donald M. Nelson, *Arsenal of Democracy*, Harcourt, Brace & Company, New York, 1946.

Hoffman Nickerson, *The Armed Horde 1793–1939*, Putnam's, New York, 1940.

———. *Arms and Policy, 1939–1944*, Putnam's, New York, 1945.

Harold Nicolson, *The Congress of Vienna*, Harcourt, Brace & Company, New York, 1946.

Frank Notestein and others, *The Future Population of Europe and the Soviet Union*, League of Nations, Geneva, 1944.

Leslie Paul, *The Annihilation of Man*, Harcourt, Brace & Company, New York, 1945.

George S. Pettee, *The Future of American Secret Intelligence*, Infantry Journal Press, Washington, 1946.

Maj. Gen. C. F. Robinson, *Foreign Logistical Organizations and Methods—A Report from the Secretary of the Army*. The Army Department, 1947.

Walter Sharp and Grayson Kirk, *Contemporary International Politics*, Farrar & Rinehart, New York, 1940.

James T. Shotwell, *War as an Instrument of National Policy*, Harcourt, Brace & Company, New York, 1939.

Leslie E. Simon, *German Research in World War II*, John Wiley & Sons, Inc., New York, 1947.

Henry DeWolf Smyth, *Atomic Energy for Military Purposes*, the Official

Report on the Development of the Atomic Bomb under the Auspices of the United States Government, Princeton University Press, 1945.

OSWALD SPENGLER, *The Decline of the West*, Alfred A. Knopf, Inc., New York, 1939.

NICHOLAS JOHN SPYKMAN, *America's Strategy in World Politics*, Harcourt, Brace & Company, New York, 1942.

———. *The Geography of the Peace*, edited by Helen R. Nicholl, Harcourt, Brace & Company, New York, 1944.

JOHN R. STEELMAN, *The Federal Research Program*, U. S. Government Printing Office, Washington, 1947.

ROBERT STRAUSZ-HUPE, *The Balance of Tomorrow*, Putnam's, New York, 1945.

LINCOLN R. THIESMEYER and JOHN E. BURCHARD, *Combat Scientists*, Little, Brown & Company, Boston, 1947.

DR. HAROLD C. UREY, "I'm a Frightened Man," as told to Michael Amrine, in *Atomic Terror Tomorrow*, the Crowell-Collier Publishing Co., New York, 1946.

GEORGE WELLER, *Bases Overseas*, Harcourt, Brace & Company, New York, 1944.

HANS W. WEIGERT and VILHJALMUR STEFANSSON, *Compass of the World*, Macmillan Company, New York, 1944.

America's Resources for World Leadership, National Industrial Conference Board, Inc., New York, 1947.

British Security, A Report by a Chatham House Study Group, Royal Institute of International Affairs, London, 1946.

Documents Under Discussion by the Atomic Energy Commission of the United Nations, compiled by the United States Mission to the United Nations, June–September, 1947.

The Effects of Atomic Bombs on Hiroshima and Nagasaki, U. S. Strategic Bombing Survey, Chairman's Office, U. S. Government Printing Office, Washington, 1946.

Essential Information on Atomic Energy, Special Committee on Atomic Energy, U. S. Senate, U. S. Government Printing Office, Washington, 1946.

Expenditures of the Federal Government, edited by John A. Krout, Academy of the Political Sciences, Columbia University, New York, 1938.

Inter-American Affairs, 1943, Columbia University Press, New York, 1944.

Inter-American Statistical Yearbook, Macmillan Company, New York, 1942.

Investigations of National Resources, Hearings Before a Subcommittee of the Committee on Public Lands, U. S. Senate, U. S. Government Printing Office, Washington, 1947.

Makers of Modern Strategy, edited by Earle, Craig and Gilbert, Princeton University Press, 1944.

Minerals Yearbook 1945, U. S. Department of the Interior, edited by H. D. Keiser, U. S. Government Printing Office, Washington, 1947.

Mission Accomplished, U. S. Army Air Forces, U. S. Government Printing Office, Washington, 1946.

One World or None, edited by Dexter Masters and Katharine Way, Whittlesey House, McGraw-Hill, New York, 1946.

A Program for National Security, Report of the President's Advisory Commission on Universal Training, U. S. Government Printing Office, Washington, 1947.

Public Reaction to the Atomic Bomb and World Affairs, A Nation-wide Survey of Attitudes and Information, Cornell University, Ithaca, New York, April, 1947.

Raw Materials in War and Peace, Associates in International Relations, Department of Social Sciences, U. S. Military Academy Printing Office, West Point, 1947.

Report to the Air Coordinating Committee of the Subcommittee on Demobilization of the Aircraft Industry, U. S. Government Printing Office, Washington, 1945.

Statesman's Year Book, edited by M. Epstein, Macmillan Company, New York, 1946.

Statistical Abstract of the United States, U. S. Department of Commerce, Bureau of the Census, U. S. Government Printing Office, Washington, 1946.

Summary Report (Pacific War), U. S. Strategic Bombing Survey, U. S. Government Printing Office, Washington, July, 1946.

The United States at War, Development and Administration of the War Program by the Federal Government, Committee on Records of War Administration, Bureau of the Budget, U. S. Government Printing Office, Washington, 1946.

Joseph and Stewart Alsop, "Are We Ready for a Pushbutton War?," *Saturday Evening Post*, September 3, 1947.

Adam Bergson, "The Fourth Five-Year Plan: Heavy Versus Consumers' Goods Industry," *Political Science Quarterly*, June 1947.

Percy W. Bidwell, "Ideals in American Foreign Policy," *International Affairs* (London), October 1946.

Robert S. Bird, "How Strong is America?," New York *Herald Tribune*, September 14, 1947.

Bernard Brodie, "The Atomic Dilemma," *Annals of the American Academy of Political and Social Sciences*, January 1947.

Bernard Brodie and Eilene Galloway, "The Atomic Bomb and the Armed Services," *Public Affairs Bulletin*, No. 55, the Library of Congress Legislative Reference Service, May 1947.

Colin Clark, "Soviet Military Potential," *Soundings* (London), September 1947.

Congressional Quarterly, March 15, 1947, Vol. v, No. 11.

Department of State Bulletin, September 7, 1947.

Gerald de Gaury, "The End of Arabian Isolation," *Foreign Affairs*, October 1946.

Samuel Grafton, "I'd Rather Be Right," New York *Post*, December 4, 1947.

Col. Clifford J. Heflin, "Mobility in the Next War," *Air University Quarterly*, Fall 1947.

William O. Hotchkiss, "Our Declining Mineral Reserves," *Yale Review*, Autumn 1947.

Brig. Gen. Robert Wood Johnson, "Dig, Son, Dig!," *Army Ordnance*, January–February 1947.

Eric Larrabee, "The Peacetime Army: Warriors Need Not Apply," *Harper's Magazine*, March 1947.

E. Willard Miller, "Some Aspects of the U.S. Mineral Self-Sufficiency," *Economic Geography*, April 1947.

Monthly Bulletin of Statistics, Statistical Office of the United Nations.

Saul K. Padover, "The American Century?," *American Scholar*, Winter 1947–48.

Stefan T. Possony, "Who's Who in the Atomic Race?," *U. S. Naval Institute Proceedings*, February 1946.

Theodor Rosebury and Elvin A. Kabat, with the assistance of Martin H. Boldt, "Bacterial Warfare, A Critical Analysis of the Available Agents, Their Possible Military Applications, and the Means for Protection Against Them," *Journal of Immunology*, May 1947.

Col. Dale O. Smith, "One-Way Combat," *Air University Quarterly*, Fall 1947.

Successful Farming, September 1947.

Arnold Toynbee, "Does History Repeat Itself?," *New York Times Sunday Magazine*, September 21, 1947.

Jacob Viner, "The Implications of the Atomic Bomb for International Relations," *Proceedings of the American Philosophical Society*, January 29, 1946.

Walter H. Voskuil, "Postwar Russia and Her Mineral Deposits," *Journal of Land and Public Utility Economics*, May 1947.

Tennessee Williams, "A Streetcar Named Success," New York *Times*, November 30, 1947.

Quincy Wright, "Atomic Dilemma: Comment," *Air Affairs*, Autumn 1947.

"X," "The Sources of Soviet Conduct," *Foreign Affairs*, July 1947.

APPENDIX I

MILITARY STRENGTHS OF THE POWERS

A

Military Potential

COUNTRY	POPULATION	AREA	STEEL PRODUCTION	COAL PRODUCTION	POWER PRODUCTION
United States	144,708,000 (Est. 10/47)	3,022,387	60.3 millions of metric tons (1946)	631,399 thousands of metric tons (1944)	228,189 millions of kilowatt hours (1944)
Russia	196,963,182 (Est. 1946)	8,390,490	16.3 millions of metric tons (1946)	153,523 thousands of metric tons (Est. 1945)	40,000 millions of kilowatt hours (1946)
Gt. Britain	47,888,958	94,279	13.1 millions of metric tons (1946)	191,644 thousands of metric tons (1944)	38,932 millions of kilowatt hours (1946)
France	39,700,000	212,659	4.4 millions of metric tons (1946)	25,260 thousands of metric tons (1944)	22,959 millions of kilowatt hours (1946)
China	457,835,475 (Est. 1936)	4,314,697	5,872 metric tons (Jan.-June 1944) (Free China)	2,306 thousands of metric tons (1946)	987.9 millions of kilowatt hours (1946)
Italy	45,800,000	119,800	1.2 millions of metric tons (1946)	Estimated 3,200 thousands of metric tons in 1947	16,923 millions of kilowatt hours (1946)

335

COUNTRY	POPULATION	AREA	STEEL PRODUCTION	COAL PRODUCTION	POWER PRODUCTION
			Western Zone Only		
Germany	65,910,800	182,741	2,986 thousands of metric tons (1946)	114,466 thousands of metric tons (1946)	21,062 millions of kilowatt hours (1946)
Japan	73,114,000 (Est. 1946)	146,690	0.6 million of metric tons (1946)	20,373 thousands of metric tons (1946)	27,062 millions of kilowatt hours (1946)

Note: German production figures of 1946 include only those of Western Germany.

Sources: *The Monthly Bulletin of Statistics*, November 1947; Committee of European Economic Cooperation, Volume II, *Technical Reports, Department of State; World Almanac; Minerals Yearbook*, 1945; *Statistical Abstract of the United States; Statesman's Year Book; Russia's Postwar Economy*, by Harry Schwartz, Syracuse University Press.

B

Estimates of Armed Forces of the "Big Five"

COUNTRY	ARMY		NAVY		AIR FORCE	
	REGULAR	RESERVES	TONNAGE	MEN	MILITARY PLANES	MEN
U. S.	650,000	Nat. Guard & Org. Res. 1,300,000	3,820,000	454,499 plus 90,486 Marines (Navy & Marine Res. 870,000) (Figures include Naval & Marine air personnel)	Air Force (O) 3,500 (R) 19,000 Navy (O) 4,500–6,000 (R) 7,000–9,000	325,000 (not including Naval air strength)
USSR	3,000,000 to 3,400,000	7,000,000 to 12,000,000	400,000 to 550,000	300,000 to 400,000	(O) 10,000–16,000 (R) 10,000–20,000	600,000 to 700,000
Gt. Britain	806,000	2,000,000 to 3,500,000	1,549,000	188,000	4,000 to 9,000 10,000 to 12,000 (includes naval air arm)	307,000
France	465,000	?	275,000	60,000	3,000	50,000 to 80,000
Nationalist China	4,500,000	?	Small Craft	22,000	300 to 450	20,000

Estimates are as of December 1, 1947. These figures change somewhat from month to month. U.S. figures represent latest official figures available as of December 1, 1947.

Reserves include organized and trained men and do not represent mobilizable man power.

Navy tonnage figures include ships in operation and in reserve of five principal categories only—carriers, battleships, cruisers, destroyers and submarines.

"Men" includes officers and enlisted men.

Military aircraft include: (O) operating aircraft—all military-type aircraft (combat and non-combat) assigned to actual operating squadrons of regular forces; (R) reserve aircraft—all military-type aircraft not in operating squadrons, inclusive of planes used by reserves.

Figures for Great Britain do not include Dominions or colonies. British Army is being reduced gradually to prewar strength. Sharp cuts in figures given above can be expected in the case of Britain in the near future. Strength for March 1, 1948, for all three British armed services is 937,000.

Russian figures are at best approximate.

China's astronomical numbers do not represent "effectives." Most are half trained, ill equipped.

Germany and Japan at present have no armed forces.

Italy's military power is limited by treaty to: Army—250,000, including 65,000 *carabinieri*; Navy—81,258 tons, 25,000 men; Air Force—350 planes, 25,000 men.

Yugoslavia's armed forces by contrast are: Army—350,000 to 400,000 men, including some 60,000 internal-security troops and semimilitary police, organized in thirty-five full or part-strength infantry divisions, two armored divisions (poorly equipped); Navy—chiefly small craft, 2,000 to 10,000 men; Air Force, perhaps 1,000 planes, all types (one third to one half combat types)—10,000 to 18,000 men. Reserves of perhaps 600,000 men. Yugoslavia is one of the strongest, in a military sense, of the Russian satellites.

It should be emphasized that the figures in this table represent estimates of *actual* strength—not projected, planned, or authorized figures. Chapter XIII amplifies the authorized and planned man-power programs of the United States.

U.S. air-power program is now undergoing considerable revision and study. Projected plans, for which funds are not yet available and which have been approved only in part by Congress, call for:

U. S. Air Force—

By June 30, 1948—

337,000 Enlisted Men
64,000 Officers
Fifty-five fully-manned regular air groups
Fifteen skeletonized groups

Eventually— Regular Force .... 6,869 planes of all types
Air National Guard .... 3,212 planes of all types
Air Reserve .... 2,360 planes of all types
Storage Reserve 8,100

Total 20,541

The U. S. Navy's present air strength, broken down (in somewhat different manner from the tabular figures) is:

Combat planes, first line (best available)   3,511
Combat planes (second line)   4,392
Combat planes, training   2,014
Transport and utility planes   1,261
Trainers   3,545

Total   14,723

Future plans for the Navy's air arm contemplate, within five years, the following numbers of aircraft:

Fleet combat aircraft   3,300
Aircraft in fleet support   2,700
Training aircraft   2,000
Reserve (storage)   2,700
Spares and overhaul   3,800

Total   14,500

APPENDIX II

UNITED STATES AND RUSSIAN MINERAL RESOURCES

Estimated Percentages of World Reserves

	COAL	IRON ORE	PETROLEUM	COPPER	LEAD	ZINC
U.S.A.	45%	34%	35%	22%	35%	34%
USSR	27%	11%	14%	16%	2%	12%

Source: *America's Resources for World Leadership*, prepared by the Conference Board, National Industrial Conference Board, Inc., New York, 1947, page 17. "Data are latest available and reflect postwar situation so far as ascertainable."

APPENDIX III

The Effects of Atomic Bombs on Hiroshima and Nagasaki, United States Strategic Bombing Survey, page 33:

A simple table shows most strikingly the comparison between the striking forces needed for atomic and for conventional raids. Against the two atomic attacks can be set the data for the most effective single urban attack, that on Tokyo on 9 March 1945, and the average effort and results from the Twentieth Air Force's campaign against Japanese cities:

	Effort and results			
	HIROSHIMA	NAGASAKI	TOKYO	AVERAGE OF 93 URBAN ATTACKS
Planes	1	1	279	173
Bomb load	1[1]	1[1]	1,667[2]	1,129[2]
Population density per square mile	35,000	65,000	130,000	[3]
Square miles destroyed	4.7	1.8	15.8	1.8
Killed and missing	70/80,000	35/40,000	83,600	1,850
Injured	70,000	40,000	102,000	1,830
Mortality rate per square mile destroyed	15,000	20,000	5,300	1,000
Casualty rate per square mile	32,000	43,000	11,800	2,000

[1] Atomic.   [2] Tons.   [3] Unknown.

APPENDIX IV

BIOLOGICAL WARFARE

Part of a paper by Dr. Franklin S. Cooper

A. *Introduction*

The use of bacteria or viruses for the initiation of epidemic diseases is a potentially important new weapon for total war. Biological warfare would undoubtedly have a powerful effect on civilian morale. Even relatively few cases of an unfamiliar disease occurring in peacetime provoke widespread uneasiness, as is evidenced by the public reaction to outbreaks of poliomyelitis or bubonic plague. As a new weapon, and one readily adaptable for use by secret agents, biological warfare might well be used in a surprise attack; it would be equally effective in a war of attrition.

In its present state as a potential but untried weapon, biological warfare can be compared with the atomic bomb just before the New Mexico tests. There was little doubt that the bomb would be tremendously effective if only it actually would explode. Theory predicted an explosion, but only experiment could give a sure answer. In the case of biological warfare, history has already answered the question.

B. *Military Characteristics*

The fact that epidemic diseases are universally known and dreaded means that biological warfare would have a tremendous impact on civilian morale. This is due in large part to the two principal and distinctive military characteristics of the bacterial weapon: First, it strikes directly at the enemy himself. It does not merely blockade his food supply so that he starves; or destroy the factories which supply his armies; or destroy his own home while he crouches in a shelter. It destroys the enemy himself, whether in his factory, his home, or in a dugout. In this it resembles gas warfare. Second, biological warfare is self-propagating; it is almost literally a "human conflagration." A thousand-plane raid is not needed to affect the entire population of a city. If enough small "fires" are set, the "conflagration" will spread even beyond the bounds of the city. A third military characteristic, important for strategic reasons, is that biological warfare does not destroy property and does not necessarily destroy life.

C. *Feasibility of Biological Warfare*

The potentialities of biological warfare seem clear enough, but thus far there has been no deliberate large-scale use. . . .

The classification of diseases may most easily be made in terms of the mode of transmission: (1) air-borne or "droplet" diseases, e.g., colds and influenza, diphtheria, measles, smallpox; (2) food or water-borne diseases, e.g., typhoid and cholera; (3) contact diseases, e.g., syphilis, gonorrhea; (4) diseases transmitted by an insect or other vector, e.g., typhus, plague, Rocky Mountain spotted fever, and malaria. The "droplet" infections lend themselves to easy dissemination and are readily transmitted from person to person in spite of all controls that have thus far been tried. It seems likely that this class of infections would be well adapted for use in biological warfare. The second and third categories can be controlled adequately by ordinary sanitary measures, except perhaps in the event of disruption of water and food supplies by intensive bombing. Vector diseases, while sometimes very important, are by their very nature adapted only to special situations, and even in such cases their intentional introduction would be rather difficult.

There are a number of factors, in addition to the route of infection, which determine the spread of a disease to epidemic proportions. Clearly, the disease must be highly infectious, or many of the persons exposed will not be affected themselves, and will not serve to transmit the disease to others. It must also be highly virulent; that is, those who contract the disease must be severely incapacitated by it. Another factor, related to infectiousness and virulence, is the susceptibility of the population as a whole to a particular disease.

The interaction between these factors is always complex, but leads to some interesting conclusions with respect to effective biological weapons. Measles will serve as a very good illustration. Measles is a virus disease, transmitted by droplets, and is highly infectious. However, a single attack usually provides long-term immunity. It is not surprising, then, that measles should be a childhood disease. When measles sweeps through a community, most of the children, and a few of the adults who have previously escaped, are infected, and the disease dies out only when susceptible persons are no longer available. A few years later, when the population again contains a substantial number of susceptible young children, a chance infection will once more set off a small epidemic. Thus few adults fail to acquire immunity during childhood; those adults who do have measles find it a severe disease. This is the usual situation in a country in which the disease is endemic. The results are very different when the disease is first introduced into a population which has had no previous experience with it. When measles was carried to the Sandwich Islands in 1774, it met with a population without previous experience and hence without immunity. The disease spread like wildfire, proved to be a very virulent disease for the adult population, and resulted in a mortality of about one in four. There have been a number of comparable cases which demonstrate that an old and highly infectious disease is likely to become a regular childhood disease of no great consequence; but that the same disease, if introduced into new surroundings, may result in a serious epidemic.

One can conclude that the usual endemic diseases will not be particularly useful as biological weapons, but rather that the diseases chosen for this purpose will be new ones to the country under attack.

The deliberate initiation of an epidemic requires the effective dissemination of the disease agent among a population, and this in turn involves the preparation of comparatively large quantities of the infectious material, its storage until a convenient time for attack, and its distribution in the enemy's country. The preparation of adequate quantities of most bacteria would be comparatively simple, although a number of the pathogens require quite complex media, and some investigation of mass culture methods would be necessary. The preparation of viruses in quantity would be somewhat more laborious. However, the development of the chick embryo technique makes this preparation possible on an adequate scale.

The processing of bacteria or viruses for storage would probably utilize the simultaneous freezing and drying of the infectious material. This method has proved thoroughly effective for preserving both the viability and the virulence of a very wide variety of disease agents. Cultures prepared in this way can be stored almost indefinitely, and will resume growth upon the addition of water.

Frozen and dried (lyophilized) cultures might be especially suitable for use in spreading air-borne diseases. The finely dispersed powder could be scattered directly from planes, or could be spread over a considerable area by a properly designed bomb. Although no extensive studies have been reported on the infectiousness of such dried powders, one would expect them to be as effective as the dust particles and dried droplets by which many air-borne diseases are commonly spread. Similarly, the optimum range of concentration, the persistence of the materials, and their ability to stand exposure to light and moisture would require some study. It seems probable that these problems could be solved, and that the intentional spreading of air-borne diseases would be a comparatively simple matter.

However, the successful development of offensive weapons is not enough to make biological warfare feasible; it is equally essential to have adequate defensive measures for the protection of the home population from the diseases employed against the enemy. Mass mechanical air filters or air-sterilization units could be used under certain conditions, although these methods are either of doubtful value or not fully developed and available. Strict quarantine is probably the most effective of all methods, but it would be extraordinarily difficult to enforce if an initial attack had succeeded in starting a widespread epidemic, or if the attack were linked with mass bombing raids.

Against specific diseases, it is possible to provide active immunization as against smallpox, or passive immunization as by the use of diphtheria antitoxin. Both methods have severe limitations, not only in the number of diseases for which effective vaccines and antisera have been developed, but also in the specificity of action, which would make it impossible to prepare in advance against unfamiliar diseases. The rapid strides in the development of chemo-therapy and antibiotics give some hope that therapeutic agents may be found which would have a generalized action against diseases, perhaps even including new ones. The virus diseases, however, are generally resistant to chemotherapy; also, it is possible to develop strains of bacteria which have overcome their normal susceptibility to control by chemotherapy. This latter point raises the unpleasant possibility that an organism which we might use offensively, depending upon chemotherapy for our own protection, might develop a resistance to the therapeutic treatment.

D. *Strategy of Biological Warfare*

One of the advantages of the bacterial weapon is its strategic flexibility. It lends itself equally well to a surprise attack by air or to use by secret agents, in which case the fact of a deliberate attack might be quite difficult to establish. It is equally adaptable to a war of attrition. The biological weapon used would be chosen to meet the strategic requirements, and might be one which is rapidly and dramatically fatal, or one which merely incapacitates its victims. From the standpoint of military advantage in a long campaign, incapacitation is probably more effective than death, as a prolonged convalescence is a severe drain on civilian personnel, materials and, ultimately, on morale.

In considering the possible use of biological warfare against the United States, one could expect the use of either a dramatically and highly fatal disease such as bubonic plague, or a highly infectious disease requiring a long convalescence such as influenza. The first would be suited to blitz tactics and would undoubtedly have a tremendous morale effect. The second would be a potent means of attrition, especially against war production and the organiza-tion of an effective defense.

A surprise attack on the United States might well begin with an influenza epidemic in our major cities, started by secret agents. Within two weeks, such an epidemic should be spreading rapidly. A mass bombing attack at this time, possibly with atomic bombs, might well be accompanied by the dissemination from aircraft of a highly fatal infection. The demoralization of our civilian population during the next several weeks might easily make us vulnerable to attack by a small, highly mobile, air-borne force.

However, the character of a surprise raid would be determined by the over-all military situation, with particular regard to the atomic bomb. If the United States were thoroughly armed with atomic bombs and prepared to retaliate instantly, it is probably unlikely that any enemy would risk the chance of detection in using secret agents to start an epidemic as the first stage of hostilities. On the other hand, if our defensive position were such that we would require several weeks before we could launch effective counterattacks or set up an effective intercept system against bombing raids, it is probable that the first overt raids would be preceded by the activities of secret agents in starting infections similar enough to naturally occurring ones not to arouse immediate widespread suspicion. In this way, an epidemic of considerable proportion could be well launched before any effective measures were taken, and the disorganization following a bombing raid would help to spread the epidemic.

The use of biological weapons in a war of attrition is comparatively easy to visualize. In a long war, plant and animal diseases would be quite as important through their effects on the food supply as diseases directed against the human population. If a long war seemed inevitable, then these methods would very probably be used. However, dependence on attrition in any future war involves a considerable risk, since there is always the chance that the enemy will develop an important new weapon which will change the entire situation. The emphasis in prewar planning can be expected to center on weapons intended to force a prompt decision.

E. *Problem of International Control*

Biological warfare poses severe problems for international inspection and control, problems that are much more difficult than those for the atomic bomb. In the first place, no extensive industrial facilities are required, and the cost of biological weapons is easily within the capabilities of small nations. This does not imply that technology is unimportant, since those countries which lead in research will be in the best position to use biological weapons and the other conventional weapons needed to implement them. Aircraft, for example, is probably as essential to biological warfare, at least after the initial attack, as it is to conventional warfare.

The development of offensive biological weapons would be exceedingly difficult to detect or control by a system of international inspection, since the development of defensive measures, a very important part of the total preparation, is largely identical with public health research. The development of offensive measures would require only a small increment in this activity, and could readily be disguised. This situation differs markedly from the large expansion of the uranium-mining industry required to convert from the production of uranium for peacetime purposes to its use for the manufacture of atomic bombs.

Finally, the use of biological weapons would be difficult to prove, and the identity of the aggressor nation might be impossible to establish with certainty. All these factors make the problem of international control of biological warfare extremely difficult. Moreover, the problem probably would be complicated rather than simplified if effective controls were established over atomic bombs and other conventional weapons. That is to say, an aggressor might be much more willing to take the chance of using biological warfare if he were certain that he did not face immediate reprisals with conventional weapons.

F. *Defensive Measures for the United States*

If one excludes the possibility of effective international control, at least for the time being, there remains the question of the action which the United States can take to protect itself against biological warfare. First and most important is clearly the maintenance of research leadership in all phases of the subject. Defensive measures are obviously important, but it would be unrealistic to limit consideration to defensive measures alone; adequate defense depends on thorough familiarity with all the offensive possibilities of the weapon. Moreover, the development of effective offensive weapons provides the means for retaliation, and a threat which might deter potential aggressors.

Also, it is important to organize an effective quarantine and damage-control system, since general civilian demoralization might be one of the worst consequences of a sudden attack. The dispersal of industrial and government facilities, and the provision of a few duplicate control centers, are necessary defensive measures against either biological warfare or atomic bombing.

APPENDIX V

ESTIMATED RESERVES OF U.S. RAW MATERIALS
(AS OF 1944)

Bureau of Mines and U. S. Geological Survey Statistics as presented in *Mineral Position of the United States* to a U. S. Senate Subcommittee on "Investigation of National Resources." Printed by U. S. Government Printing Office, Washington, December 1947 for the Committee on Public Lands.

Estimated "Commercial" Reserves in Years in Known Deposits in the United States at the 1935–44 Average Consumption Rate:

MINERAL	RESERVE IN YEARS
Magnesium	Unlimited
Nitrates	"
Salt	"
Bituminous coal & lignite	4,386
Phosphate rock	600
Helium	235

Mineral	Reserve in Years
Anthracite	187
Molybdenum	157
Rutile	124
Potash	99
Iron ore	76
Ilmenite	73
Arsenic*	55
Natural gas	55
Cobalt*	53
Sulfur	39
Bismuth	36
Fluorspar	33
Bauxite	23
Zinc	20
Gold	19
Copper	19
Petroleum	15
Silver*	13
Cadmium*	11
Lead	10
Vanadium	8
Manganese	4
Platinum metals	3
Antimony*	3
Mercury	2
Tungsten	2
Chromite	1

Reserves Negligible—Quantitative Comparisons Not Significant

Mica (strategic)
Asbestos (long-fiber)
Graphite (flake)
Nickel*

Tin
Industrial diamonds
Quartz crystal

* Obtained chiefly as by-products. Output dependent on rate of production of associated metals.

U.S. Mineral Position—Actual, Impending, and Potential

Based on known "commercial" reserves, outlook for noteworthy discovery, and the possibility that known submarginal resources can be made available by technologic progress and improved economic conditions.

RELATIVE SELF-SUFFICIENCY

Actual and Impending
(Based on present technologic and economic conditions and on known "commercial" reserves)

Potential
(If technologic and economic changes permit use of known submarginal resources)

A. VIRTUAL SELF-SUFFICIENCY ASSURED FOR A LONG TIME:

Bituminous coal & lignite
Anthracite
Natural gas
Magnesium
Molybdenum
Fluorspar (metallurgical)
Helium
Magnesite
Nitrates
Phosphate rock
Potash
Salt
Sulfur

A. VIRTUAL SELF-SUFFICIENCY:

Bituminous coal & lignite
Anthracite
Natural gas
Petroleum
Aluminum ores
Copper
Iron ore
Magnesium
Manganese
Molybdenum
Titanium
Vanadium
Fluorspar (all grades)
Graphite (flake)
Helium
Magnesite
Nitrates
Phosphate rock
Potash
Salt
Sulfur

B. COMPLETE OR VIRTUAL DEPENDENCE ON FOREIGN SOURCES:

1. Small or remote expectation of improving position through discovery:
   Chromite
   Ferro-grade manganese
   Nickel*
   Platinum metals
   Tin
   Industrial diamonds
   Quartz crystals
   Asbestos (spinning quality)
2. Good expectation of improving position through discovery:
   Cobalt*
   Graphite (flake)

B. COMPLETE OR VIRTUAL DEPENDENCE ON FOREIGN SOURCES:

Platinum metals
Tin
Industrial diamonds
Quartz crystals
Asbestos (spinning quality)

Actual and Impending	*Potential*
C. PARTIAL DEPENDENCE ON FOREIGN SOURCES, ACTUAL OR IMPENDING:	C. PARTIAL DEPENDENCE ON FOREIGN SOURCES:

1. Good expectation of improving position through discovery:

Petroleum
Arsenic*
Bismuth*
Cadmium*
Copper
Iron ore
Lead
Mercury
Tantalum*
Tungsten
Zinc
Fluorspar (acid grade)

2. Little hope of improving position through discovery:

Antimony*
Vanadium
High-grade bauxite
Strategic mica

Antimony
Arsenic
Bismuth
Cadmium
Cobalt
Chromite
Lead
Mercury
Nickel
Tantalum
Tungsten
Zinc
Strategic mica

* Domestic production chiefly by-products.
Source: Bureau of Mines and U.S. Geological Survey Statistics as presented in *Mineral Position of the United States* to a U. S. Senate Subcommittee on "Investigation of National Resources," U. S. Government Printing Office, Washington, December 1947. Printed for the Committee on Public Lands.

APPENDIX VI

"STRATEGIC" AND CRITICAL RAW MATERIALS
As Listed by the Army and Navy Munitions Board, 1946

("Materials for which stock-piling is deemed the only satisfactory means of insuring an adequate supply for a future emergency.")

Agar
Antimony
Asbestos:[1]
   Rhodesian chrysotile
   South African amosite

Bauxite
Beryl
Bismuth
Cadmium
Castor oil[2]

[1] Require special storage conditions.
[2] Require rotation of stocks.

Celestite
Chromite:
    Metallurgical grade
    Refractory grade:
        Rhodesian origin
        Other origin
Cobalt
Coconut oil[2]
Columbite
Copper
Cordage fibers:[2]
    Manila
    Sisal
Corundum
Diamonds, industrial
Emetine
Graphite:
    Amorphous lump
    Flake
Hyoscine
Iodine[1]
Jewel bearings:
    Instrument jewels, except V jewels
    Sapphire and ruby V jewels
    Watch and timekeeping device jewels
Kapok[2]
Kyanite, Indian
Lead
Manganese ore:
    Battery grade
    Metallurgical grade
Mercury

Mica:
    Muscovite block and film, good stained and better
    Muscovite splittings
    Phlogopite splittings
Monazite
Nickel
Opium[1,3]
Palm Oil[2]
Pepper
Platinum group metals:
    Iridium
    Platinum
Pyrethrum[2]
Quartz crystals
Quebracho
Quinidine
Quinine[1]
Rapeseed oil[2]
Rubber:[1,2]
    Crude rubber
    Natural rubber latex
Rutile
Sapphire, and ruby
Shellac[2]
Sperm oil[2]
Talc, steatite, block or lava
Tantalite
Tin
Tung oil[2]
Tungsten
Vanadium
Zinc
Zirconium ores:
    Baddeleyite
    Zircon

---

[1] Require special storage conditions.
[2] Require rotation of stocks.
[3] Stocks to be held by Treasury Department, Bureau of Narcotics.

Source: *Raw Materials in War and Peace*, Associates in International Relations, Department of Social Sciences, United States Military Academy, 1947, page 160.

APPENDIX VII
U.S. OVERSEAS BASES

PACIFIC

Major Base Areas

HAWAIIAN Is. Major air, ground, naval installations in active status.
MARIANAS Is. Major air, ground, naval installations in active status.
ALEUTIAN-ALASKA. Major air, ground and secondary naval installations in active status.
RYUKYUS. Major air, ground and secondary naval installations in active status.

Secondary Bases

PHILIPPINES. Secondary air, ground and naval installations in reduced operational status.
MIDWAY. Air, ground and secondary naval installations in reduced operational status.
SAMOA. Air and naval station in caretaker status.

Subsidiary Air Bases and Anchorages

MANUS. Air and naval installations in caretaker status (Australian control).
ENIWETOK. Air facilities in maintenance for transients—naval facilities in caretaker status.
KWAJALEIN. Air facilities in reduced operations—naval facilities in caretaker status.
TRUK. Caretaker status except service for transient aircraft.
PALAU. Maintenance status.
JOHNSTON. Air facilities in reduced operational status.
PALMYRA. Caretaker status except service for transient aircraft.
MAJURO. Caretaker status except service for transient aircraft.
CANTON. Only facilities for emergency air service.
MARCUS. Caretaker status except for weather and transient aircraft (Air Force).
IWO JIMA. Reduced Air Force facilities for transient aircraft.

ATLANTIC

Major Base Areas

NEWFOUNDLAND. Air, ground and secondary naval facilities in active status.
PUERTO RICO. Air, ground and secondary naval facilities in active status.
CANAL ZONE. Air, ground and secondary naval facilities in active status.
Naval installations in the Caribbean are distributed among Guantánamo, San Juan and Trinidad because of the undeveloped status of Roosevelt Roads, Puerto Rico.

Secondary Bases

BERMUDA. Air and secondary naval facilities in operational status.

ST. THOMAS. Air and submarine base in caretaker status.

Subsidiary Air Bases

GREAT EXUMA. Aviation facilities in a caretaker status with service for transient aircraft.

JAMAICA. Aviation facilities in a caretaker status with service for transient aircraft.

ANTIGUA. Aviation facilities in a caretaker status with service for transient aircraft.

ST. LUCIA. Aviation facilities in a caretaker status with service for transient aircraft.

BRITISH GUIANA. Aviation facilities in a caretaker status with service for transient aircraft.

See text of Chapter VII and footnotes for a discussion of the special base situation in Labrador, Greenland, Iceland, the Azores and Brazil.

APPENDIX VIII

POSTWAR U.S. MILITARY ORGANIZATION

UNITED STATES AIR FORCE
Chief of
Staff
The Air Staff

UNITED STATES

1. Strategic Air Command
   Eighth Air Force and Fifteenth Air Force
2. Tactical Air Command
   Ninth and Twelfth Air Forces
3. Air Defense Command
   First, Second, Fourth, Tenth, Eleventh, and Fourteenth Air Forces[1] (National Guard and Reserve with a cadre of regulars)
4. Air Training Command
5. Air Material Command
6. Air Transport Command
7. Air Proving Ground Command
8. Air University
9. Bolling Field Command

[1] The six air forces of the air defense command may be merged into four by a projected reorganization.

EUROPE: United States Air Forces in Europe
JAPAN: Far East Air Forces
        Fifth, Thirteenth and Twentieth
Caribbean Air Command
Alaskan Air Command
Seventh Air Force (Hawaii)

UNITED STATES ARMY

The Chief of Staff   Headquarters, Army Ground Forces

UNITED STATES

ARMIES: First, Second, Third, Fourth, Fifth, and Sixth Armies (headquarters
    cadres only; chiefly administrative and training, not operational).
    2nd Infantry (below strength)
    2nd Armored (one-third to one-half strength)
    82nd Airborne (to be brought up to full strength)

Activated but skeletonized divisions, cadres, training and housekeeping units
    only:
    3rd Armored Division
    4th Division
    5th Division
    9th Division

OCCUPATIONAL FORCES AND OVERSEAS

For command purposes the commanding generals of occupation forces are
under the Chief of Staff.

As military governors they go through the chain of command to the Joint
Chiefs of Staff, and for policy also to the State Department.

Headquarters, U.S. Army, Europe
1. U.S. Ground and Service Forces, Germany
    1st Infantry Div.
2. U.S. Forces, Austria
3. TRUST—Trieste United States Troops (5,000 men)

C-in-C, Far East

JAPAN: Eighth Army: (I Corps) 24th and 25th Divisions; (IX Corps) 1st
    Cavalry and 11th Airborne
KOREA: XXIV Corps: 6th and 7th Infantry Divisions.
U.S. Army, Caribbean (Headquarters at Panama)
    (includes Panama Canal Zone and all Caribbean bases)
U.S. Army, Alaska
    (includes Aleutians)
U.S. Army, Pacific
    (includes Central and South Pacific)

UNITED STATES NAVY

UNITED STATES NAVY

Chief of Naval Operations

United States Pacific Fleet	United States Atlantic Fleet
First Task Fleet	Second Task Fleet
Naval Forces—Western Pacific	Operational Development Force
Naval Forces Far East	*Naval Forces Eastern Atlantic and Mediterranean
*(Fleet Components from PacFlt, Logistic Support by ComPacFlt.)	(Fleet Components from LantFlt, Logistics Support by ComLantFlt.)
Alaskan Sea Frontier	Naval Forces Germany
(Fleet Components from PacFlt, Logistic Support by ComPacFlt.)	(Under operational control of Commander in Chief Europe to assist in occupation.)
Reserve Fleet (Operating directly under CNO)	Reserve Fleet (Operating directly under CNO)
* Fleet Component assigned as directed by CNO.	* Operating directly under CNO.

THE NAVY

(In active Operating Commission)

Atlantic

Six carriers	Cruisers
Six escort carriers	More than sixty destroyers
One battleship	Thirty to forty submarines

Pacific

Six carriers	Cruisers
Four escort carriers	More than sixty destroyers
One battleship	Thirty to forty submarines

Units of the Atlantic Fleet are rotated to duty in "Naval Forces Eastern Atlantic and Mediterranean" and units of the Pacific Fleet to "Naval Forces Far East."

In addition to the forces outlined above, the Navy maintains very sizable forces, including a number of battleships in reduced commission for training reserves, etc., and these could be brought up to full strength quickly. Thousands of other combat vessels are preserved in the "mothball fleet." Hundreds of auxiliaries, including amphibious "lift" for $2\frac{1}{2}$ divisions, are in operation or reserve.

The Marines maintain in this country two divisions (below war strength)—the First and Second—and sizable forces in Hawaii, the Marianas and elsewhere, which could provide a third Marine Division. A battalion landing team is stationed in China and another—minus some units—is aboard ship in the Mediterranean.

THEATER COMMANDS

The world has been divided into a number of geographical "theaters," and unified commands for most of these theaters have been established. One "theater," the United States, has no unified command.

The theater commands, with the names of the officers (and the services to which they belong), who were assigned as theater commanders in late 1947, follows:

Alaskan Command	Lt. Gen. Nathan F. Twining (Air Force)
Caribbean Defense Command	Lt. Gen. W. D. Crittenberger (Army)
European Command	Lt. Gen. Lucius D. Clay (Army)
Pacific Command	Admiral DeWitt C. Ramsay (Navy)
Far East Command	General Douglas MacArthur (Army)
Atlantic Command	Admiral W. H. P. Blandy (Navy)
Northeast Command	Unassigned

With the withdrawal of American troops from Italy, the Mediterranean Theater Command has been abolished.

General MacArthur wears two hats; he is also "SCAP," or Supreme Commander, Allied Powers, in Japan.

INDEX

Publications of the

COUNCIL ON FOREIGN RELATIONS

Foreign Affairs (quarterly), edited by Hamilton Fish Armstrong.

The United States in World Affairs (annual). Volumes for 1931, 1932 and 1933 by Walter Lippmann and William O. Scroggs; for 1934-1935, 1936, 1937, 1938, 1939 and 1940 by Whitney H. Shepardson and William O. Scroggs; for 1945-1947 by John C. Campbell.

Political Handbook of the World (annual), edited by Walter H. Mallory.

Survey of American Foreign-Relations (in four volumes, 1928-1931), prepared under the direction of Charles P. Howland.

The Foreign Affairs Reader, edited by Hamilton Fish Armstrong.

The Study of International Relations in American Colleges and Universities, by Grayson Kirk.

Foreign Affairs Bibliography, 1932-1942, by Robert Gale Woolbert.

The Struggle for Airways in Latin America, by William A. M. Burden.

World Economy in Transition, by Eugene Staley.

Mobilizing Civilian America, by Harold J. Tobin and Percy W. Bidwell.

The Far Eastern Crisis, by Henry L. Stimson.

The Invisible Tariff, by Percy W. Bidwell.

Raw Materials in Peace and War, by Eugene Staley.

Our Trade with Britain, by Percy W. Bidwell.

Peaceful Change, by Frederick Sherwood Dunn.

Can We Be Neutral?, by Allen W. Dulles and Hamilton Fish Armstrong.

Ores and Industry in the Far East, by H. Foster Bain.

Limits of Land Settlement, prepared under the direction of Isaiah Bowman.

International Security, by Philip C. Jessup.

American Agencies Interested in International Affairs, compiled by Ruth Savord.

Dollars in Latin America, by Willy Feuerlein and Elizabeth Hannan.

New Directions in Our Trade Policy, by William Diebold, Jr.

International Air Transport and National Policy, by Oliver J. Lissitzyn.

The United States in a Multi-National Economy, by Jacob Viner and others.

The Problem of Germany, by Hoyt Price and Carl E. Schorske.

The Price of Power, by Hanson W. Baldwin.

Set in Linotype Janson
Format by A. W. Rushmore
Manufactured by The Haddon Craftsmen
Published by HARPER *&* BROTHERS
New York and London

DATE DUE

FEB 22 '66			
MAR 9 '68			
GAYLORD			PRINTED IN U.S.A

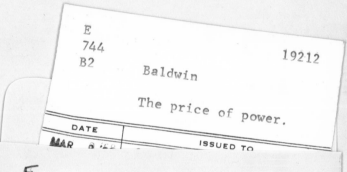

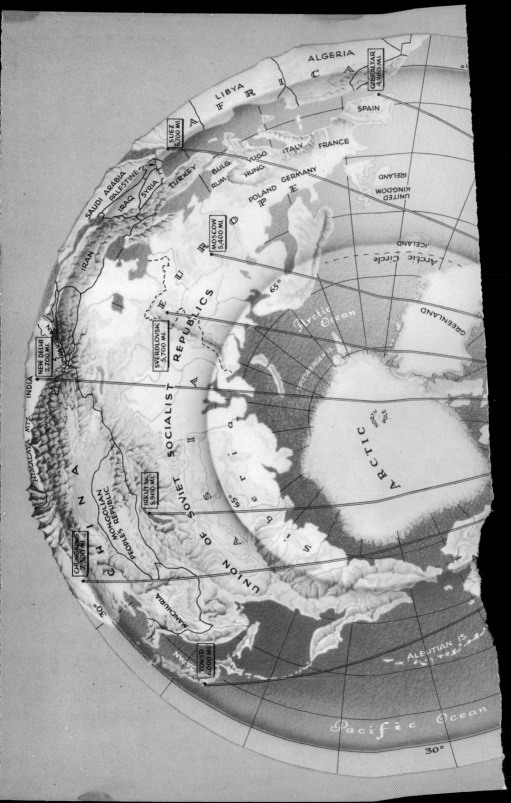